Ford Cortina III 1600 & 2000 ohc Owners Workshop Manual

D1336983

by J H Haynes
Member of the Guild of Motoring Writers

and P G Strasman
MISTC

Models covered:
Cortina 1600L & XL Saloon & Estate
Cortina 1600 GXL Saloon
Cortina 1600 GT Saloon
Cortina 2000L & XL Saloon & Estate
Cortina 2000 GXL Saloon
Cortina 2000 GT Saloon
Cortina 2000E Saloon & Estate

ISBN 0 85696 295 3

© Haynes Publishing Group 1976, 1979, 1981, 1983

ABCDi

Printed in England *(295 - 10J3)*

HAYNES PUBLISHING GROUP
SPARKFORD YEOVIL SOMERSET BA22 7JJ ENGLAND
distributed in the USA by
HAYNES PUBLICATIONS INC
861 LAWRENCE DRIVE
NEWBURY PARK
CALIFORNIA 91320
USA

Acknowledgements

Thanks are due to the Ford Motor Company for the supply of technical information and certain illustrations, to Castrol Limited for providing lubrication data, and to the Champion Sparking Plug Company Limited who supplied the illustrations showing the various spark plug conditions. The bodywork repair photographs used in this manual were provided by Lloyds Industries Limited who supply 'Turtle Wax', 'Dupli-color Holts', and other Holts range products.

The section of Chapter 10 dealing with the suppression of radio interference, was originated by Mr I. P. Davey, and was first published in *Motor* magazine.

Lastly, thanks are due to all of those people at Sparkford who helped in the production of this manual. Particularly, Brian Horsfall and Les Brazier who carried out the mechanical work and took the photographs respectively; Stanley Randolph who planned the layout of each page and Rod Grainger the editor.

About this manual

Its aims

The aim of this Manual is to help you get the best value from your car. It can do so in several ways. It can help you decide what work must be done (even should you choose to get it done by a garage), provide information on routine maintenance and servicing, and give a logical course of action and diagnosis when random faults occur. However, it is hoped that you will make full use of the Manual by tackling the work yourself. On simpler jobs it may even be quicker than booking the car into a garage, and having to go there twice, to leave and collect it. Perhaps most important, a lot of money can be saved by avoiding the costs the garage must charge to cover its labour and overheads.

The Manual has drawings and descriptions to show the function of the various components so that their layout can be understood. Then the tasks are described and photographed in a step-by-step sequence so that even a novice can do the work.

Its arrangement

The manual is divided into thirteen Chapters, each covering a logical sub-division of the vehicle. The Chapters are each divided into consecutively numbered Sections and the Sections into paragraphs (or sub-sections), with decimal numbers following on from the Section they are in, eg 5.1, 5.2, 5.3 etc.

It is freely illustrated, especially in those parts where there is a detailed sequence of operations to be carried out. There are two forms of illustration: figures and photographs. The figures are numbered in sequence with decimal numbers, according to their position in the Chapter: eg Fig. 6.4 is the 4th drawing/ illustration in Chapter 6. Photographs are numbered (either individually or in related groups) the same as the Section or sub-section of the text where the operation they show is described.

There is an alphabetical index at the back of the manual as well as a contents list at the front.

References to the 'left' or 'right' of the vehicle are in the sense of a person in the driver's seat facing forwards.

Whilst every care is taken to ensure that the information in this manual is correct no liability can be accepted by the authors or publishers for loss, damage or injury caused by any errors in, or omissions from, the information given.

Contents

Introduction to the Ford Cortina Mk III

The Cortina MkIII models were introduced in 1970. All 2000cc models and the 1600GT were fitted with a new overhead-camshaft engine. Other 1300cc/1600cc models of the Cortina MkIII introduced at the same time, retained the overhead valve pushrod engine from the earlier Cortina MkII range, (the Cortina MkIII ohv models are the subject of another manual).

In September 1973, several changes were made. The ohc engine became a standard fitting in all 1600cc models. Some fairly major modifications were made to the suspension and drive-line of all models and the car interior was redesigned.

September 1973 also saw the introduction of the 2000E as a direct replacement for the 2000 GXL model.

An Estate version of the 2000E was introduced in September 1974. Other minor changes to the Cortina III include improved interior trim for the 2000GT model and similar modifications to 'L' models in December 1974.

October 1975 saw several further modifications to trim, both interior and exterior, and the standard fitment to all models of such items as servo brakes, heated rear window, hazard flashers, etc.

In August 1976 the Cortina Mk III was discontinued to be superseded by the Mk IV range.

1972 Ford Cortina 2000 GXL (now superseded by 2000E)

1973 Ford Cortina 2000 E saloon

1973 Ford Cortina XL 1600 2-door saloon

1974 Ford Cortina 2000E Estate Car

1975 Ford Cortina 2000 GT Saloon

Routine maintenance

Maintenance is essential for ensuring safety and desirable for the purpose of getting the best in terms of performance and economy from your car. Over the years the need for periodic lubrication - oiling, greasing and so on - has been drastically reduced if not totally eliminated. This has unfortunately tended to lead some owners to think that because no such action is required, components either no longer exist, or will last for ever. This is a serious delusion. It follows therefore that the largest initial element of maintenance is visual examination. This may lead to repairs or renewals, but should help avoid breakdowns.

In the summary given here the 'essential for safety' items are **shown in bold type.** They must be attended to at the regular frequencies shown in order to avoid the possibility of accidents and loss of life. Other neglect results in unreliability, increased running costs, more rapid wear and more rapid depreciation of the vehicle in general.

Every 250 miles (400 km) or weekly - whichever comes first

Steering
Check the tyre pressures.
Examine tyres for wear or damage.
Is steering smooth and accurate?

Brakes
Check reservoir fluid level.
Is there any fall off in braking efficiency?
Try an emergency stop.

Lights, wipers and horns
Do all bulbs work at the front and rear?
Are the headlamp beams aligned properly?
Do the wipers and horns work?
Check windshield washer fluid level.

Engine
Check the engine oil level and top-up if required.
Check the radiator coolant level and top-up if required.
Check the battery electrolyte level and top-up to the level of the separators with distilled water.

Checking windscreen washer fluid level

Engine oil dipstick

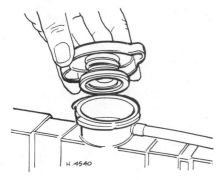
Removing radiator cap

Checking battery electrolyte level

At the first 3000 miles (4800 km) only

Renew the engine oil.

Every 6000 miles (9600 km)

Check tension of alternator drivebelt.
Clean fuel pump filter.
Check wear in disc pads.
Check rear brake shoe lining wear.
Renew engine oil and filter.
Check fluid level in brake master cylinder and top-up as necessary.
Check transmission oil level and top-up if necessary.
Check rear axle oil level and top-up if necessary.
Check and adjust the clutch cable free movement.
Inspect steering and suspension components for wear.
Check and adjust valve clearances.
With rocker cover removed, remove distributor rotor and crank engine on starter motor. Check that oil is discharged from the lubrication tube nozzles onto the cam followers.
Clean and re-gap spark plugs.
Inspect brake lines and flexible hoses for damage or deterioration.
Check exhaust system for leaks or broken mountings.
Check carburettor adjustment.
Change position of roadwheels to even out tyre wear, if wished.

Lubricate door hinges, locks etc.
Clean crankcase ventilation P.V.C. valve.

Every 12000 miles (1900 km)

Check distributor contact points and renew if necessary.
Renew spark plugs.
Renew fuel evaporative emission control carbon canister filter (where fitted).
Check ignition timing.
Check front wheel alignment

Every 18000 miles (29000 km)

Renew air cleaner element.

Every 24000 miles (38000 km) or at two yearly intervals

Drain cooling system and refill with 'long-life' type antifreeze mixture.
Clean, repack with grease and adjust front wheel bearings.

Every 36000 miles (58000 km)

Bleed hydraulic system, renew all system seals and refill with clean, fresh fluid.
Remove plugs and grease front suspension upper swivel balljoints.

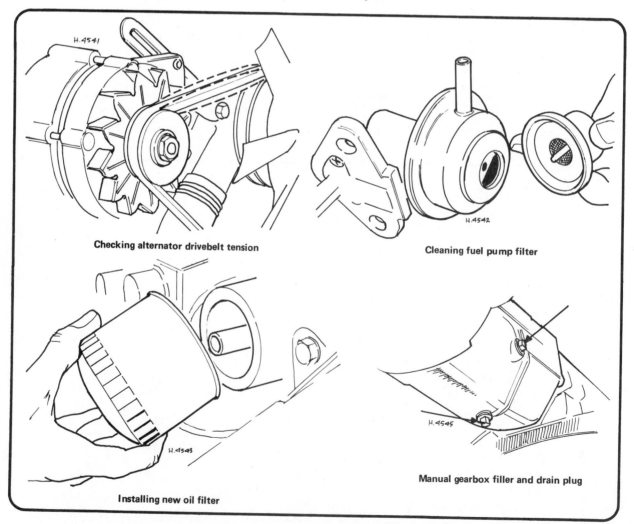

Checking alternator drivebelt tension

Cleaning fuel pump filter

Installing new oil filter

Manual gearbox filler and drain plug

9

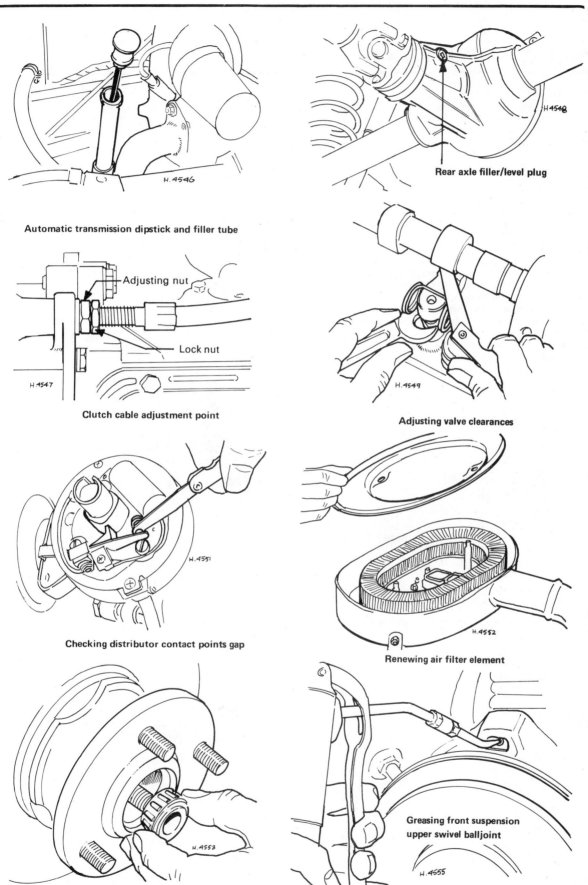

Automatic transmission dipstick and filler tube

Rear axle filler/level plug

Clutch cable adjustment point

Adjusting nut

Lock nut

Adjusting valve clearances

Checking distributor contact points gap

Renewing air filter element

Removing front wheel outer bearing

Greasing front suspension upper swivel balljoint

Jacking and Towing

Jacking points

To change a wheel in an emergency, use the jack supplied with the vehicle. Ensure that the roadwheel nuts are released before jacking-up the car and make sure that the arm of the jack is fully engaged with the body bracket and that the base of the jack is standing on a firm level surface.

The jack supplied with the vehicle is not suitable for use when raising the vehicle for maintenance or repair operations. For this work, use a trolley, hydraulic or screw type jack located under the front crossmember, bodyframe side-members or rear axle casing, as illustrated. Always supplement the jack with axle stands or blocks before crawling beneath the car.

Towing points

If your vehicle is being towed, make sure that the tow rope is attached to a towing eye or the front crossmember. If the vehicle is equipped with automatic transmission, the distance towed must not exceed 15 miles (24 km), nor the speed 30 mph (48 km/h), otherwise serious damage to the transmission may result. If these limits are likely to be exceeded, disconnect and remove the propeller shaft.

If you are towing another vehicle, attach the tow rope to the lower suspension arm bracket at the axle tube.

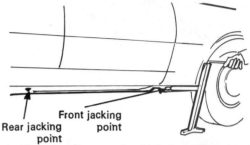
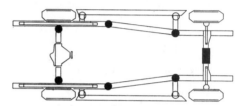

Jacking points (for use only with jack supplied with vehicle)

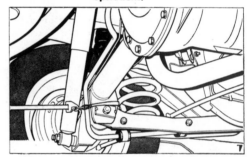

Vehicle jacking points (for maintenance and repair operations)

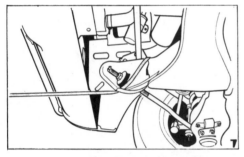

Tow rope attachment to front of vehicle

Tow rope attachment to rear of vehicle

Quick reference capacities

Engine oil capacity:

Excluding filter (oil change only)	5.3 Imp. pints (3.0 litres)	
With new filter	6.6 Imp. pints (3.75 litres)	

Cooling system:	**Up to 1974**	**1974 onwards**
1600cc	11.4 Imp. pints (6.5 litres)	10.0 Imp. pints (5.8 litres)
2000cc	12.4 Imp. pints (7.1 litres)	10.75 Imp. pints (6.1 litres)

Fuel tank capacity ... ... 11.9 Imp. gals. (54.0 litres)

Gearbox capacity:

1600cc	1.75 Imp. pints (1.00 litres)
2000cc	2.9 Imp. pints (1.66 litres)

Automatic transmission fluid capacity:

Borg-Warner	11.25 Imp. pints (6.4 litres)
Ford Bordeaux	10.5 Imp. pints (6.0 litres)

Rear axle capacity:

1600cc	1.76 Imp. pints (1.0 litre)
2000cc	1.94 Imp. pints (1.1 litres)

Buying spare parts and vehicle identification numbers

Buying spare parts

Spare parts are available from many sources, for example: Ford garages, other garages and accessory shops, and motor factors. Our advice regarding spare part sources is as follows:

Officially appointed Ford garages - This is the best source of parts which are peculiar to your car and are otherwise not generally available (eg; complete cylinder heads, internal gearbox components, badges, interior trim etc). It is also the only place at which you should buy parts if your car is still under warranty - non-Ford components may invalidate the warranty. To be sure of obtaining the correct parts it will always be necessary to give the storeman your car's vehicle identification number, and if possible, to take the 'old' part along for positive identification. Remember that many parts are available on a factory exchange scheme - any parts returned should always be clean! It obviously makes good sense to go straight to the specialists on your car for this type of part for they are best equipped to supply you.

Other garages and accessory shops - These are often very good places to buy materials and components needed for the maintenance of your car (eg; oil filters, spark plugs, bulbs, fan belts, oils and greases, touch-up paint, filler paste, etc). They also sell general accessories, usually have convenient opening hours, charge lower prices and can often be found not far from home.

Motor factors - Good factors will stock all of the more important components which wear out relatively quickly (eg; clutch components, pistons, valves, exhaust systems, brake cylinders/pipes/hoses/seals/shoes and pads etc). Motor factors will often provide new or reconditioned components on a part exchange basis - this can save a considerable amount of money.

Vehicle identification numbers

Although many individual parts, and in some cases sub-assemblies, fit a number of different models it is dangerous to assume that just because they look the same, they are the same. Differences are not always easy to detect except by serial numbers. Make sure therefore, that the appropriate identity number for the model or sub-assembly is known and quoted when a spare part is ordered.

The vehicle identification plate is mounted on the right-hand side of the front body panel and many be seen once the bonnet is open. Record the numbers from your car on the blank spaces of the accompanying illustration. You can then take the manual with you when buying parts; also the exploded drawings throughout the manual can be used to point out and identify the components required.

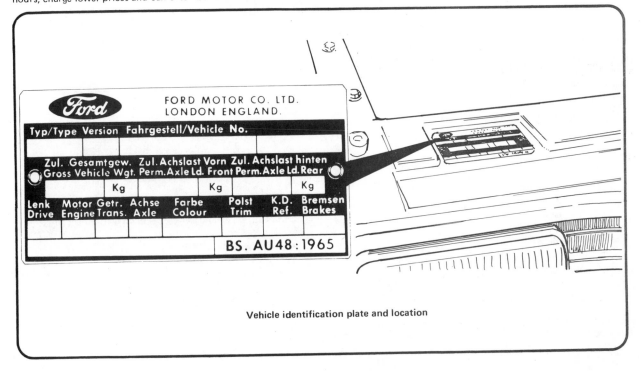

Vehicle identification plate and location

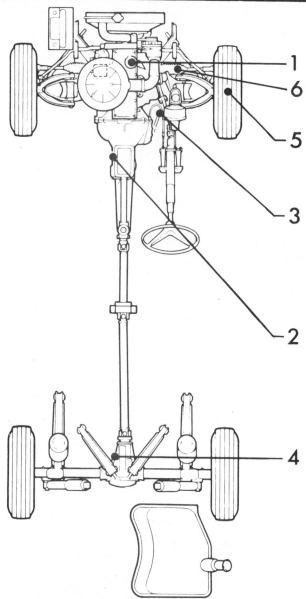

Recommended lubricants

Component								Castrol Product
1 Engine	...	...	...	...	...	...	...	Castrol GTX
2 Gearbox (manual)	...	...	...	...	...	...	...	Castrol Hypoy Light (80 EP)
3 Gearbox (automatic):								
Borg-Warner		...	...	...	...	...	...	Ford auto trans fluid M-2C33F (Castrol TQF)
Bordeaux		...	...	...	...	...	...	Ford auto trans fluid SQ-M2C-9007-AA (Castrol TQF)
4 Rear axle (differential)		...	...	...	...	...	...	Castrol Hypoy B (90 EP)
5 Front wheel bearings		...	...	...	...	...	...	Castrol LM Grease
6 Steering	...	...	...	...	...	...	...	Castrol Hypoy B (90 EP)

Note: The above are general recommendations. Lubrication requirements vary from territory-to-territory and depend on the usage to which the vehicle is put - consult the operators handbook supplied with your car.

Chapter 1 Engine

Contents

Specifications

Engine (general)

	1600 cc	2000 cc
Engine type	Four in-line, single overhead camshaft	
Firing order	1 - 3 - 4 - 2	
Bore	3.451 in. (87.65 mm)	3.575 in. (90.8 mm)
Stroke	2.6 in. (66.00 mm)	3.03 in. (76.95 mm)
Cubic capacity	1593 cc (97.2 cu in.)	1993 cc (115.9 cu in.)
Compression ratio	9.2 : 1	
Maximum continuous engine speed (rpm)	6300	5850
Engine bhp (DIN):		
Standard	72 @ 5500 rpm	98 @ 5500 rpm
GT	88 @ 5700 rpm	
Max. torque (DIN):		
Standard	86 lb/ft @ 2700 rpm	111 lb/ft @ 3500 rpm
GT	91 lb/ft @ 4000 rpm	

Cylinder block

	1600 (all models)		2000 (all models)	
Cast identification marks	16		20	
Number of main bearings	5		5	
Cylinder bore dia. grades:				
Standard grade:	inches	mm	inches	mm
1	3.4508–3.4512	(87.650–87.660)	3.5748–3.5752	(90.800–90.810)
2	3.4512–3.4516	(87.660–87.670)	3.5752–3.5756	(90.810–90.820)
3	3.4516–3.4520	(87.670–87.680)	3.5756–3.5760	(90.820–90.830)
4	3.4520–3.4524	(87.680–87.690)	3.5760–3.5764	(90.830–90.840)
Oversize A	3.4709–3.4713	(88.160–88.170)	3.5949–3.5953	(91.310–91.320)
Oversize B	3.4713–3.4717	(88.170–88.180)	3.5953–3.5957	(91.320–91.330)
Oversize C	3.4717–3.4720	(88.180–88.190)	3.5957–3.5961	(91.330–91.340)
Standard supp. in service	3.4520–3.4524	(87.680–87.690)	3.5760–3.5764	(90.830–90.840)
Oversize 0.5	3.4717–3.4720	(88.180–88.190)	3.5957–3.5961	(91.330–91.340)
Oversize 1.0	3.4913–3.4917	(88.680–88.690)	3.6154–3.6157	(91.830–91.840)

Spigot bearing length in (mm)	1.072–1.070 (27.22–27.17)
Main bearing liners fitted:	
Inner diameter:	
Standard:	
RED in (mm)	2.2446–2.2456 (57.014–57.038)
BLUE in (mm)	2.2442–2.2452 (57.004–57.028)
Crankshaft:	
Undersize:	
0.25 RED in (mm)	2.2348–2.2357 (56.764–56.788)
BLUE in (mm)	2.2344–2.2354 (56.754–56.778)
0.50 in (mm)	2.2250–2.2263 (56.514–56.548)
0.75 in (mm)	2.2151–2.2164 (56.264–56.298)
1.00 in (mm)	2.2053–2.2066 (56.014–56.048)
Main bearing parent bore dia:	
RED in (mm)	2.3866–2.3870 (60.620–60.630)
BLUE in (mm)	2.3870–2.3874 (60.630–60.640)

Crankshaft

Endfloat in (mm)	0.0032–0.0110 (0.08–0.28)
Main bearing journal diameters:	
Standard:	
RED in (mm)	2.2441–2.2437 (57.000–56.990)
BLUE in (mm)	2.2437–2.2433 (56.990–56.980)
Undersize:	
0.25 in (mm)	2.2338–2.2335 (56.740–56.730)
0.50 in (mm)	2.2244–2.2240 (56.500–56.490)
0.75 in (mm)	2.2146–2.2142 (56.250–56.240)
1.00 in (mm)	2.2047–2.2043 (56.000–55.990)
Thrust washer thickness:	
Standard in (mm)	0.091–0.0925 (2.3–2.35)
Undersize in (mm)	0.098–0.100 (2.5–2.55)
Main bearing clearance in (mm)	0.0005–0.0019 (0.014–0.048)
Crankpin journal diameter:	
Standard:	
RED in (mm)	2.0472–2.0468 (52.000–51.990)
BLUE in (mm)	2.0468–2.0465 (51.990–51.980)
Undersize:	
0.25 RED in (mm)	2.0374–2.0370 (51.750–51.740)
0.25 BLUE in (mm)	2.0370–2.0366 (51.740–51.730)
0.50 in (mm)	2.0276–2.0272 (51.500–51.490)
0.75 in (mm)	2.0177–2.0173 (51.250–51.240)

Camshaft

Drive	Toothed belt
Thrust plate thickness:	
Type 1 in (mm)	0.158 (4.01)
Type 2 in (mm)	0.157 (3.98)
Width of camshaft groove in (mm)	$0.1600 \begin{smallmatrix} +0.0028 \\ -0.0000 \end{smallmatrix} \left(4.064 \begin{smallmatrix} +0.070 \\ -0.000 \end{smallmatrix} \right)$

1600

Cam lift in (mm)	0.2338 (5.938)
Cam heel to toe dimensions in (mm)	1.418–1.412 (36.01–35.87)

1600 GT and 2000

Cam lift in (mm)	0.2518 (6.397)
Cam heel to toe dimensions in (mm)	1.435–1.430 (36.46–36.32)

Journal diameter (all models):
    Front in (mm) ... ...   1.6539—1.6531 (42.01—41.99)
    Centre in (mm) ... ...   1.7606—1.7528 (44.72—44.52)
    Rear in (mm) ... ...   1.7720—1.7713 (45.01—44.99)
Bearing - inside diameter (all models):
    Front in (mm) ... ...   1.6557—1.6549 (42.055—42.035)
    Centre in (mm) ... ...   1.7588—1.7580 (44.675—44.655)
    Rear in (mm) ... ...   1.7381—1.7730 (45.055—45.035)
Camshaft endfloat in (mm) ... ...   0.002—0.0035 (0.05—0.09)
Identification colour ... ...   White (1600) Yellow (1600 GT/2000)

Pistons

	1600 (all models)	2000 (all models)
Piston diameter:		
Standard:		
Grade 1 in (mm)	3.4490—3.4494 (87.605—87.615)	3.5730—3.5734 (90.755—90.765)
2 in (mm)	3.4494—3.4498 (87.615—87.625)	3.5734—3.5738 (90.765—90.775)
3 in (mm)	3.4498—3.4502 (87.625—87.635)	3.5738—3.5742 (90.775—90.785)
4 in (mm)	3.4502—3.4506 (87.635—87.645)	3.5742—3.5746 (90.785—90.795)
Standard supplied in service in (mm) ...	3.4500—3.4510 (87.630—87.655)	3.5740—3.5750 (90.780—90.805)
Oversize supplied in service:		
0.5 in (mm)	3.4697—3.4707 (88.130—88.155)	3.5937—3.5947 (91.280—91.305)
1.0 in (mm)	3.4894—3.4904 (88.630—88.655)	3.6134—3.6144 (91.780—91.805)

	1600 and 2000 (all models)
Piston clearance in cylinder bore in (mm)	0.001—0.0024 (0.025—0.060)
Ring gap (in situ):	
Top in (mm)	0.015—0.023 (0.38—0.58)
Centre in (mm)	0.015—0.023 (0.38—0.58)
Bottom in (mm)	0.0157—0.055 (0.4—1.4)
Ring gap position:	
Top	150º from one side of the helical expander gap
Centre	150º from the side opposite the helical expander gap
	Top mark towards piston crown
Bottom	Helical expander: opposite the marked piston front side
	Intermediate rings: 1 in (25 mm) each side of helical expander gap

Gudgeon pins

Length in (mm)	2.83—2.87 (72—72.8)
Diameter:	
RED in (mm)	0.94465—0.94476 (23.994—23.997)
BLUE in (mm)	0.94476—0.94488 (23.997—24.000)
YELLOW in (mm)	0.94488—0.94500 (24.000—24.003)
Interference fit in piston in (mm)	0.0002—0.00043 (0.005—0.011)
Clearance in small end bush in (mm)	0.0007—0.00153 (0.018—0.039)

Connecting rods

Big end bore:	
RED in (mm)	2.1653—2.1657 (55.00—55.01)
BLUE in (mm)	2.1657—2.1661 (55.01—55.02)
Small end bush diameter in (mm)	0.9434—0.9439 (23.964—23.976)
Inside diameter:	
Standard:	
RED in (mm)	2.0478—2.0487 (52.014—52.038)
BLUE in (mm)	2.0474—2.0483 (52.004—52.028)
Undersize:	
0.25 RED in (mm)	2.0379—2.0388 (51.764—51.788)
0.25 BLUE in (mm)	2.0376—2.0385 (51.754—51.778)
0.50 in (mm)	2.0281—2.0294 (51.514—51.548)
0.75 in (mm)	2.0183—2.0196 (51.264—51.298)
1.00 in (mm)	2.0084—2.0100 (51.014—51.048)
Crankpin to bearing liner clearance:	
Standard in (mm)	0.00055—0.0018 (0.014—0.048)
Undersize in (mm)	0.00055—0.0023 (0.014—0.058)

Cylinder head

	1600 models	2000 models
Cast identification number	6	0

	1600 and 2000 (all models)
Valve seat angle	44º 30' 45º

Valve guide inside diameter, inlet and exhaust:
    Standard in (mm) ... ...   0.3174—0.3184 (8.063—8.088)
    Oversize:
        0.2 in (mm) ... ...   0.3253—0.3263 (8.263—8.288)
        0.4 in (mm) ... ...   0.3332—0.3342 (8.463—8.488)
Parent bore for camshaft bearing liners:
    Front in (mm) ... ...   1.6557—1.6549 (42.055—42.035)
    Centre in (mm) ... ...   1.7589—1.7580 (44.675—44.655)
    Rear in (mm) ... ...   1.7738—1.7730 (45.055—45.035)

Valves

1600 and 2000 (all models)

Valve clearances (cold):
    Inlet in (mm) 0.008 (0.20)
    Exhaust in (mm) 0.010 (0.25)

	1600 models	1600 GT and 2000 models
Inlet opens	16° BTDC	18° BTDC
Inlet closes	60° ABDC	70° ABDC
Exhaust opens	58° BBDC	64° BBDC
Exhaust closes	18° ATDC	24° ATDC

Inlet valve

	1600 models	1600 GT and 2000 models
Length in (mm)	4.449 ± 0.016 (113 ± 0.4)	4.3760 (111.15)
Valve head diameter in (mm)	1.516 ± 0.008 (38.5 ± 0.2)	1.654 ± 0.008 (42 ± 0.2)

Valve stem diameter:
    Standard in (mm) ... ...   0.3167—0.3159 (8.043—8.025)
    Oversize:
        0.2 in (mm) ... ...   0.3245—0.3238 (8.243—8.225)
        0.4 in (mm) ... ...   0.3324—0.3317 (8.443—8.425)
Valve stem to guide clearance in (mm) ... ...   0.0008—0.0025 (0.020—0.063)

| Valve lift in (mm) ... ... | 0.3730 (9.474) | 0.3993 (10.142) |

1600 and 2000 (all models)

Valve spring free-length in (mm) 1.73 (44)

	1600 models	2000 models
Spring load, valve open lb (kp)	169.4 ± 6.6 (77 ± 3)	176 ± 6 (80 ± 3)

1600 and 2000 (all models)

Spring load, valve closed lb (kp) ... ...   68 ± 4 (31 ± 2)
Spring length, compressed in (mm) 0.945 (24)

Exhaust valves

	1600 models	1600 GT and 2000 models
Length in (mm)	4.449 ± 0.19 (113 ± 0.5)	4.37 ± 0.19 (111 ± 0.5)

	1600	1600 GT	2000
Valve head diameter in (mm)	1.18 ± 0.08 (30 ± 0.2)	1.34 ± 0.08 (34 ± 0.2)	1.42 ± 0.08 (36 ± 0.2)

1600 and 2000 (all models)

Valve stem diameter:
    Standard in (mm) ... ...   0.3156—0.3149 (8.017—7.999)
    Oversize:
        0.2 in (mm) ... ...   0.3235—0.3228 (8.217—8.199)
        0.4 in (mm) ... ...   0.3314—0.3307 (8.417—8.399)
Valve stem to guide clearance in (mm) ... ...   0.0034—0.0035 (0.086—0.089)

	1600	1600 GT and 2000
Valve lift in (mm)	0.3728 (9.47)	0.3992 (10.14)

1600 and 2000 (all models)

Valve spring free length in (mm) 1.732 (44)

	1600 models	2000 models
Spring load, valve open lb (kp)	170 ± 6 (77 ± 3)	176 ± 6 (80 ± 3)

1600 and 2000 (all models)

Spring load, valve closed lb (kp) ... ...   68.3 ± 4.4 (31 ± 2)
Spring length, compressed in (mm) 0.95 (24)

Engine lubrication data (all models)
    Oil change without renewal of filter. Imp. pints (litres) ...   5.3 (3.0)
    Oil change with renewal of filter. Imp. pints (litres) 6.6 (3.75)

Minimum oil pressure:

At 700 rpm lb f in^2 (kp/cm^2) ...	...	...	...	16 (1.1)
At 1,500 rpm lb f in^2 (kp/cm^2) ...	...	...	...	36 (2.5)
Relief valve opens at lb f in^2 (kp/cm^2) ...	...	...	...	57—67 (4.0—4.7)
Oil pump outer rotor and housing clearance in (mm)	...	...		0.006—0.012 (0.15—0.30)
Inner and outer rotor clearance in (mm) ...	...	...	...	0.002—0.008 (0.05—0.20)
Inner and outer rotor endfloat in (mm) ...	...	...	...	0.0012—0.004 (0.03—0.10)

Torque wrench settings

	lb f ft	kg fm
Main bearing caps ...	64.5—74.5	9.0—10.4
Flywheel ...	46.5—50.9	6.5—7.1
Oil pump ...	12—15	1.7—2.1
Oil pump cover ...	6.4—9.3	0.9—1.3
Oil sump:		
First stage ...	0.7—1.4	0.1—0.2
Second stage ...	4.3—5.7	0.6—0.8
Third stage ...	4.3—5.7	0.6—0.8
Oil drain plug ...	15—20	2.1—2.8
Cylinder head:		
First stage ...	28.5—39.5	4.0—5.5
Second stage ...	39.5—50	5.5—7.0
Third stage ...	64.5—79	9.0—11.0
Rocker cover:		
1st to 6th bolt ... (Sequence (1))	3.6—5.0	0.5—0.7
7th to 8th bolt ... (2)	1.4—1.8	0.2—0.25
9th and 10th bolt ... (3)	3.6—5.0	0.5—0.7
7th and 8th bolt ... (4)	3.6—5.0	0.5—0.7
Spark plugs ...	14.3—20	2.0—2.8

1 General description

Engines fitted to models covered by the manual are of the four cylinder overhead camshaft design and available in two capacities, 1600 cc and 2000 cc. An exploded view identifying the main components is shown in Fig. 1.1.

The cylinder head is of the crossflow design with the inlet manifold one side and the exhaust manifold on the other. As flat top pistons are used the combustion chambers are contained in the cylinder head.

The combined crankcase and cylinder block is made of cast iron and houses the pistons and crankshaft. Attached to the underside of the crankcase is a pressed steel sump which acts as a reservoir for the engine oil. Full information on the lubricating system will be found in Section 24.

The cast iron cylinder head is mounted on top of the cylinder block and acts as a support for the overhead camshaft. The slightly angled valves operate directly in the cylinder head and are controlled by the camshaft via cam followers. The camshaft is operated by a toothed reinforced composite rubber belt from the crankshaft. To eliminate backlash and prevent slackness of the belt a spring loaded tensioner in the form of a jockey wheel is in contact with the back of the belt. It serves two further functions, to keep the belt away from the water pump and also to increase the contact area of the camshaft and crankshaft sprocket.

The drive belt also drives the balance shaft sprocket and it is from this shaft that the oil pump, distributor and fuel pump operate.

The inlet manifold is mounted on the left-hand side of the cylinder head and to this the carburettor is fitted. A water jacket is incorporated in the inlet manifold so that the petrol/air charge may be correctly prepared before entering the combustion chambers.

The exhaust manifold is mounted on the right-hand side of the cylinder head and connects to a single downpipe and silencer system.

Aluminium alloy pistons are connected to the crankshaft by 'H' section forged steel connecting rods and gudgeon pins. The gudgeon pin is a press fit in the small end of the connecting rod but a floating fit in the piston boss. Two compression rings and one scraper ring, all located above the gudgeon pin, are fitted.

The forged crankshaft runs in five main bearings and endfloat is accommodated by fitting thrust washers either side of the centre main bearing.

Before commencing any overhaul work on the engine refer to Section 8, where information is given about special tools that are required to remove the cylinder head drive belt tensioner and oil pump.

2 Major operations possible with engine in place

The following major operations can be carried out to the engine with it in place:
1 *Removal and replacement of camshaft*
2 *Removal and replacement of cylinder head*
3 *Removal and replacement of camshaft drivebelt*
4 *Removal and replacement of balance shaft*
5 *Removal and replacement of engine front mountings*

3 Major operations requiring engine removal

The following major operations can be carried out with the engine out of the body frame on the bench or floor:
1 *Removal and replacement of the main bearings*
2 *Removal and replacement of the crankshaft*
3 *Removal and replacement of the flywheel*
4 *Removal and replacement of the crankshaft rear oil seal*
5 *Removal and replacement of oil pump*
6 *Removal and replacement of sump*
7 *Removal and replacement of big end bearings*
8 *Removal and replacement of pistons and connecting rods*

4 Methods of engine removal

The engine may be lifted out either on its own or in unit with the gearbox. On models fitted with automatic transmission it is recommended that the engine be lifted out on its own, unless a substantial crane or overhead hoist is available, because of the weight factor. If the engine and gearbox are removed as a unit they have to be lifted out at a very steep angle, so make sure

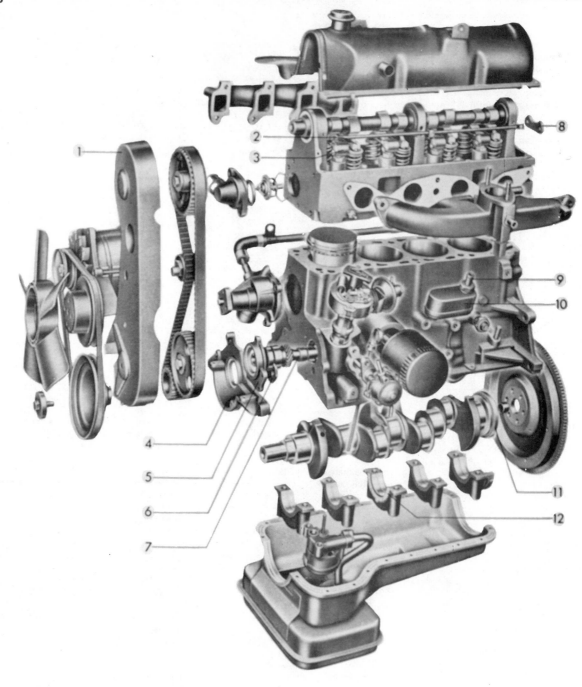

Fig. 1.1. Exploded view of the engine

1	Timing cover	4	Crankshaft front cover	6	Retaining plate	10	Oil separator
2	Cam follower arm	5	Auxiliary shaft front cover	7	Auxiliary shaft	11	Crankshaft rear oil seal
3	Spring			8	Crankshaft thrust plate	12	Thrust washers
				9	Crankcase ventilation valve		

that there is sufficient lifting height available.

5   Engine removal with gearbox

1   The do-it-yourself owner should be able to remove the power unit fairly easily in about 4 hours. It is essential to have a good hoist and two axle stands if an inspection pit is not available.

2   The sequence of operations listed in this Section is not critical as the position of the person undertaking the work, or the tool in his hand, will determine to a certain extent the order in which the work is tackled. Obviously the power unit cannot be removed until everything is disconnected from it and the following sequence will ensure that nothing is forgotten.

3   Open the bonnet and using a soft pencil mark the outline position of both the hinges at the bonnet to act as a datum for refitting.

4   With the help of a second person to take the weight of the bonnet undo and remove the hinge to bonnet securing bolts with plain and spring washers. There are two bolts to each hinge.

5   Lift away the bonnet and put in a safe place where it will not be scratched. Remove the battery as described in Chapter 10, Section 2.

6   Place a container having a capacity of at least 8 Imp. pints (4.55 litres) under the engine sump and remove the oil drain plug. Allow the oil to drain out and then refit the plug.

7   Refer to Chapter 3, Section 2, and remove the air cleaner assembly from the top of the carburettor.

8   Mark the HT leads so that they may be refitted in their original positions and detach from the spark plugs.

9   Release the HT lead rubber moulding from the clip on the top of the cover.

10 Spring back the clips securing the distributor cap to the distributor body. Lift off the distributor cap.

11 Detach the HT lead from the centre of the ignition coil. Remove the distributor cap from the engine compartment.

12 Refer to Chapter 2, Section 2, and drain the cooling system.

13 Slacken the clip that secures the heater hose to the water pump. Pull off the hose.

14 Slacken the clip that secures the heater hose to the heater unit. Pull off the hose.

15 Slacken the clips that secure the hoses to the automatic choke and pull off the two hoses.

16 Slacken the clip securing the water hose to the adaptor elbow on the side of the inlet manifold and pull off the hose.

17 Slacken the clip that secures the fuel feed pipe to the carburettor float chamber and pull off the hose. Plug the end to stop dirt ingress or fuel loss due to syphoning.

18 Detach the throttle control inner cable from the operating rod (photo).

19 Unscrew the throttle control outer cable securing nut and detach the cable from the mounting bracket (photo).

20 Detach the vacuum pipe from the vacuum unit on the side of the distributor (photo).

21 Undo and remove the four nuts and washers that secure the carburettor to the inlet manifold. Carefully lift the carburettor up and away from the studs on the manifold.

22 The combined insulation spacer and gasket may now be lifted from the studs. Note that it is marked 'TOP FRONT' and it must be refitted the correct way round.

23 Slacken the clip securing the hose to the manifold branch pipe adaptor and pull off the hose.

24 Slacken the clip securing the hose to the adaptor at the centre of the manifold and pull off the hose.

25 Undo and remove the self lock nuts and bolts securing the inlet manifold to the side of the cylinder head.

26 Note that one of the manifold securing bolts also retains the air cleaner support bracket (photo).

27 Lift away the inlet manifold (photo).

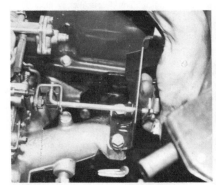

5.18 Detaching throttle cable from operating rod

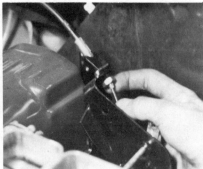

5.19 Detaching throttle cable assembly from mounting bracket

5.20 Detaching vacuum pipe from distributor

5.26 Air cleaner support bracket retained by one manifold bolt

5.27 Lifting away inlet manifold

5.33 Crankcase ventilation valve removal

28 Carefully lift away the inlet manifold gasket.
29 Undo and remove the two nuts that secure the exhaust downpipe clamp plate to the exhaust manifold.
30 Slide the clamp plate down the exhaust pipe.
31 Refer to Chapter 2, Section 5, and remove the radiator.
32 Detach the thermal transmitter electric cable from the inlet manifold side of the cylinder head.
33 Pull the crankcase ventilation valve and hose from the oil separator located on the left-hand side of the cylinder block (photo).
34 Detach the oil pressure warning light cable from the switch located below the oil separator.
35 Detach the Lucar terminal connector from the starter motor solenoid (photo). Also detach the terminal connector from the rear of the alternator. If tight a screwdriver will be of assistance.
36 Make a note of the electrical cable connections on the rear of the starter motor solenoid and detach the cables (photos).
37 Undo and remove the distributor clamp bolt and clamp (photo). Lift away the distributor.
38 Undo and remove the bolt that secures the cable terminal to the engine just in front of the fuel pump (photo).
39 Undo and remove the two bolts and spring washers that secure the fuel pump to the cylinder block (photo).
40 Place the fuel pump on the battery tray (photo). Withdraw the pump operating rod from the cylinder block and put in a safe place.
41 Slacken the alternator securing bolts and push the alternator towards the engine. Lift away the fan belt.
42 Undo and remove the four bolts that secure the fan pulley to the water pump pulley hub. Lift away the fan and pulley (photo).
43 Working under the car slacken the exhaust downpipe to silencer clamp.
44 Detach the exhaust pipe rubber mounting from the body mounted bracket and pull the exhaust system to one side to give better access. Tie in position with string or wire (photo).
45 *Models fitted with centre console proceed to paragraph 49; otherwise as follows:*
46 Carefully ease the gearchange lever gaiter from the body panel and slide it up the gearlever.
47 Using a screwdriver bend back the locking tabs on the lock ring and carefully unscrew the lock ring and gearchange lever retainer.
48 The gearchange lever can now be lifted upwards and away from the gearbox.
49 *Models fitted with centre console:* Undo and remove the screws that secure the parcel tray and lift away the parcel tray.
50 Unlock the nut located at the base of the gearchange lever knob. Unscrew the gearchange lever knob and locknut.
51 Undo and remove the centre console and instrument cluster mounting screws.
52 Move the console unit until it is possible to gain access to the rear of the instrument cluster. Make a note of the electrical cable connections and detach from the rear of the instruments.
53 Undo and remove the centre bolt from the handbrake lever compensator and pull the lever handle fully up. The console unit may now be lifted away from inside the car.
54 *All models:* Mark the mating flanges of the propeller shaft and final drive so that they may be reconnected in their original positions and undo and remove the four securing bolts.
55 Where a split type propeller shaft is fitted, undo and remove the centre bearing retainer securing bolts, spring and plain washers.
56 Wrap some polythene around the end of the gearbox and secure with string or wire to stop oil running out..
57 Pull off the plug attached to the reverse light switch located on the side of the remote control housing.
58 Using a pair of circlip pliers remove the circlip retaining the speedometer drive cable end to the gearbox extension housing.
59 Pull the speedometer drive cable away from the side of the extension housing.
60 Using a pair of pliers detach the clutch operating cable from the actuating arm that protrudes from the side of the clutch

housing. On some models it will be necessary to pull back the rubber gaiter first.
61 Pull the clutch cable assembly through the locating hole in the flange on the clutch housing.
62 Suitably support the weight of the gearbox by using either a jack or an axle stand. Using a rope sling passed under the engine mountings support the weight of the engine (photo).
63 Undo and remove the one bolt that secures the rubber mountings to the gearbox extension housing.
64 Undo and remove the four bolts, spring and plain washers that secure the gearbox support crossmember to the body. Lift away the crossmember.
65 Undo and remove the two engine mountings lower securing nut and large plain washer.
66 Check that no electric cables or controls have been left connected and are tucked well out of the way.
67 The complete unit may now be removed from the car. Commence by removing the support from the rear of the gearbox and carefully lower the end to the ground. It will be beneficial if a piece of wood planking is placed between the end of the gearbox and the floor so that it can act as a skid.
68 Carefully raise the engine and pull slightly forward. It will now be necessary to tilt the engine at a very steep angle so that the sump clears the front grille panels. Continue to raise the engine until the sump is just above the front panel (photos).
69 A second person should now lift the rear of the gearbox over the front panel, and when all is clear lower the unit to the floor.
70 Thoroughly wash the exterior with paraffin or water soluble cleaner. Wash off with a strong water jet and dry thoroughly.
71 The gearbox may now be separated from the engine. Undo and remove the bolts that secure the starter motor to the bellhousing flange. Lift away the starter motor.
72 Remove the rear engine cover plate and bracket assembly from the clutch housing.
73 Undo and remove the remaining bolts that secure the clutch bell housing to the rear of the engine. The gearbox may now be parted from the engine. **DO NOT** allow the weight of the gearbox to hang on the input shaft (first motion shaft).

6 Engine removal without gearbox

1 Follow the instructions given in Section 5, paragraphs 1 to 44, inclusive.
2 Suitably support the weight of the gearbox by using either a jack or an axle stand. Using a rope sling passed under the engine mountings support the weight of the engine.
3 Undo and remove the two engine mounting lower securing nuts and large plain washers.
4 Undo and remove the bolts that secure the starter motor to the gearbox flange. Lift away the starter motor.
5 Remove the rear engine cover plate and bracket assembly from the clutch housing. Detach the bracket assembly from the cylinder block and swing it back out of the way.
6 Undo and remove the remaining bolts that secure the clutch bell housing to the rear of the engine.
7 Follow the instructions given in Section 5, paragraphs 66, 68 and 70.

7 Engine removal without automatic transmission

The procedure is similar to that described in Section 6 of this Chapter, but it will be necessary to refer to Chapter 6, Section 9 for the precautionary measures to be taken when separating the engine from the automatic transmission.

8 Engine - dismantling (general)

1 It is best to mount the engine on a dismantling stand, but if this is not available, stand the engine on a strong bench at a

5.35 Removal of starter solenoid Lucar cable terminal

5.36A Detachment of cables at rear of solenoid

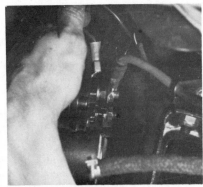
5.36B Detachment of third cable from rear of starter motor

5.37 Removal of distributor clamp and clamp bolt

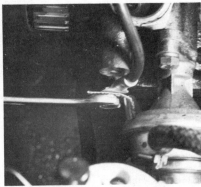
5.38 Detachment of earth cable from engine

5.39 Removal of fuel pump securing bolts

5.40 Fuel pump removed from engine

5.42 Removal of fan and pulley

5.44 Detachment of exhaust pipe rubber

5.62 Lifting rope sling positioned around engine mounting brackets

5.68A Engine removal - Stage 1

5.68B Engine removal - Stage 2

comfortable working height. Failing this, it will have to be stripped down on the floor.

2   During the dismantling process, the greatest care should be taken to keep the exposed parts free from dirt. As an aid to achieving this, thoroughly clean down the outside of the engine, first removing all traces of oil and congealed dirt.

3   A good grease solvent will make the job much easier, for, after the solvent has been applied and allowed to stand for a time, a vigorous jet of water will wash off the solvent and grease with it. If the dirt is thick and deeply embedded, work the solvent into it with a strong stiff brush.

4   Finally wipe down the exterior of the engine with a rag and only then, when it is quite clean, should the dismantling process begin. As the engine is stripped, clean each part in a bath of paraffin or petrol. Never immerse parts with oilways in paraffin eg; crankshaft. To clean these parts, wipe down carefully with a petrol dampened rag. Oilways can be cleaned out with wire. If an airline is available, all parts can be blown dry and the oilways blown through as an added precaution.

6   Re-use of old gaskets is false economy. To avoid the possibility of trouble after the engine has been reassembled **always** use new gaskets throughout.

7   Do not throw away the old gaskets, for sometimes it happens that an immediate replacement cannot be found and the old gasket is then very useful as a template. Hang up the gaskets as they are removed.

8   To strip the engine, it is best to work from the top down. The crankcase provides a firm base on which the engine can be supported in an upright position. When the stage is reached where the crankshaft must be removed, the engine can be turned on its side and all other work carried out with it in this position.

9   Wherever possible replace nuts, bolts and washers finger tight from wherever they were removed. This helps to avoid loss and muddle. If they cannot be replaced then arrange them in a fashion that it is clear from whence they came.

10 Before dismantling begins it is important that three special tools are obtained otherwise certain work cannot be carried out. The special tools are shown in the photo, and will enable the cylinder head bolts, the oil pump bolts and the valve springs to be removed.

9   Engine - removing ancillary components

Before basic engine dismantling begins, it is necessary to strip it of ancillary components

    a) Fuel system components
       Carburettor and manifold assembly
       Exhaust manifold
       Fuel pump
       Fuel line
    b) Ignition system components
       Spark plugs
       Distributor
    c) Electrical system components
       Alternator
       Starter motor
    d) Cooling system components
       Fan and hub
       Water pump
       Thermostat housing and thermostat
       Water temperature indicator sender unit
    e) Engine
       Oil filter
       Oil pressure sender unit
       Oil level dipstick
       Oil filler cap and top cover
       Engine mountings
       Crankcase ventilation valve and oil separator
    f) Clutch
       Clutch pressure plate assembly
       Clutch friction plate assembly

    g) Where emission control systems are installed (see Chapter 3) remove the air pump, valves and hoses or disconnect the decel valve.

All nuts and bolts associated with the foregoing. Some of these items have to be removed for individual servicing or renewal periodically and details can be found in the appropriate Chapter.

1 0 Cylinder head - removal (engine in car)

1   Open the bonnet and using a soft pencil mark the outline of both the hinges at the bonnet to act as a datum for refitting.

2   With the help of a second person to take the weight of the bonnet undo and remove the hinge to bonnet securing bolts with plain and spring washers. There are two bolts to each hinge.

3   Lift away the bonnet and put in a safe place where it will not be scratched.

4   Refer to Chapter 10, Section 2, and remove the battery.

5   Place a container having a capacity of at least 8 Imp. pints (4.55 litres) under the engine and sump and remove the oil drain plug. Allow the oil to drain out and then refit the plug.

6   Refer to Chapter 3, Section 2, and remove the air cleaner assembly from the top of the carburettor.

7   Mark the HT leads so that they may be refitted in their original positions and detach from the spark plugs.

8   Release the HT lead rubber moulding from the clip on the top of the cover.

9   Spring back the clips securing the distributor cap to the distributor body. Lift off the distributor cap.

10 Detach the HT lead from the centre of the ignition coil. Remove the distributor cap from the engine compartment.

11 Refer to Chapter 2, Section 2, and drain the cooling system.

12 Refer to Chapter 3, Section 16 or 20, and remove the carburettor.

13 The combined insulation spacer and gasket may now be lifted from the studs. Note that it is marked 'TOP FRONT' and it must be refitted the correct way round.

14 Slacken the clip securing the hose to the inlet manifold branch pipe adaptor and pull off the hose.

15 Slacken the clip securing the hose to the adaptor at the centre of the manifold and pull off the hose.

16 Undo and remove the self lock nuts and bolts securing the inlet manifold to the side of the cylinder head. Note that one of the manifold securing bolts also retains the air cleaner support bracket.

17 Lift away the inlet manifold and recover the manifold gasket.

18 Undo and remove the two nuts that secure the exhaust downpipe and clamp plate to the exhaust manifold.

19 Slide the clamp plate down the exhaust pipe.

20 Detach the thermal transmitter electric cable from the inlet manifold side of the cylinder head (photo).

21 Slacken the radiator top hose clips and completely remove the hose (photo).

22 Undo and remove the bolts, spring and plain washers that secure the top cover to the cylinder head (photos).

23 Lift away the top cover (photo).

24 Undo and remove the two self locking nuts that secure the heat deflector plate to the top of the exhaust manifold. Lift away the deflector plate (photo).

25 Undo and remove the bolts, spring and plain washers that secure the toothed drivebelt guard (photo).

26 Lift away the guard (photo).

27 Release the tension from the drivebelt by slackening the spring loaded roller mounting plate securing bolt (photo).

28 Lift the toothed drivebelt from the camshaft sprocket (photo).

29 Using the special tool (21 - 002) together with a socket wrench (photo), slacken the cylinder head securing bolts in a diagonal and progressive manner until all are free from tension. Remove the ten bolts noting that because of the special shape of the bolt head no washers are used. Unfortunately there is no other tool

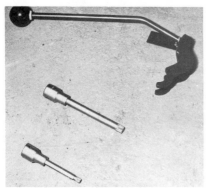

8.10 Three special tools necessary for dismantling

10.20 Thermal transmitter electric cable detachment

10.21 Slackening radiator top hose clip

10.22A Removing top cover front securing bolts

10.22B Top cover flange securing bolts

10.23 Top cover removal

10.24 Removing heat deflector plate

10.25 Removing belt guard securing bolts

10.26 Belt guard removal

10.27 Releasing belt tensioner mounting plate securing bolt

10.28 Removing belt from camshaft sprocket

10.29 Slackening cylinder head securing bolts

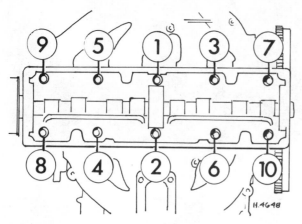

Fig. 1.2. Correct order for slackening or tightening cylinder head
bolts (Secs. 10 and 57)

suitable to slot into the bolt head so do not attempt to improvise
which will only cause damage to the bolt (Fig. 1.2).
30 The cylinder head may now be removed by lifting upwards
(photo). If the head is stuck, try to rock it to break the seal.
Under no circumstances try to prise it apart from the cylinder
block with a screwdriver or cold chisel, as damage may be done
to the faces of the cylinder head and block. If the head will not
readily free, temporarily refit the battery and turn the engine
over using the starter motor, as the compression in the cylinders
will often break the cylinder head joint. If this fails to work,
strike the head sharply with a plastic headed or wooden hammer,
or with a metal hammer with an interposed piece of wood to
cushion the blow. Under no circumstances hit the head directly
with a metal hammer as this may cause the casting to fracture.
Several sharp taps with the hammer, at the same time pulling
upwards, should free the head. Lift the head off and place to one
side (photo).

11 Cylinder head - removal (engine on bench)

The procedure for removing the cylinder head with the
engine on the bench is similar to that for removal when the
engine is in the car, with the exception of disconnecting the
controls and services. Refer to Section 10, and follow the
sequence given in paragraphs 22 to 30, inclusive.

12 Auxiliary shaft - removal

1   Using a metal bar lock the shaft sprocket and with an open

ended spanner undo and remove the bolt and washer that
secures the sprocket to the shaft (photo).
2   Undo and remove the three bolts and spring washers that
secure the shaft timing cover to the cylinder block (photo).
3   Lift away the timing cover (photo).
4   Undo and remove the two crosshead screws that secure the
shaft thrust plate to the cylinder block (photo).
5   Lift away the thrust plate (photo).
6   The shaft may now be drawn forwards and then lifted
away (photo).

13 Flywheel and sump - removal

1   With the clutch removed, as described in Chapter 5, lock the
flywheel using a screwdriver in mesh with the starter ring gear
and undo the six bolts that secure the flywheel to the crankshaft
in a diagonal and progressive manner (photo). Lift away the
bolts.
2   Mark the relative position of the flywheel and crankshaft
and then lift away the flywheel (photo).
3   Undo the remaining engine backplate securing bolts and
ease the backplate from the two dowels. Lift away the backplate
(photo).
4   Undo and remove the bolts that secure the sump to the
underside of the crankcase (photo).
5   Lift away the sump and its gasket (photo).

14 Oil pump and strainer - removal

1   Undo and remove the screw and spring washer that secures
the oil pump pick-up pipe support bracket to the crankcase.
2   Using special tool (21 - 012) undo the two special bolts that
secure the oil pump to the underside of the crankcase. Unfortunately there is no other tool suitable to slot into the screw head
so do not attempt to improvise which will only cause damage to
the screw (photo).
3   Lift away the oil pump and strainer assembly (photo).
4   Carefully lift away the oil pump drive making a special note
of which way round it is fitted (photo).

15 Crankshaft pulley, sprocket and timing cover - removal

1   Lock the crankshaft using a block of soft wood placed
between a crankshaft web and the crankcase then using a socket
and suitable extension, undo the bolt that secures the crankshaft
pulley. Recover the large diameter plain washer.
2   Using a large screwdriver ease the pulley from the crankshaft.
Recover the large diameter thrust washer.
3   Again using the screwdriver ease the sprocket from the
crankshaft (photo).

10.30A Cylinder head removal

10.30B Engine with cylinder head
removed

12.1 Auxiliary shaft sprocket securing
bolt removal

12.2 Removing auxiliary shaft timing cover securing bolts

12.3 Removing auxiliary shaft timing cover

12.4 Removal of auxiliary shaft thrust plate securing screws

12.5 Lifting away thrust plate

12.6 Withdrawal of auxiliary shaft

13.1 Removal of flywheel securing bolts

13.2 Lifting away flywheel

13.3 Backplate removal

13.4 Removal of sump securing bolts

13.5 Lifting away sump

14.2 Removal of oil pump securing bolts

14.3 Lifting away oil pump and pick up pipe

14.4 Oil pump drive shaft removal

15.3 Removal of sprocket from crankshaft

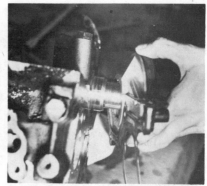

15.5 Removal of timing cover and gasket

16.1 Piston identification marks stamped on crown

16.3 Lifting away big-end cap

17.1 Main bearing - cap identification marks

17.3 Lifting away No. 2 main bearing-cap

17.4 Rear main bearing-cap removal

17.8 Lifting away crankshaft rear oil seal

17.9 Cylinder block and crankcase with crankshaft removed

18.6 Lifting away crankshaft pulley

18.8 Drive belt removal

4   Undo and remove the bolts and spring washers that secure the timing cover to the front of the crankcase.
5   Lift away the timing cover and the gasket (photo).

16 Pistons, connecting rods and big-end bearings - removal

1   Note that the pistons have an arrow marked on the crown showing the forward facing side (photo). Inspect the big-end bearing caps and connecting rods to make sure identification marks are visible. This is to ensure that the correct end caps are fitted to the correct connecting rods and the connecting rods placed in their respective bores (Fig. 1.3).
2   Undo the big-end nuts and place to one side in the order in which they were removed.
3   Remove the big-end caps, taking care to keep them in the right order and the correct way round. Also ensure that the shell bearings are kept with their correct connecting rods unless the rods are to be renewed (photo).
4   If the big-end caps are difficult to remove, they may be gently tapped with a soft hammer.
5   To remove the shell bearings, press the bearing opposite the groove in both the connecting rod and its cap, and the bearing will slide out easily.
6   Withdraw the pistons and connecting rods upwards and ensure they are kept in the correct order for replacement in the same bore as they were originally fitted.

17 Crankshaft and main bearings - removal

With the engine removed from the car and separated from the gearbox, and the drivebelt, crankshaft pulley and sprocket, flywheel and backplate, oil pump, big-end bearings and pistons all dismantled, proceed to remove the crankshaft and main bearings.
1   Make sure that identification marks are visible on the main bearing end caps, so that they may be refitted in their original positions and also the correct way round (photo).
2   Undo by one turn at a time the bolts which hold the five bearing caps.
3   Lift away each main bearing cap and the bottom half of each bearing shell, taking care to keep the bearing shell in the right caps (photo).
4   When removing the rear main bearing end cap note that this also retains the crankshaft rear oil seal (photo).
5   When removing the centre main bearing, note the bottom semi-circular halves of the thrust washers, one half lying on either side of the main bearing. Lay them with the centre main bearing along the correct side.
6   As the centre and rear bearing end caps are accurately located by dowels it may be necessary to gently tap the end caps to release them.
7   Slightly rotate the crankshaft to free the upper halves of the bearing shells and thrust washers which can be extracted and placed over the correct bearing cap.
8   Carefully lift away the crankshaft rear oil seal (photo).
9   Remove the crankshaft by lifting it away from the crankcase (photo).

18 Camshaft drivebelt - removal (engine in car)

It is possible to remove the camshaft drivebelt with the engine in-situ but experience is such that this type of belt is very reliable and unlikely to break or stretch considerably. However, during a major engine overhaul it is recommended that a new belt is fitted. To renew the belt, engine in the car:
1   Refer to Chapter 2, Section 2, and drain the cooling system. Slacken the top hose securing clips and remove the top hose.
2   Slacken the alternator mounting bolts and push the unit towards the engine. Lift away the fan belt.
3   Undo and remove the bolts that secure the drivebelt guard

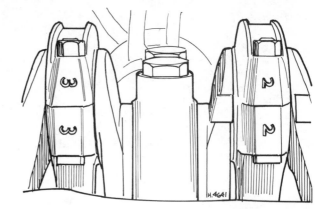

Fig. 1.3. Big-end bearing cap and connecting rod identification marks (Sec. 16)

to the front of the engine. Lift away the guard.
4   Slacken the belt tensioner mounting plate securing bolt and release the tension on the belt.
5   Place the car in gear (manual gearbox only), and apply the brakes firmly. Undo and remove the bolt and plain washer that secure the crankshaft pulley to the nose of the crankshaft. On vehicles fitted with automatic transmission, the starter must be removed and the ring gear jammed to prevent the crankshaft rotating.
6   Using a screwdriver carefully ease off the pulley (photo).
7   Recover the plain large diameter thrust washer.
8   The drivebelt may now be lifted away (photo).

19 Valves - removal

1   To enable the valves to be removed a special valve spring compressor is required. This has a part number of '21 - 005'. However, it was found that it was just possible to use a universal valve spring compressor provided extreme caution was taken.
2   Make a special note of how the cam follower springs are fitted and using a screwdriver remove these from the cam followers (photo).
3   Back off fully the cam follower adjustment and remove the cam followers. Keep these in their respective order so that they can be refitted in their original positions.
4   Using the valve spring compressor, contract the valve springs and lift out the collets (photo).
5   Remove the spring cap and spring and using a screwdriver prise the oil retainer caps out of their seats. Remove each valve and keep in its respective order unless they are so badly worn that they are to be renewed. If they are going to be used again, place them in a sheet of card having eight numbered holes corresponding with the relative positions of the valves when fitted. Also keep the valve springs cups etc., in the correct order.
6   If necessary unscrew the ball head bolts.

20 Camshaft - removal

It is not necessary to remove the engine from the car in order to remove the camshaft. However, it will be necessary to remove the cylinder head first (Section 10) as the camshaft has to be withdrawn from the rear.
1   Undo and remove the bolts, and spring washers and bracket that secure the camshaft lubrication pipe. Lift away the pipe (photo).
2   Carefully inspect the fine oil drillings in the pipe to make sure that none are blocked. (photo)
3   Using a metal bar lock the camshaft drive sprocket then

19.2 Cam follower spring removal

19.4 Compressing valve spring

20.1 Removing camshaft lubrication pipe (Later models have a modified oil pipe)

20.2 Camshaft lubrication pipe oil holes (Later models have a modified oil pipe)

20.3 Using a metal bar to lock camshaft sprocket

20.4 Removal of camshaft sprocket

20.5 Removing camshaft thrust plate securing bolts

20.6 Camshaft thrust plate removal

20.8 Tapping camshaft through bearings

20.9 Camshaft removal

20.10 Camshaft oil seal removal

21.3 Thermostat housing removal

undo and remove the sprocket securing bolt and washer (photo).

4 Using a soft faced hammer or screwdriver ease the sprocket from the camshaft (photo).

5 Undo and remove the two bolts and spring washers that secure the camshaft thrust plate to the rear bearing support (photo).

6 Lift away the thrust plate noting which way round it is fitted (photo).

7 Remove the cam follower springs and then the cam followers as detailed in Section 19, paragraphs 2 and 3.

8 The camshaft may now be removed by using a soft faced hammer and tapping rearwards. Take care not to cut the fingers when the camshaft is being handled as the sides of the lobes can be sharp (photo).

9 Lift the camshaft through the bearing inserts as the lobes can damage the soft metal bearing surfaces (photo).

10 If the oil seal has hardened or become damaged, it may be removed by prising it out with a screwdriver (photo).

21 Thermostat housing and belt tensioner - removal

1 Removal of these parts will usually only be necessary if the cylinder head is to be completely dismantled.

2 Undo and remove the two bolts and spring washers that secure the thermostat housing to the front face of the cylinder head.

3 Lift away the thermostat housing and recover its gasket (photo).

4 Undo and remove the bolt and spring washer that secures the belt tensioner to the cylinder head. It will be necessary to override the tension using a screwdriver as a lever (photos).

5 Using tool number '21 - 012' (the tool for removal of the oil pump securing bolts) unscrew the tensioner mounting plate and spring shaped bolt and lift away the tensioner assembly (photo).

22 Gudgeon pin - removal

Interference fit type gudgeon pins are used and it is important that no damage is caused during removal and refitting. Because of this, should it be necessary to fit new pistons, take the parts along to the local Ford garage who will have the special equipment to do this job.

23 Piston ring - removal

1 To remove the piston rings, slide them carefully over the top of the piston, taking care not to scratch the aluminium alloy; never slide them off the bottom of the piston skirt. It is very easy to break the cast iron piston rings if they are pulled off roughly, so this operation should be done with extreme care. It is helpful to make use of an old 0.020 inch (0.508 mm) feeler gauge.

2 Lift one end of the piston ring to be removed out of its groove and insert under it the end of the feeler gauge.

3 Turn the feeler gauge slowly round the piston and, as the ring comes out of its groove, apply slight upward pressure so that it rests on the land above. It can then be eased off the piston with the feeler gauge stopping it from slipping into an empty groove if it is any but the top piston ring that is being removed.

24 Lubrication and crankcase ventilation systems - description

1 The pressed steel oil sump is attached to the underside of the crankcase and acts as a reservoir for the engine oil. The oil pump draws oil through a strainer located under the oil surface, passes it along a short passage and into the full flow oil filter. The freshly filtered oil flows from the centre of the filter element and enters the main gallery. Five small drillings connect the main gallery to the five main bearings. The big-end bearings are supplied with oil by the front and rear main bearings via skew oil bores.

When the crankshaft is rotating, oil is thrown from the hole in each big-end bearing and splashes the thrust side of the piston and bore.

2 The auxiliary shaft is lubricated directly from the main oil gallery. The distributor shaft is supplied with oil passing along a drilling inside the auxiliary shaft.

3 A further three drillings connect the main oil gallery to the overhead camshaft. The centre camshaft bearing has a semi-circular groove from which oil is passed along a pipe running parallel with the camshaft. The pipe is drilled opposite to each cam and cam follower so providing lubrication to the cams and cam followers. Oil then passes back to the sump, via large drillings in the cylinder head and cylinder block.

A semi enclosed engine ventilation system is used to control crankcase vapour. It is controlled by the amount of air drawn in by the engine when running and the throughput of the regulator valve (Fig. 1.5).

4 The system is known as the P.C.V. system (Positive Crankcase Ventilation) and the advantage of the system is that should the 'blow-by' exceed the capacity of the P.C.V.valve, excess fumes are fed into the engine through the air cleaner. This is caused by the rise in crankcase pressure which creates a reverse flow in the air intake pipe.

5 Periodically, pull the valve and hose from the rubber grommet of the oil separator and inspect the valve for free-movement. If it is sticky in action or is choked with sludge, dismantle it and clean the components.

6 Occasionally check the security and condition of the system connecting hoses.

21.4A Removal of belt tensioner mounting plate securing bolt

21.4B Easing off the belt spring tension with a screwdriver

21.5 Using special tool to remove mounting plate and spring securing bolt from belt tensioner

H.4647

Fig. 1.4. Circulation of lubricant through the engine (Sec. 24)

OIL FILLER CAP

Fig. 1.5. The semi-enclosed engine ventilation system (Sec. 24)

Fig. 1.6. Exploded and sectional views of P.C.V. valve (Sec. 24)

1 Valve body
2 Spring
3 Piston

4 Washer
5 Circlip

Large Throttle Openings

Small Throttle Openings

25 Oil pump - dismantling, inspection and reassembly

1 If oil pump wear is suspected it is possible to obtain a repair kit. Check for wear first as described later in this Section and if confirmed, obtain an overhaul kit or a new pump. The two rotors are a matched pair and form a single replacement unit. Where the rotor assembly is to be re-used the outer rotor, prior to dismantling, must be marked on its front face in order to ensure correct reassembly.

2 Undo and remove the two bolts and spring washers that secure the intake cowl to the oil pump body. Lift away the cowl and its gasket (Fig. 1.7).

3 Note the relative position of the oil pump cover and body and then undo and remove the three bolts and spring washers. Lift away the cover.

4 Carefully remove the rotors from the housing.

5 Using a centre punch tap a hole in the centre of the pressure relief valve sealing plug, (make a note to obtain a new one).

6 Screw in a self tapping screw and using an open ended spanner withdraw the sealing plug as shown in Fig. 1.8.

7 Thoroughly clean all parts in petrol or paraffin and wipe dry using a non-fluffy rag. The necessary clearances may now be checked using a machined straight-edge (a good steel rule) and a set of feeler gauges. The critical clearances are between the lobes of the centre rotor and convex faces of the outer rotor; between the rotor and the pump body; and between both rotors and the end cover plate.

8 The rotor lobe clearance may be checked using feeler gauges and should be within the limits 0.002 - 0.008 in (0.05 - 0.20 mm).

9 The clearance between the outer rotor and pump body should be within the limits 0.006 - 0.012 in (0.15 - 0.30 mm) (Fig. 1.9)

10 The endfloat clearance may be measured by placing a steel straight-edge across the end of the pump and measuring the gap between the rotors and the straight-edge. The gap in either rotor should be within the limits 0.0012 - 0.004 in (0.03 - 0.10 mm), as shown in Fig. 1.10.

11 If the only excessive clearances are endfloat it is possible to reduce them by removing the rotors and lapping the face of the body on a flat bed until the necessary clearances are obtained. It must be emphasised, however, that the face of the body must remain perfectly flat and square to the axis of the rotor spindle otherwise the clearances will not be equal and the end cover will not be a pressure tight fit to the body. It is worth trying, of course, if the pump is in need of renewal anyway but unless done properly, it could seriously jeopardise the rest of the overhaul. Any variations in the other two clearances should be overcome with a new unit.

12 With all parts scrupulously clean first refit the relief valve and spring and lightly lubricate with engine oil.

13 Using a suitable diameter drift drive in a new sealing plug, flat side outwards until it is flush with the intake cowl bearing face.

14 Well lubricate both rotors with engine oil and insert into the body. Fit the oil pump cover and secure with the three bolts in a diagonal and progressive manner to a final torque wrench setting of 6.4 - 9.3 lb f ft (0.9 - 1.3 kg f m).

15 Fit the intermediate shaft into the rotor driveshaft and make sure that the rotor turns freely.

16 Fit the cowl to the pump body, using a new gasket and secure

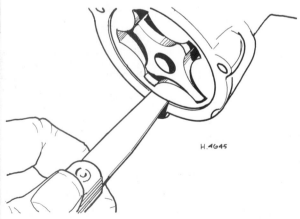

Fig. 1.7. Components of oil pump (Sec. 25)

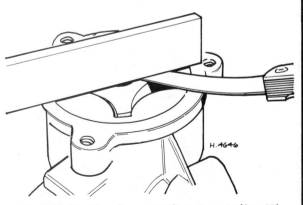

Fig. 1.8. Removal of sealing plug from oil pump pressure relief valve (Sec. 25)

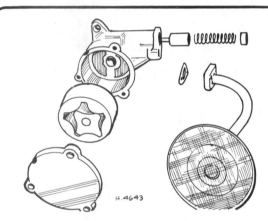

Fig. 1.9. Checking oil pump outer rotor and body clearance (Sec. 25)

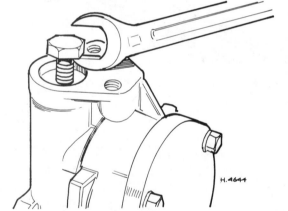

Fig. 1.10. Checking oil pump endfloat clearance (Sec. 25)

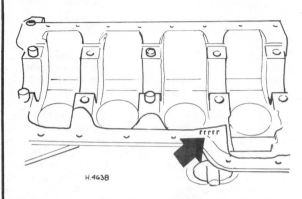

H.4638

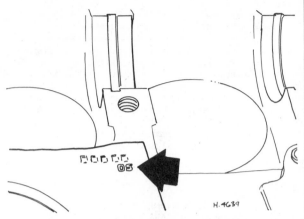

H.4639

A With either the crankshaft main or big end bearings a bearing comprises the bore, crankshaft journal and two bearing liner halves. The main bearing bore and also the crankshaft journal are marked with blue colour if of minimum size within the tolerance grade and with red colour if of maximum size within the tolerance grade. The parent bore in the cylinder block is marked with letters

r   red   b   blue

B The parent bore identification letters are stamped on the oil sump side of the machined face of the cylinder block. Where the code letters are followed by the letters 'OS' the parent bores are of 0.4 mm oversize

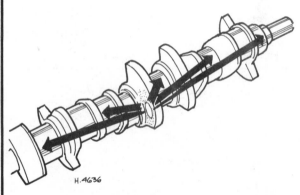

H.4636

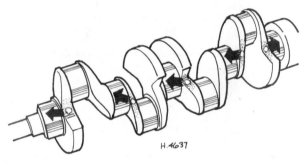

H.4637

C If all main bearing journals are within the same tolerance grade, a red or blue colour mark is to be found on the crankshaft web behind the centre bearing

D If the main bearing journals vary in tolerance the colour marks are to be found on the narrow side of the web behind the respective bearing, but for the rear bearing in front.

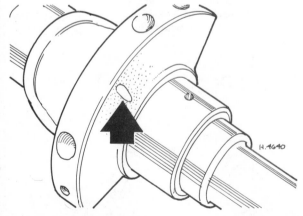

H.4640

Fig. 1.11. Crankshaft identification codes

E If the main bearing journals have been ground to undersize a colour line is to be found on the front web

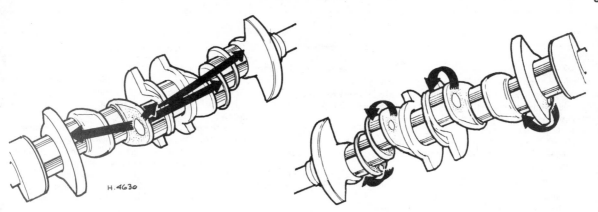

H.4630

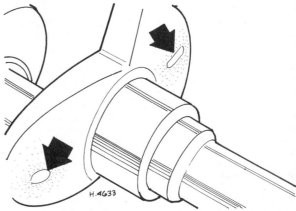

F   If all big-end bearings are within the same tolerance grade a red or blue paint spot is to be found on the web behind the third bearing journal

G   If all the big-end bearings are of a different tolerance grade, the paint spot is to be found on the web behind the respective journal

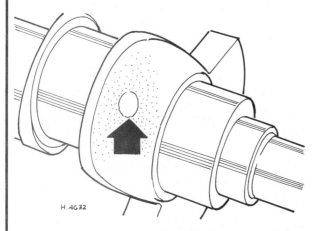

H.4632

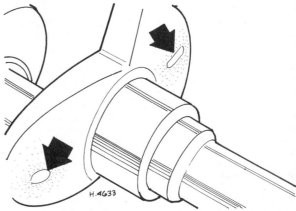

H.4633

H   If the big-end journals are undersize the front side of the counterweight is marked with a paint spot

I   If the main bearing and big-end bearing journals have been ground undersize, the crankshaft is marked by a paint stripe and a paint spot on the front web

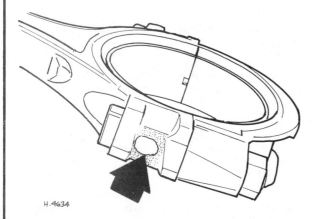

H.4634

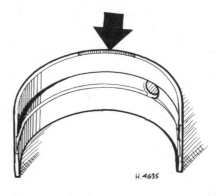

H.4635

J   A red or blue paint spot for connecting rod identification is next to the big-end bore

K   A red or blue paint spot for bearing shell identification is on the outer edge of the shell. If oversize shells are fitted they are marked on their outer face - see Specifications

Fig. 1.12. Crankshaft main and big-end bearing identification codes

with the two bolts.

26 Oil filter - removal and refitting

The oil filter is a complete throw away cartridge screwed into the left-hand side of the cylinder block. Simply unscrew the old unit, clean the seating on the block and lubricate with engine oil. Screw the new one into position taking care not to cross the thread. Continue until the sealing ring just touches the block face then tighten between three quarters of a turn and a full turn using the hands only. Always run the engine and check for signs of leaks after installation.

27 Engine components - examination for wear

When the engine has been stripped down and all parts properly cleaned decisions have to be made as to what needs renewal and the following sections tell the examiner what to look for. In any border line case it is always best to decide in favour of a new part. Even if a part may still be serviceable its life will have been reduced by wear and the degree of trouble needed to replace it in the future must be taken into consideration. However, these things are relative and it depends on whether a quick 'survival' job is being done or whether the car as a whole is being regarded as having many thousands of miles of useful and economical life remaining.

28 Crankshaft - examination and renovation

1   Look at the main bearing journals and the crankpins and if there are any scratches or score marks then the shaft will need regrinding. Such conditions will nearly always be accompanied by similar deterioration in the matching bearing shells.
2   Each bearing journal should also be round and can be checked with a micrometer or caliper gauge around the periphery at several points. If there is more than 0.001 in of ovality regrinding is necessary.
3   A main Ford agent or motor engineering specialist will be able to decide to what extent regrinding is necessary and also supply the special undersize shell bearing to match whatever may need grinding off.
4   Before taking the crankshaft for regrinding check also the cylinder bores and pistons as it may be advantageous to have the whole engine done at the same time.

29 Crankshaft, main and big-end bearings - examination and renovation

1   With careful servicing and regular oil and filter changes bearings will last for a very long time but they can still fail for unforeseen reasons. With big-end bearings the indication is a regular rhythmic loud knocking from the crankcase. The frequency depends on engine speed and is particularly noticeable when the engine is under load. This symptom is accompanied by a fall in oil pressure although this is not normally noticeable unless an oil pressure gauge is fitted. Main bearing failure is usually indicated by serious vibration, particularly at higher engine revolutions, accompanied by a more significant drop in oil pressure and a 'rumbling' noise.
2   Big-end bearings can be removed with the engine still in the car. If the failure is sudden and the engine has a low mileage since new or overhaul this is possibly worth doing. Bearing shells in good condition have bearing surfaces with a smooth, even matt silver/grey colour all over. Worn bearings will show patches of a different colour when the bearing metal has worn away and exposed the underlay. Damaged bearings will be pitted or scored. It is always well worthwhile fitting new shells as their cost is relatively low. If the crankshaft is in good condition it is merely a question of obtaining another set of standard size. A reground crankshaft will need new bearing shells as a matter of course.

30 Cylinder bores - examination and renovation

1   A new cylinder is perfectly round and the walls parallel throughout its length. The action of the piston tends to wear the walls at right angles to the gudgeon pin due to side thrust. This wear takes place principally on that section of the cylinder swept by the piston rings.
2   It is possible to get an indication of bore wear by removing the cylinder head with the engine still in the car. With the piston down in the bore first signs of wear can be seen and felt just below the top of the bore where the top piston ring reaches and there will be a noticeable lip. If there is no lip it is fairly reasonable to expect that bore wear is not severe and any lack of compression or excessive oil consumption is due to worn or broken piston rings or pistons (see Section 31).
3   If it is possible to obtain a bore measuring micrometer, measure the bore in the thrust plane below the lip and again at the bottom of the cylinder in the same plane. If the difference is more than 0.003 inch then a rebore is necessary. Similarly, a difference of 0.003 inch or more across the bore diameter is a sign of ovality calling for rebore.
4   Any bore which is significantly scratched or scored will need reboring. This symptom usually indicates that the piston or rings are damaged also. In the event of only one cylinder being in need of reboring it will still be necessary for all four to be bored and fitted with new oversize pistons and rings. Your Ford agent or local motor engineering specialist will be able to rebore and obtain the necessary matched pistons. If the crankshaft is undergoing regrinding also, it is a good idea to let the same firm renovate and reassemble the crankshaft and pistons to the block. A reputable firm normally gives a guarantee for such work. In cases where engines have been rebored already to their maximum, new cylinder liners are available which may be fitted. In such cases the same reboring processes have to be followed and the services of a specialist engineering firm are required.

31 Pistons and piston rings - inspection and testing

1   Worn pistons and rings can usually be diagnosed when the symptoms of excessive oil consumption and lower compression occur and are sometimes, though not always, associated with worn cylinder bores. Compression testers that fit into the spark plug hole are available and these can indicate where low compression is occurring. Wear usually accelerates the more it is left so when the symptoms occur, early action can possibly save the expense of a rebore.
2   Another symptom of piston wear is piston slap - a knocking noise from the crankcase not to be confused with big-end bearing failure. It can be heard clearly at low engine speed when there is no load (idling for example) and is much less audible when the engine speed increases. Piston wear usually occurs in the skirt or lower end of the piston and is indicated by vertical streaks in the worn area which is always on the thrust side. It can also be seen where the skirt thickness is different.
3   Piston ring wear can be checked by first removing the rings from the pistons as described in Section 23. Then place the rings in the cylinder bores from the top, pushing them down about 1½ inches (38.1 mm) with the head of a piston (from which the rings have been removed) so that they rest square in the cylinder. Then measure the gap at the ends of the ring with a feeler gauge. If it exceeds 0.023 inch (0.58 mm) for the two top compression rings, or 0.055 inch (1.4 mm) for the lower oil control ring then they need renewal.
4   The grooves in which the rings locate in the piston can also become enlarged in use. The clearance between ring and piston, in the groove, should not exceed 0.004 inch (0.102 mm) for the top two compression rings and 0.003 inch (0.076 mm) for the lower oil control ring.
5   However, it is rare that a piston is only worn in the ring grooves and the need to replace them for this fault alone is hardly ever encountered. Wherever pistons are renewed the

weight of the four piston/connecting rod assemblies should be kept within the limit variations of 8 gms. to maintain engine balance.

32 Connecting rods and gudgeon pins - examination and renovation

1   Gudgeon pins are a shrink fit into the connecting rods. Neither of these would normally need replacement unless the pistons were being changed, in which case the new pistons would automatically be supplied with new gudgeon pins.

2   Connecting rods are not subject to wear but in extreme circumstances such as engine seizure they could be distorted. Such conditions may be visually apparent but where doubt exists they should be changed. The bearing caps should also be examined for indications of filing down which may have been attempted in the mistaken idea that bearing slackness could be remedied in this way. If there are such signs then the connecting rods should be replaced.

33 Camshaft and camshaft bearings - examination and renovation

1   The camshaft bearing bushes should be examined for signs of scoring and pitting. If they need renewal they will have to be dealt with professionally as, although it may be relatively easy to remove the old bushes, the correct fitting of new ones requires special tools. If they are not fitted evenly and square from the very start they can be distorted thus causing localised wear in a very short time. See your Ford dealer or local engineering specialist for this work.

2   The camshaft itself may show signs of wear on the bearing journals, or cam lobes. The main decision to take is what degree of wear justifies replacement, which is costly. Any signs of scoring or damage to the bearing journals cannot be removed by regrinding. Renewal of the whole camshaft is the only solution. When overhauling the valve gear, check that oil is being ejected from the nozzles onto the cam followers. Turn the engine on the starter to observe this.

3   The cam lobes themselves may show signs of ridging or pitting on the high points. If ridging is light then it may be possible to smooth it out with fine emery. The cam lobes however, are surface hardened and once this is penetrated wear will be very rapid thereafter.

34 Cam followers - examination

The faces of the cam followers which bear on the camshaft should show no signs of pitting, scoring or other forms of wear. They should not be a loose sloppy fit on the ballheaded bolt.

Inspect the face which bears onto the valve stem and if pitted the cam follower must be renewed.

35 Valves and valve seats - examination and renovation

1   With the valves removed from the cylinder heads examine the heads for signs of cracking, burning away and pitting of the edge where it seats in the port. The seats of the valves in the cylinder head should also be examined for the same signs. Usually it is the valve that deteriorates first but if a bad valve is not rectified the seat will suffer and this is more difficult to repair.

2   Provided there are no obvious signs of serious pitting the valve should be ground with its seat. This may be done by placing a smear of carborundum paste on the edge of the valve and, using a suction type valve holder, grinding the valve in situ. This is done with a semi-rotary action, rotating the handle of the valve holder between the hands and lifting it occasionally to redistribute the traces of paste. Use a coarse paste to start

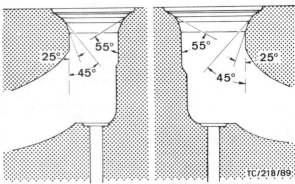

Fig. 1.13. Valve seat angles (Sec. 35)

with. As soon as a matt grey unbroken line appears on both the valve and seat the valve is 'ground in'. All traces of carbon should also be cleaned from the head and neck of the valve stem. A wire brush mounted in a power drill is a quick and effective way of doing this.

3   If the valve requires renewal it should be ground into the seat in the same way as the old valve.

4   Another form of valve wear can occur on the stem where it runs in the guide in the cylinder head. This can be detected by trying to rock the valve from side to side. If there is any movement at all it is an indication that the valve stem or guide is worn. Check the stem first with a micrometer at points along and around its length and if they are not within the specified size new valves will probably solve the problem. If the guides are worn, however, they will need reboring for oversize valves or for fitting guide inserts. The valve seats will also need recutting to ensure they are concentric with the stems. This work should be given to your Ford dealer or local engineering works.

5   When valve seats are badly burnt or pitted, requiring renewal, inserts may be fitted - or replaced if already fitted once before - and once again this is a specialist task to be carried out by a suitable engineering firm.

6   When all valve grinding is completed it is essential that every trace of grinding paste is removed from the valves and ports in the cylinder head. This should be done by thorough washing in petrol or paraffin and blowing out with a jet of air. If particles of carborundum should work their way into the engine they would cause havoc with bearings or cylinder walls.

36 Timing gears and belt - examination and renovation

1   Any wear which takes place in the timing mechanism will be on the teeth of the drive belt or due to stretch of the fabric. Whenever the engine is to be stripped for major overhaul a new belt should be fitted.

2   It is very unusual for the timing gears (sprockets) to wear at the teeth. If the securing bolt/nuts have been loose it is possible for the keyway or hub bore to wear. Check these two points and if damage or wear is evident a new gear must be obtained.

37 Flywheel ring gear - examination and renovation

1   If the ring gear is badly worn or has missing teeth it should be renewed. The old ring can be removed from the flywheel by cutting a notch between two teeth with a hacksaw and then splitting it with a cold chisel.

2   To fit a new ring gear requires heating the ring to 400°F (204°C). This can be done by polishing four equal spaced sections of the gear laying it on a suitable heat resistant surface (such as fire bricks) and heating it evenly with a blow lamp or torch until the polished areas turn a light yellow tinge. Do not overheat or the hard wearing properties will be lost. The gear has a chamfered inner edge which should go against the shoulder

when put on the flywheel. When hot enough place the gear in position quickly, tapping it home, if necessary and let it cool naturally without quenching in any way.

38 Cylinder head and piston crowns - decarbonization

1   When the cylinder head is removed, either in the course of an overhaul or for inspection of bores or valve condition when the engine is in the car, it is normal to remove all carbon deposits from the piston crowns and heads.

2   This is best done with a cup shaped wire brush and an electric drill and is fairly straightforward when the engine is dismantled and the pistons removed. Sometimes hard spots of carbon are not exactly removed except by a scraper. When cleaning the pistons with a scraper, take care not to damage the surface of the piston in any way.

3   When the engine is in the car certain precautions must be taken when decarbonising the piston crowns in order to prevent dislodged pieces of carbon falling into the interior of the engine which could cause damage to cylinder bores, piston and rings - or if allowed into the water passages - damage to the water pump. Turn the engine so that the piston being worked on is at the top of its stroke and then mask off the adjacent cylinder bores and all surrounding water jacket orifices with paper and adhesive tape. Press grease into the gap all round the piston to keep carbon particles out and then scrape all carbon away by hand carefully. Do not use a power drill and wire brush when the engine is in the car as it will virtually be impossible to keep all the carbon dust clear of the engine. When completed, carefully clear out the grease around the rim of the piston with a match-stick or something similar - bringing any carbon particles with it. Repeat the process on the other piston crown. It is not recommended that a ring of carbon is left round the edge of the piston on the theory that it will aid oil consumption. This was valid in the earlier days of long stroke low revving engines but modern engines, fuels and lubricants cause less carbon deposits anyway and any left behind tends merely to cause hot spots.

39 Valve guides - inspection

Examine the valve guides internally for wear. If the valves are a very loose fit in the guides and there is the slightest suspicion of lateral rocking using a new valve, then the guides will have to be reamed and oversize valves, fitted. This is a job best left to the local Ford garage.

40 Sump - inspection

Wash out the sump in petrol and wipe dry. Inspect the exterior for signs of damage or excessive rust: If evident, a new sump must be obtained. To ensure an oil tight joint scrape away all traces of the old gasket from the cylinder block mating face.

41 Engine reassembly - general

All components of the engine must be cleaned of oil, sludge and old gaskets and the working area should also be cleared and clean. In addition to the normal range of good quality socket spanners and general tools which are essential, the following must be available before reassembling begins:
1   *Complete set of new gaskets (photo).*
2   *Supply of clean rags.*
3   *Clean oil can full of clean engine oil.*
4   *Torque spanner.*
5   *All new spare parts as necessary.*

42 Crankshaft - installation

Ensure that the crankcase is thoroughly clean and that all oilways are clear. A thin twist drill or a piece of wire is useful for cleaning them out. If possible blow them out with compressed air.

Treat the crankshaft in the same fashion, and then inject engine oil into the crankshaft oilways.

Commence work of rebuilding the engine by replacing the crankshaft and main bearings:

1   Wipe the bearing shell locations in the crankcase with a soft, non-fluffy rag.

2   Wipe the crankshaft journals with a soft, non-fluffy rag.

3   If the old main bearing shells are to be renewed (not to do so, is a false economy unless they are virtually new) fit the five upper halves of the main bearing shells to their location in the crankcase (photo).

4   Identify each main bearing cap and place in order. The number is cast onto the cap and with intermediate caps an arrow is also marked so that the cap is fitted the correct way round. (photo)

5   Wipe the end cap bearing shell location with a soft non-fluffy rag.

6   Fit the bearing half shell onto each main bearing cap (photo).

7   Fit the bearing half shell into each location in the crank-case.

8   Apply a little grease to each side of the centre main bearing so as to retain the thrust washers (photo).

9   Fit the upper halves of the thrust washers into their grooves either side of the main bearing. The slots must face outwards (photo).

10 Lubricate the crankshaft journals and the upper and lower main bearing shells with engine oil (photo).

11 Carefully lower the crankshaft into the crankcase (photo).

12 Lubricate the crankshaft main bearing journals again and then fit No. 1 bearing cap (photo). Fit the two securing bolts but do not tighten yet.

13 Apply a little gasket cement to the crankshaft rear main bearing end cap location (photo).

14 Next fit No. 5 end cap (photo). Fit the two securing bolts but as before do not tighten yet.

15 Apply a little grease to either side of the centre main bearing end cap so as to retain the thrust washers. Fit the thrust washers with the tag located in the groove and the slots facing outwards (photo).

16 Fit the centre main bearing end cap and the two securing bolts. Then refit the intermediate main bearing end caps. Make sure that the arrows point towards the front of the engine. (photo)

17 Lightly tighten all main cap securing bolts and then fully tighten in a progressive manner to a final torque wrench setting of 64.5 - 74.5 lb ft (9.0 - 10.4 kg m) (photo).

18 Using a screwdriver ease the crankshaft fully forwards and with feeler gauges check the clearance between the crankshaft journal side and the thrust washers. The clearance must not exceed 0.0032 - 0.0110 in (0.08 - 0.28 mm). Undersize thrust washers are available (photo).

19 Test the crankshaft for freedom of rotation. Should it be stiff to turn or possess high spots, a most careful inspection must be made with a micrometer, preferably by a qualified mechanic, to get to the root of the trouble. It is very seldom that any trouble of this nature will be experienced when fitting the crankshaft.

43 Pistons and connecting rods - reassembly

As a press type gudgeon pin is used (see Section 22) this operation must be carried out by the local Ford garage.

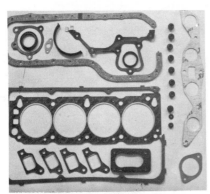
41.1 Items found in gasket set

42.3 Inserting bearing shells into crankcase

42.4 Main bearing cap identification marks

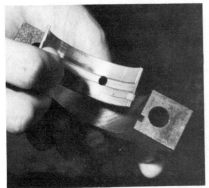
42.6 Fitting bearing shell to main bearing cap

42.8 Applying grease to either side of centre main bearing

42.9 Fitting thrust washers to centre main bearing

42.10 Lubricating bearing shells

42.11 Fitting crankshaft to crankcase

42.12 Refitting No. 1 main bearing cap Note identification mark

42.13 Applying gasket cement to rear main bearing cap location

42.14 Refitting rear main bearing cap

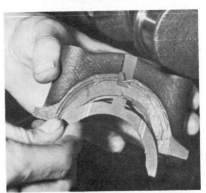
42.15 Fitting thrust washers to centre main bearing cap

42.16 All main bearing caps in position

42.17 Tightening main bearing cap securing bolts

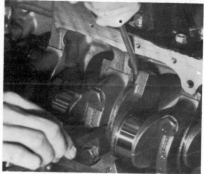

42.18 Using feeler gauge to check end-float

44 Piston rings - replacement

1   Check that the piston ring grooves and oilways are thoroughly clean and unblocked. Piston rings must always be fitted over the head of the piston and never from the bottom.
2   The easiest method to use when fitting rings is to wrap a .020 in (0.5080 mm) feeler gauge round the top of the piston and place the rings one at a time, starting with the bottom oil control ring, over the feeler gauge.
3   The feeler gauge, complete with ring can then be slid down the piston over the other piston ring grooves until the correct groove is reached. The piston ring is then slid gently off the feeler gauge into the groove.
4   An alternative method is to fit the rings by holding them slightly open with the thumbs and both of the index fingers. This method requires a steady hand and great care as it is easy to open the ring too much and break it.

Fig. 1.14. Piston identification mark relative to piston lubrication jet hole (Sec. 45)

45 Pistons - replacement

The piston, complete with connecting rods, can be fitted to the cylinder bores in the following sequence:
1   With a wad of clean rag wipe the cylinder bores clean.
2   The pistons, complete with connecting rods, are fitted to their bores from the top of the block.
3   Locate the piston ring gaps in the following manner (photo):
   Top: 150° from one side of the helical expander gap.
   Centre: 150° from the side opposite the helical expander gap.
   Bottom: Helical expander: opposite the marked piston front side.
   Intermediate rings: 1 inch (25 mm) each side of the helical expander gap.
4   Well lubricate the piston and rings with engine oil (photo).
5   Fit a universal piston ring compressor and prepare to insert the first piston into the bore. Make sure it is the correct piston-connecting rod assembly for that particular bore, that the connecting rod is the correct way round and that the front of the piston is towards the front of the bore, ie; towards the front of the engine (photo).
6   Again lubricate the piston skirt and insert into the bore up to the bottom of the piston ring compressor (photos).
7   Gently but firmly tap the piston through the piston ring compressor and into the cylinder bore with a wooden or plastic faced hammer (photo).

46 Connecting rods to crankshaft - reassembly

1   Wipe clean the connecting rod half of the big-end bearing

cap and the underside of the shell bearing and fit the shell bearing in position with its locating tongue engaged with the corresponding cut out in the rod.
2   If the old bearings are nearly new and are being refitted then ensure they are replaced in their correct locations on the correct rods.
3   Generously lubricate the crankpin journals with engine oil and turn the crankshaft so that the crankpin is in the most advantageous position for the connecting rods to be drawn onto it.
4   Wipe clean the connecting rod bearing cap and back of the shell bearing, and fit the shell bearing in position ensuring that the locating tongue at the back of the bearing engages with the locating groove in the connecting rod cap.
5   Generously lubricate the shell bearing and offer up the connecting rod bearing cap to the connecting rod.
6   Refit the connecting rod nuts (photo).
7   Tighten the bolts with a torque wrench set to 35 lb f ft (4.8 kg f m) (photo).
8   When all the connecting rods have been fitted, rotate the crankshaft to check that everything is free, and that there are no high spots causing binding. The bottom half of the engine is now nearly built up.

47 Oil pump - refitting

1   Wipe the mating faces of the oil pump and underside of the cylinder block.
2   Insert the hexagonal drive shaft into the end of the oil pump (photo).
3   Offer up the oil pump and refit the two special bolts. Using

45.3 Positioning ring gaps

45.4 Lubricating pistons prior to refitting

45.5 Piston identification marks

45.6A Inserting connecting rod into cylinder bore

45.6B Piston ring compressor correctly positioned

45.7 Pushing piston down bore

46.6 Refitting big-end cap securing nuts

46.7 Tightening big-end cap securing nuts

47.2 Inserting oil pump drive shaft

47.3 Tightening oil pump securing bolts

48.1 Refitting rectangular shaped seals to rear of crankshaft

48.2 Fitting seal into rear main bearing cap

the special tool (21 - 012) and a torque wrench tighten the two bolts to a torque wrench setting of 12 - 15 lb f ft (1.7 - 2.1 kg f m) (photo).
4   Refit the one bolt and spring washer that secures the oil pump pick-up pipe support bracket to the crankcase.

48 Crankshaft rear oil seal - installation

1   Apply some gasket cement to the slot on either side of the rear main bearing end cap and insert a rectangular shaped seal (photo).
2   Apply some gasket cement to the slot in the rear main bearing end cap and carefully insert the shaped seal (photo).
3   Lightly smear some grease on the crankshaft rear oil seal and carefully ease it over the end of the crankshaft. The spring

must be inwards (photo).
4   Using a soft metal drift carefully tap the seal into position (photo).

49 Auxiliary shaft and timing cover - refitting

1   Carefully insert the auxiliary shaft into the front face of the cylinder block (photo).
2   Position the thrust plate into its groove in the auxiliary shaft - countersunk faces of the holes facing outwards - and refit the two crosshead screws (photo).
3   Tighten the two crosshead screws using a crosshead screwdriver and an open-ended spanner (photo).
4   Smear some grease on the cylinder block face of a new gasket and carefully fit into position (photo).

48.3 Refitting crankshaft rear oil seal

48.4 Tapping crankshaft rear oil seal into position

49.1 Refitting auxiliary shaft

49.2 Locating auxiliary shaft thrust plate

49.3 Tightening auxiliary shaft thrust plate securing screws

49.4 Positioning new gasket on cylinder block front face

49.6A Refitting crankshaft timing cover

49.6B Tightening crankshaft timing cover securing bolts

49.8 Tightening auxiliary shaft timing cover securing bolts

5   Apply some gasket cement to the slot in the underside of the crankshaft timing cover. Insert the shaped seal.
6   Offer up the timing cover and secure with the bolts and spring washers (photos).
7   Smear some grease onto the seal located in the shaft timing cover and carefully ease the cover over the end of the auxiliary shaft.
8   Secure the auxiliary shaft timing cover with the four bolts and spring washers (photo).

50 Sump - installation

1   Wipe the mating faces of the underside of the crankcase and the sump.
2   Smear some Castrol LM grease on the underside of the crankcase.
3   Fit the sump gasket making sure that the bolt holes line up (Fig. 1.15).
4   Offer the sump up to the gasket taking care not to dislodge the gasket and secure in position with the bolts (photo).
5   Tighten the sump bolts in a progressive manner, to a final torque wrench setting of 4.3 - 5.7 lb f ft (0.6 - 0.8 kg f m) (Fig. 1.16).

51 Crankshaft sprocket and pulley and auxiliary shaft sprocket - refitting

1   Check that the keyways in the end of the crankshaft are clean and the keys are free from burrs. Fit the keys into the keyways (photo).

2   Slide the sprocket into position on the crankshaft. This sprocket is the small diameter one (photo).
3   Ease the drive belt into mesh with the crankshaft sprocket (photo).
4   Slide the large diameter plain washer onto the crankshaft (photo).
5   Check that the keyway in the end of the balance shaft is clean and the key is free of burrs. Fit the key to the keyway.
6   Slide the sprocket onto the end of the auxiliary shaft (photo).
7   Slide the pulley onto the end of the crankshaft (photo).
8   Refit the bolt and thick plain washer to the end of the crankshaft (photo).
9   Lock the crankshaft pulley with a metal bar and using a socket wrench fully tighten the bolt (photo).

52 Water pump - refitting

1   Make sure that all traces of the old gasket are removed and then smear some grease on the gasket face of the cylinder block.
2   Fit a new gasket to the cylinder block
3   Offer up the water pump and secure in position with the four bolts and spring washers (photo).

53 Flywheel and clutch - refitting

1   Remove all traces of the shaped seal from the backplate and apply a little adhesive to the backplate. Fit a new seal to the backplate (photo).
2   Wipe the mating faces of the backplate and cylinder block

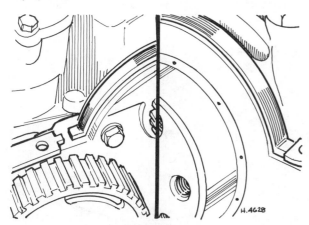

Fig. 1.15. Correct fitment of sump gasket at front and rear main bearing caps (Sec. 50)

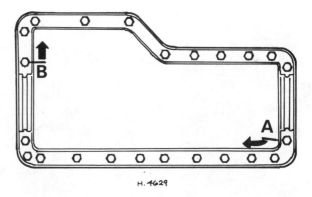

Fig. 1.16. Correct order for tightening sump bolts (Sec. 50)

50.4 New gaskets fitted to greased underside of crankcase, ready for sump

51.1 Refitting Woodruff key to crankshaft

51.2 Sliding on crankshaft sprocket

51.3 Fitting drive belt to crankshaft sprocket

51.4 Refitting large diameter plain washer

51.6 Fitting sprocket to auxiliary shaft

51.7 Refitting crankshaft pulley

51.8 Crankshaft pulley securing bolt and large washer

51.9 Tightening crankshaft pulley securing bolt

52.3 Water pump is offered up to mating face fitted with new gasket

53.1 Fitting new gasket to backplate

53.2 Backplate located on dowels in rear of cylinder block

53.5 Fully tightening flywheel securing bolts

53.6 Refitting clutch

53.8 Fully tightening clutch securing bolts once disc has been centralised

and carefully fit the backplate to the two dowels (photo).

3   Wipe the mating faces of the flywheel and crankshaft and offer up the flywheel to the crankshaft aligning the previously made marks unless new parts have been fitted.

4   Fit the six crankshaft securing bolts and lightly tighten.

5   Lock the flywheel using a screwdriver engaged in the starter ring gear and tighten the securing bolts in a diagonal and progressive manner to a final torque wrench setting of **46.5 - 50.9 lb f ft (6.5 - 7.1 kg f m)** (photo).

6   Refit the clutch disc and pressure plate assembly to the flywheel making sure the disc is the right way round (photo).

7   Secure the pressure plate assembly with the six retaining bolts and spring washers.

8   Centralise the clutch disc using an old input shaft or piece of wooden dowel and fully tighten the retaining bolts (photo).

54 Valves - refitting

1   With the valves suitably ground in (see Section 35) and kept in their correct order start with No. 1 cylinder and insert the valve into its guide (photo).

2   Lubricate the valve stem with engine oil and slide on a new oil seal. The spring must be uppermost as shown in the photo.

3   Fit the valve spring and cap (photo).

4   Using a universal valve spring compressor, compress the valve spring until the split collets can be slid into position (photo). Note these collets have serrations which engage in slots in the valve stem. Release the valve spring compressor.

5   Repeat this procedure until all eight valves and valve springs are fitted.

55 Camshaft - installation

1   If the oil seal was removed (Section 20) a new one should be fitted taking care that it is fitted the correct way round. Gently tap it into position so that it does not tilt (photo).

2   Apply some grease to the lip of the oil seal. Wipe the three bearing surfaces with a clean, non-fluffy rag.

3   Lift the camshaft through the bearing taking care not to damage the bearing surfaces with the sharp edges of the cam lobes. Also take care not to cut the fingers (photo).

4   When the journals are ready to be inserted into the bearings lubricate the bearings with engine oil (photo).

5   Push the camshaft through the bearings until the locating groove in the rear of the camshaft is just rearwards of the bearing carrier.

6   Slide the thrust plate into engagement with the camshaft taking care to fit it the correct way round as previously noted (photo).

7   Secure the thrust plate with the two bolts and spring washers (photo).

8   Check that the keyway in the end of the camshaft is clean and the key is free of burrs. Fit the key into the keyway (photo).

9   Locate the tag on the camshaft sprocket backplate and this must locate in the second groove in the camshaft sprocket (photo).

10 Fit the camshaft sprocket backplate, tag facing outwards (photo).

11 Fit the camshaft sprocket to the end of the camshaft and with a soft faced hammer make sure it is fully home (photo).

12 Refit the sprocket securing bolt and thick plain washer (photo).

54.1 Inserting valve into valve guide

54.2 Sliding seal down valve stem

54.3 Replacing valve spring cap

54.4 Refitting valve collets

55.1 Camshaft oil seal correctly fitted

55.3 Threading camshaft through bearings

55.4 Lubricating camshaft bearings

55.6 Locating camshaft thrust plate

55.7 Tightening camshaft thrust plate retaining bolts

55.8 Fitting Woodruff key to camshaft

55.9 Camshaft sprocket backplate tag

55.10 Camshaft sprocket backplate refitted

55.11 Refitting camshaft sprocket

55.12 Camshaft sprocket securing bolt and plain washer

56.1 Slackening ball headed bolt locknut

56.2 Passing cam follower under camshaft

56.3 Cup located over ball headed bolt

56.4 Cam follower spring engaged with the anchor

56 Cam followers - refitting

1   Undo the ball headed bolt locknut and screw down the bolt fully. This will facilitate refitting the cam followers (photo).
2   Rotate the camshaft until the cam lobe is away from the top of the cylinder head. Pass the cam follower under the back of the cam until the cup is over the ball headed bolt (photo).
3   Engage the cup with the ball headed bolt (photo).
4   Refit the cam follower spring by engaging the ends of the spring with the anchor on the ball headed bolt (photo).
5   Using the fingers pull the spring up and then over the top of the cam follower (photos).
6   Repeat the above sequence for the remaining seven cam followers.
7   Check that the jet holes in the camshaft lubrication pipe are free and offer up to the camshaft bearing pedestals (photo).
8   Refit the pipe securing bolts and spring washers.

57 Cylinder head - refitting

1   Wipe the mating faces of the cylinder head and cylinder block.
2   Carefully place a new gasket on the cylinder block and check to ensure that it is the correct way up, and the right way round (photo).
3   Gently lower the cylinder head being as accurate as possible first time, so that the gasket is not dislodged (photo).
4   Refit the cylinder head bolts taking care not to damage the gasket if it has moved (photo).
5   Using the special tool (21 - 002) lightly tighten all the bolts (photo).
6   Tighten the cylinder head bolts progressively to a final torque wrench setting of 64.5 - 79 lb f ft (9.0 - 11.0 kg f m) (photo), in the order shown in Fig. 1.2.

58 Camshaft drivebelt tensioner and thermostat housing - refitting

1   Thread the shaped bolt through the spring and tensioner plate and screw the bolt into the cylinder head (photo).
2   Tighten the bolt securely using special tool '21 - 012'.
3   Using a screwdriver to overcome the tension of the spring, position the plate so that its securing bolt can be screwed into the cylinder head (photo).
4   Clean the mating faces of the cylinder head and thermostat housing and fit a new gasket.
5   Offer up the thermostat housing and secure in position with the two bolts and spring washers.
6   Tighten the bolts to a torque wrench setting of 12 - 15 lb f ft (1.66 - 2.07 kg f m).

59 Camshaft drivebelt - refitting and timing

1   Rotate the crankshaft until No 1 piston is at its TDC position. This is indicated by the crankshaft sprocket keyway being uppermost and, if the pulley is fitted, by the timing marks indicating TDC (see Chapter 4). If the distributor is fitted, also check that the rotor is pointing to No 1 spark plug electrode (see Fig 1.17).
2   Rotate the camshaft until the pointer is in alignment with the dot mark on the front bearing pedestal (photo). To achieve this always rotate the camshaft in the direction shown in Fig. 1. 17.
3   Engage the drivebelt with the crankshaft sprocket and auxiliary shaft sprocket. Pass the back of the belt over the tensioner jockey wheel and then slide it into mesh with the camshaft sprocket.
4   Slacken the tensioner plate securing bolt and allow the tensioner to settle by rotating the crankshaft twice. Retighten

56.5A Cam follower spring being lifted over cam follower

56.5B Cam follower spring correctly fitted

56.7 Replacing lubrication pipe

57.2 Positioning cylinder head gasket on top of cylinder block

57.3 Lowering cylinder head onto gasket

57.4 Refitting cylinder head bolts

57.5 Special tool engaged in cylinder head bolt

57.6 Tightening cylinder head bolts

58.1 Refitting drive belt tensioner

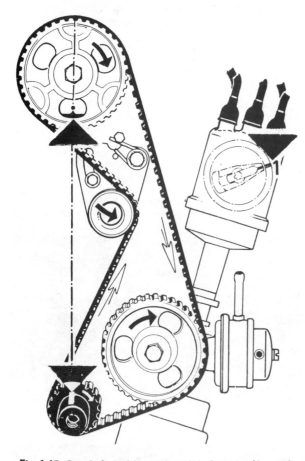

Fig. 1.17. Camshaft, ignition and crankshaft timing (Sec. 59)

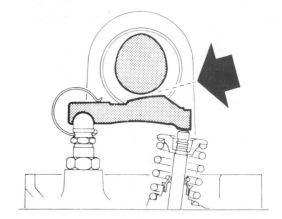

Fig. 1.18. Cam follower and camshaft clearance

This will ensure that the cam follower will be at the back of the cam.

2   Using feeler gauges as shown in this photo check the clearance which should be as follows:

    Inlet   0.008 in (0.20 mm)
    Exhaust   0.010 in (0.25 mm)

3   If adjustment is necessary, using open ended spanners slacken the ball headed bolt securing locknut (photo).

4   Screw the ball headed bolt up or down as necessary until the required clearance is obtained (photo). Retighten the locknut.

5   An alternative method of adjustment is to work to the following table.

Valves open	Valves to adjust
1 ex and 4 in	6 in and 7 ex
6 in and 7 ex	1 ex and 4 in
2 in and 5 ex	3 ex and 8 in
3 ex and 8 in	2 in and 5 ex

the tensioner plate securing bolt.

5   Line up the timing marks and check that these are correct indicating the belt has been correctly refitted (photo).

6   Refit the drivebelt guard, easing the guard into engagement with the bolt and large plain washer located under the water pump (photos).

7   Refit the guard securing bolts and tighten fully.

60 Valve clearances - checking and adjustment

1   With the engine top cover removed, turn the crankshaft until each cam in turn points vertically upwards.

61 Engine/gearbox - reconnecting

If the engine was removed in unit with the gearbox it may be re-attached in the following manner:

1   With the engine on the floor and a wood block under the front of the sump, lift up the gearbox and insert the gearbox input shaft in the centre of the clutch and push so that the input shaft splines pass through the internal splines of the clutch disc.

2   If difficulty is experienced in engaging the splines, try turning the gearbox slightly but on no account allow the weight of the gearbox to rest on the input shaft as it is easily bent.

3   With the gearbox correctly positioned on the engine backplate support its weight using a wooden block (photo).

58.3 Using screwdriver to relieve tension of spring

59.2 Lining up camshaft timing marks

59.5 Drive belt fitted

59.6A Replacing drive belt guard

59.6B Locating guard between washer and pedestal

60.2 Checking cam follower clearance

60.3 Slackening ball headed bolt locknut

60.4 Adjusting ball headed bolt

61.3 Gearbox located ready for attachment to engine

61.5A Refitting starter motor

61.5B Securing starter motor to engine

62.3 Engine positioned over front panels

4 Secure the gearbox to the engine and backplate with the bolts and spring washers.

5 Refit the starter motor to its aperture in the backplate and secure with the two bolts and spring washers (photos).

6 Refit the support bar located between the engine and clutch bellhousing.

62 Engine - installation (with gearbox)

1 Pass a rope sling around the engine mountings and raise the complete power unit from the floor.

2 Check that all cables and controls in the engine compartment are tucked well out of the way and that the exhaust downpipe is tied to the steering column.

3 Place an old blanket over the front of the car to avoid scratching of the grille or front panel. Lift up the power unit sufficiently so that the sump passes over the front panel (photo).

4 An assistant should now lift up the gearbox extension housing whilst the engine is pushed rearwards. Ease the gearbox through the engine compartment and then gradually lower the engine (photo).

5 If a trolley jack is available have it ready under the car to accept the weight of the rear of the gearbox. Alternatively use a piece of wood (photo).

6 Continue to lower the engine and ease the gearbox rearwards until the engine is central within the engine compartment.

7 Locate the engine front mounting studs within the bracket in the front crossmember using a metal bar (photo).

8 Jack up the rear of the gearbox and secure the engine mountings with the nuts and plain washers.

9 Attach the gearbox crossmember to the gearbox extension housing and secure with the shaped metal plate and bolt (photo).

10 Secure the gearbox crossmember to the body attached brackets using the four special dowel bolts and spring washers (photo).

11 Remove the engine suspension rope and the trolley jack (if used) from the gearbox.

12 Working under the car first reconnect the reverse light switch terminal connector (photo).

13 Reconnect the speedometer inner cable to the drive gear and push the outer cable fully up to the extension housing machined recess.

14 Secure the speedometer cable to the gearbox using the circlip. Make sure that it is correctly seated (photo).

15 Check that the clutch release cable nylon bush is correctly located in the gearbox clutch housing flange and fixed through the clutch release cable.

16 Thread the clutch cable through the rubber gaiter (if fitted) and reconnect the clutch inner cable to the relase arm. (photo)

17 Adjust the cable until there is a clearance of 0.12 in (3.5 mm) between the adjusting nut and its abutment on the bell housing (photo). (See also Chapter 5, Section 2).

18 Refit the rubber gaiter (if fitted) (photo).

19 Wipe clean the gearbox mainshaft splines and lubricate with a little Castrol Hypoy Light (EP 80).

20 Offer up the propeller shaft and engage the propeller shaft splines with those of the mainshaft (photo).

21 Where a split type propeller shaft is fitted secure the centre bearing housing to the brackets mounted on the body with the two bolts, spring and plain washers (photo).

22 Align the marks that were previously made on the propeller shaft and final drive flanges and secure with the four bolts and spring washers (photo).

23 Release the exhaust downpipe and offer up to the exhaust manifold. Push up the clamp plate and secure with the two nuts. These nuts should be tightened a turn at a time to ensure that the downpipe seats correctly.

24 Reconnect the exhaust pipe intermediate support rubber to the body mounted bracket (photo).

25 Remove the gearbox filler plug and check the oil level. Top-up as necessary with gearbox oil. The total capacity is 1.58 Imp. pints (0.9 litres).

26 Refit the filler plug and lightly tighten. The plug has a ½ inch square socket so if a socket set is available the ratchet wrench will just fit nicely.

27 Now turning to the engine compartment reconnect the cables to the rear of the starter motor solenoid as noted upon removal. Secure with the nut (photo).

28 The distributor may now be refitted. Look up the initial static advance for the particular model in the specifications given in Chapter 4.

29 Turn the engine until No. 1 piston is coming up to TDC on the compression stroke. This can be checked by removing No. 1 spark plug and feeling the pressure being developed in the cylinder. Alternatively remove the oil filler cap and note when the cam is in the upright position.

30 Refer to Chapter 4, Section 14, and refit the distributor to the engine (photos).

31 Wipe the oil filter mating face of the cylinder block and smear a little grease on the oil filter seal. Screw the new unit into position taking care not to cross the thread. Continue until the sealing ring just touches the block face then tighten a half turn.

32 Insert the fuel pump operating rod in the side of the cylinder block just below the distributor body (photo).

33 Refit the fuel pump and insulation washer and secure with the two bolts and spring washers (photo).

34 Refit the earth cables to the side of the cylinder block just below the fuel pump and secure them with the bolt and washer (photo).

35 Refit the main fuel line connection to the fuel pump.

36 Refit the water pump pulley and fan blades to the water pump hub and secure with the four bolts, plain and spring washers. Tighten these bolts to a torque wrench setting of 5 - 7 lb f ft (0.69 - 0.97 kg f m).

37 Remove all traces of old gasket from the inlet manifold side of the cylinder head and inlet manifold. Fit a new gasket.

62.4 Gearbox placed ready for pushing down below bulkhead

62.5 Trolley jack under rear of gearbox extension housing

62.7 Engine mounting being aligned on crossmember

62.9 Gearbox crossmember attachment to gearbox extension housing

62.10 Crossmember to body mounted bracket attachment

62.12 Connector being attached to reverse light switch

62.14 Speedometer cable secured by circlip

62.16 Clutch cable threaded through rubber gaiter

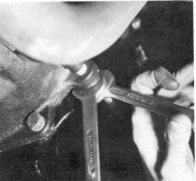

62.17 Clutch cable adjustment

62.18 Rubber gaiter refitted to clutch housing

62.20 Sliding propeller shaft into engagement with mainshaft

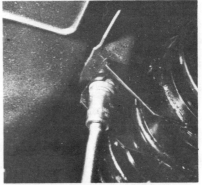

62.21 Propeller shaft centre bearing housing attachment to body

62.22 Propeller shaft and final drive flange reconnection

62.24 Exhaust pipe rubber mounting reconnected to body mounted bracket

62.27 Reconnecting starter motor cables

62.30A Replacing distributor

62.30B Securing distributor with clamp and bolt

62.32 Inserting fuel pump operating rod

62.33 Securing fuel pump to cylinder block

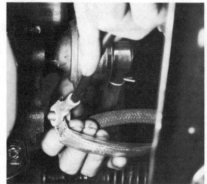
62.34 Reconnecting earth cables to cylinder block

62.38 Refitting inlet manifold to cylinder head, fitted with new gasket

62.40 The carburettor insulator washer and gasket. The gasket face is marked TOP FRONT to ensure correct fitment

62.43 Connecting water hose to automatic choke and inlet manifold

62.44 Connecting crankcase breather hose to inlet manifold

62.45 Connecting servo unit vacuum hose to inlet manifold

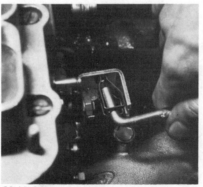
62.46 Connecting throttle control rod to carburettor

62.47 Reconnecting throttle control cable to operating rod

38 Refit the inlet manifold to the side of the cylinder head (photo).

39 Secure the inlet manifold with the nuts, bolts and washers.

40 Fit the insulator washer to the inlet manifold taking care to ensure that it is the correct way round (photo).

41 Refit the carburettor to the inlet manifold.

42 Secure the carburettor to the inlet manifold studs with the spring washer.

43 Reconnect the hose located between the automatic choke and inlet manifold. Tighten the two clips (photo).

44 Reconnect the crankcase breather pipe to the union adjacent to the water hose connection on the inlet manifold. Tighten the hose clip (photo).

45 Refit the servo unit vacuum hose to the union on the pipe of the inlet manifold. Tighten the hose clip (photo).

46 Reconnect the throttle control rod to the carburettor (photo).

47 Reconnect the throttle control cable to the carburettor throttle operating rod (photo).

48 Refit the fuel pipe from the fuel pump to the carburettor. Tighten the hose clip (photo).

49 Reconnect the throttle return spring (photo).

50 The alternator may now be refitted. Offer it up to its mounting bracket on the right-hand side of the cylinder block and insert the two lower mounting bolts with spring washers and spacer on the bolt and plain washer on the front (photo).

51 Refit the adjustment link to the side of the cylinder block and then attach the alternator to the adjustment link. Adjust the tension until there is 0.5 in (12.7 mm) of lateral movement at the mid point position of the belt run between the alternator pulley and the water pump. Tighten all securing bolts.

52 Refit the terminal connector to the rear of the alternator.

53 Secure the terminal connector with the spring clip (photo).

54 Carefully replace the radiator and secure with the four bolts and plain washers.

55 Locate the cowl in the rear of the radiator (if fitted) and secure with the four bolts and washers (photo).

56 Reconnect the radiator top and bottom hoses and tighten the hose clips (photo).

57 Refit the heater hose to the union on the side of the water pump and secure with the clips (photo).

58 Place new gaskets on the engine top cover and position on the top of the cylinder head (photo).

59 Secure the top cover with the ten bolts and spring washers see photo, and Fig. 1.19.

60 Make sure the sump drain plug is tight and then refill the engine with 6.6 Imp. pints (3.75 litres) of engine oil.

61 Reconnect the lower heater hose to the thermostatic choke union on the side of the carburettor. Secure with the hose clip.

62 Place the battery on its tray and secure with the clamp, bolt and washers.

63 Reconnect the battery positive and then negative terminals. Also reconnect the distributor HT leads to the spark plugs and to the centre of the ignition coil (Fig. 1.20).

64 Screw in the oil pressure switch and tighten with an open ended spanner. Reconnect the electric terminal (photo).

65 Fit the oil separator to the left-hand side of the engine the correct way round as shown in this photo and insert the P.C.V. valve in the top.

66 Refit the air cleaner to the carburettor, as described in Chapter 3, Section 2.

67 Reconnect the LT cable to the side of the distributor.

68 Refill the cooling system as described in Chapter 2, Section 4.

69 *Models fitted with centre console:* Place the console in its approximate fitted position and release the handbrake.

70 Refit the centre bolt to the handbrake lever compensator and tighten securely.

71 Move the console unit rearwards until it is possible to gain access to the rear of the instrument cluster. Remake the

62.48 Reconnecting fuel pipe to float chamber

62.49 Throttle return spring refitted

62.50 Alternator lower mounting bolts

62.53 Spring clip securing alternator connector

62.55 Refitting radiator cowl

62.56 Reconnecting radiator top hose

62.57 Heater hose being reconnected to water pump

62.58 Refitting top cover, complete with new gaskets

62.59 Securing top cover to cylinder head and drive belt guard

62.64 Refitting oil pressure switch

62.65 Refitting oil separator to crankcase

62.75 Selector rod in extension housing ready to accept gear change lever.

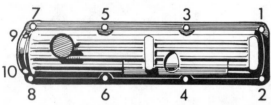
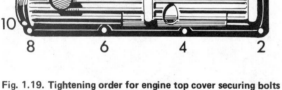

Fig. 1.19. Tightening order for engine top cover securing bolts (Sec. 62)

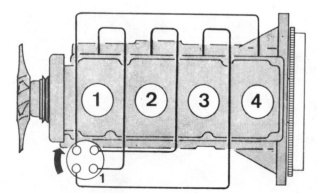

Fig. 1.20. Correct fitment of H.T. leads (Sec. 62)

electrical connections at the rear of the instrument making reference to the note made prior to disconnection.

72 Move the console unit forwards again and secure with the self tapping screws.

73 Apply some grease to the end of the gearchange lever and refit. Screw down the lever and tighten the locknut.

74 Replace the parcel tray and secure with the self tapping screws.

75 *Models fitted with parcel tray:* Apply some grease to the end of the gearchange lever and lower it into engagement with the selector rod (photo).

76 Carefully screw on the lock ring and gearchange lever retainer. Using a screwdriver, bend down several of the lock ring locking tabs.

77 Refit the gaiter over the gearchange lever and re-attach it to the body panel.

78 Refer to Chapter 3, Section 2, and refit the air cleaner assembly.

79 With the help of an assistant refit the bonnet and secure the hinges with the bolts, spring and plain washers in their original positions.

80 Generally check that all wires, hoses, controls and attachments have been reconnected and the engine should be ready to start.

81 On vehicles having emission control systems, reconnect components and hoses.

63 Engine - installation (without gearbox)

The sequence of operations is basically identical to that for refitting the engine with the gearbox attached. The exception being work carried out on detaching the gearbox. These differences will have become evident during the removal stage. Follow the instructions found in Section 62, leaving out the paragraphs referring to the gearbox.

64 Engine - initial start-up after major overhaul or repair

1 Make sure that the battery is fully charged and that all lubricants, coolant and fuel are replenished.

2 If the fuel system has been dismantled it will require several revolutions of the engine on the starter motor to pump the petrol up to the carburettor. An initial 'prime' of about 1/3 of a cupful of petrol poured down the air intake of the carburettor will help the engine to fire quickly, thus relieving the load on the battery. Do not overdo this however as flooding may result.

3 As soon as the engine fires and runs, keep it going at a fast tickover only (no faster) and bring it up to normal working temperature.

4 As the engine warms up there will be odd smells and some smoke from parts getting hot and burning off oil deposits. The signs to look for are leaks of water or oil which will be obvious, if serious. Check also the exhaust pipe and manifold connections as these do not always find their exact gas tight position until the warmth and vibration have acted on them and it is almost certain that they will need tightening further. This should be done, of course, with the engine stopped.

5 When normal running temperature has been reached, adjust the engine idle speed as described in Chapter 3.

6 Stop the engine and wait a few minutes to see if any lubricant or coolant is dripping out when the engine is stationary.

7 After the engine has run for 20 minutes remove the engine top cover and recheck the tightness of the cylinder head bolts. Also check the tightness of the sump bolts. In both cases use a torque wrench.

8 Road test the car to check that the timing is correct and that the engine is giving the necessary smoothness and power. Do not race the engine - if new bearings and/or pistons have been fitted it should be treated as a new engine and run in at a reduced speed for the first 1000 miles (2000 km).

65 Fault diagnosis - Engine

Symptom	Cause	Remedy
Engine turns over but will not start	Ignition damp or wet	Wipe dry the distributor cap and ignition leads
	Ignition leads to spark plugs loose	Check and tighten at both spark plug and distributor cap ends
	Shorted or disconnected low tension leads	Check the wiring on the CB and SW terminals of the coil and to the distributor
	Dirty, incorrectly set or pitted contact breaker points	Clean, file smooth and adjust
	Faulty condenser	Check contact breaker points for arcing, remove and fit new condenser
	Defective ignition switch	By-pass switch with wire
	Ignition LT leads connected wrong way round	Remove and replace leads to coil in correct order
	Faulty coil	Remove and fit new coil
	Contact breaker point spring earthed or broken	Check spring is not touching metal part of distributor. Check insulator washers are correctly placed. Renew points if the spring is broken
	No petrol in petrol tank	Refill tank!
	Vapour lock in fuel line (in hot conditions or at high altitude)	Blow into petrol tank, allow engine to cool, or apply a cold wet rag to the fuel line in engine compartment
	Blocked float chamber needle valve	Remove, clean and replace
	Fuel pump filter blocked	Remove, clean and replace
	Choked or blocked carburettor jets	Dismantle and clean
	Faulty fuel pump	Remove, overhaul and replace
	Too much choke allowing too rich a mixture to wet plugs	Remove and dry spark plugs or with wide open throttle, push-start the car (manual gearbox only)
	Float damaged or leaking or needle not seating	Remove, examine, clean and replace float and needle valve as necessary
	Float lever incorrectly adjusted	Remove and adjust correctly
Engine stalls and will not start	Ignition failure - sudden	Check over low and high tension circuits for breaks in wiring
	Ignition failure - misfiring precludes total stoppage	Check contact breaker points, clean and adjust. Renew condenser if faulty
	Ignition failure - in severe rain or after traversing water splash	Dry out ignition leads and distributor cap
	No petrol in petrol tank	Refill tank
	Petrol tank breather choked	Remove petrol cap and clean out breather hole or pipe
	Sudden obstruction in carburettor	Check jets, filter, and needle valve in float chamber for blockage
	Water in fuel system	Drain tank and blow out fuel lines

Symptom	Cause	Remedy
Engine misfires or idles unevenly	Ignition leads loose	Check and tighten as necessary at spark plug and distributor cap ends
	Battery leads loose on terminals	Check and tighten terminal leads
	Battery earth strap loose on body attachment point	Check and tighten earth lead to body attachment point
	Engine earth lead loose	Tighten lead
	Low tension leads to SW and CB terminals on coil loose	Check and tighten leads if found loose
	Low tension lead from CB terminal side to distributor loose	Check and tighten if found loose
	Dirty, or incorrectly gapped spark plugs	Remove, clean and regap
	Dirty, incorrectly set or pitted contact breaker points	Clean, file smooth and adjust
	Tracking across distributor cap	Remove and fit new cap
	Ignition too retarded	Check and adjust ignition timing
	Faulty coil	Remove and fit new coil
	Mixture too weak	Check jets, float chamber needle valve and filters for obstruction. Clean as necessary. Carburettor incorrectly adjusted
	Air leak in carburettor	Remove and overhaul carburettor
	Air leak at inlet manifold to cylinder head, or inlet manifold to carburettor	Test by pouring oil along joints. Bubbles indicate leak. Renew manifold gasket as appropriate.
	Incorrect valve clearances	Adjust cam follower clearances
	Burnt out exhaust valves	Remove cylinder head and renew defective valves
	Sticking or leaking valves	Remove cylinder head, clean, check and renew valves as necessary
	Wear or broken valve springs	Check and renew as necessary
	Worn valve guides or stems	Renew valves
	Worn pistons and piston rings	Dismantle engine, renew pistons and rings
Lack of power and poor compression	Burnt out exhaust valves	Remove cylinder head, renew defective valves
	Sticking or leaking valves	Remove cylinder head, clean, check and renew valves as necessary
	Worn valve guides and stems	Remove cylinder head and renew valves
	Weak or broken valve springs	Remove cylinder head, renew defective springs
	Blown cylinder head gasket (accompanied by increase in noise)	Remove cylinder head and fit new gasket
	Worn pistons and piston rings	Dismantle engine, renew pistons and rings
	Worn or scored cylinder bores	Dismantle engine, rebore, renew pistons and rings
	Ignition timing wrongly set. Too advanced or retarded	Check and reset ignition timing
	Contact breaker points incorrectly gapped	Check and reset contact breaker points
	Incorrect valve clearances	Adjust cam follower clearances
	Incorrectly set spark plugs	Remove, clean and regap
	Carburettor too rich or too weak	Tune carburettor for optimum performance
	Dirty contact breaker points	Remove, clean and replace
	Fuel filters blocked causing top end fuel starvation	Dismantle, inspect, clean, and replace all fuel filters
	Distributor automatic balance weights or vacuum advance and retard mechanisms not functioning correctly	Overhaul distributor
	Faulty fuel pump giving top end fuel starvation	Remove, overhaul, or fit exchange reconditioned fuel pump
Excessive oil consumption	Badly worn, perished or missing valve stem oil seals	Remove, fit new oil seals to valve stems
	Excessively worn valve stems and valve guides	Remove cylinder head and fit new valves
	Worn piston rings	Fit oil control rings to existing pistons or purchase new pistons
	Worn pistons and cylinder bores	Fit new pistons and rings, rebore cylinders
	Excessive piston ring gap allowing blow-by	Fit new piston rings and set gap correctly
	Piston oil return holes choked	Decarbonise engine and pistons

Symptom	Cause	Remedy
Oil being lost due to leaks	Leaking oil filter gasket	Inspect and fit new gasket as necessary
	Leaking top cover gasket	Inspect and fit new gasket as necessary
	Leaking timing case gasket	Inspect and fit new gasket as necessary
	Leaking sump gasket	Inspect and fit new gasket as necessary
	Loose sump plug	Tighten, fit new gasket as necessary
Unusual noises from engine	Worn valve gear (noisy tapping from top cover	Inspect and renew cam followers and ball headed bolts
	Worn big-end bearing (regular heavy knocking)	Drop sump, if bearings broken up clean out oil pump and oilways, fit new bearings. If bearings not broken but worn fit bearing shells
	Worn main bearings (rumbling and vibration)	Drop sump, remove crankshaft, if bearings worn but not broken up, renew. If broken up strip oil pump and clean out
	Worn crankshaft (knocking, rumbling and vibration	Regrind crankshaft, fit new main and big-end bearings
Engine fails to turn over when starter button operated	Discharged or defective battery	Charge or renew battery, push-start car (manual gearbox only)
	Dirty or loose battery leads	Clean and tighten both terminals and earth ends of earth lead
	Defective starter solenoid or switch	Run a heavy duty wire direct from the battery to the starter motor or by-pass the solenoid
	Engine earth strap disconnected	Check and retighten strap
	Defective starter motor	Remove and recondition

Chapter 2 Cooling system

Contents

Specifications

System type

... ...   Pressurised, assisted by pump and fan

Thermostat

Type	Wax
Location	Top water outlet tube
Starts to open	85 - 89°C (185 - 192°F)
Fully open	99 - 102°C (210 - 216°F)

Radiator

Type	Corrugated fin
Pressure cap opens	13 lb sq in (0.91 kg cm^2)

Fan

1600 models	7 blades 12.5 in (317.5 mm)
2000 models:	
Standard	7 blades 12.5 in (317.5 mm)
Optional	6 blades 14.0 in (355.6 mm)

Cooling system capacity (including heater)

	Up to 1974	1974 onwards
1600 models	11.4 Imp. pints (6.5 litres)	10.0 Imp. pints (5.8 litres)
2000 models	12.4 Imp. pints (7.1 litres)	10.75 Imp. pints (6.1 litres)

Torque wrench settings

	lb f ft	kg f m
Fan blade	5 - 7	0.69 - 0.97
Water pump	5 - 7	0.69 - 0.97
Thermostat housing	12 - 15	1.66 - 2.07

1 General description

The engine cooling water is circulated by a thermo-syphon water pump assisted system, and the whole system is pressurised. This is both to prevent the loss of water down the overflow pipe with the radiator cap in position and to prevent premature boiling in adverse conditions. The radiator cap is pressurised to 13 lb/sq. in (0.91 kg/cm^2). This has the effect of considerably increasing the boiling point of the coolant. If the water temperature goes above the increased boiling point the extra pressure in the system forces the internal part of the cap off its seat, thus exposing the overflow pipe down which the steam from the boiling water escapes thereby relieving the pressure. It is, therefore, important to check that the radiator cap is in good condition and that the spring behind the sealing washer has not weakened. The cooling system comprises the radiator, top and bottom water hoses, heater hoses, the impeller water pump (mounted on the front of the engine, it carries the fan blades,

and is driven by the fan belt), the thermostat and the two drain taps. The inlet manifold is water heated.

The system functions in the following fashion: Cold water in the bottom of the radiator circulates up the lower radiator hose to the water pump where it is pushed round the water passages in the cylinder block, helping to keep the cylinder bores and pistons cool.

The water then travels up into the cylinder head and circulates round the combustion spaces and valve seats absorbing more heat, and then, when the engine is at its correct operating temperature, travels out of the cylinder head, past the open thermostat into the upper radiator hose and so into the radiator header tank.

The water travels down the radiator where it is rapidly cooled by the in-rush of cold air through the radiator core, which is created by both the fan and the motion of the car. The water, now much cooler, reaches the bottom of the radiator when the cycle is repeated.

When the engine is cold the thermostat (which is a valve that

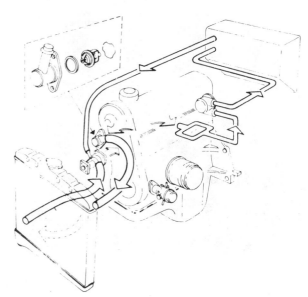

Fig. 2.1. Cooling system water circulation (Sec. 1)

opens and closes according to the temperature of the water) maintains the circulation of the same water in the engine.

Only when the correct minimum operating temperature has been reached, as shown in the Specification, does the thermostat begin to open, allowing water to return to the radiator.

2 Cooling system - draining

1 If the engine is cold, remove the filler cap from the radiator by turning the cap anti-clockwise. If the engine is hot, then turn the filler cap very slightly until pressure in the system has had time to be released. Use a rag over the cap to protect your hand from escaping steam. If with the engine very hot the cap is released suddenly, the drop in pressure can result in the water boiling. With the pressure released the cap can be removed.
2 If antifreeze is used in the cooling system, drain it into a bowl having a capacity of at least 13 Imp. pints (7.39 litres for re-use.
3 Open the drain plug located on the rear of the radiator lower tank next to the bottom hose. Also remove the engine drain plug

2.3 Cylinder block drain plug removal

which is located at the rear left-hand side of the cylinder block (photo).
4 When the water has finished running, probe the drain plug orifices with a short piece of wire to dislodge any particles of rust or sediment which may be causing a blockage.
5 It is important to note that the heater cannot be drained completely during the cold weather so an antifreeze solution must be used. Always use an antifreeze with an ethylene glycol or glycerine base.

3 Cooling system - flushing

1 In time the cooling system will gradually lose its efficiency as the radiator becomes choked with rust, scale deposits from the water, and other sediment. To clean the system out, remove the radiator filler cap and drain plug and leave a hose running in the filler cap neck for ten to fifteen minutes.
2 In very bad cases the radiator should be reverse flushed. This can be done with the radiator in position. The cylinder block plug is removed and a hose with a suitable tapered adaptor placed in the drain plug hole. Water under pressure is then forced through the radiator and out of the header tank filler cap neck.
3 It is recommended that some polythene sheeting is placed over the engine to stop water finding its way into the electrical system.
4 The hose should now be removed and placed in the radiator cap filler neck, and the radiator washed out in the usual manner.

4 Cooling system - filling

1 Refit the cylinder block and radiator drain plugs.
2 Fill the system slowly to ensure that no air lock develops. If a heater is fitted, check that the valve in the heater is open (control at HOT), otherwise an air lock may form in the heater. The best type of water to use in the cooling system is rain water; use this whenever possible.
3 Do not fill the system higher than within a ½ inch (12.7 mm) of the filler neck. Overfilling will merely result in wastage, which is especially to be avoided when antifreeze is in use.
4 It is usually found that air locks develop in the heater radiator so the system should be vented during refilling by detaching the heater supply hose from the elbow connection on the water outlet housing.
5 Pour coolant into the radiator filler neck whilst the end of the heater supply hose is held at the elbow connection height. When a constant stream of water flows from the supply hose quickly refit the hose. If venting is not carried out it is possible for the engine to overheat. Should the engine overheat for no apparent reason then the system should be vented before seeking other causes.
6 Only use antifreze mixture with a glycerine or ethylene glycol base.
7 Replace the filler cap and turn it firmly clockwise to lock it in position.

5 Radiator - removal, inspection and cleaning

1 Drain the cooling system, as described in Section 2 of this Chapter.
2 Slacken the two clips which hold the top and bottom radiator hoses on the radiator and carefully pull off the two hoses.
3 Undo and remove the four bolts that secure the radiator shroud to the radiator side panels and move the shroud over the fan blades. This is only applicable when a shroud is fitted. (photo)
4 Undo and remove the four bolts that secure the radiator to the front panel. The radiator may now be lifted upwards and away from the engine compartment. The fragile matrix must not be touched by the fan blades as it easily punctures. (photo)
5 Lift the radiator shroud from over the fan blades and remove

5.3 Radiator shroud repositioned over fan blades

5.4 Radiator removal

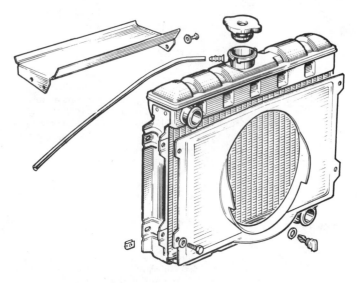

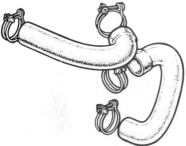

Fig. 2.2. Radiator assembly (Sec. 5)

from the engine compartment.

6   With the radiator away from the car any leaks can be soldered or repaired with a suitable substance. Clean out the inside of the radiator by flushing as described earlier in this Chapter. When the radiator is out of the car it is advantageous to turn it upside down and reverse flush. Clean the exterior of the radiator by carefully using a compressed air jet or a strong jet of water to clear away any road dirt, flies etc.

7   Inspect the radiator hoses for cracks, internal or external perishing and damage by overtightening of the securing clips. Also inspect the overflow pipe. Renew the hoses if suspect. Examine the radiator hose clips and renew them if they are rusted or distorted.

8   The drain plug and washer should be renewed if leaking or with worn threads, but first ensure the leak is not caused by a faulty fibre washer.

6   Radiator - installation

1   Refitting the radiator and shroud (if fitted) is the reverse

sequence to removal (see Section 5).

2   If new hoses are to be fitted they can be a little difficult to fit on to the radiator so lubricate them with a little soap.

3   Refill the cooling system, as described in Section 4.

4   A clearance of 0.8 in (20.0 mm) must be maintained between the bottom hose and the stabilizer bar to prevent chafing. Make sure that the upper end of the hose is pushed well up onto the water pump (Fig. 2.3).

7   Thermostat - removal, testing and refitting

1   Partially drain the cooling system (usually 4 Imp. pints (2.27 litres) is enough), as described in Section 2.

2   Slacken the top radiator hose to the thermostat housing and remove the hose.

3   Undo and remove the two bolts and spring washers that secure the thermostat housing to the cylinder head.

4   Carefully lift the thermostat housing away from the cylinder head. Recover the joint washer adhering to either the housing or cylinder head.

5   Using a screwdriver ease the clip securing the thermostat to the housing (Fig. 2.4). Note which way round the thermostat is fitted in the housing and also that the bridge is 90° to the outlet. (photo)

6   The thermostat may now be withdrawn from the housing. Recover the seal from inside the housing. (photo)

7   Test the thermostat for correct functioning by suspending it on a string in a saucepan of cold water together with a thermometer. Heat the water and note the temperature at which the thermostat begins to open. This should be 85 - 89°C (185 - 192°F). It is advantageous in winter to fit a thermostat that does not open too early. Continue heating the water until the thermostat is fully open. Then let it cool down naturally.

8   If the thermostat does not fully open in boiling water, or does not close down as the water cools, then it must be discarded and a new one fitted. Should the thermostat be stuck open when cold this will usually be apparent when removing it from the housing.

9   Refitting the thermostat is the reverse sequence to removal. Always ensure that the thermostat housing and cylinder head mating faces are clean and flat. If the thermostat housing is badly corroded fit a new housing. Always use a new paper gasket. Tighten the two securing bolts to a torque wrench setting of 12 - 15 lb f ft (1.66 - 2.07 kg f m).

10 If a new winter thermostat is fitted, provided the summer one is still functioning correctly, it can be placed on the one side and refitted in the spring. Thermostats should last for two to three years before renewal becomes desirable.

8   Water pump - removal and refitting

1   Drain the cooling system, as described in Section 2.

2   Refer to Section 5 and remove the radiator (and shroud if fitted).

3   Slacken the alternator mounting bolts and push the alternator towards the cylinder block. Lift away the fan belt.

4   Undo and remove the four bolts and washers that secure the fan assembly to the water pump spindle hub. Lift away the fan and pulley (Fig. 2.5).

Fig. 2.4. Using screwdriver to release thermostat retaining clip (Sec. 7)

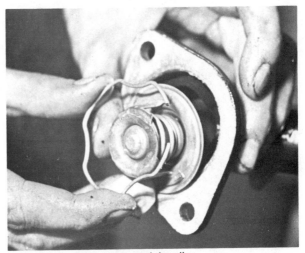

7.5 Removal of thermostat retaining clips

7.6 Removal of sealing ring

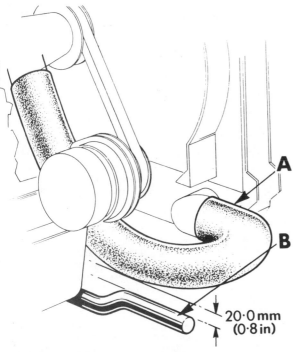

20·0 mm (0·8 in)

Fig. 2.3. Radiator bottom hose (A) to stabilizer bar (B) clearance diagram (Sec. 6)

Fig. 2.5. Fan and pulley removal (Sec. 8)

Fig. 2.6. Water pump removal (Sec. 8)

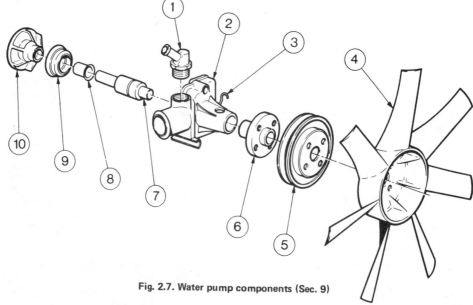

Fig. 2.7. Water pump components (Sec. 9)

1 *Heater connection*	7 *Shaft and bearing*
2 *Pump body*	*assembly*
3 *Bearing retainer*	8 *Slinger*
4 *Cooling fan*	9 *Seal assembly*
5 *Fan pulley*	10 *Impeller*
6 *Pulley hub*	

5   Slacken the clip that secures the heater hose to the water pump. Pull the hose from its union on the water pump.

6   Undo and remove the four bolts and spring washers that secure the water pump to the cylinder block. Lift away the water pump and recover the gasket (Fig. 2.6).

7   Refitting the water pump is the reverse sequence to removal. The following additional points should however be noted:

    a) *Make sure the mating faces of the cylinder block and water pump are clean. Always use a new gasket.*

    b) *Tighten the water pump securing bolts to a torque wrench setting of 5 - 7 lb f ft (0.69 - 0.97 kg f m).*

    c) *Tighten the water pump fan and pulley bolts to a torque wrench setting of 5 - 7 lb f ft (0.69 - 0.97 kg f m).*

9   Water pump - dismantling and overhaul

1   Before undertaking the dismantling of a water pump to effect a repair, check that all parts are available. It may be quicker and

more economical to replace the complete unit.

2   Refer to Fig. 2.7 and using a universal three leg puller and suitable thrust block draw the hub from the shaft.

3   Carefully pull out the bearing retaining clip from the slot in the water pump housing. On some water pumps this clip is not fitted.

4   Using a soft faced hammer drive the shaft and bearing assembly out towards the rear of the pump body.

5   The impeller vane is removed from the spindle by using a universal three leg puller and suitable thrust block.

6   Remove the seal and the slinger by splitting the latter with the aid of a sharp cold chisel.

7   Carefully inspect the condition of the shaft and bearing assembly and if it shows signs of wear or corrosion, new parts should be obtained. If it was found that coolant was leaking from the pump, a new seal should be obtained. If it was evident that the pulley hub or impeller were a loose fit they must be renewed. The repair kit available comprises a new shaft and bearing assembly, a slinger seal, bush, clip and gasket.

8   To reassemble the water pump first fit the shaft and bearing assembly to the housing, larger end of the shaft to the front of the housing, and press the assembly into the housing until the front of the bearing is flush with the pump housing.
9   Refit the bearing locating wire.
10 Next press the pump pulley onto the front end of the shaft until the end of the shaft is flush with the end of the hub.
11 Press the new slinger (flanged end first) onto the shaft until the non-flanged end is approximately 0.5 in (13 mm) from the shaft end. To act as a rough guide the flanged end on the slinger will be just in line with the impeller side of the window in the water pump body.
12 Place the new seal over the shaft and into the counterbore in the water pump housing and then press the impeller into the shaft until a clearance of 0.03 inch (0.76 mm) is obtained between the impeller and the housing face (Fig. 2.8). Whilst this is being carried out the slinger will be pushed into its final position by the impeller.

10 Fan belt - removal and refitting

If the fan belt is worn or has stretched unduly, it should be renewed. The most usual reason for replacement is that the belt has broken in service. It is recommended that a spare belt be always carried in the car.
1   Loosen the alternator mounting bolts and move the alternator towards the engine (Fig. 2.9).
2   Slip the old belt over the crankshaft, alternator and water pump pulley wheels and lift it off over the fan blades.
3   Put a new belt onto the three pulleys and adjust it as described in Section 11. **Note:** After fitting a new belt it will require adjustment after 250 miles (400 km).

11 Fan belt - adjustment

1   It is important to keep the fan belt correctly adjusted and it is considered that this should be a regular maintenance task every 6,000 miles (10,000 km). If the belt is loose it will slip, wear rapidly and cause the alternator and water pump to malfunction. If the belt is too tight the alternator and water pump bearings will wear rapidly causing premature failure of these components.
2   The fan belt tension is correct when there is 0.5 in (12.7 mm) of lateral movement at the mid-point position of the belt run between the alternator pulley and the water pump (Fig. 2.10).

3   To adjust the fan belt, slacken the alternator securing bolts and move the alternator in or out until the correct tension is obtained. It is easier if the alternator bolts are only slackened a little so it requires some effort to move the alternator. In this way the tension of the belt can be arrived at more quickly than by making frequent adjustment.
4   When the correct adjustment has been obtained fully tighten the alternator mounting bolts.

12 Temperature gauge - fault diagnosis

1   If the temperature gauge fails to work, either the gauge, the sender unit, the wiring or the connections are at fault.
2   It is not possible to repair the gauge or the sender unit and they must be replaced by new units if at fault.
3   First check the wiring connections are sound. Check the wiring for breaks using an ohmmeter. The sender unit and gauge should be tested by substitution.

13 Temperature gauge and sender unit - removal and refitting

1   Information on the removal of the gauge will be found in Chapter 10, with the exception of the GT models where the gauge is fitted to the centre console. Removal of the console is

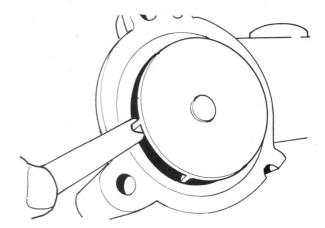

Fig. 2.8. Checking slinger clearance with feeler gauges (Sec. 9)

Fig. 2.9. Alternator mountings (Sec. 10)

Fig. 2.10. Correct total deflection of fan belt (Sec. 11)

simply effected by unscrewing the self tapping screws.
2   To remove the sender unit, disconnect the wires leading into the unit at its connector and unscrew the unit with a spanner. The unit is locked in the cylinder head just below the manifold on the left-hand side. Refitting is the reverse sequence to removal.

14 Antifreeze precautions

1 In circumstances where it is likely that the temperature will drop below freezing it is essential that some of the water is drained and an adequate amount of ethylene glycol antifreeze such as Castrol antifreeze is added to the cooling system.
2 If Castrol antifreeze is not available, any antifreeze which conforms with specifications BS3151 or BS3152 can be used. Never use an antifreeze with an alcohol base as evaporation is too high.
3 Castrol antifreeze with an anti-corrosion additive can be left in the cooling system for up to two years, but after six months it is advisable to have the specific gravity of the coolant checked at your local garage, and thereafter once every three months.
4 The table below gives the amount of antifreeze and degree of protection.

Anti-freeze %	Commences to freeze °C	°F	Frozen solid °C	°F	Amount of anti-freeze Imp. pints	litres
25	-13	9	-26	-15	2½	1.42
33 1/3	-19	-2	-36	-33	3	1.71
50	-36	-33	-48	-53	4½	2.56

Note: Never use antifreeze in the windscreen washer reservoir as it will cause damage to the paintwork.

15 Fault diagnosis - Cooling system

Symptom	Cause	Remedy
Overheating	Insufficient water in cooling system	Top up radiator
	Fan belt slipping (accompanied by a shrieking noise on rapid engine acceleration)	Tighten fan belt to recommended tension or replace if worn
	Radiator core blocked or radiator grille restricted	Reverse flush radiator, remove obstructions
	Bottom water hose collapsed, impeding flow	Remove and fit new hose
	Thermostat not opening properly	Remove and fit new thermostat
	Ignition advance and retard incorrectly set (accompanied by loss of power, and perhaps, misfiring)	Check and reset ignition timing
	Carburettor incorrectly adjusted (mixture too weak)	Tune carburettor
	Exhaust system partially blocked	Check exhaust pipe for constrictive dents and blockages
	Oil level in sump too low	Top up sump to full mark on dipstick
	Blown cylinder head gasket (water/steam being forced down the radiator overflow pipe under pressure)	Remove cylinder head, fit new gasket
	Engine not yet run-in	Run-in slowly and carefully
	Brakes binding	Check and adjust brakes if necessary
Cool running	Thermostat jammed open	Remove and renew thermostat
	Incorrect thermostat fitted allowing premature opening of valve	Remove and replace with new thermostat which opens at a higher temperature
	Thermostat missing	Check and fit correct thermostat
Loss of cooling water	Loose clips on water hose	Check and tighten clips if necessary
	Top, bottom or by-pass water hoses perished and leaking	Check and replace any faulty hoses
	Radiator core leaking	Remove radiator and repair
	Thermostat gasket leaking	Inspect and renew gasket
	Radiator pressure cap spring worn or seal ineffective	Renew radiator pressure cap
	Blown cylinder head gasket (pressure in system forcing water/steam down overflow pipe	Remove cylinder head and fit new gasket
	Cylinder wall or head cracked	Dismantle engine, despatch to engineering works for repair

Chapter 3
Carburation; fuel and emission control systems

Contents

Specifications

Fuel pump
Type	Mechanical driven by pushrod from auxiliary shaft
Delivery pressure	3.75 to 5.0 lb/in^2 (0.26 - 0.35 kg/cm^2)
Inlet vacuum	8.5 in (21.60 cm) Hg

Fuel tank
Capacity	11.9 Imp. gallons (54 litres)

Fuel filter
Fuel filter	Nylon mesh, located in fuel line

Air cleaner
Air cleaner	Replaceable paper element

Carburettor applications

Index	Engine	Carburettor type	Transmission type	Ford identification number *
(a)	1600 ohc	Ford downdraught	Manual	71 - HW - 9510 - AGA
(b)	1600 ohc	Ford downdraught	Manual or automatic	71 - HW - 9510 - AJA
(c)	1600 ohc (exhaust emission)	Ford downdraught	Manual	71 - HW - 9510 - YA
(d)	1600 ohc (exhaust emission)	Ford downdraught	Automatic	71 - HW - 9510 - AHA
(e)	1600 ohc GT (exhaust emission)	Weber	Manual	71 - HF - 9510 - BC
(f)	1600 ohc GT	Weber	Automatic	71 - HF - 9510 - CB
(g)	2000 ohc	Weber	Manual	71 - HF - 9510 - DC
(h)	2000 ohc	Weber	Automatic	71 - HF - 9510 - EC

Note: All Weber carburettors have automatic choke mechanism

* Ford identification numbers may vary slightly from those quoted. Where this is the case, working procedures and specifications will remain the same.

Ford downdraught carburettors (all models)
Throttle barrel diameter	1.42 in (36.0 mm)
Venturi diameter	1.10 in (28.0 mm)
Main jet	137
Float level	1.10 in (28.0 mm)
Float travel	0.26 in (6.57 mm)
Choke plate pull down	0.09 in (2.30 mm)
De-choke	0.21 in (5.33 mm)
Accelerator pump stroke	0.10 in (2.54 mm)
Idling speed:	
Manual transmission	730 to 770 rpm
Automatic transmission	775 to 825 rpm
Fast idle speed	(a) 1900 rpm (b) 2100 rpm (c) 2100 rpm (d) 2300 rpm

Weber carburettors
See carburettor application list on page 63

	Index * (e)	Index * (f)	Index * (g)	Index * (h)
Venturi diameter:				
Primary	1.02 in (26 mm)	1.02 in (26 mm)	1.02 in (26 mm)	1.02 in (26 mm)
Secondary	1.06 in (27 mm)	1.06 in (27 mm)	1.06 in (27 mm)	1.06 in (27 mm)
Main jet:				
Primary	140	135	140	140
Secondary	140	145	140	140
Air correction jet:				
Primary	170	170	170	170
Secondary	140	140	160	160
Emulsion tube:				
Primary	F50	F50	F50	F50
Secondary	F6	F6	F50	F50
Idling jet:				
Primary	55	55	60	55
Secondary	45	45	50	50
Accelerator pump jet	Special	Special	50	50
Needle valve	0.08 in (2.0 mm)	0.08 in (2.0 mm)	0.08 in (2.0 mm)	0.08 in (2.0 mm)
Idling speed:				
Manual transmission	750	750	700	700
Automatic transmission	800	800	800	800
Fast idle speed	3200 rpm	3000 rpm	3000 rpm	3000 rpm
Fast idle setting	0.033 in (0.85 mm)	0.039 in (1.00 mm)	0.039 to 0.433 in (1.00 to 1.10 mm)	0.039 to 0.433 in (1.00 to 1.10 mm)

	Index * (e)	Index * (f)	Index * (g)	Index * (h)
Float level:				
Upper	1.38 to 1.39 in (35 to 35.5 mm)	1.38 to 1.39 in (35 to 35.5 mm)	1.61 to 1.63 in (40.75 to 41.25 mm)	1.61 to 1.63 in ** (40.75 to 41.25 mm)
Lower	1.97 to 2.02 in (50.5 to 52 mm)	1.97 to 2.02 in (50.5 to 52 mm)	1.97 to 2.02 in (50.5 to 52 mm)	1.97 to 2.02 in (50.5 to 52 mm)
Choke plate pull down	0.177 in (4.50 mm)	0.118 in (3.00 mm)	0.158 in (4.00 mm)	0.158 in (4.00 mm)

** *If plastic float fitted, 1.38 to 1.40 in (35.0 to 35.5 mm)*

Torque wrench settings

	lb f ft	kg f m
Fuel pump to cylinder block	12 - 15	1.7 - 2.1
Air cleaner body to carburettor	6 - 9	0.83 - 1.22
Air cleaner cover to body	2.5 - 3	0.34 - 0.41
Carburettor attachment nuts	5 - 7	0.7 - 1.0
Fuel tank retaining straps	Tighten until 1.6 - 1.8 in (40 - 45 mm) of thread is protruding through the nut	

1 General description

The fuel system comprises an 11.9 Imp. gallon (54.0 litre) fuel tank, a mechanically operated fuel pump, a filter and a Ford or Weber carburettor.

The fuel tank is positioned below the luggage compartment and is held in position by two retaining straps. The filler pipe neck is integral with the tank and passes through the right-hand quarter panel.

The combined fuel outlet and sender unit is located in the front face of the tank. Fuel tank ventilation is via the filler cap.

The mechanical fuel pump is connected to the fuel tank by a nylon pipe. It is located on the left-hand side of the engine and is driven by an auxiliary shaft. Located in the fuel pump is a nylon filter and access is gained via a sediment cap.

A Nitrile rubber flexible hose connects the carburettor to the fuel pump.

Incorporated in the hose between the carburettor and fuel pump is a line filter and the direction of petrol flow is indicated by an arrow on the housing.

The air cleaner fitted to all models is of the renewable paper element type.

2 Air cleaner - removal, refitting and servicing

The renewable paper element type air cleaner is fitted onto the top of the carburettor installation and is retained in position by securing nuts and on a flange at the top of the carburettor. Additional support brackets are used. To remove the air cleaner assembly proceed as follows:

1 Note the direction in which the air intake is pointing as on some models it is adjustable to a cold or hot weather position.

2 Undo and remove the bolt and spring washer that secures the support bracket to the top cover.

3 Undo and remove the bolt and spring washer that secures the air cleaner long support bracket located next to the

distributor.

4   Undo and remove the four self-tapping screws on the top cover.

5   There is one additional screw that should be removed and this is located above the air intake.

6   Carefully lift away the top cover (photo). At this stage the element may be lifted out.

7   If it is necessary to remove the lower body, first bend back the lock tabs and then undo and remove the four securing nuts (photo).

8   Lift away the two tab washers and the reinforcement plate (photo).

9   The lower body together with the support brackets may now be removed from the top of the carburettor (photo).

10   Refitting the air cleaner is the reverse sequence to removal.

Servicing

The element may be cleaned by using a compressed air jet in the reverse direction to air flow by holding the jet nozzle at least 5 inches (127 mm) away from the element at its centre and blowing outwards. Then hold the element in the vertical position and gently tap until all dirt and dust is removed.

Inspect the element for signs of splitting, cracking, pin holes or permanent distortion and, if evident, a new element should be fitted. A new element must be fitted after 15,000 miles (25,000 km) or earlier if the car is being operated in very dusty conditions.

3   Fuel pump - routine servicing

1   At intervals of 3,000 miles (5,000 km) undo and pull the fuel pipe from the pump inlet tube.

2   Undo and remove the centre screw and 'O' ring and lift off the sediment cap, filter and seal. (photo)

3   Thoroughly clean the sediment cap, filter and pumping chamber using a paintbrush and clean petrol to remove any sediment. (photo)

4   Reassembly is the reverse sequence to dismantling. Do not overtighten the centre screw as it could distort the sediment cap.

4   Fuel pump - description

The mechanical fuel pump is mounted on the left-hand side of the engine and is driven by an auxiliary shaft. It is not recommended that this type of pump be dismantled for repair other than cleaning the filter and sediment cap. Should a fault appear in the pump it may be tested and if confirmed it must be discarded and a new one obtained. One of two designs may be fitted, this depending on the availability at the time of production of the car.

5   Fuel pump - removal and refitting

1   Remove the inlet and outlet pipes at the pump and plug the ends to stop petrol loss or dirt finding its way into the fuel system.

2   Undo and remove two bolts and spring washers that secure the pump to the cylinder block.

3   Lift away the fuel pump and gasket and recover the pushrod.

4   Refitting the fuel pump is the reverse sequence to removal but there are several additional points that should be noted:

    a)   *Do not forget to refit the pushrod.*

    b)   *Tighten the pump securing bolts to a torque wrench setting of 12 - 15 lb f ft (1.7 - 2.1 kg fm).*

    c)   *Before reconnecting the pipe from the fuel tank to the pump inlet, move the end to a position lower than the*

2.6 Lifting away air cleaner top

2.7 Undoing four air cleaner body to carburettor retaining nuts

2.8 Lifting away reinforcement plate

2.9 Removal of air cleaner body

3.2 Lifting away fuel pump sediment cap, filter and seal

3.3 Removal of filter from sediment cap of fuel pump

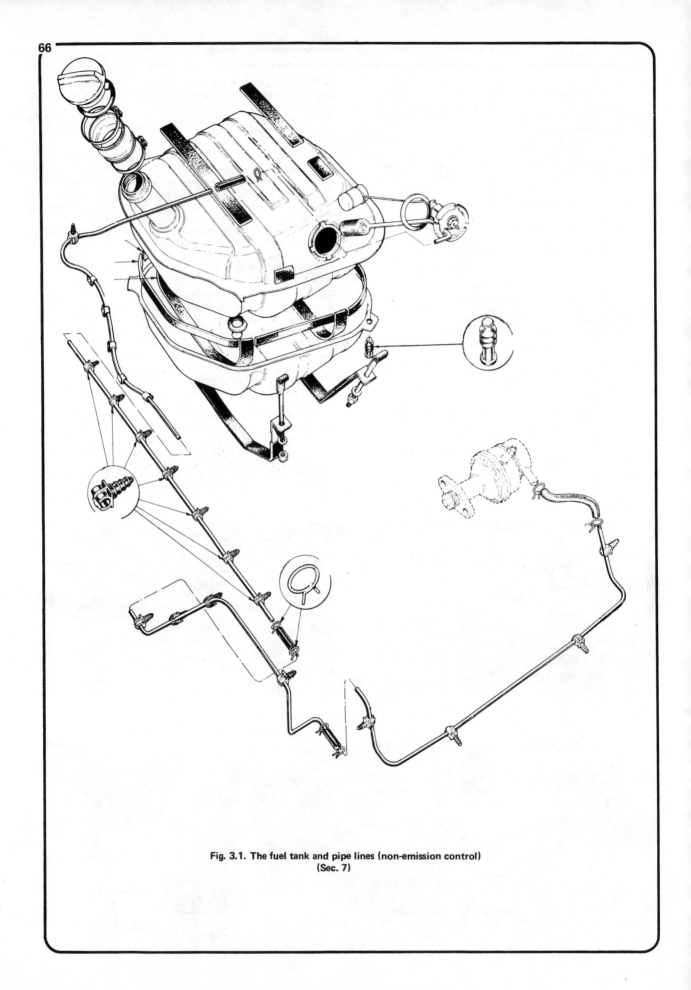

Fig. 3.1. The fuel tank and pipe lines (non-emission control)
(Sec. 7)

*fuel tank so that fuel can syphon out. Quickly connect
the pipe to the pump inlet.*
d) *Disconnect the pipe at the carburettor and turn the engine
over until petrol issues from the open end. Quickly
connect the pipe to the carburettor union.*

6 Fuel pump - testing

Presuming that the fuel lines and unions are in good condition and that there are no leaks anywhere, check the performance of the fuel pump in the following manner. Disconnect
the fuel pipe at the carburettor inlet union, and the high tension
lead to the coil and, with a suitable container or large rag in
position to catch the ejected fuel, turn the engine over. A good
spurt of petrol should emerge from the end of the pipe every
second revolution.

7 Fuel tank - removal and refitting

1   The fuel tank is positioned at the rear of the car and is
supported on two straps.
2   Remove the filler cap and, using a length of rubber hose or
plastic pipe approximately 0.25 in (6.35 mm) bore, syphon as
much petrol out as possible until the level is below the level of
the sender unit.
3   Disconnect the battery earth terminal, release the fuel gauge
sender unit wire and also the fuel feed pipe from the sender unit.
4   Using two screwdrivers in the slots in the sender unit retaining ring unscrew the sender unit from the fuel tank. Lift away
the sealing ring and the sender unit noting that the float must
hang downwards.
5   Undo and remove the tank strap retaining nuts and lower
the tank.
6   Refitting is the reverse sequence to removal. Tighten the
support strap securing nuts until 1.6 - 1.8 in (40 - 45 mm) of
thread is protruding through the nut.
7   Refill the fuel tank and reconnect the battery earth terminal. Test the operation of the fuel gauge sender unit by
switching on the ignition. Wait 30 seconds and observe the gauge
reading.

8 Fuel tank - cleaning

1   With time it is likely that sediment will collect in the bottom
of the fuel tank. Condensation, resulting in rust and other impurities, will usually be found in the fuel tank of any car more
than three or four years old.
2   When the tank is removed it should be vigorously flushed out
and turned upside down. If facilities are available at the local
garage the tank may be steam cleaned and the exterior repainted
with a lead based paint.
3   Never weld or bring a naked light close to an empty fuel tank
until it has been steam cleaned out for at least two hours or
washed internally with boiling water and detergent and allowed to
stand for at least three hours.
4   Any small holes may be repaired using a special preparation
such as Holts Petro-Patch which gives satisfactory results provided that the instructions are rigidly adhered to.

9 Fuel gauge sender unit - removal and refitting

1   The fuel gauge sender unit can be removed with the fuel tank
in position. (Refer to Section 7, paragraphs 2 to 4).
2   If the operation of the sender unit is suspect, check that the
rheostat is not damaged and that the wiper contact is bearing
against the coil.
3   Replacement is a straightforward reversal of the removal
sequence. Always fit a new seal to the recess in the tank to
ensure no leaks develop.

4   The float arm should hang downwards. Test the operation of
the fuel gauge sender unit by switching on the ignition. Wait 30
seconds and observe the gauge reading.

10 Fuel line filter - removal and refitting

1   Slacken the two hose clips and ease off the inlet and outlet
pipes. Plug the ends of the pipes to stop dirt ingress or loss of
petrol. Lift away the filter (Fig. 3.2).
2   The filter should be renewed at intervals of 18,000 miles
(30,000 km) or when fuel starvation symptoms are experienced.
3   Refitting the fuel line filter is the reverse sequence to removal. There is an arrow on the filter body which indicates the
direction of fuel flow as it must not be fitted the wrong way
round.

11 Accelerator pedal and shaft - removal and refitting

1   Release the accelerator cable retaining clip from the shaft
extension and detach the cable.
2   Withdraw the two shaft retaining clips and slide out the shaft.
It will be found beneficial if one bush is rotated through 45°
and with a screwdriver easing the bush from the bracket.
3   If desired the pedal may be detached from the pedal shaft
spigot by prising the pedal flange out of engagement with a
screwdriver. Lift away the pedal spring.
4   Inspect the pedal shaft bushes and if worn they should be
renewed.
5   It will now be necessary to check the adjustment as described
in Section 13.

12 Accelerator cable - removal and refitting

1   Working under the bonnet slide the clip from the inner cable
socket and the throttle shaft ball so as to disconnect the inner
cable (Fig. 3.3).
2   Slacken the two lock nuts that retain the outer cable to the
bracket on the inlet manifold. Detach the outer cable.
3   Withdraw the clip and disconnect the inner cable from the
lever on the accelerator pedal shaft.
4   Undo and remove the screw thereby releasing the throttle
cable from the engine compartment rear bulkhead panel.
5   The cable may now be drawn through the aperture in the
bulkhead.
6   Refitting and reconnecting the accelerator cable is the reverse sequence to removal.
7   It will now be necessary to adjust the linkage, as described in
Section 13.

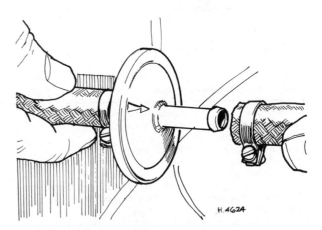

**Fig. 3.2. Fuel line filter (arrow shows direction of flow
through unit) (Sec. 10)**

Fig. 3.3. Accelerator cable to pedal attachment (Sec. 12)

Fig. 3.4. Accelerator linkage adjustment point (Sec. 13)

Fig. 3.5. Ford automatic choke carburettor (Sec. 15)

13 Accelerator linkage - adjustment

1   Working under the bonnet unscrew the outer cable lock nuts to their respective ends of the threaded section (Fig. 3.4).
2   Detach the throttle return spring.
3   An assistant should now depress and hold the throttle pedal in the fully open position.
4   The throttle disc should now be fully opened and the nut nearest to the outer cable adjusted until all slackness is removed from the inner cable and the throttle plate is just maintained in the fully open position.
5   Tighten the second nut so as to hold the cable in this set position.
6   Release the accelerator pedal and refit the throttle return spring.

14 Carburettors - dismantling and reassembly (general)

1   With time the component parts of the carburettor will wear and petrol consumption will increase. The diameter of the drillings and jets may alter due to erosion and air and fuel leaks may develop around the spindles and other moving parts. Because of the high degree of precision involved, it is best to purchase an exchange rebuilt carburettor. This is one of the few instances where it is better to take the latter course rather than rebuild the component itself.
2   It may be necessary to partially dismantle the carburettor to clear a blocked jet or renew a gasket. Providing care is taken there is no reason why the carburettor may not be completely reconditioned at home, but ensure a full repair kit can be obtained before you strip the carburettor down. **Never** poke out jets with wire but to clean them out blow them out with compressed air or with air from a car tyre pump.

15 Carburettor (Ford downdraught) - description

The carburettor is of single, downdraught type, incorporating idling, main, power valve and accelerator pump systems. A fully automatic or manual choke may be fitted and the float chamber is externally vented.
A connection for the distributor vacuum pipe is provided and throttle speed and volume control screws.

16 Carburettor (Ford downdraught) - removal and refitting

1   Open the bonnet and remove the air cleaner assembly, as detailed in Section 2, of this Chapter.
2   Partially drain the cooling system and collect in a suitable capacity container if antifreeze is in use.
3   Slacken the clips securing the hoses to the automatic choke housing and carefully separate the hoses from the housing. With manual choke, disconnect the cable.
4   Slacken the fuel pipe retaining clip at the float chamber union and detach the flexible hose.
5   Release the distributor automatic advance pipe from the side of the carburettor.
6   Disconnect the throttle control shaft from the throttle shaft.
7   Undo the two nuts that secure the carburettor flange and remove the nuts and spring washers.
8   Carefully lift away the carburettor and its gasket.
9   Replacement is a straightforward reversal of the removal sequence but note the following additional points:
    a) *Remove all traces of the old carburettor gasket, clean the mating flanges and fit a new gasket in place.*
    b) *Refill the cooling system as described in Chapter 2, Section 4.*

17 Carburettor (Ford downdraught) - adjustments in-situ

These adjustments may be carried out with the unit in position on the inlet manifold.

(a)   Slow running adjustment

1   In view of the increasing awareness of the dangers of exhaust pollution, it is recommended that the slow running (idling) setting is made using a CO meter (exhaust gas analyser). With the engine at normal operating temperature and the throttle speed screw set to give the specified idling speed, connect the analyser and adjust the mixture screw until the carbon monoxide emission level indicated on the meter is below 3%. Readjust the throttle speed screw if necessary to give the specified idle speed (Fig. 3.7).
2   Where an exhaust gas analyser is not available, a device such as a 'Colortune' may be used or as a temporary adjustment,

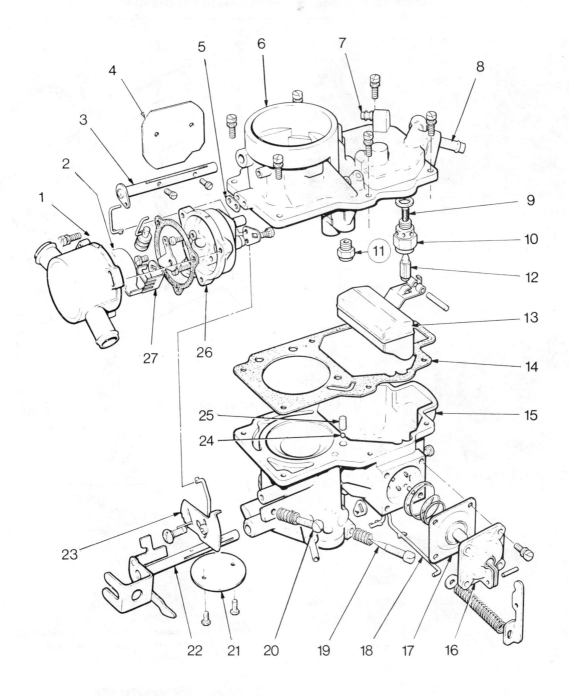

Fig. 3.6. Exploded view of Ford automatic choke carburettor

1	Thermostatic spring cover	8	Fuel inlet nozzle	14	Gasket	21	Throttle plate
2	Thermostatic spring	9	Filter	15	Lower body	22	Throttle plate spindle
3	Choke valve plate spindle	10	Fuel inlet needle valve	16	Accelerator pump cover	23	Fast idle cam
4	Choke plate		seat	17	Diaphragm	24	Ball
5	Gasket	11	Main jet	18	Pump rod	25	Weight
6	Upper body	12	Fuel inlet needle valve	19	Mixture control screw	26	Automatic choke housing
7	External vent	13	Float	20	Throttle speed screw	27	Operating lever

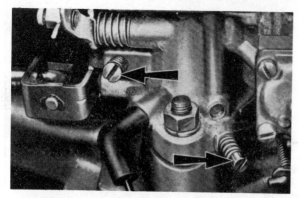

Fig. 3.7. Ford carburettor throttle speed screw (left) and mixture screw (right) (Sec. 17)

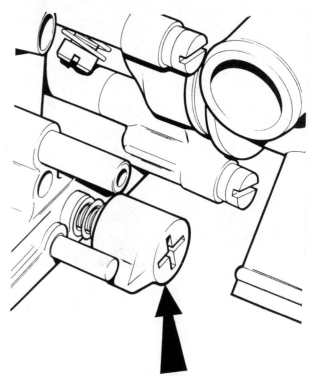

Fig. 3.8. Carburettor mixture screw limiter cap (Sec. 17)

Fig. 3.9. Removing the upper body (Ford carburettor) (Sec. 17)

Fig. 3.10. Checking float level adjustment (Ford carburettor) (Sec. 17)

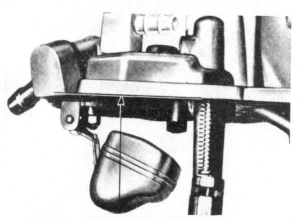

Fig. 3.11. Checking float travel (Ford carburettor) (Sec. 17)

Fig. 3.12. Checking accelerator pump stroke (Ford carburettor) (Sec. 17)

set the throttle speed screw to give a slightly higher than recommended idle speed and then unscrew the mixture screw until the engine speed is at its highest point and any further rotation causes the speed to drop. Now screw the mixture control screw in until the idling speed drops by about 25 rpm indicating a slightly weakened mixture.

On some vehicles equipped with emission control systems, the mixture screw is fitted with a limiter cap. This restricts the adjustment travel to within one turn of the factory set position. If the cap is removed (by cutting it off) then a new one must be pressed onto the mixture screw after its position has been set using an exhaust gas analyser (CO meter).

(b)   Float level adjustment

3   Remove the air cleaner and either disconnect the choke cable or with an automatic choke, proceed as described in the next paragraph.

4   Disconnect the water hoses from the automatic choke housing. If the hoses are retained in an upright position, there will be no loss of coolant and the system will not therefore have to be drained.

5   Disconnect the fuel inlet pipe and the vent pipe from the carburettor.

6   Remove the upper body securing screws, lift the upper body away, disengaging the choke link at the same time. As the upper body is withdrawn, the accelerator pump discharge valve will be exposed and if the throttle linkage is actuated, it is possible for the valve and weight to be ejected. These components will cause serious damage to the engine is they should fall down the carburettor throat.

7   Hold the carburettor upper body vertically so that the float hangs downward.

8   Measure the distance between the bottom of the float to the mating face of the upper body. The distance should be 1.10 in (28.0 mm).

9   Now hold the upper body in a horizontal attitude so that the float is fully suspended and measure the distance between the bottom of the float and the mating face of the upper body. The distance should be 1.36 in (34.57 mm). The foregoing dimensions may be adjusted by bending the tabs on the float arm.

10   Reassembly is a reversal of dismantling.

(c)   Accelerator pump stroke - adjustment

11   Unscrew the throttle speed screw until it no longer contacts the throttle lever.

12   Depress the accelerator pump diaphragm plunger fully and then check the clearance between the end of the plunger and the operating lever using a twist drill or other suitable gauge, 0.10 in (2.54 mm) in diameter.

13   If necessary, bend the accelerator pump rod to provide the correct clearance. Reset the throttle speed screw to give the original idling speed.

18 Carburettor (Ford downdraught) - dismantling and reassembly

1   Remove the screw which retains the fast idle cam and then remove the cam.

2   Unscrew the retaining screws and remove the upper body.

3   Remove the choke thermostatic spring housing (3 screws) and the automatic choke housing (2 screws).

4   Dismantle the choke housing components (piston, link and lever) and withdraw the choke link operating shaft and plate assembly.

5   Remove the pivot pin and withdraw the float and fuel inlet needle valve.

6   Unscrew the needle valve seat and remove it together with the filter screen.

7   Remove the main jet.

8   Invert the lower body to eject the accelerator pump ball valve and weight.

9   Do not dismantle the choke valve plate or spindle unless absolutely essential.

10   Remove the accelerator pump cover and disengage the cover from the operating link. Withdraw the diaphragm and return spring.

11   Do not dismantle the throttle valve plate unless absolutely essential.

12   Unscrew and remove the throttle speed and mixture control screws.

13   With the carburettor now completely dismantled, wash all components in clean fuel and renew any components which are worn. Should the choke or throttle valve plate spindles have worn in the carburettor body, then the carburettor should be renewed complete.

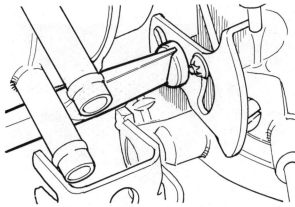

Fig. 3.13. Removing fast idle cam screw (Ford carburettor) (Sec. 18)

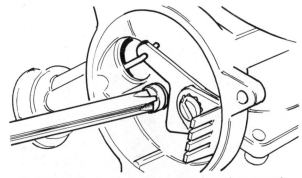

Fig. 3.14. Removing the securing screws from the automatic choke housing (Ford carburettor) (Sec. 18)

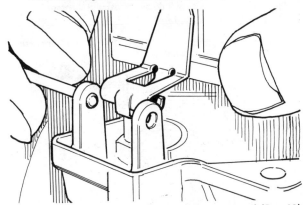

Fig. 3.15. Removing float pivot pin (Ford carburettor) (Sec. 18)

Fig. 3.16. Removing accelerator pump cover (Ford carburettor) (Sec. 18)

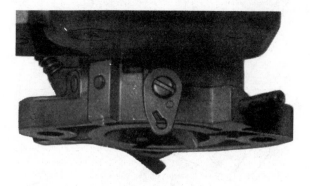

Fig. 3.17. Throttle lever to spindle alignment (Ford carburettor) (Sec. 18)

Fig. 3.18. Correct installation of throttle plate (Ford carburettor) (Sec. 18)

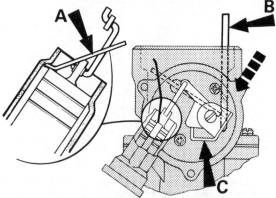

Fig. 3.19. Choke plate pull down adjustment diagram (Ford carburettor) (Sec. 18)

A Wire to trap piston
B Twist drill used as guide
C Thermostat lever extension

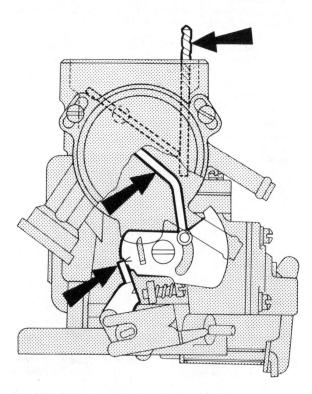

Fig. 3.20. Fast idle cam to throttle lever fast idle tab alignment (Ford carburettor) (Sec. 18)

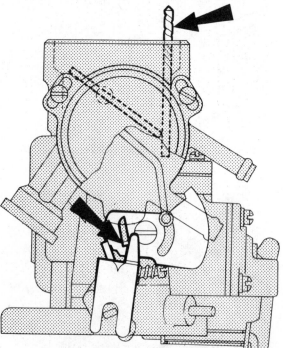

Fig. 3.21. Fast idle cam projection and de-choke setting diagram (Ford carburettor) (Sec. 18)

14 Blow through all jets and passages with air from a tyre pump, never probe them with wire or they will be damaged and the calibration upset.

15 Obtain a repair kit which will contain all the necessary gaskets for use during reassembly.

16 Reassembly is a reversal of dismantling but the following points should be noted.

17 If the plate has been removed from the throttle spindle then it must be refitted in relation to the throttle valve plate as illustrated.

18 Should the throttle valve have been dismantled, then it must be refitted so that the two punch marks are furthest from the mixture control screw.

19 When reassembling the float, check the float travel as described in Section 17 (b).

20 Check the choke plate pull down. To do this on auto. choke units depress the vacuum piston until the vacuum bleed port is exposed. Insert a piece of thin wire so that when the piston is

raised, it will be trapped by the wire. Now close the choke plate until its movement is stopped by the linkage. Open the throttle as necessary for the fast idle tab to clear the cam. Use a twist drill (0.09 in - 2.30 mm diameter) to check the gap between the bottom of the choke plate and the carburettor body. If necessary, bend the extension of the choke thermostat lever at the point where it abuts the triangular shaped piston operating lever.

21 Using the same drill placed between the edge of the choke plate and the carburettor body, open the throttle as necessary for the fast idle cam to attain its natural attitude. Check that the 'V' mark on the fast idle cam lines up with the top corner of the throttle lever fast idle tab. Bend the fast idle cam link as necessary to achieve this.

22 Check the de-choke setting by first opening the throttle slightly so that the choke plate closes by the action of the bi-metal spring. Open the throttle fully and hold it against the stop. Now check the clearance between the bottom of the choke plate and the carburettor body. Use a twist drill for this purpose, 0.21 in (5.33 mm) in diameter. If necessary, bend the projection on the fast idle cam.

23 Where the foregoing adjustments have all been correctly carried out and yet the fast idle speed is incorrect under cold starting conditions, the tab which contacts the stops of the fast idle cam should be bent as necessary to achieve the specified speed.

24 When installing the thermostatic spring and cover, engage the spring in the centre slot of the operating lever and ensure that the cover and housing marks are in alignment.

25 *On manual choke carburettors:* close the choke valve plate with the fingers and measure the gap between the edge of the valve plate and the internal wall of the carburettor intake. Use a twist drill to measure the clearance which should be between 0.14 and 0.16 inch (3.6 to 4.1 mm). If necessary, bend the tab on the choke spindle to correct. If the fast idle speed is incorrect during full choke starts, bend the tab which contacts the throttle fast idle cam.

19 Carburettor (Weber dual barrel) - description

The component parts of this carburettor are shown in Fig. 3.24 and it will be seen that it is of the dual barrel design having vertical downdraft and incorporating a fully automatic strangler type choke to ensure easy starting whilst the engine is cold. The float chamber is internally vented.

The carburettor body comprises two castings which form the upper and lower bodies. The upper body incorporates the float chamber cover, float pivot brackets, fuel inlet union, gauze filter, spring loaded needle valve, twin air intakes, choke plates and the section of the power valve controlled by vacuum.

Incorporated in the lower body is the float chamber, accelerator pump, two throttle barrels and integral main ventures, throttle plates, spindles, levers, jets and the petrol power valve.

The throttle plate opening is in a preset sequence so that the primary starts to open first and is then followed by the secondary in such a manner that both plates reach full throttle position at the same time. The primary barrel, throttle plate and venturi are smaller than the secondary, whereas the auxiliary venturi size is identical in both the primary and secondary barrels.

All the carburation systems are located in the lower body and the main progression systems operate in both barrels, whilst the idling and the power valve systems operate in the primary barrel only and the full load enrichment system in the secondary barrel.

The accelerator pump discharges fuel into the primary barrel.

A connection for the vacuum required to control the distributor advance/retard vacuum unit is located on the lower body.

20 Carburettor (Weber) - removal and installation

1   The procedure is very similar to that described for the Ford carburettor, in Section 16, except that four nuts are used to secure the unit to the manifold.

21 Carburettor (Weber) - dismantling and reassembly

1   Before dismantling wash the exterior of the carburettor and wipe dry using a non-fluffy rag. Select a clean area of the workbench and lay several layers of newspaper on the top. Obtain several small containers for putting some of the small parts in, which could be easily lost. Whenever a part is to be removed look at it first so that it may be refitted in its original position. As each part is removed place it in order along one edge of the newspaper so that by using this method reassembly is made easier.

2   All parts of the carburettor are shown in Fig. 3.24.

3   Unscrew and remove the fuel filter retainer from the upper body. Recover the cylindrical filter.

4   Disconnect the choke plate operating rod at its upper end (Fig. 3.22).

5   Undo and remove the screws and spring washers that retain the upper body to the lower body. Lift away the upper body and the gasket.

6   Carefully extract the float pivot pin and lift out the float assembly followed by the needle valve (Fig. 3.23).

7   Using a box spanner unscrew the needle valve carrier.

8   Undo and remove the three screws and spring washers that secure the spring loaded diaphragm cover. Lift away the cover and spring.

9   Undo and remove the four screws and spring washers that secure the accelerator pump cover to the lower body. Lift away the cover gasket, diaphragm and spring.

10 If necessary using a parallel pin punch, drive out the pivot pin from the plain end and lift away the accelerator pump lever.

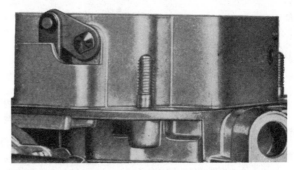

Fig. 3.22. Choke plate rod upper end attachment (Weber) (Sec. 21)

Fig. 3.23. Float pivot pin removal (Weber) (Sec. 21)

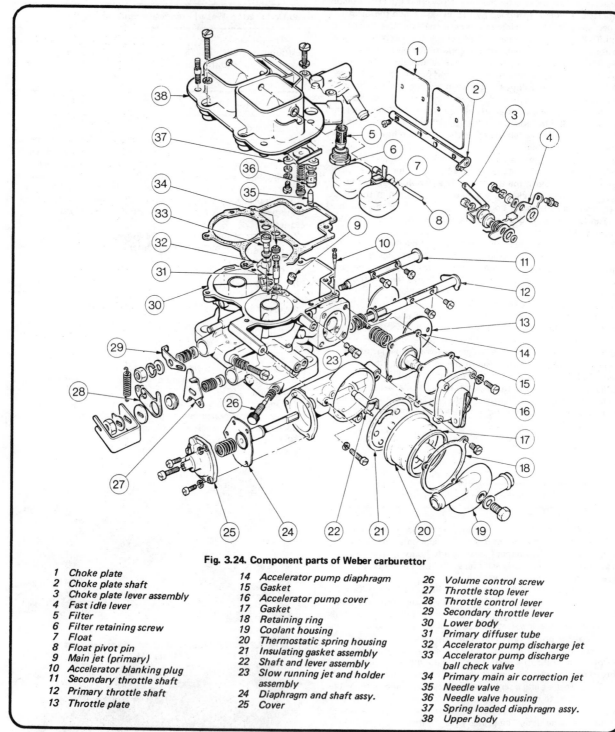

Fig. 3.24. Component parts of Weber carburettor

1	Choke plate	14	Accelerator pump diaphragm	26	Volume control screw
2	Choke plate shaft	15	Gasket	27	Throttle stop lever
3	Choke plate lever assembly	16	Accelerator pump cover	28	Throttle control lever
4	Fast idle lever	17	Gasket	29	Secondary throttle lever
5	Filter	18	Retaining ring	30	Lower body
6	Filter retaining screw	19	Coolant housing	31	Primary diffuser tube
7	Float	20	Thermostatic spring housing	32	Accelerator pump discharge jet
8	Float pivot pin	21	Insulating gasket assembly	33	Accelerator pump discharge
9	Main jet (primary)	22	Shaft and lever assembly		ball check valve
10	Accelerator blanking plug	23	Slow running jet and holder	34	Primary main air correction jet
11	Secondary throttle shaft		assembly	35	Needle valve
12	Primary throttle shaft	24	Diaphragm and shaft assy.	36	Needle valve housing
13	Throttle plate	25	Cover	37	Spring loaded diaphragm assy.
				38	Upper body

11 Also if necessary remove the split pin (or clip) that retains the upper end of the choke plate operating rod to the spindle lever and detach. Remove the dust seal from the air cleaner flange.

12 Undo the two screws that secure each choke plate to the shaft. Lift away the choke plates. Remove the burrs from the threaded holes and then withdraw the shaft.

13 Obtain a selection of screwdrivers with the ends in good condition and square so that the jets may be removed without damage.

14 Unscrew the primary and secondary main jets from the base

of the float chamber. **Do not** remove the power valve from the centre of the base of the float chamber (Fig. 3.25).

15 Unscrew and remove the accelerator pump discharge valve from the top of the carburettor body together with the discharge jet (Fig. 3.26).

16 Unscrew the air correction jets from the top of the lower carburettor body. Invert the latter and slide out the emulsion tubes.

17 Unscrew the two idling jet holders, one from either side of the carburettor body and remove the idling jets (Fig. 3.27).

18 Remove the volume control screw and spring from the base

of the body.

19 Unhook the secondary throttle return spring from the secondary throttle control lever and then unscrew the nut located on the primary throttle shaft. Remove the throttle control lever, spacer, secondary throttle control lever, bush, wave washer, fast idle lever, washer, slow running stop lever and spring from the spindle (Fig. 3.28).

20 Unscrew and remove the nut, washer and lever from the secondary throttle spindle.

21 Undo the two screws that secure each throttle plate to the shaft. Lift away the two throttle plates. Remove the burrs from the threaded holes and then withdraw the shaft.

22 Undo and remove the retaining screws, washer, choke operating lever and spring.

23 Undo and remove the centre screw to release the water housing and its gasket. Lift away the water housing.

24 Unscrew the three clamping ring screws, lift away the rings, thermostatic spring housing and insulating gasket.

25 Undo and remove the screws to release the diaphragm and spindle assembly.

26 Dismantling is now complete and all parts should be thoroughly washed and cleaned in petrol. Remove any sediment in the float chamber and drillings but take care not to scratch the fine drillings whilst doing so. Remove all traces of old gaskets using a sharp knife. When all parts are clean reassembly can begin.

27 To reassemble first insert the fuel filter into the upper body and screw in the retaining plug.

28 Insert the choke spindle in its bore, locate the choke plate in the shaft with the minus (-) sign uppermost. Secure the choke plates in position with two screws each. Peen over the threaded ends to lock.

29 Fit the dust seal to the air cleaner mounting flange.

30 Carefully insert the choke rod through the seal and connect it to the choke spindle lever.

31 Position the spring loaded diaphragm assembly in the upper body and secure with three screws and spring washers.

32 Using a box spanner screw in the needle valve housing. A new fibre washer should always be fitted under the housing.

33 Fit the needle valve into the housing (make sure it is the correct way up). Offer up the float to the pivot bracket and retain in position with the pivot pin.

34 Refer to Section 22 and check the float level settings.

35 The emulsion tubes, air correction jets and the primary and secondary main jets may next be refitted to their locations in the lower body.

36 Position the idling jets within their holders and then fit the assemblies together with new 'O' rings, one to each side of the lower body.

37 Locate the discharge valve, fitted with a new washer to both on the top and lower face, onto the discharge valve and secure the assembly to the lower body.

38 Position a new gasket, diaphragm and spring onto the accelerator pump cover and secure the cover assembly with the four screws and spring washers.

39 Refit the volume control screw and spring to the base of the lower body.

40 Slide the throttle shafts into their appropriate bores and fit the throttle plates into the shafts so that the 78° mark is towards the base of the lower body. Secure the throttle plates with two screws each and peen over the ends to stop them working loose.

41 Fit the lever and washer onto the secondary throttle spindle and secure with the nut and spring washer.

Fig. 3.25. Removal of primary and secondary main jets (Weber) (Sec. 21)

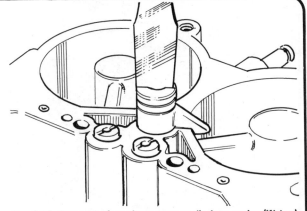

Fig. 3.26. Removal of accelerator pump discharge valve (Weber) (Sec. 21)

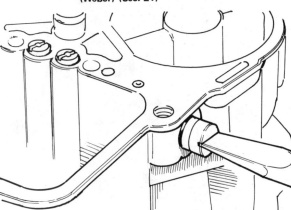

Fig. 3.27. Idling jet holder removal (Weber) (Sec. 21)

Fig. 3.28. Throttle return spring location (Weber) (Sec. 21)

42 Slide the following parts onto the primary throttle shaft: spring, slow running stop lever, washer, fast idle lever, wave washer, bush, secondary throttle control lever, spacer and throttle control lever. Secure with the plain washer and nut. Refer to Fig. 3.29.

43 Next engage the secondary throttle return spring with the throttle control lever. Locate the choke operating lever, spring and washer and retain in position with the screw.

44 Fit a new gasket onto the top face of the lower body and offer up the upper body to the lower body. Secure the two body halves with the retaining screws and spring washers.

45 With the primary throttle closed against its stop, check that the secondary throttle plate is closed in the bore; adjust the secondary throttle stop screw as necessary.

46 Refit the accelerator pump lever and secure with the pin. Carefully drive the pin home until the serrated end is flush with the casting.

47 The automatic choke is all that remains to be fitted. Position

Fig. 3.29. Correct assembly order of parts on primary throttle shaft (Weber) (Sec. 21)

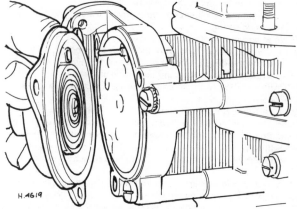

Fig. 3.30. Locating thermostatic spring loop in crankpin (Weber) (Sec. 21)

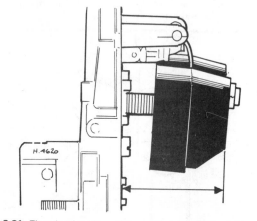

Fig. 3.31. Float level setting - 1st measurement (Weber) (Sec. 22)

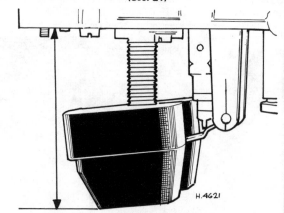

Fig. 3.32. Float level setting - 2nd measurement (Weber) (Sec. 22)

Fig. 3.33. Choke and plate pull down measurement (Weber) (Sec. 23)

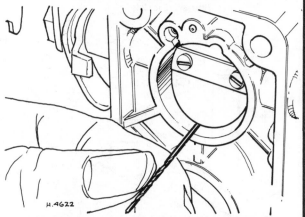

Fig. 3.34. Fast idle adjustment - carburettor removed from engine (Weber) (Sec. 24)

the diaphragm and shaft assembly within the inner choke housing. Locate the spring and cover on the diaphragm and retain with the screws.

48 Place the insulation gasket on the inner housing and follow this with the thermostatic spring housing. Take care to ensure that the spring loop engages with the crankpin (Fig. 3.30).

49 Line up the locating marks and secure the housing with the locking ring and screws.

50 Refer to the relevant sections and check and then adjust the fast idle setting, choke plate pull down and choke plate opening.

22 Carburettor (Weber) - float level adjustment

1 Since the height of the float is important to the maintenance of a correct flow of fuel, the correct height must be obtained by measurement and adjustment.

2 Refer to Section 2 and remove the air cleaner assembly.

3 Detach the fuel supply pipe and plug the end to stop dirt ingress.

4 Detach the choke plate operating rod.

5 Undo and remove the screws and spring washers that secure the upper body to the lower body. Lift away the upper body.

6 Carefully examine the float for signs of puncture which may be tested by inserting in warm water and watching for air bubbles.

7 Inspect the float arm for signs of fracture, damage or bending and, if satisfactory, hold the upper body in the vertical position with the float hanging down as shown in Fig. 3.31.

8 Measure the distance between the bottom of the float and the body and adjust if necessary, to the dimensions given in the Specifications at the beginning of this Chapter. Adjustment is made at the tab which rests against the needle valve.

9 Now hold the upper body in the horizontal position so that the float is suspended. Measure the distance from the bottom of the float to the body. Adjust if necessary to the dimensions as given in the Specifications at the beginning of this Chapter. Adjustment is made by bending the tab that rests against the needle valve body. See Fig. 3.32.

10 Reassemble the carburettor upper body which is the reverse sequence to removal.

23 Carburettor (Weber) - choke plate pull down adjustment

1 To check the choke control first take off the air cleaner as described in Section 2 of this Chapter.

2 With the choke fully closed, hold the choke lever against its stop.

3 Using a finger, carefully open the choke plates against the action of the toggle spring and, using a drill of suitable diameter (see Specifications) check the clearance between the lower edge of the choke plate and the carburettor body (Fig. 3.33).

4 If it is necessary to make an adjustment partially drain the cooling system and remove the thermostatic spring housing and adjust the screw under the blanking plug at the rear of the pull down diaphragm.

5 The phasing may be checked with the fast idle screw against the cam stop. This is done with the drill at the lower edge of the choke plate and carburettor body.

24 Carburettor (Weber) - fast idle adjustment

1 This adjustment is best carried out with the assistance of an electronic tachometer fitted to the ignition system.

2 Start the engine and run until it reaches its normal operating temperature, then stop it.

3 Set the automatic choke on the high cam position by opening the throttle, fully closing the choke plates, then releasing the throttle again to allow the choke plates to fully open.

4 Without disturbing the throttle, start the engine and adjust the fast idle speed to the specified rpm by turning the screw on

Fig. 3.35. Slow running adjustment - volume control screw (Weber) (Sec. 25)

the fast idle lever.

5 It is possible to carry out this adjustment with the carburettor removed by measuring the clearance between the primary throttle plate and carburettor body adjacent to the progression holes. Adjust as necessary. (Fig. 3.34).

25 Carburettor (Weber) - slow running adjustment

This adjustment must be made using an exhaust gas analyser. The volume adjustment screw must be turned as necessary to give 2.5% - 3.5% exhaust CO emission at the idle speed given in the Specifications at the beginning of this Chapter.

As a rough setting however turn the throttle stop screw clockwise so that the engine is running at a fast idle, then turn the volume control screw in either direction until the engine just runs evenly. Continue these adjustments until the engine will run slowly but smoothly with regular firing and no hint of stalling (Fig. 3.35).

26 Emission control system

In some operating territories, the fume emission control equipment which is fitted to Cortina models is designed to reduce atmospheric pollution to minimal levels without affecting engine performance or economy of running more than is absolutely necessary.

This pollution occurs in three ways: (i) blow-by gas (unburned mixture) which leaks past the piston rings during the compression stroke and into the engine crankcase; (ii) fuel vapour caused by evaporation of fuel stored in the fuel tank and carburettor; (iii) exhaust gas discharged as the normal products of combustion through the vehicle exhaust pipe.

1 *The crankcase ventilation system (P.C.V.)* is described in Chapter 1, Section 24.

2 *The fuel evaporative control system* is designed to minimize the escape of fuel vapour from the fuel tank and carburettor bowl to atmosphere.

3 The main components of the system comprise a vapour separator, a three way control valve (or control orifice on later models) and a charcoal canister. The vapour is retained in the carbon canister which is purged by manifold vacuum when the engine is running, the vapour being drawn into and burned in the engine combustion chambers.

4 *Exhaust emission control* may be accomplished by one of several methods according to the stringency of the regulations:

   (i)   A *deceleration valve* which is sensitive to manifold

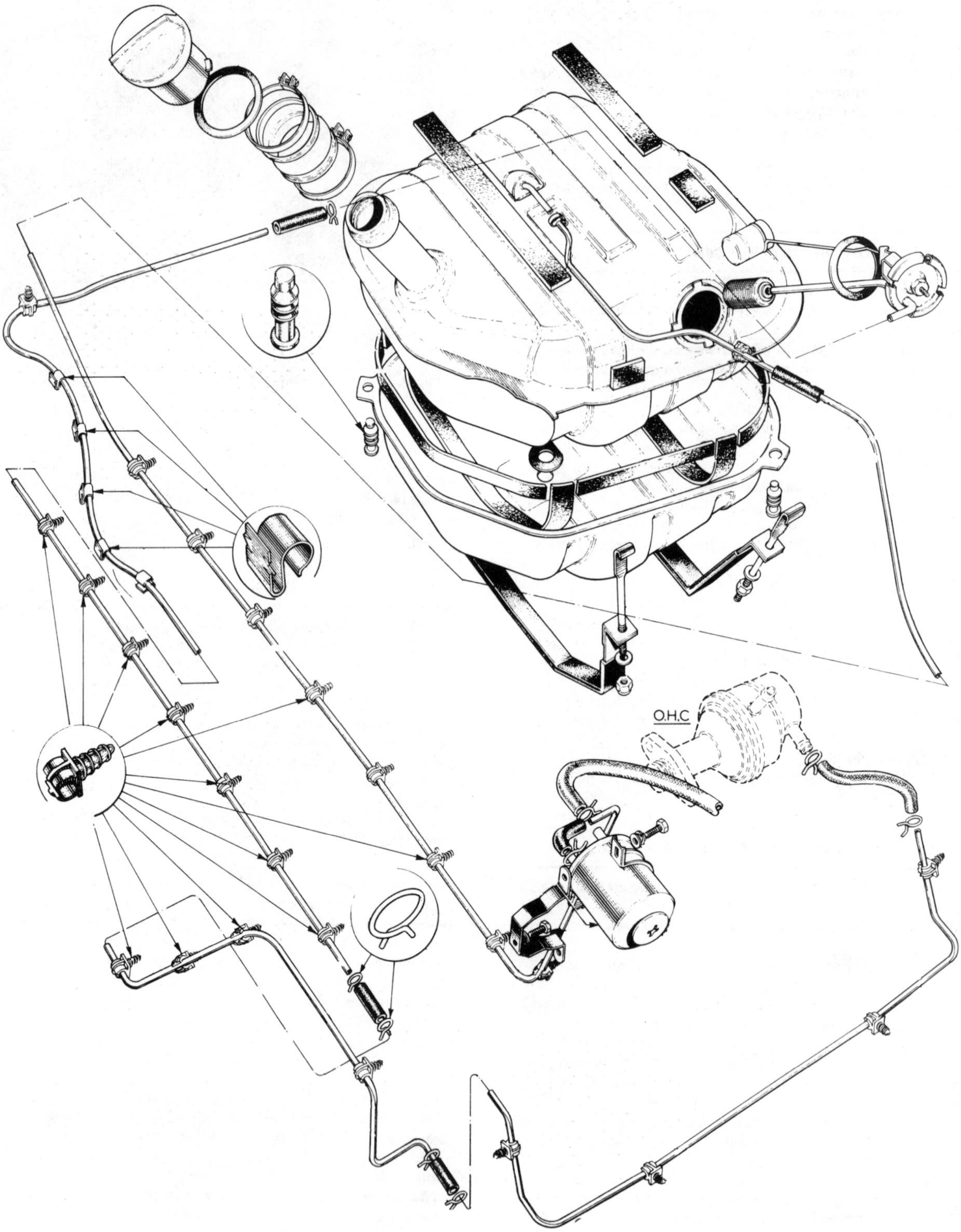

O.H.C

Fig. 3.36. Fuel evaporative emission control system (Sec. 26)

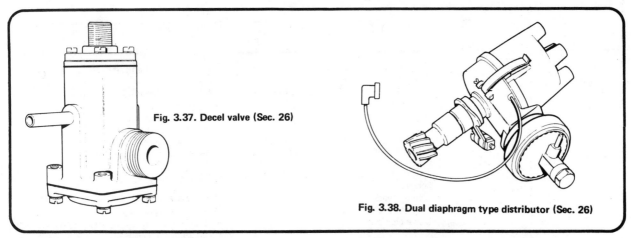

Fig. 3.37. Decel valve (Sec. 26)

Fig. 3.38. Dual diaphragm type distributor (Sec. 26)

vacuum. During deceleration when manifold vacuum is high the valve is opened to admit a greater volume of combustible mixture. This causes more complete combustion and reduces the emission of toxic fumes.

(ii) *A dual diaphragm distributor* may be used to provide additional retardation of the ignition during deceleration.

(iii) *Air injection system.* The system comprises a belt-driven air injection pump and the necessary valves and connecting hoses to provide a controlled supply of air to the area of the exhaust valves where it dilutes the exhaust gases and helps to burn the unburned portion of the exhaust gases in the exhaust system.

The diverter valve is actuated by a sharp increase in manifold vacuum and under these conditions, the valve shuts off the injected air to prevent backfiring during this period of richer mixture.

On engine overrun, the air generated by the air pump is expelled to atmosphere through the diverter valve and muffler. At high engine speeds, excess air pressure is released through the pressure relief valve of the diverter valve.

(iv) *Automatic temperature controlled air cleaner,* usually installed in conjunction with the air injection system; the air cleaner intake incorporates a temperature senitive valve which controls the volume of air drawn from the engine compartment or from the area around the exhaust manifold, using a deflector. By maintaining the carburettor intake air at a constant temperature, approximately 100ºF (40ºC), the carburettor calibrations can be reduced to leaner levels to reduce hydrocarbon emissions.

5   Maintenance consists chiefly of checking the security and condition of the system hoses. Every 15,000 miles (24,000 km) renew the element in the carbon canister. Maintain the correct drivebelt tension (½ in total deflection) of the air pump drivebelt.

6   It is emphasised that the efficiency of any emission control system depends in part on the state of tune of the basic engine components - ignition, valve clearances, carburettor settings, and these must always be maintained as described in the appropriate Chapters of this manual.

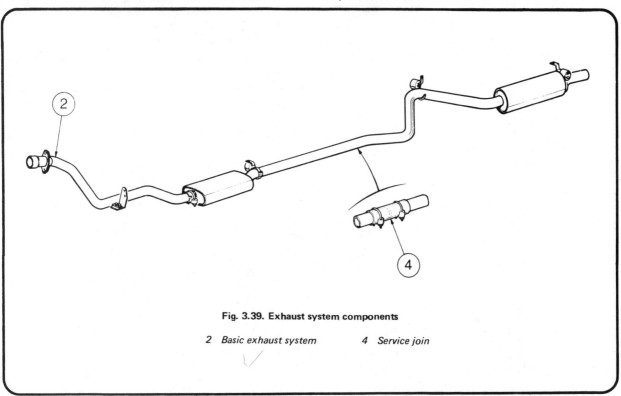

Fig. 3.39. Exhaust system components

2   *Basic exhaust system*   4   *Service join*

27 Fault diagnosis - fuel system and carburation

Symptom	Cause	Remedy
Fuel consumption excessive	Air cleaner choked and dirty giving rich mixture	Remove, clean and replace air cleaner element
	Fuel leaking from carburettor, fuel pumps, or fuel lines	Check for and eliminate all fuel leaks Tighten fuel line union nuts
	Float chamber flooding	Check and adjust float level
	Generally worn carburettor	Remove, overhaul and replace
	Distributor condenser faulty	Remove and fit new unit
	Balance weights or vacuum advance mechanism in distributor faulty	Remove and overhaul distributor
	Carburettor incorrectly adjusted mixture too rich	Tune and adjust carburettor
	Idling speed too high	Adjust idling speed
	Contact breaker gap incorrect	Check and reset gap
	Valve clearances incorrect	Check cam follower to valve stem clearances and adjust as necessary
	Incorrectly set spark plugs	Remove, clean and re-gap
	Tyres under-inflated	Check tyre pressures and inflate if necessary
	Wrong spark plugs fitted	Remove and replace with correct units
	Brakes dragging	Check and adjust brakes
Insufficient fuel delivery or weak mixture due to air leaks	Petrol tank air vent restricted	Remove petrol cap and clean out air vent
	Partially clogged filters in pump and carburettor	Remove and clean filters Remove and clean out float chamber and needle valve assembly
	Incorrectly seating valves in fuel pump	Remove, and fit new fuel pump
	Fuel pump diaphragm leaking or damaged	Remove and fit new fuel pump
	Gasket in fuel pump damaged	Remove, and fit new fuel pump
	Fuel pump valves sticking due to petrol gumming	Remove and throughly clean fuel pump
	Too little fuel in fuel tank (prevalent when climbing steep hills)	Refill fuel tank
	Union joints on pipe connections loose	Tighten joints and check for air leaks
	Split in fuel pipe on suction side of fuel pump	Examine, locate and repair
	Inlet manifold to block or inlet manifold to carburettor gasket leaking	Test by pouring oil along joints - bubbles indicate leak. Renew gasket as appropriate

28 Fault diagnosis - emission control systems

Symptom	Reason
P.C.V. system Escaping fumes from engine	Clogged P.C.V. valve Split or collapsed hoses
Fuel evaporative emission control system Fuel odour and /or rough running engine	Choked carbon canister Stuck filler cap valve Collapsed or split hoses
Air injection system Fume emission from exhaust pipe	Slack air pump drive belt Split or broken hoses Clogged pump air filter Defective air pump Leaking pressure relief valve

Chapter 4 Ignition system

Contents

Specifications

Spark plugs

Type	1600 Autolite BF 22
	2000 Autolite BF 32
Size	18 mm
Plug gap	0.025 in (0.64 mm)

Coil

Type ... ...   Oil filled low voltage used in conjunction with 1.5 ohm ballast resistor

	Autolite	Bosch
Resistance at 20°C (68°F)		
Primary	0.95 - 1.2 ohms	1.2 to 1.3 ohms
Secondary	5.900 - 6.900 ohms	7000 to 9300 ohms

Distributor

Type	Ford (Motorcraft) or Bosch	
Application:		Colour code
1600	Bosch 71 - HM - 12100 - SA	(Black)
1600 GT	Bosch 71 - HM - 12100 - DA	(Blue)
	or	
	Ford 71 - BB - 12100 - UB	(Red)
2000	Ford 71 - BB - 12100 - UB	(Red)
Contact points gap setting:		
Bosch	0.018 in (0.45 mm)	
Ford (Motorcraft)	0.025 in (0.64 mm)	
Rotation of rotor	Clockwise from top	
Automatic advance	Mechanical and vacuum	
Drive	Skew gear	
Initial static advance:		
1600 (except GT)	6° BTDC	
2000 and 1600 GT	4° BTDC (up to 1976), 8° BTDC (1976)	
Firing order	1 3 4 2	
Condenser capacity	0.21 - 0.25 m.fd.	
Contact breaker spring tension	15 - 19 oz (430 - 530 gms)	
Dwell angle	48—52°	

---

1 General description

In order that the engine can run correctly it is necessary for an electrical spark to ignite the fuel/air mixture in the combustion chamber at exactly the right moment in relation to engine speed and load. The ignition system is based on feeding low tension voltage from the battery to the coil where it is converted to high tension voltage. The high tension voltage is powerful enough to jump the spark plug gap in the cylinders many times a second under high compression pressures, providing that the system is in good condition and that all adjustments are correct.

The ignition system is divided into two circuits, low tension and high tension.

The low tension circuit (sometimes known as the primary) consists of the battery, lead to the control box, lead to the ignition switch, lead from the ignition switch to the low tension or primary coil windings (terminal SW), and the lead from the low tension coil windings (coil terminal CB) to the contact breaker points and condenser in the distributor.

The high tension circuit consists of the high tension or secondary coil windings, the heavy ignition lead from the centre of the coil to the centre of the distributor cap, the rotor arm and the spark plug leads and spark plugs.

The system functions in the following manner: Low tension voltage is changed in the coil into high tension voltage by the opening and closing of the contact breaker points in the low tension circuit. High tension voltage is then fed via the carbon brush in the centre of the distributor cap to the rotor arm of the distributor cap, and each time it comes in line with one of the four metal segments in the cap, which are connected to the spark plug leads, the opening and closing of the contact breaker points causes the high tension voltage to build up, jump the gap from the rotor arm to the appropriate metal segment and so via the spark plug lead to the spark plug, where it finally jumps the spark plug gap before going to earth.

The ignition is advanced and retarded automatically, to ensure the spark occurs at just the right instant for the particular load at the prevailing engine speed.

The ignition advance is controlled both mechanically and by a vacuum operated system. The mechanical governor comprises two lead weights, which move out from the distributor shaft as the engine speed rises due to centrifugal force. As they move outwards they rotate the cam relative to the distributor shaft, and so advance the spark. The weights are held in position by two light springs and it is the tension of the springs which is largely responsible for correct spark advancement.

The vacuum control consists of a diaphragm, one side of which is connected via a small bore tube to the carburettor, and the other side to the contact breaker plate. Depression in the inlet manifold and carburettor, which varies with engine speed and throttle opening, causes the diaphragm to move, so moving the contact breaker plate, and advancing or retarding the spark. A fine degree of control is achieved by a spring in the vacuum assembly.

The wiring harness includes a high resistance wire in the ignition coil feed circuit and it is very important that only a 'ballast resistor' type ignition coil is used. This lead is identified by its white with pink colour tracer colour coding and has a resistance of 1.4 - 1.6 ohms. The starter solenoid has an extra terminal so that a wire from the solenoid to the coil supplies current direct to the coil when the starter motor is operated. The ballast resistor wire is therefore by-passed and battery voltage is fed to the ignition system so giving easier starting.

2 Contact breaker points - adjustment

1   To adjust the contact breaker points to the correct gap, first release the two clips securing the distributor cap to the distributor body, and lift away the cap. Clean the cap inside and out with a dry cloth. It is unlikely that the four segments will be badly burned or scored, but if they are the cap will have to be renewed.

2   Inspect the carbon brush contact located in the top of the cap to ensure that it is not broken and stands proud of the plastic surface.

3   Lift away the rotor arm and check the contact spring on the top of the rotor arm. It must be clean and have adequate tension to ensure good contact.

4   Gently prise the contact breaker points open to examine the condition of their faces. If they are rough, pitted or dirty it will be necessary to remove them for resurfacing, or for replacement points to be fitted.

5   Presuming the points are satisfactory, or that they have been cleaned or replaced, measure the gap between the points with

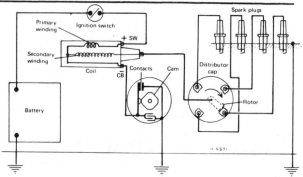

Fig. 4.1. Ignition system theoretical wiring diagram (Sec. 1)

feeler gauges, by turning the crankshaft until the heel of the breaker arm is on the highest point of the cam. The gap should be:

Bosch	*0.018 in (0.45 mm)*
Ford	*0.025 in (0.64 mm)*

6   If the gap varies from the amount slacken the contact plate securing screw/s, Bosch distributor 1 screw, Ford distributor 2 screws (photo).

7   Adjust the contact gap by inserting a screwdriver in the notched hole in the contact breaker plate. Turn clockwise to increase, and anticlockwise to decrease, the gap. When the gap is correct, tighten the securing screw/s and check the gap again. (photo)

8   Replace the rotor arm and distributor cap. Retain in position with the two clips.

3 Contact breaker points - removal and refitting

1   If the contact breaker points are burned, pitted or badly worn, they must be removed and either replaced or their faces must be filed smooth. The contact breaker points fitted to the Ford distributor are mounted on the breaker plate and the assembly must be renewed as a complete unit as opposed to the Bosch distributor where the contact breaker points may be renewed as a set.

2   Lift off the rotor arm by pulling it straight up from the top end of the cam spindle.

Bosch

a) Detach the low tension lead terminal from the internal terminal post and then undo and remove the screw that retains the contact breaker assembly to the base plate. Lift away the two contact breaker points.

b) To refit the points first locate the fixed point and lightly tighten the retaining screw. Smear a trace of grease onto the cam to lubricate the moving point heel and then fit the moving point pivot and then reset the gap as described in Section 2.

Ford

a) Slacken the self tapping screw that secures the condenser and low tension lead to the contact breaker point assembly. Slide out the forked ends of the lead terminals

b) Undo and remove the two screws that secure the contact breaker points base plate to the distributor base plate. Lift away the points assembly.

c) To refit the points is the reverse sequence to removal. Smear a trace of grease onto the cam to lubricate the moving point heel, and then reset the gap, as described in Section 2.

3   Should the contact breaker points be badly worn, a new set must be fitted. As an emergency measure clean the faces with fine emery paper folded over a thin steel rule. It is necessary to rub the pitted point right down to the stage where all the pitting has disappeared. When the surfaces are flat a feeler gauge can be used to reset the gap.

4   Finally replace the rotor arm and distributor cap. Retain in position with the two clips.

2.6 Slackening contact plate screw (Ford)

2.7 Resetting contact breaker points (Ford)

4 Condenser - removal, testing and refitting

1 The purpose of the condenser (sometimes known as a capacitor) is to ensure that when the contact breaker points open there is no sparking across them which would waste voltage and cause wear.

2 The condenser is fitted in parallel with the contact breaker points. If it develops a short circuit, it will cause ignition failure as the contact breaker points will be prevented from correctly interrupting the low tension circuit.

3 If the engine becomes very difficult to start or begins to miss after several miles of running and the breaker points show signs of excessive burning then the condition of the condenser must be suspect. One further test can be made by separating the points by hand with the ignition switched on. If this is accompanied by a bright flash, it is indicative that the condenser has failed.

4 Without special test equipment the only safe way to diagnose condenser trouble is to replace a suspected unit with a new one and note if there is any improvement.

5 To remove the condenser from the distributor take off the distributor cap and rotor arm.

6 **Bosch:** Release the condenser cable from the side of the distributor body and then undo and remove the screw that secures the condenser to the side of the distributor body. Lift away the condenser.

7 **Ford:** Slacken the self tapping screw holding the condenser lead and low tension lead to the contact breaker points. Slide out the forked terminal on the end of the condenser low tension lead. Undo and remove the condenser retaining screw and remove the condenser from the breaker plate.

8 To refit the condenser, simply reverse the order of removal.

5 Distributor - lubrication

1 It is important that the distributor cam is lubricated with vaseline (petroleum jelly) or grease at 3,000 miles (5,000 km) or 3 monthly intervals. Also the automatic timing control weights and cam spindle are lubricated with engine oil.

2 Great care should be taken not to use too much lubricant as any excess that finds its way onto the contact breaker points could cause burning and misfiring.

3 To gain access to the cam spindle, lift away the distributor cap and rotor arm. Apply no more than two drops of engine oil onto the felt pad. This will run down the spindle when the engine is hot and lubricate the bearings.

4 To lubricate the automatic timing control allow a few drops of oil to pass through the holes in the contact breaker base plate through which the four sided cam emerges. Apply not more than one drop of oil to the pivot post of the moving contact breaker point. Wipe away excess oil and refit the rotor arm and distributor cap.

6 Distributor - removal

1 To remove the distributor from the engine, mark the four spark plug leads so that they may be refitted to the correct plugs and pull off the four spark plugs lead connectors.

2 Disconnect the high tension lead from the centre of the distributor cap by gripping the end cap and pulling. Also disconnect the low tension lead from the ignition coil.

3 Pull off the rubber union holding the vacuum pipe to the distributor vacuum advance housing. Refer to the note in paragraph 5.

4 Remove the distributor body clamp bolt which holds the distributor clamp plate to the engine and lift out the distributor (Fig. 4.2).

5 **Note:** If it is not wished to disturb the timing turn the crankshaft until the timing marks are in line and the rotor arm is pointing to number 1 spark plug segment in the distributor cap.

H.4610

Fig. 4.2. Distributor clamp plate and securing bolt (Sec. 6)

This will facilitate refitting the distributor providing the crank-shaft is not moved whilst the distributor is away from the engine. Mark the position of the rotor in relation to the distributor body.

7 Distributor (Bosch) - dismantling

1 With the distributor on the bench, release the two spring clips

retaining the cap and lift away the cap (Fig. 4.3).
2 Pull the rotor arm off the distributor cam spindle.
3 Remove the contact breaker points, as described in Section 3.
4 Unscrew and remove the condenser securing screw and lift away the condenser and connector.
5 Next carefully remove the 'U' shaped clip from the pull rod of the vacuum unit.
6 Undo and remove the two screws that secure the vacuum unit to the side of the distributor body. Lift away the vacuum

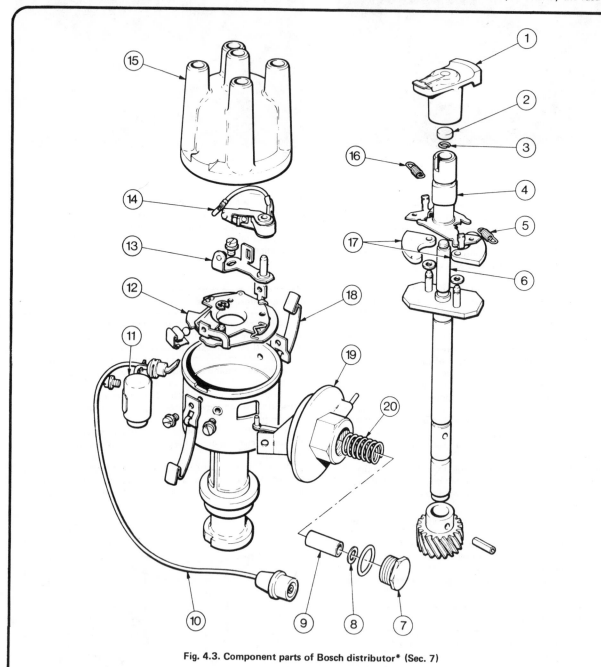

Fig. 4.3. Component parts of Bosch distributor* (Sec. 7)

1	Rotor	6	Shaft	11	Condenser	16	Spring
2	Felt	7	Plug	12	Base plate	17	Advance weights
3	Circlip	8	Plate	13	Points assembly	18	Clip
4	Cam	9	Spacer	14	Points assembly	19	Vacuum unit
5	Advance spring	10	LT lead	15	Cap	20	Spring

* Distributors fitted from 1972 onwards may differ slightly in detail.

unit.

7 Undo and remove the screws that secure the distributor cap spring clip retainer to the side of the distributor body. Lift away the two clips and retainers. This will also release the breaker plate assembly.

8 Lift away the contact breaker plate assembly from the inside of the distributor body.

9 Separate the breaker plate by removing the spring clip that holds the lower and upper plates together.

10 It is important that the primary and secondary springs of

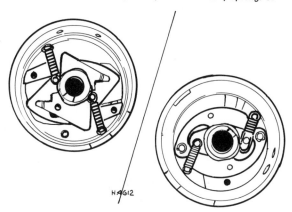

Fig. 4.4. Springs correctly located on centrifugal weights (Bosch) (Sec. 7)

(left) Early type   *(right) Later type*

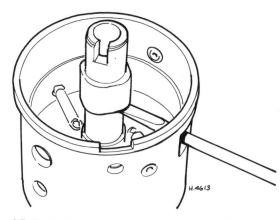

Fig. 4.5. Removal of cam from cam spindle (Bosch) (Sec. 7)

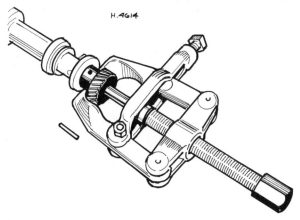

Fig. 4.6. Removal of drive gear (Bosch) (Secs. 7 and 8)

the automatic advance system are refitted in their original position during reassembly so the springs, weights and upper plate must be marked accordingly.

11 Refer to Fig. 4.4 and unhook the springs from the posts on the centrifugal weights.

12 Using a screwdriver as shown in Fig. 4.5 release the cam from the cam spindle and recover the felt pad, lock ring, and thrust washers from the cam. Release the two springs from the cam plate and lift away the centrifugal weights and washers.

13 Should it be necessary to remove the drive gear, using a suitable diameter parallel pin punch tap out the gear lock pin.

14 The gear may now be drawn off the shaft with a universal puller as shown in Fig. 4.6. If there are no means of holding the legs these must be bound together with wire to stop them springing apart during removal.

15 Finally withdraw the shaft from the distributor body.

8 Distributor (Ford) - dismantling

1 Refer to Section 7, and follow the instructions given in paragraphs 1 and 2. The component parts are shown in Fig. 4.7.

2 Next prise off the small circlip from the vacuum unit pivot post.

3 Take out the two screws that hold the breaker plate to the distributor body and lift away.

4 Undo and remove the condenser retaining screw and lift away the condenser.

5 Take off the circlip, flat washer and wave washer from the pivot post. Separate the two plates by bringing the holding down screw through the keyhole slot in the lower plate. Be careful not to lose the spring now left on the pivot post.

6 Pull the low tension wire and grommet from the lower plate.

7 Undo the two screws holding the vacuum unit to the body. Take off the unit.

8 To dismantle the vacuum unit, unscrew the bolt on the end of the unit and withdraw the vacuum spring, stop and shims.

9 The mechanical advance is next removed but first make a careful note of the assembly particularly which spring fits which post and the position of the advance springs. Then remove the advance spring. (photo)

10 Prise off the circlips from the governor weight pivot pins and take out the weights.

11 Dismantle the spindle by taking out the felt pad in the top of the spindle. Expand the exposed circlip and take it out.

12 Now mark which slot in the mechanical advance plate is occupied by the advance stop which stands up from the action plate, and lift the cam from the spindle.

8.9 Mechanical advance mechanism (Ford). Note different size springs

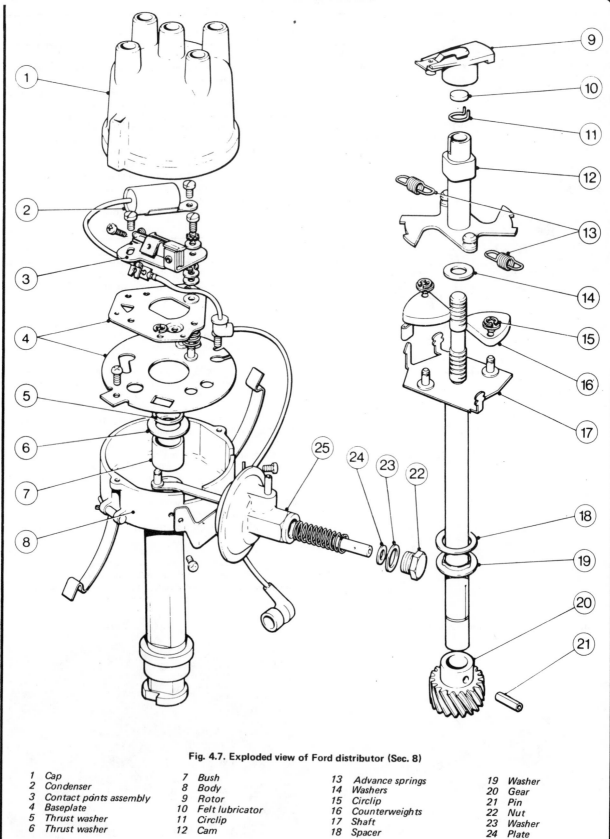

Fig. 4.7. Exploded view of Ford distributor (Sec. 8)

1	Cap	7	Bush	13	Advance springs	19 Washer
2	Condenser	8	Body	14	Washers	20 Gear
3	Contact points assembly	9	Rotor	15	Circlip	21 Pin
4	Baseplate	10	Felt lubricator	16	Counterweights	22 Nut
5	Thrust washer	11	Circlip	17	Shaft	23 Washer
6	Thrust washer	12	Cam	18	Spacer	24 Plate
						25 Vacuum unit

13 It is only necessary to remove the spindle and lower plate if it is excessively worn. If this is the case, with a suitable diameter parallel pin punch tap out the gear lock pin.

14 The gear may now be drawn off the shaft with a universal puller as shown in Fig. 4.6. If there are no means of holding the legs these must be bound together with wire to stop them springing apart during removal.

15 Finally withdraw the shaft from the distributor body.

9 Distributor - inspection and repair

1 Check the contact breaker points for wear, as described in Section 3. Check the distributor cap for signs of tracking indicated by a thin black line between the segments. Replace the cap if any signs of tracking are found.

2 If the metal portion of the rotor arm is badly burned or loose, renew the arm. If only slightly burned clean the end with a fine file. Check that the contact spring has adequate pressure and the bearing surface is clean and in good condition.

3 Check that the carbon brush in the distributor cap is unbroken and stands proud of its holder.

4 Examine the centrifugal weights and pivots for wear and the advance springs for slackness. They can best be checked by comparing with new parts. If they are slack they must be renewed.

5 Check the points assembly for fit on the breaker plate, and the cam follower for wear.

6 Examine the fit of the spindle in the distributor body. If there is excessive side movement it will be necessary either to fit a new bush or obtain a new body.

10 Distributor (Bosch) - reassembly

1 To reassemble first refit the two centrifugal weight washers onto the cam spindle. Smear a little grease onto the centrifugal weight contact faces and pivots and replace the weights in their original positions.

2 Lubricate the upper end of the spindle with engine oil and slide on the cam. Hook the two springs onto the weight retainers so that they are refitted in their original positions.

3 Position the thrust washer and lock ring in the cam. Carefully manipulate the lock ring into position using a thin electrician's screwdriver.

4 Refit the felt pad and thoroughly soak with engine oil.

5 Lubricate the distributor spindle with engine oil and insert it into the housing. The gear may now be tapped into position taking care to line up the lock pin holes in the gear and spindle. Support the spindle whilst performing this operation.

6 Fit a new lock pin to the gear and spindle and make sure that it is symmetrically positioned.

7 Locate the lower breaker plate in the distributor body. Place the distributor cap retaining spring clip and retainers on the outside of the distributor body and secure the retainers and lower breaker plate with the two screws.

8 Position the contact breaker point assembly in the breaker plate in such a manner that the entire lower surface of the assembly contacts the plate. Refit the contact breaker point assembly securing screw but do not fully tighten yet.

9 Hook the diaphragm assembly pull rod into contact with the pivot pin.

10 Secure the diaphragm to the distributor body with the two screws. Also refit the condenser to the terminal side of the diaphragm bracket securing screw. The condenser must firmly contact its lower stop on the housing.

11 Apply a little grease or petroleum jelly to the cam and also to the heel of the breaker lever.

12 Reset the contact breaker points, as described in Section 2, and then replace the rotor arm and distributor cap.

11 Distributor (Ford) - reassembly

1 Reassembly is a straightforward reversal of the dismantling process but there are several points which must be noted.

2 Lubricate with engine oil the balance weights and other parts of the mechanical advance mechanism, the distributor shaft and the portion of the shaft on which the cam bears, during assembly. Do not oil excessively, but ensure these parts are adequately lubricated.

3 When fitting the spindle, first replace the thrust washers below the lower breaker plate before inserting into the distributor body. Next fit the wave washer and thrust washer at the lower end and replace the drive gear. Secure it with a new pin.

4 Assemble the upper and lower spindle with the advance stop in the correct slot (the one which was marked) in the mechanical advance plate.

5 After assembling the advance weights and springs, check that they move freely without binding.

6 Before assembling the breaker plates make sure that the nylon bearing studs are correctly located in their holes in the upper breaker plate, and the small earth spring is fitted on the pivot post. (photo)

7 As the upper breaker plate is being refitted pass the holding down stud through the keyhole slot in the lower plate. (photo)

8 Hold the upper plate in position and refit the wave washer, flat washer and circlip. (photo)

9 When all is assembled reset the contact breaker points, as described in Section 2.

12 Distributor - installation

1 If a new shaft or gear has not been fitted (ie; the original parts are still being used), it will not be necessary to re-time the ignition.

2 Insert the distributor into its location with the vacuum advance assembly to the rear.

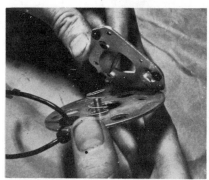
11.6 Reassembly of breaker plates (Ford)

11.7 Breaker plates correctly assembled (Ford)

11.8 Fitting spring clip to breaker plate post (Ford)

3 Notice that the rotor arm rotates as the gears mesh. The rotor arm must settle in exactly the same direction that it was in before the distributor was removed. To do this lift out the assembly far enough to rotate the shaft one tooth at a time lowering it home to check the direction of the rotor arm. When it points in the desired direction with the assembly fully home fit the distributor clamp plate, bolt and plain washer.

4 With the distributor assembly fitted reconnect the low tension lead from the side of the distributor to the CB terminal on the coil. Reconnect the HT lead to the centre of the distributor cap and refit the rubber union of the vacuum pipe which runs from the induction manifold to the side of the vacuum advance unit.

5 If the engine has been disturbed, refer to Section 14.

---

13 Spark plugs and HT leads

---

1 The correct functioning of the spark plugs is vital for the correct running and efficiency of the engine.

2 At intervals of 3,000 miles (5,000 km), the plugs should be removed, examined, cleaned, and if worn excessively, renewed. The condition of the spark plugs will also tell much about the overall condition of the engine (Fig. 4.8).

3 If the insulator nose of the spark plug is clean and white, with no deposits, this is indicative of a weak mixture, or too hot a plug (a hot plug transfers heat away from the electrode slowly - a cold plug transfers it away quickly).

4 The plugs fitted as standard are as listed in Specifications at the head of this Chapter. If the tip and insulator nose are covered with hard black looking deposits, then this is indicative that the mixture is too rich. Should the plug be black and oily, then it is likely that the engine is fairly worn, as well as the mixture being too rich.

5 If the insulator nose is covered with light tan to greyish brown deposits, then the mixture is correct and it is likely that the engine is in good condition.

6 If there are any traces of long brown tapering stains on the outside of the white portion of the plug, then the plug will have to be renewed, as this shows that there is a faulty joint between the plug body and the insulator, and compression is being allowed to leak away.

7 Plugs should be cleaned by a sand blasting machine which will free them from carbon more thoroughly than cleaning by hand. The machine will also test the condition of the plugs under compression. Any plug that fails to spark at the recommended pressure should be renewed.

8 The spark plug gap is of considerable importance, as, if it is too large or too small, the size of the spark and its efficiency will be seriously impaired. The spark plug gap should be set to the figure given in Specifications at the beginning of this Chapter.

9 To set it, measure the gap with a feeler gauge, and then bend open, or close, the outer plug electrode until the correct gap is achieved. The centre electrode should never be bent as this may crack the insulation and cause plug failure if nothing worse.

10 When replacing the plugs, remember to use new plug washers, and replace the leads from the distributor in the correct firing order, which is 1 3 4 2 (No. 1 cylinder being the one nearest the radiator).

11 The plug leads require no routine attention other than being kept clean and wiped over regularly.

12 At intervals of 3,000 miles (5,000 km) or 3 months, however, pull the leads off the plugs and distributor one at a time and make sure no water has found its way onto the connections. Remove any corrosion from the brass ends, wipe the collars on top of the distributor, and refit the leads.

---

14 Ignition timing

---

1 When a new gear or shaft has been fitted or the engine has been rotated, or if a new assembly is being fitted, it will be necessary to retime the ignition. Carry it out this way:

2 Look up the initial advance (static) for the particular model in the Specifications at the beginning of this Chapter.

3 Turn the engine until No. 1 piston is coming up to TDC on the compression stroke. This can be checked by removing No. 1 spark plug and feeling the pressure being developed in the cylinder or by removing the oil filler cap and noting when the cam is in the upright position. If this check is not made it is all too easy to set the timing 180° out. The engine can most easily be turned by engaging top gear and edging the car along (except automatic).

4 Continue turning the engine until the appropriate timing mark on the crankshaft pulley is in line with the pointer. This setting must be correct for the initial advance for the engine which has already been looked up (Fig. 4.9). For later models, the crankshaft pulley is marked by a heavy mark, indicating TDC, and then thick lines at 4°, 8° and 12° BTDC and thin lines at 2°, 6° and 10° BTDC.

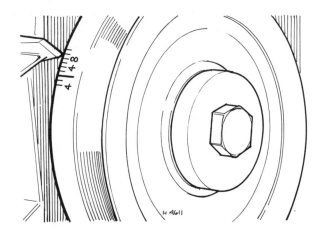

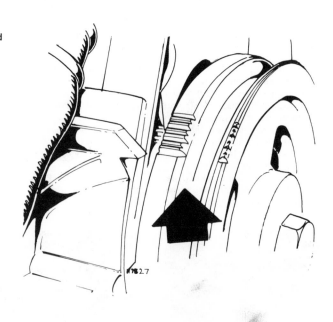

Fig.4.9. Ignition timing marks (alternative types) — typical

Measuring plug gap. A feeler gauge of the correct size (see ignition system specifications) should have a slight 'drag' when slid between the electrodes. Adjust gap if necessary

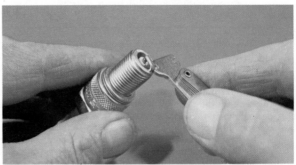

Adjusting plug gap. The plug gap is adjusted by bending the earth electrode inwards, or outwards, as necessary until the correct clearance is obtained. Note the use of the correct tool

Normal. Grey-brown deposits, lightly coated core nose. Gap increasing by around 0.001 in (0.025 mm) per 1000 miles (1600 km). Plugs ideally suited to engine, and engine in good condition

Carbon fouling. Dry, black, sooty deposits. Will cause weak spark and eventually misfire. Fault: over-rich fuel mixture. Check: carburettor mixture settings, float level and jet sizes; choke operation and cleanliness of air filter. Plugs can be re-used after cleaning

Oil fouling. Wet, oily deposits. Will cause weak spark and eventually misfire. Fault: worn bores/piston rings or valve guides; sometimes occurs (temporarily) during running-in period. Plugs can be re-used after thorough cleaning

Overheating. Electrodes have glazed appearance, core nose very white – few deposits. Fault: plug overheating. Check: plug value, ignition timing, fuel octane rating (too low) and fuel mixture (too weak). Discard plugs and cure fault immediately

Electrode damage. Electrodes burned away; core nose has burned, glazed appearance. Fault: pre-ignition. Check: as for 'Overheating' but may be more severe. Discard plugs and remedy fault before piston or valve damage occurs

Split core nose (may appear initially as a crack). Damage is self-evident, but cracks will only show after cleaning. Fault: pre-ignition or wrong gap-setting technique. Check: ignition timing, cooling system, fuel octane rating (too low) and fuel mixture (too weak). Discard plugs, rectify fault immediately

5   Now with the vacuum advance unit pointing to the rear of the engine and the rotor arm in the same position as was noted before removal insert the distributor into its location. Notice that the rotor arm rotates as the gears mesh. Lift out the distributor far enough to rotate the shaft one tooth at a time, lowering it home to check the direction of the rotor arm. When it points in the desired direction with the assembly fully home fit the distributor clamp plate, bolt and plain washer. Do not fully tighten yet.

6   Gently turn the distributor body until the contact breaker points are just opening when the rotor is pointing at the contact in the distributor cap which is connected to No. 1 spark plug. A convenient way is to put a mark on the outside of the distributor body in line with the segment in the cover, so that it shows when the cover is removed.

7   If this position cannot be reached check that the drive gear has meshed on the correct tooth by lifting out the distributor once more. If necessary, rotate the drive shaft gear one tooth and try again.

8   Tighten the distributor body clamp enough to hold the distributor, but do not overtighten.

9   Set in this way the timing should be approximately correct but small adjustments may have to be made following a road test.

10 The setting of a distributor including the amount of vacuum and mechanical advance can only be accurately carried out on an electric tester. Alterations to the vacuum advance shims or tension on the mechanical advance unit springs will change the characteristics of the unit.

11 Since the ignition timing setting enables the firing point to be correctly related to the grade of fuel used, the fullest advantage of a change of grade from that recommended for the engine will only be attained by readjustment of the ignition setting.

15 Ignition system - fault finding

By far the majority of breakdown and running troubles are caused by faults in the ignition system either in the low tension or high tension circuits.

There are two main symptoms indicating ignition faults. Either the engine will not start or fire, or the engine is difficult to start and misfires. If it is a regular misfire, ie; the engine is running on only two or three cylinders, the fault is almost sure to be in the secondary or high tension circuit. If the misfiring is intermittent, the fault could be in either the high or low tension circuits. If the car stops suddenly, or will not start at all, it is likely that the fault is in the low tension circuit. Loss of power and overheating, apart from faulty carburation settings, are normally due to faults in the distributor or to incorrect ignition timing.

16 Fault diagnosis - engine fails to start

1   If the engine fails to start and the car was running normally when it was last used, first check there is fuel in the petrol tank. If the engine turns over normally on the starter motor and the battery is evidently well charged, then the fault may be in either the high or low tension circuits. First check the HT circuit. **Note:** If the battery is known to be fully charged, the ignition light comes on, and the starter motor fails to turn the engine **check the tightness of the leads on the battery terminals** and also the secureness of the earth lead to its **connection to the body.** It is quite common for the leads to have worked loose, even if they look and feel secure. If one of the battery terminal posts gets very hot when trying to work the starter motor this is a sure indication of a faulty connection to that terminal.

2   One of the commonest reasons for bad starting is wet or damp spark plug leads and distributor. Remove the distributor cap. If condensation is visible internally dry the cap with a rag and also wipe over the leads. Replace the cap.

3   If the engine still fails to start, check that current is reaching the plugs, by disconnecting each plug lead in turn at the spark plug end, and holding the end of the cable about 3/16 inch

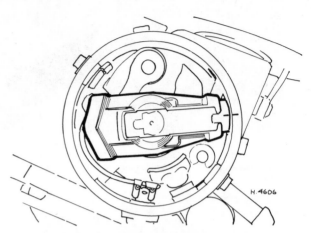

Fig. 4.10. Alignment of distributor rotor and body marks after correct installation of distributor (no. 1 piston at T.D.C.) (Sec. 14)

(5 mm) away from the cylinder block. Spin the engine on the starter motor.

4   Sparking between the end of the cable and the block should be fairly strong with a strong regular blue spark. (Hold the lead with rubber to avoid electric shocks). If current is reaching the plugs, then remove them and clean and regap them to 0.025 inch (0.64 mm). The engine should now start.

5   If there is no spark at the plug leads take off the HT lead from the centre of the distributor cap and hold it to the block as before. Spin the engine on the starter once more. A rapid succession of blue sparks between the end of the lead and the block indicate that the coil is in order and that the distributor cap is cracked, the rotor arm faulty, or the carbon brush in the top of the distributor cap is not making good contact with the spring on the rotor arm. Possibly, the points are in bad condition. Clean and reset them as described in this Chapter, Section 2 or 3.

6   If there are no sparks from the end of the lead from the coil check the connections at the coil end of the lead. If it is in order start checking the low tension circuit.

7   Use a 12v voltmeter or a 12v bulb and two lengths of wire. With the ignition switched on and the points open, test between the low tension wire to the coil (it is marked SW or +) and earth. No reading indicates a break in the supply from the ignition switch. Check the connections at the switch to see if any are loose. Refit them and the engine should run. A reading shows a faulty coil or condenser, or broken lead between the coil and the distributor.

8   Take the condenser wire off the points assembly and with the points open test between the moving point and earth. If there is now a reading then the fault is in the condenser. Fit a new one and the fault is cleared.

9   With no reading from the moving point to earth, take a reading between earth and the CB terminal of the coil. A reading here shows a broken wire which will need to be replaced between the coil and distributor. No reading confirms that the coil has failed and must be replaced, after which the engine will run once more. Remember to refit the condenser wire to the points assembly. For these tests it is sufficient to separate the points with a piece of dry paper while testing with the points open.

17 Fault diagnosis - engine misfires

1   If the engine misfires regularly run it at a fast idling speed. Pull off each of the plug caps in turn and listen to the note of the engine. Hold the plug cap in a dry cloth or with a rubber glove as additional protection against a shock from the HT supply.

2   No difference in engine running will be noticed when the lead from the defective circuit is removed. Removing the lead from one of the good cylinders will accentuate the misfire.

3   Remove the plug lead from the end of the defective plug and hold it about 3/16 inch (5 mm) away from the block. Re-start the engine. If the sparking is fairly strong and regular the fault must lie in the spark plug.

4   The plug may be loose, the insulation may be cracked, or the points may have burnt away giving too wide a gap for the spark to jump. Worse still, one of the points may have broken off. Either renew the plug, or clean it, reset the gap, and then test it.

5   If there is no spark at the end of the plug lead, or if it is weak and intermittent, check the ignition lead from the distributor to the plug. If the insulation is cracked or perished, renew the lead. Check the connections at the distributor cap.

6   If there is still no spark, examine the distributor cap carefully for tracking. This can be recognised by a very thin black line running between two or more electrodes, or between an electrode and some other part of the distributor. These lines are paths which now conduct electricity across the cap thus letting it run to earth. The only answer is a new distributor cap.

7   Apart from the ignition timing being incorrect, other causes of misfiring have already been dealt with under the section dealing with the failure of the engine to start. To recap - these are that:

   a) *The coil may be faulty giving an intermittent misfire;*
   b) *There may be a damaged wire or loose connection in the low tension circuit;*
   c) *The condenser may be short circuiting; or*
   d) *There may be a mechanical fault in the distributor (broken driving spindle or contact breaker spring).*

8   If the ignition timing is too far retarded, it should be noted that the engine will tend to overheat, and there will be a quite noticeable drop in power. If the engine is overheating and the power is down, and the ignition timing is correct, then the carburettor should be checked, as it is likely that this is where the fault lies.

Chapter 5 Clutch

Contents

Specifications

Clutch

Type	Laycock single dry plate diaphragm spring, cable operated	
Lining material	Ferodo RYZ	
	1600 GT and 2000	**1600 (except GT)**
Lining diameter:		
Inner	5.67 in (144.0 mm)	5.00 in (127.0 mm)
Outer	8.46 in (215.0 mm)	7.64 in (189.0 mm)
Lining thickness	0.33 in (8.4 mm)	0.28 in (7.2 mm)
Lining thickness (minimum)	0.12 in (3.0 mm)	0.08 in (2.0 mm)
Dampers		Two driven fibre plates
Number of torsion springs	6	4
Pedal free-play (measured at bellhousing)	0.12 to 0.14 in (3.05 to 3.56 mm)	
Total pedal stroke	6.50 in (165 mm) plus 0.75 in (19 mm) allowance for wear	

Torque wrench settings

	lb f ft	**kg fm**
Clutch to flywheel bolts	12 - 17	1.6 - 2.07
Bellhousing to gearbox	40 - 45	5.5 - 6.22

1 General description

All models covered by this manual are fitted with a single diaphragm spring clutch. The unit comprises a steel cover which is dowelled and bolted to the rear face of the flywheel and contains the pressure plate, diaphragm spring and fulcrum rings.

The clutch disc is free to slide along the splined first motion shaft and is held in position between the flywheel and the pressure plate by the pressure of the pressure plate spring. Friction lining material is rivetted to the clutch disc and it has a spring cushioned hub to absorb transmission shocks and to help ensure a smooth take off.

The circular diaphragm spring is mounted on shoulder pins and held in place in the cover by two fulcrum rings. The spring is also held to the pressure plate by three spring steel clips which are rivetted in position.

The clutch is actuated by a cable controlled by the clutch pedal. The clutch release mechanism consists of a release fork and bearing which are in permanent contact with the release fingers on the pressure plate assembly. There should therefore never be any free play at the release fork. Wear of the friction material in the clutch is adjusted out by means of a cable adjuster at the lower end of the cable where it passes through the bellhousing.

Depressing the clutch pedal actuates the clutch release arm by means of the cable. The release arms pushes the release bearing forwards to bear against the release fingers so moving the centre of the diaphragm spring inwards. The spring is sandwiched between two annular rings which act as fulcrum points. As the centre of the spring is pushed in, the outside of the spring is pushed out, so moving the pressure plate backwards and disengaging the pressure plate from the clutch disc.

When the clutch pedal is released the diaphragm spring forces the pressure plate into contact with the high friction linings on the clutch disc and at the same time pushes the clutch disc a fraction of an inch forwards on its splines so engaging the clutch disc with the flywheel. The clutch disc is now firmly sandwiched between the pressure plate and the flywheel so the drive is taken up.

2 Routine maintenance and clutch adjustment

1 Every 6,000 miles (10,000 km) adjust the clutch cable to compensate for wear in the linings.
2 The clutch should be adjusted until there is a clearance of between 0.12 and 0.14 in (3.05 and 3.56 mm) between the adjusting nut and its abutment on the bellhousing, as shown in Fig. 5.2.
3 To obtain the correct adjustment slacken off the locknut and with an assistant pulling the clutch pedal onto its stop turn the adjusting nut until the correct clearance has been obtained.
4 Hold the adjusting nut steady to prevent it moving and re-tighten the locknut. Check the clearance again.
5 When a new clutch friction plate has been fitted it will be found that the cable will require fairly extensive adjustment, particularly if the old friction plate was well worn before renewal.

3 Clutch - removal

This job may be carried out with the engine either in or out

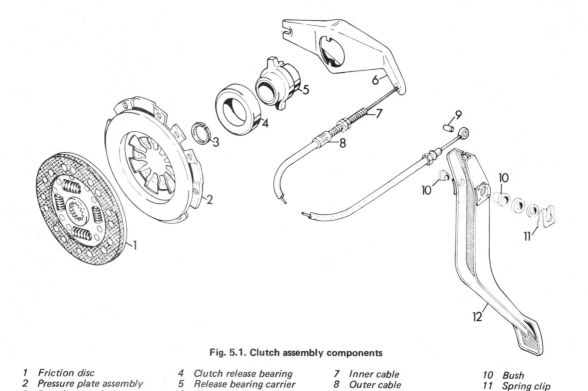

Fig. 5.1. Clutch assembly components

1 Friction disc	4 Clutch release bearing	7 Inner cable	10 Bush
2 Pressure plate assembly	5 Release bearing carrier	8 Outer cable	11 Spring clip
3 Ring (if fitted)	6 Clutch actuating arm	9 Pin	12 Clutch pedal

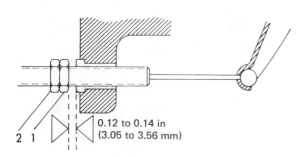

0.12 to 0.14 in
(3.05 to 3.56 mm)

Fig. 5.2. Clutch clearance (Sec. 2)

1 Adjustment nut   2 Locknut

of the car. The gearbox must be detached from the rear of the engine as described in Chapter 6. Then proceed as follows:

1 With a file or scriber mark the relative position of the clutch cover and flywheel which will ensure identical positioning on replacement. This is not necessary if a new clutch is to be fitted.

2 Undo and remove, in a diagonal and progressive manner, the six bolts and spring washers that secure the clutch cover to the flywheel. This will prevent distortion of the cover and also the cover suddenly flying off due to binding on the dowels.

3 With all the bolts removed lift the clutch assembly from the locating dowels. Note which way round the friction plate is fitted and lift it from the clutch cover.

4 Clutch - dismantling and inspection

1 It is not practical to dismantle the pressure plate assembly and the term 'dismantling' is usually used for simply fitting a new clutch friction plate.

2 If a new clutch disc is being fitted it is a false economy not to renew the release bearing at the same time. This will preclude having to replace it at a later date when wear on the clutch linings is still very small.

3 If the pressure plate assembly requires renewal an exchange unit must be purchased. This will have been accurately set up and balanced to very fine limits.

4 Examine the clutch disc friction linings for wear and loose rivets and the disc for rim distortion, cracks, broken hub springs, and worn splines. The surface of the friction linings may be highly glazed, but as long as the clutch material pattern can be clearly seen this is satisfactory. Compare the amount of lining wear with a new clutch disc at the stores in your local garage or measure the lining thickness (see Specifications). If worn the friction plate must be renewed.

5 It is always best to renew the clutch driven plate as an assembly to preclude further trouble, but, if it is wished to merely renew the linings, the rivets should be drilled out and not knocked out with a punch. The manufacturers do not advise that only the linings are renewed and personal experience dictates that it is far more satisfactory to renew the driven plate complete rather than to try and economise by only fitting new friction linings.

6 Check the machined faces of the flywheel and the pressure plate. If either is grooved it should be machined until smooth, or renewed.

7 If the pressure plate is cracked or split it is essential that an exchange unit is fitted, also if the pressure of the diaphragm spring is suspect.

8 Check the release bearing for smoothness of operation. There should be no harshness or slackness in it. It should spin reasonably freely bearing in mind it has been pre-packed with grease.

5 Clutch - installation

1   It is important that no oil or grease gets on the clutch plate
friction linings, or the pressure plate and flywheel faces. It is advisable to replace the clutch with clean hands and to wipe down
the pressure plate and flywheel faces with a clean rag before
assembly begins.
2   Place the clutch plate against the flywheel, ensuring that it is
the correct way round. The projecting torsion spring plate should
be furthest from the flywheel.
3   Replace the clutch cover assembly loosely on the dowels.
Replace the six bolts and spring washers and tighten them finger
tight so that the clutch plate is gripped but can still be moved.
4   The clutch disc must now be centralised so that when the
engine and gearbox are mated, the gearbox first motion shaft
splines will pass through the splines in the centre of the driven
plate.
5   Centralisation can be carried out quite easily by inserting a
round bar or long screwdriver through the hole in the centre of
the clutch, so that the end of the bar rests in the small hole in the
end of the crankshaft containing the spigot bush. Ideally an old
Ford first motion shaft should be used.
6   Using the first motion shaft spigot bush as a fulcrum, moving
the bar sideways or up and down will move the clutch disc in
whichever direction is necessary to achieve centralisation.
7   Centralisation is easily judged by removing the bar and viewing
the driven plate hub in relation to the hole in the centre of the
clutch cover plate diaphragm spring. When the hub appears exactly in the centre of the hole all is correct. Alternatively the first
motion shaft will fit the bush and centre of the clutch hub
exactly, obviating the need for visual alignment.
8   Tighten the clutch bolts firmly in a diagonal sequence to
ensure that the cover plate is pulled down evenly and without
distortion of the flange (Fig. 5.4). Finally tighten the bolts to a
torque wrench setting of 12 - 15 lb f ft (1.6 - 2.07 kg fm).

6 Clutch cable - removal and refitting

1   Open the bonnet, and for safety reasons disconnect the
battery.
2   Carefully prise out the rubber bung from the upper bulkhead
over the pedal assembly.
3   Chock the rear wheels, jack up the front of the car and support on firmly based stands. Ease off the rubber grommet from
the side of the clutch housing located as shown in Fig. 5.5.
4   Push the clutch pedal hard against the stop and with an open
ended spanner slacken the locknut and clutch adjustment nut.
These are located on the clutch bellhousing.
5   It will now be possible to lift the cable ball end from the
slotted end of the release lever. Whilst this is being done take
great care not to accidentally disengage the release lever from
the bearing hub.
6   Lever the cable eye end and pin from the cable retention bush
in the pedal with a small screwdriver (See Figs. 5.7 and 5.8).
7   Withdraw the pin from the eye and withdraw the cable assembly from the abutment tube in the dash panel.
8   Replacement is a straightforward reversal of the removal
sequence. Well lubricate the pivot pin. Refer to Section 2 and
adjust the cable.

7 Clutch release bearing - removal and refitting

1   With the gearbox and engine separated to provide access to
the clutch, attention can be given to the release bearing located
in the bellhousing, over the input shaft.
2   The release bearing is a relatively inexpensive but important
component and unless it is nearly new it is a mistake not to replace it during an overhaul of the clutch.
3   To remove the release bearing, first pull off the release arm
rubber gaiter.

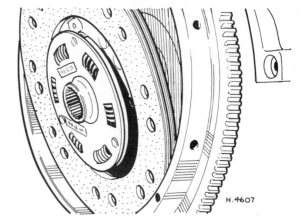

Fig. 5.3. Clutch plate installation (Sec. 5)

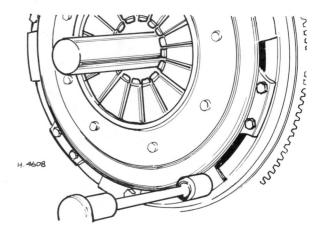

Fig. 5.4. Tightening clutch securing bolts (Sec. 5)

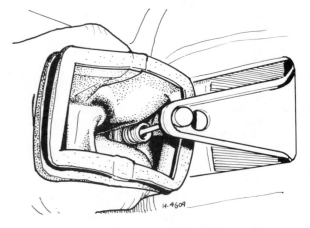

Fig. 5.5. Removal of rubber grommet from side of clutch
bellhousing (Sec. 6)

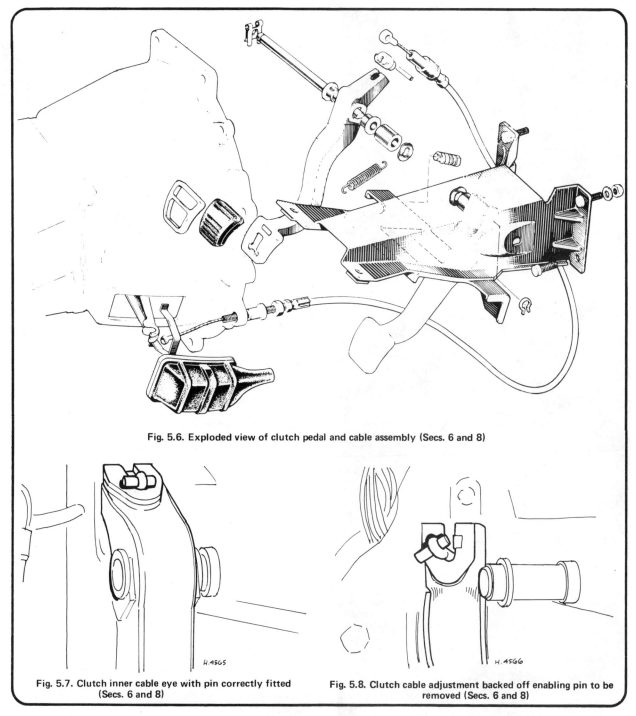

Fig. 5.6. Exploded view of clutch pedal and cable assembly (Secs. 6 and 8)

Fig. 5.7. Clutch inner cable eye with pin correctly fitted
(Secs. 6 and 8)

Fig. 5.8. Clutch cable adjustment backed off enabling pin to be
removed (Secs. 6 and 8)

4   The release bearing and arm can be separately withdrawn from
the clutch housing (photos). Alternatively they may be removed
as an assembly.
5   To free the bearing from the release arm simply unhook it and
then with the aid of two wooden blocks and a vice press off the
release bearing from its hub. Note which way round the bearing
is fitted (photo).
6   Replacement is a straightforward reversal of removal.

---

8   Clutch pedal - removal and installation

1   The clutch pedal is removed and replaced in the same manner
as the brake pedal, once the cable has been released from the
pedal.
2   A full description of how to remove and replace the brake
pedal can be found in Chapter 9, Section 15 (See also Figs. 5.6,
5.7 and 5.8).

---

9   Clutch - fault diagnosis

There are four main faults to which the clutch and release
mechanism are prone. They may occur by themselves or in conjunction with any of the other faults. They are clutch squeal,
slip, spin and judder.

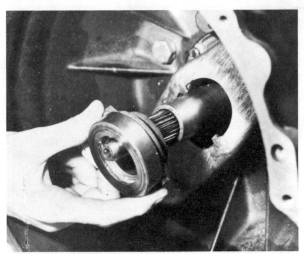

7.4A Release bearing removal

7.4B Release arm removal

7.5 Removal of clutch release bearing by rotating through 90⁰

Clutch squeal

1   If on taking up the drive or when changing gear, the clutch squeals, this is a sure indication of a badly worn clutch release bearing.

2   As well as regular wear due to normal use, wear of the clutch release bearing is much accentuated if the clutch is ridden, or held down for long periods in gear, with the engine running. To minimise wear of this component the car should always be taken out of gear at traffic lights and for similar holdups.

Clutch slip

1   Clutch slip is a self evident condition which occurs when the clutch friction plate is badly worn, when oil or grease have got onto the flywheel or pressure plate faces, or when the pressure plate itself is faulty.

2   The reason for clutch slip is that, due to one of the faults listed above, there is either insufficient pressure from the pressure plate, or insufficient friction from the friction plate to ensure solid drive.

3   If small amounts of oil get onto the clutch, they will be burnt off under the heat of clutch engagement, and in the process, gradually darken the linings. Excessive oil on the clutch will burn off leaving a carbon deposit which can cause quite bad slip, or fierceness, spin and judder.

4   If clutch slip is suspected, and confirmation of this condition is required, there are several   tests which can be made.

5   With the engine in second or third gear and pulling lightly up a moderate incline sudden depression of the accelerator pedal may cause the engine to increase its speed without any increase in road speed. Easing off on the accelerator will then give a definite drop in engine speed without the car slowing.

6   In extreme cases of clutch slip the engine will race under normal acceleration conditions.

7   If slip is due to oil or grease on the linings a temporary cure can sometimes be effected by squirting carbon tetrachloride into the clutch. The permanent cure is, of course, to renew the clutch driven plate and trace and rectify the oil leak.

Clutch spin

1   Clutch spin is a condition which occurs when the release arm travel is excessive, there is an obstruction in the clutch either on the primary gear splines or in the operating lever itself, or the oil may have partially burnt off the clutch linings and have left a resinous deposit which is causing the clutch disc to stick to the pressure plate or flywheel.

2   The reason for clutch spin is that due to any, or a combination of, the faults just listed, the clutch pressure plate is not complete-ly freeing from the centre plate even with the clutch pedal fully depressed.

3   If clutch spin is suspected, the condition can be confirmed by extreme difficulty in engaging first gear from rest, difficulty in changing gear, and very sudden take up of the clutch drive at the fully depressed end of   the clutch pedal travel as the clutch is released.

4   Check that the clutch cable is correctly adjusted and, if in order, the fault lies internally in the clutch. It will then be necessary to remove the clutch for examination, and to check the gearbox input shaft.

Clutch judder

1   Clutch judder is a self evident condition which occurs when the gearbox or engine mountings are loose or too flexible, when there is oil on the faces of the clutch friction plate, or when the clutch pressure plate has been incorrectly adjusted during assembly.

2   The reason for clutch judder is that due to one of the faults just listed, the clutch pressure plate is not freeing smoothly from the friction disc, and is snatching.

3   Clutch judder normally occurs when the clutch pedal is released in first or reverse gears, and the whole car shudders as it moves backwards or forwards.

Chapter 6
Manual Gearbox and automatic transmission

Contents

Specifications

Manual gearbox

Number of gears	4 forward, 1 reverse
Type of gears	Helical constant mesh
Synchromesh	All forward gears
Countershaft gear train endfloat	0.006 — 0.018 in (0.15 — 0.45 mm)
Thrust washer thickness	0.061 — 0.063 in (1.55 — 1.60 mm)
Countershaft diameter	0.6818 — 0.6823 in (17.317 — 17.329 mm)
Oil capacity	1600 cc 1.75 Imp. pints (1.00 litre); 2000 cc 2.9 Imp. pints (1.66 litres)

	1600 and 2000	1600 GT
Ratios:		
First	3.65 : 1	2.97 : 1
Second	1.97 : 1	2.01 : 1
Third	1.37 : 1	1.43 : 1
Top	1.00 : 1	1.00 : 1
Reverse	3.66 : 1	3.32 : 1

Automatic transmission (up to 1974)

Type	Borg Warner BW 35
Torque converter ratio range	Infinitely variable between 1 : 1 and 1.91 : 1 operating in all gears
Lubricant capacity	11.25 Imp. pints (6.4 litres)
Gear ratio:	
Low	2.395 : 1
Intermediate	1.450 : 1
Top	1 : 1
Reverse	2.094 : 1
Oil cooler type	Tubes/fins
Oil cooler hoses:	
Inner diameter	0.272 — 0.300 in (6.91 — 7.62 mm)
Wall thickness	0.232 — 0.315 in (5.89 — 8.00 mm)

Automatic transmission (1974 onwards)

Type	Ford Bordeaux
Torque converter ratio	2.02 : 1
Lubricant capacity	10.5 Imp. pints (6 litres)
Gear ratios:	
Low	2.47 : 1
Intermediate	1.47 : 1
Top	1 : 1
Reverse	2.11 : 1

Torque wrench settings

	lb f ft	kg fm
Manual gearbox		
Gearbox top cover	8 – 9	1.1 – 1.3
Gearbox spigot bearing	8 – 9	1.1 – 1.3
Extension housing to gearbox	33 – 36	4.6 – 5.0
Automatic transmission (Borg-Warner)		
Torque converter to drive plate	25 – 35	3.5 – 4.1
Converter housing to transmission case	8 – 13	1.1 – 1.8
Starter inhibitor switch locknut	4 – 6	0.6 – 0.8
Centre support to transmission case	30 – 40	4.1 – 5.5
Oil sump to transmission case	8 – 13	1.1 – 1.8
Oil drain plug	9 – 12	1.4 – 1.6
Automatic transmission (Ford)		
Torque converter housing to transmission	26 – 39	3.6 – 5.3
Torque converter to driveplate	26 – 30	3.6 – 4.1
Fluid pan to transmission	12 – 17	1.6 – 2.4
Inhibitor switch	12 – 15	1.6 – 2.0
Torque converter housing to engine	22 – 27	3.0 – 3.7
Torque converter drain plug	20 – 30	2.7 – 4.0

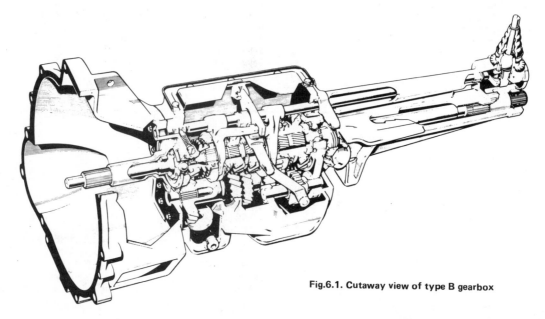

Fig.6.1. Cutaway view of type B gearbox

1 General description (manual gearbox)

The gearbox fitted to all models contains four constant mesh helically cut forward gears and one straight cut reverse gear. Synchromesh is fitted between 1st and 2nd, 2nd and 3rd and 3rd and 4th. The individual cast iron bellhousing and gearbox casings are bolted together whereas the gearbox extension housing is of cast aluminium and incorporates the remote control gearchange system.

The gearbox is of simple design using a minimum number of components. Where close tolerances and limits are required, manufacturing tolerances are compensated for and excessive end float or backlash eliminated by the fitting of selective circlips, located as shown in Fig. 6.2. When overhauling the gearbox always use new circlips, never replace ones that have already been used.

The gear selector mechanism is unusual in that the selector forks are free to slide on one selector rod which also serves as the gearchange shaft. At the gearbox end of this rod lies the selector arm, which, depending on the position of the gearlever, places the appropriate selector fork in the position necessary for the synchroniser sleeve to engage with the dog teeth on the gear selected.

It is impossible to select two gears at once because of an

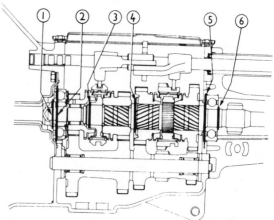

Fig.6.2. Location of selective fit circlips on type B gearbox (Sec.1)

interlock guard plate which pivots on the right-hand side of the gearbox casing. The selector forks when not in use are positively held by the guard plate in their disengaged positions.

2 Gearbox - removal and installation

1 The gearbox can be removed in unit with the engine through the engine compartment as described in Chapter 1, Section 5. Alternatively the gearbox can be separated from the rear of the engine at the bellhousing and the gearbox lowered from under the car. The latter method is easier and quicker than the former.

2 If a hoist or an inspection pit are not available then run the back of the car up a pair of ramps or jack it up and fit axle stands. Next jack up the front of the car and support on axle stands

3 For safety reasons, disconnect the battery earth terminal.

4 Working inside the car, push the front seats rearwards as far as possible.

5 Models fitted with parcel tray instead of centre console proceed to paragraph 9, otherwise continue as follows.

6 Carefully ease the gearchange lever gaiter from the body panel and slide it up the gear lever. (photo)

7 Using a screwdriver bend back the locking tabs on the lock ring and very carefully unscrew the lock ring and gearchange lever retainer. (photo)

8 The gearchange lever can now be lifted upwards and away from the gearbox. (photo)

9 *Models fitted with centre console:* Undo and remove the screws that secure the parcel tray bolts and lift away the parcel tray.

10 Unlock the nut located at the base of the gearchange lever. Unscrew the gearchange lever and locknut.

11 Undo and remove the centre console and instrument cluster mounting screws.

12 Move the console unit until it is possible to gain access to the rear of the instrument cluster. Make a note of the electrical cable connections and detach from the rear of the instruments.

13 Undo and remove the centre bolt from the handbrake lever compensator and pull the lever handle fully up. The console unit may now be lifted away from inside the car.

14 *All models.* Mark the mating flanges of the propeller shaft and final drive so that they may be reconnected in their original positions and undo and remove the four securing bolts.

15 Where a split type propeller shaft is fitted, undo and remove the centre bearing retainer securing bolts, spring and plain washers. (photo)

16 Draw the propeller shaft rearwards so detaching the front end from the rear of the gearbox and lift away from under the car.

17 Wrap some polythene around the end of the gearbox and secure with string or wire to stop any oil running out.

18 Make a note of the cable connections to the starter motor

2.6 Sliding gaiter up gear lever

2.7 Bending back lock ring tabs with screwdriver

2.8 Lifting away gearchange lever

2.15 Removal of centre bearing retainer securing bolt

and detach the cables.

19 Undo and remove the bolts that secure the starter motor to the gearbox flange. Lift away the starter motor.

20 Remove the rear engine cover plate and bracket assembly from the clutch housing. Detach the bracket assembly from the cylinder block and swing it back out of the way. This bracket is shown in Fig. 6.3.

21 Pull off the plug attached to the reverse light switch located on the side of the remote control housing.

22 Using a pair of circlip pliers remove the circlip retaining the speedometer drive cable end to the gearbox extension housing (photo).

23 Pull the speedometer drive cable away from the side of the extension housing.

24 Using a pair of pliers detach the clutch operating cable from the actuating arm that protrudes from the side of the clutch housing (photo). On some models it will be necessary to pull back the rubber gaiter first.

25 Pull the clutch cable assembly through the locating hole in the flange on the clutch housing.

26 Suitably support the weight of the gearbox by either using a jack or an axle stand. Insert a wooden chock between the sump and engine support so that the engine does not drop when the gearbox is removed.

27 Undo and remove the remaining bolts that secure the clutch bellhousing to the rear of the engine.

28 Undo and remove the exhaust pipe securing nuts at the exhaust manifold and the exhaust mounting bracket. Push the assembly away from the gearbox and tie back with string.

29 Undo and remove the one bolt that secures the rubber mounting to the gearbox extension housing.

30 Undo and remove the four bolts, spring and plain washers that secure the gearbox support crossmember to the body. (photo)

31 Lift away the crossmember. (photo)

32 The assistance of a second person is now required who should be ready to help in taking the weight of the gearbox.

33 **Do not** allow the weight of the gearbox to hang on the input shaft (first motion shaft) as it is easily bent. Carefully separate the gearbox from the engine by sliding it rearwards out of the clutch housing. It will be necessary to lower the jack or stand to give clearance of the gearbox from the underside of the body.

34 If major work is to be undertaken on the gearbox it is recommended that the exterior be washed with paraffin or 'Gunk' and dried with a non-fluffy rag.

35 Refitting the gearbox is the reverse sequence to removal but the following additional points should be noted:

a) Make sure that the engine cover plate gasket is correctly positioned.

b) Adjust the clutch control cable in such a manner that after two pedal applications, a clearance of 0.12 to 0.14 in (3.05 to 3.56 mm) exists between the adjuster nut and its abutment.

c) Before refitting the gearchange lever well grease the fork

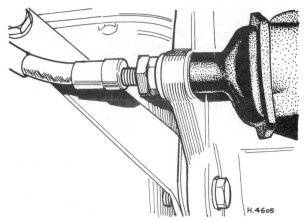

Fig. 6.3. Location of bracket between engine and clutch housing (Sec. 2)

ends.

d) Refill the gearbox with the correct gear oil.

3 Gearbox - dismantling

1 Place the complete unit on a firm bench or table and ensure that you have the following tools available, in addition to the normal range of spanners etc.

a) Good quality circlip pliers, 2 pairs - 1 expanding and 1 contracting

b) Copper headed mallet, at least 2 lb (0.14 kg)

c) Drifts, steel and brass 0.375 inch (9.525 mm) diameter

d) Small containers for needle rollers

e) Engineer's vice mounted on firm bench

f) Selection of metal tubing

Any attempt to dismantle the gearbox without the foregoing is not impossible, but will certainly be very difficult and inconvenient.

2 Read the whole of this Section before starting work.

3 The internal parts of the gearbox are shown in Fig. 6.4.

4 Undo and remove the ten bolts and shakeproof washers that secure the top cover to the main casing.

5 Lift away the top cover and its gasket. (photo)

6 Detach the release bearing from the release lever by turning the carrier through 90° and pulling forwards. (photo)

7 This photo shows the cut-outs in the release bearing carrier that have to be lined up with the two protrusions in the release lever to enable removal of the bearing carrier.

8 Undo and remove the four bolts and spring washers that secure the clutch housing to the gearbox main case. (photo)

9 Draw the clutch housing forwards away from the main case.

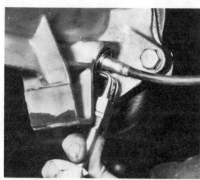

2.22 Speedometer cable retaining circlip

2.24 Detaching clutch inner cable from actuating arm

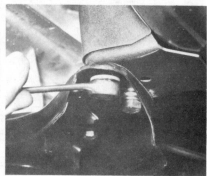

2.30 Removal of gearbox support crossmember to body securing bolt

2.31 Crossmember removal

3.5 Gearbox top cover removal

3.6 Release bearing removal

10 Using a suitably sized Allen key unscrew the side plug that retains the selector rail blocker bar. (photo)

11 Withdraw the spring and blocker bar. (photo)

12 Using a suitable diameter parallel pin punch tap out the spring pin that secures the reverse selector boss to the selector rail. (photo) Allow to drop into the bottom of the gearbox main case.

13 Again using a parallel pin punch and working through the gearchange lever aperture tap out the extension housing rear cover. (photo)

14 Undo and remove the four bolts and spring washers that secure the extension housing to the main casing.

15 Carefully pull the selector rail through the extension housing. It will be found necessary to ease each selector fork boss from the selector rail as it is withdrawn. (photo)

16 This photo shows the selector forks in position but with the selector rail removed.

17 Lift the selector forks up which will at the same time pivot the lock plate up. (photo)

18 Detach the selector forks from the lock plate. (photo)

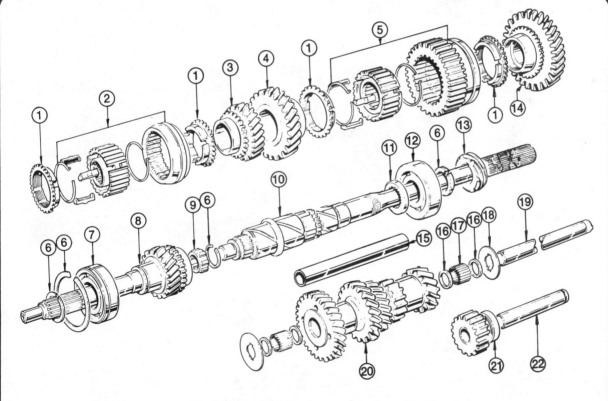

Fig. 6.4. Type B gearbox internal components (Sec.3)

1	Synchroniser sleeve		gear)	11	Oil scoop ring
2	Synchroniser hub (3rd/top	6	Circlip	12	Mainshaft bearing
	gear)	7	Input shaft bearing	13	Speedometer driven gear
3	3rd gear	8	Input shaft	14	1st gear
4	2nd gear	9	Needle roller bearing	15	Spacer sleeve
5	Synchroniser hub (1st/2nd	10	Mainshaft	16	Spacer shim

17 Needle roller (19 off)
18 Thrust washer
19 Countershaft
20 Countershaft gear train
21 Reverse idler gear
22 Idler shaft

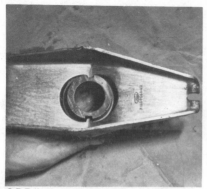

3.7 Release bearing located in release lever

3.8 Removal of clutch housing to gearbox securing bolts

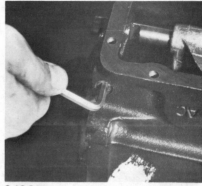

3.10 Selector rail blocker bar plug removal

3.11 Blocker bar and spring removal

3.12 Reverse selector boss spring pin removal

3.13 Extension housing rear cover removal

3.15 Selector rail removal

3.16 Selector forks correctly located in main casing

3.17 Selector fork removal

3.18 Detaching selector forks from lock plate

3.19 Lock plate spring pin removal

3.21 Spigot bearing and 'O' ring removal

19 Using a suitable diameter rod tap out the spring pin on which the lock plate pivots. (photo)

20 Undo and remove the four bolts and spring washers that secure the spigot bearing to the front face of the main case.

21 Lift away the spigot bearing from over the input shaft. Recover the 'O' ring. (photo)

22 Working in the small space between the mainshaft constant mesh gearteeth and the main case, compress the circlip using a pair of pointed pliers and release it from its location groove in the main case. (photo)

23 Rotate the extension housing until the cutaway is in such a position that the countershaft can be drawn from the main casing. This position is shown in photo 3.25.

24 Using a suitable diameter soft metal drift tap the countershaft rearwards until it is possible to pull it from the rear face of the main case. (photo)

25 Remove the countershaft from the main case. (photo)

26 Allow the countershaft gear train to drop to the bottom of the main case.

27 Using a parallel pin punch or tapered soft metal drift, tap the outer track of the input shaft bearing forwards until there is a gap between the circlip located in the outer circumference of the outer track. (photo)

28 Using a screwdriver with the blade between the circlip and main case gently prise the bearing from the facia of the main case. (photo)

29 Lift the caged bearing from the spigot end of the mainshaft. (photo)

30 Lift the synchroniser sleeve from the 3rd and top synchroniser hub. (photo)

31 The extension housing and mainshaft asembly may now be drawn rearwards from the main case. (photo)

32 Lift the countershaft geartrain from inside the main case. Note which way round it is fitted (photo). Recover the two countershaft thrust washers.

33 Using a suitable diameter drift carefully tap the idler shaft

3.22 Rear bearing retaining circlip removal

3.24 Countershaft removal using a drift

3.25 Lifting away countershaft

3.27 Using pin punch to move input shaft bearing outer track

3.28 Prising bearing outer track from main casing with screwdriver

3.29 Mainshaft caged bearing removal

3.30 Synchroniser sleeve removal

3.31 Removal of extension housing and mainshaft assembly

3.32 Countershaft gear train removal

rearwards. (photo)

34 Note which way round the idler shaft and reverse idler gear are fitted and lift away the shaft, gear and spacer sleeve.

35 To separate the mainshaft from the extension housing, first using a pair of pointed pliers compress the circlip located in the space between the 1st gear and the extension housing face. Carefully disengage it from its groove. (photo)

36 Using a soft faced hammer tap the end of the mainshaft so releasing the mainshaft bearing outer track from its bore in the extension housing. (photo)

37 Lift the mainshaft forwards and away from the extension housing. (photo)

38 The gearbox is now completely stripped out from the main casing and extension housing.

39 Clean out the interior thoroughly and check for dropped needle rollers and spring pins.

40 The mainshaft is dismantled next. With the mainshaft on the bench, using a pair of circlip pliers expand the circlip that retains the 3rd and top synchromesh hub on the mainshaft. Lift away the circlip. (photo)

41 Lift the 3rd and top synchromesh sleeve and hub assembly from the end of the mainshaft. Note which way round it is fitted. Lift away the synchroniser sleeve from the coned face of the 3rd gear (photo). Keep these parts together and if possible do not separate the synchromesh sleeve from the hub.

42 Slide the 3rd speed gear from the mainshaft.

43 Using a pair of circlip pliers expand the circlip that retains the 2nd speed gear and thrust washer on the mainshaft. (photo)

44 Slide the circlip and the thrust washer from the mainshaft. (photo)

45 The 2nd speed gear and synchroniser sleeve may next be lifted away from the mainshaft. (photo)

46 Using a pair of circlip pliers expand the circlip located at the rear of the mainshaft bearing, lift it from its groove and slide it down the mainshaft towards the speedometer drive gear. (photo)

47 Place the mainshaft on soft faces placed on the jaws of a bench vice so that the rear end is uppermost and the face of the 1st gear is on the vice. Note the exact location of the speedometer drive gear.

48 Using a soft faced hammer drive the mainshaft through the gear and bearing assembly. It may be found that the speedometer drive gear is tight and in extreme cases it may be necessary to gently heat it with a blow torch.

49 It should be noted that the 1st and 2nd gear synchroniser hub is an integral part of the mainshaft and no attempt may be made to remove it (see photo 3.52).

50 Lift away the speedometer drive gear, small circlip, bearing, oil scoop ring, large circlip, 1st gear and synchroniser sleeve (photo).

51 This photo shows the order of the parts as they are removed from the mainshaft.

52 The mainshaft is now dismantled with the exception of the synchroniser hub which stays on (photo). Mark the synchromesh sleeve, hub and blocker bars for each synchromesh unit so that

they may be refitted in their original positions.

53 Slide the synchromesh sleeve from the hub and lift away the blocker bars and springs.

54 The input shaft assembly may be dismantled by first removing the circlip using a pair of circlip pliers. (photo)

55 Place the drive gear on the top of the vice with the outer track of the race resting on soft faces.

56 Using a soft faced hammer drive the input shaft through the race inner track. The strain placed on the bearing does not matter, as the bearing would not be removed unless it was being renewed. Alternatively use a three legged universal puller.

57 Lift away the race from the drive gear noting that the circlip groove on the outer track is offset towards the front.

58 To assemble the input shaft, place the race against soft metal (old shell bearing suitably straightened) on the top of the jaws of the vice and, using a drift located in the mainshaft spigot bearing holes in the rear of the input shaft, drift the shaft into the bearing. Make quite sure the bearing is the correct way round. Alternatively use a piece of long tube of suitable diameter (photo).

59 Refit the circlip that secures the bearing and also the one located in the bearing outer track.

4 Gearbox - inspection

1 It is assumed that the gearbox has been dismantled for reasons of excessive noise, lack of synchromesh on certain gears, or for failure to stay in gear. If anything more drastic than this exists (eg; total failure, seizure, or gear case cracked) it would be better to leave well alone and look for a replacement, either a second-hand or exchange unit.

2 Examine all gears for excessively worn, chipped or damaged teeth. Any such gears should be replaced. It will usually be found that if a tooth is damaged in the countershaft gear train the mating gear teeth on the mainshaft will also be damaged.

3 Check all synchroniser sleeves for wear on the bearing surface which normally have clearly defined oil reservoir grooves in them. If these are smooth or obviously uneven, replacement is essential. Also, when fitted to their mating cones - as they would be when in operation - there should be no rock. This would signify ovality, or lack of concentricity. One of the most satisfactory ways of checking is by comparing the fit of a new sleeve on the hub with the old one. If the grooves of the sleeve are obviously worn or damaged (causing engagement difficulties) the sleeve should be renewed.

4 All ball bearings should be checked for chatter. It is advisable to replace these anyway, even though they may not appear to be too badly worn.

5 Circlips which in this particular gearbox are all important in locating bearings, gears and hubs, should also be checked to ensure that they are not distorted or damaged. In any case a selection of new circlips of varying thickness should be obtained to compensate for variations in new components fitted, or wear in old ones.

3.33 Idler shaft removal

3.35 Circlip being released from extension housing

3.36 Mainshaft being tapped through extension housing

3.37 Lifting away mainshaft

3.40 Circlip removal from end of main-shaft

3.41 Removing 3rd and top synchromesh sleeve and hub assembly

3.43 2nd speed gear and thrust washer retaining circlip removal

3.44 Lifting away circlip and thrust washer

3.45 2nd speed gear and synchroniser sleeve removal

3.46 Mainshaft rear bearing retaining circlip removal

3.50 Lifting away speedometer drive gear small circlip, bearing, oil scoop ring, large circlip, 1st gear and synchroniser sleeve

3.51 Mainshaft with components of photo 3.50 in correct order

3.52 Synchroniser hub which cannot be removed from mainshaft

3.54 Input shaft bearing retaining circlip

3.58 Input shaft bearing refitting

6   The thrust washers at the ends of the countershaft gear train should also be replaced as they will almost certainly have worn, if the gearbox is of any age.

7   The caged bearing between the input shaft and the mainshaft will usually be found in good order, but if in any doubt replace the needles as necessary.

8   The sliding hubs themselves are also subject to wear and where the fault has been failure of any gear to remain engaged, or actual difficulty in engagement, then the hub is one of the likely suspects.

9   The ends of the splines are machined in such a way as to form a 'keystone' effect on engagement with the corresponding mainshaft gear. Do not confuse this with wear. Check also that the blocker bars (sliding keys) are not sloppy and move freely. If there is any rock or backlash between the inner and outer sections of the hub, the whole assembly must be renewed, particularly if there has been a complaint of jumping out of gear.

5   Gearbox - reassembly

1   Start by reassembling the mainshaft. Fit the two springs into the synchromesh hub which is part of the mainshaft. (photo)

2   Fit the blocker bars into the grooves in the hub and grasp using the thumb and index finger. (photo)

3   Carefully slide the sleeve onto the hub so retaining the blocker bars. The grooved end should be towards the front of the mainshaft. (photo)

4   Fit the synchroniser sleeve and 1st gear to the mainshaft. (photo)

5   Slide the oil scoop ring, larger diameter to the rear of the mainshaft, and bearing onto the mainshaft. (photo)

6   Using a piece of suitable diameter tube drift the bearing into position on the mainshaft. (photo)

7   Slide the 2nd gear synchroniser sleeve and 2nd gear onto the mainshaft. (photo)

8   Fit a new circlip into the groove on the mainshaft so retaining the 2nd gear.

9   Fit a new circlip into the groove on the mainshaft at the rear of the bearing. (photo)

10   Using a suitable diameter tube drive the speedometer drive gear into position on the mainshaft as noted during removal. (photo)

11   Slide the 3rd gear, synchroniser sleeve and hub assembly onto the front of the mainshaft. (photo)

12   Retain the assembly with a new circlip. Make sure that it is correctly seated in its groove. (photo)

13   Using a screwdriver ease a new large diameter circlip over the mainshaft bearing and into the gap between 1st gear and the bearing. (photo)

14   The mainshaft is now completely reassembled and may be refitted to the extension housing.

15   Lay the extension housing on its side and carefully insert the mainshaft. (photo)

16   Place the extension housing on the edge of the bench so that the mainshaft end can protrude when fully home. Using a soft faced hammer drive the mainshaft bearing into the extension housing bore. (photo)

17   Using a pair of pointed pliers and small screwdriver refit the bearing retaining circlip. This is a fiddle and can take time. (photo)

18   Apply grease to the mating face of the extension housing and fit a new gasket. (photo)

19   Check to see that the reverse relay arm is free yet without signs of wear otherwise it should be renewed. (photo)

20   Place the reverse idler gear into its location in the main casing and engage it with the reverse relay arm. Slide in the idler shaft, plain end first and push fully home. (photo)

21   The countershaft gear train needle roller bearings are next reassembled. (photo)

5.1 Fitting springs into synchromesh hub

5.2 Fitting blocker bars to synchromesh hub

5.3 Synchromesh sleeve being slid into hub

5.4 Fitting synchroniser sleeve and 1st gear outer mainshaft

5.5 Fitting oil scoop ring and bearing onto mainshaft

5.6 Drifting bearing onto mainshaft

5.7 2nd gear synchroniser sleeve and 2nd gear being fitted to mainshaft

5.9 Rear bearing retaining circlip refitting

5.10 Drifting the speedometer drive gear onto mainshaft

5.11 3rd gear, synchroniser sleeve and hub assembly

5.12 Fitting circlip to mainshaft to retain 3rd gear assembly

5.13 Easing circlip over mainshaft bearing and into position between 1st gear and bearing

5.15 Fitting mainshaft into extension housing - stage 1

5.16 Drifting mainshaft bearing into extension housing - stage 2

5.17 Fitting bearing retaining circlip

5.18 Fitting new gasket to greased face of extension housing

5.19 Reverse relay arm

5.20 Fitting reverse idler gear and shaft into main casing

5.21 Component parts of countershaft

5.24 Inserting spacer shim into countershaft bore

5.26 Fitting needle rollers into countershaft bore

5.27 Inserting second spacer shim into countershaft bore

5.29 Fitting second set of needle rollers into countershaft bore - stage 2

5.32 Fitting thrust washers to greased face of countershaft gear train

5.33 Fitting countershaft gear train into main casing

5.34 Inserting mainshaft into main casing

5.35 Fitting caged bearing into input shaft

5.37 Drifting input shaft into its final fitted position

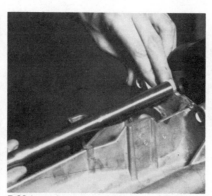
5.39 Inserting countershaft into main casing

5.40 Correct positioning of countershaft cutaway

22 Slide the spacer tube into the countershaft gear train bore.

23 Smear some grease in either end of the bore.

24 Insert one of the spacer shims. (photo)

25 Refer to photo 5.21 and it will be seen that the longer needle rollers are fitted to the smaller diameter end of the countershaft gear train bore.

26 Fit the smaller needle rollers into the forward end of the bore. Do not handle the needle rollers more than absolutely necessary as they will warm up and therefore not adhere to the grease. (photo)

27 With the first set of needle rollers in position carefully fit the second spacer shim. (photo)

28 Obtain a piece of bar or tube having approximately the same diameter as the countershaft and the same length as the countershaft gear train. Slide this halfway into the bore of the countershaft gear train so acting as a retainer for the needle rollers.

29 Insert a spacer shim into the rear end of the countershaft gear train bore and fit the second set of needle rollers in the same manner as for the first set. (photo)

30 Fit the last spacer shim and push the previously obtained bar or tube through the second set of needle roller bearings.

31 Smear grease on each thrust washer face of the countershaft gear train.

32 Fit the thrust washers to the countershaft gear train. (photo)

33 Carefully lower the countershaft gear train into the main casing making sure that the thrust washers are not dislodged. (photo)

34 Support the main casing on the bench so that it is upright and then insert the mainshaft through the rear face of the main casing. (photo)

35 Apply some grease to the caged bearing that fits into the bore in the rear of the input shaft. Fit the bearing into the bore. (photo)

36 Fit the synchroniser sleeve to the taper on the rear of the input shaft and insert the input shaft into the front face of the main case. Manipulate the mainshaft spigot so that it enters the caged bearing in the rear of the input shaft.

37 Using a soft faced hammer on the spigot at the front of the input shaft, tap the shaft until the bearing outer track circlip is fully home in its recess in the main casing. (photo)

38 Insert the gearbox and turn the extension housing until the cutaway is positioned such that the countershaft can be inserted through the main casing rear face.

39 Turn the input shaft and mainshaft so that the countershaft gear train can drop into engagement. Visually line up the countershaft bore hole in the main case with the centre of the countershaft gear train and slide the countershaft into position. The milled end of the countershaft is towards the rear of the main case. (photo)

40 Turn the countershaft until it is positioned as shown in this photo. Tap in until the main part of the shaft is flush with rear face. (photo)

41 Check that the idler shaft and countershaft protrusions will line up with the slots in the extension housing and push the extension housing up to the rear face of the main casing.

42 Secure the extension housing with the bolts and spring washers.

43 Smear some grease on the groove in the front face of the main casing and fit a new 'O' ring seal. (photo)

44 Slide the spigot bearing over the input shaft. Make sure the slight internal recess is towards the bottom, or line up the marks made during dismantling. (photo)

45 Secure the spigot bearing with the four bolts and spring washers (photo). Tighten in a diagonal manner to ensure that the 'O' ring seals correctly.

46 Slide the selector rail through the extension housing until the end protrudes into the main casing. (photo)

47 The selector forks may next be fitted into the main casing as shown in this photo. Check to ensure that the fork ends engage into the sleeve grooves.

48 Slide the reverse selector boss into the lock plate. (photo)

49 The selector rail can now be passed through the selector fork

5.43 Fitting new 'O' ring to front face of main casing

5.44 Sliding spigot bearing over input shaft

5.45 Securing spigot bearing to main casing

5.46 Fitting selector rail into extension housing

5.47 Fitting selector forks to main casing

5.48 Sliding reverse selector boss into the lock plate

5.49 Sliding selector rail through selector forks

5.50 Fitting spring pin to reverse selector boss and rail

5.51 Fitting lock plate mounting spring pin

5.52 Fitting blanking plug to main case rear face

5.56 Fitting new gasket and top cover

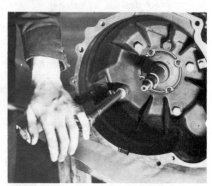

5.59 Securing clutch housing with bolts and spring washers

bosses until the cutaway is just at the rear of the front face. (photo)

50 Line up the hole in the reverse selector boss and selector rail and insert the spring pin to lock the two parts together. (photo)

51 Fit the spring pin to the lock plate mounting and tap fully home. (photo)

52 Refit the blanking plug to the main case rear face. (photo)

53 Insert the selector rail blocker bar and spring into the drilling in the front left-hand side of the main case (photos 3.10 and 3.11).

54 Screw in the side plug and tighten with an Allen key.

55 Fit the extension housing rear cover; smear some sealing compound on the outer circumference. Do not tap it down the bore more than necessary otherwise it could cause problems in selecting gears.

56 Smear some grease on the top face of the main case, fit the new gasket and then replace the top cover. (photo)

57 Secure the top cover with the ten bolts and shakeproof washers.

58 Wipe the mating faces of the clutch housing and main casing and offer up the clutch housing.

59 Secure the clutch housing with the four bolts and spring washers. (photo)

60 Fit the clutch release arm to the clutch housing and then the release bearing to the release arm. Turn through 90° to lock.

61 The gearbox is now ready for refitting. Do not forget to refill with the correct grade of oil.

6 Automatic transmission - general description

The automatic transmission takes the place of the clutch and gearbox, which are, of course, mounted behind the engine.

The system comprises two main components:

1 A three element hydrokinetic torque converter coupling, capable of torque multiplication at an infinitely variable ratio.

2 A torque/speed responsive and hydraulically operated epicyclic gearbox comprising a planetary gearset providing three forward ratios and one reverse ratio. Due to the complexity of the automatic transmission unit, if performance is not up to standard, or overhaul is necessary, it is imperative that this be left to the local main agents who will have the special equipment for fault diagnosis and rectification.

The content of the following sections is therefore confined to supplying general information and any service information and instruction that can be used by the owner.

3 During 1974, an automatic transmission of Ford manufacture was introduced in place of the previously fitted Borg-Warner type. The new unit has a large aluminium content which helps to reduce its overall weight and it is of compact dimensions. A transmission oil cooler is fitted as standard and ensures cooler operation of the transmission under trailer towing conditions. A vacuum connection to the inlet manifold provides smoother and more consistent downshifts under load than is the case with units not incorporating this facility.

4 The information given in this Chapter in respect of the Borg-Warner transmission will generally apply to the Ford unit but reference should be made to Specifications for the oil capacity and other details.

7 Automatic transmission (Borg-Warner) - fluid level checking

1 Every 6000 miles (10,000 km) bring the engine transmission to its normal operating temperature. Running the vehicle on the road for a minimum distance of 5 miles (8 km) will achieve this.

2 Select 'P' and allow the engine to idle for two or three minutes.

3 Switch off the engine and immediately withdraw the transmission dipstick. Wipe it clean, re-insert it, withdraw it for the

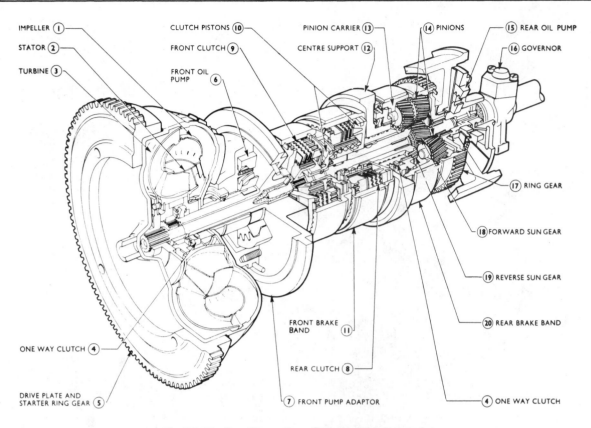

IMPELLER (1)
STATOR (2)
TURBINE (3)
CLUTCH PISTONS (10)
FRONT CLUTCH (9)
FRONT OIL PUMP (6)
PINION CARRIER (13)
CENTRE SUPPORT (12)
(14) PINIONS
(15) REAR OIL PUMP
(16) GOVERNOR
(17) RING GEAR
(18) FORWARD SUN GEAR
(19) REVERSE SUN GEAR
(20) REAR BRAKE BAND
(4) ONE WAY CLUTCH
ONE WAY CLUTCH (4)
DRIVE PLATE AND STARTER RING GEAR (5)
FRONT BRAKE BAND (11)
REAR CLUTCH (8)
(7) FRONT PUMP ADAPTOR

Fig. 6.5. The Borg Warner Type 35 Automatic transmission

second time and read off the level.

4   Top-up if necessary with specified fluid to the 'FULL' mark. The difference between the 'LOW' and 'FULL' marks on the dipstick is 1 Imp. pint (0.6 litre).

5   Always keep the exterior of the transmission unit clean and free from mud and oil and the air intake grilles must not be obstructed.

8   Automatic transmission (Ford) - fluid level checking

1   The procedure is identical to that described in the preceding Section, except that the engine should be allowed to idle while the level is checked.

2   The identity of the two alternative types of transmission can be established by observing the shape of the dipstick knob.

9   Automatic transmission (Borg-Warner) - removal and installation

Any suspected faults must be referred to the main agent before unit removal, as with this type of transmission the fault must be confirmed, using specialist equipment, before it has been removed from the car.

1   Open the engine compartment lid and place old blankets over the wings to prevent accidental scratching of the paintwork.

2   Undo and remove the battery earth connection nut and bolt from the battery terminal.

3   Remove the air cleaner and the starter motor.

4   Position the vehicle on a ramp or over an inspection pit or if these are not available, jack it up and support securely under the bodyframe. Make sure that there is sufficient clearance under the vehicle to permit withdrawal of the transmission

5   Unscrew and remove the upper bolts which secure the torque

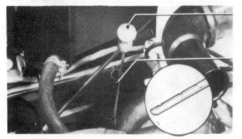

Dipstick

Filling tube

Fig. 6.6. Borg Warner type dipstick (Sec. 7)

Fig. 6.7. Ford type dipstick (Sec. 8)

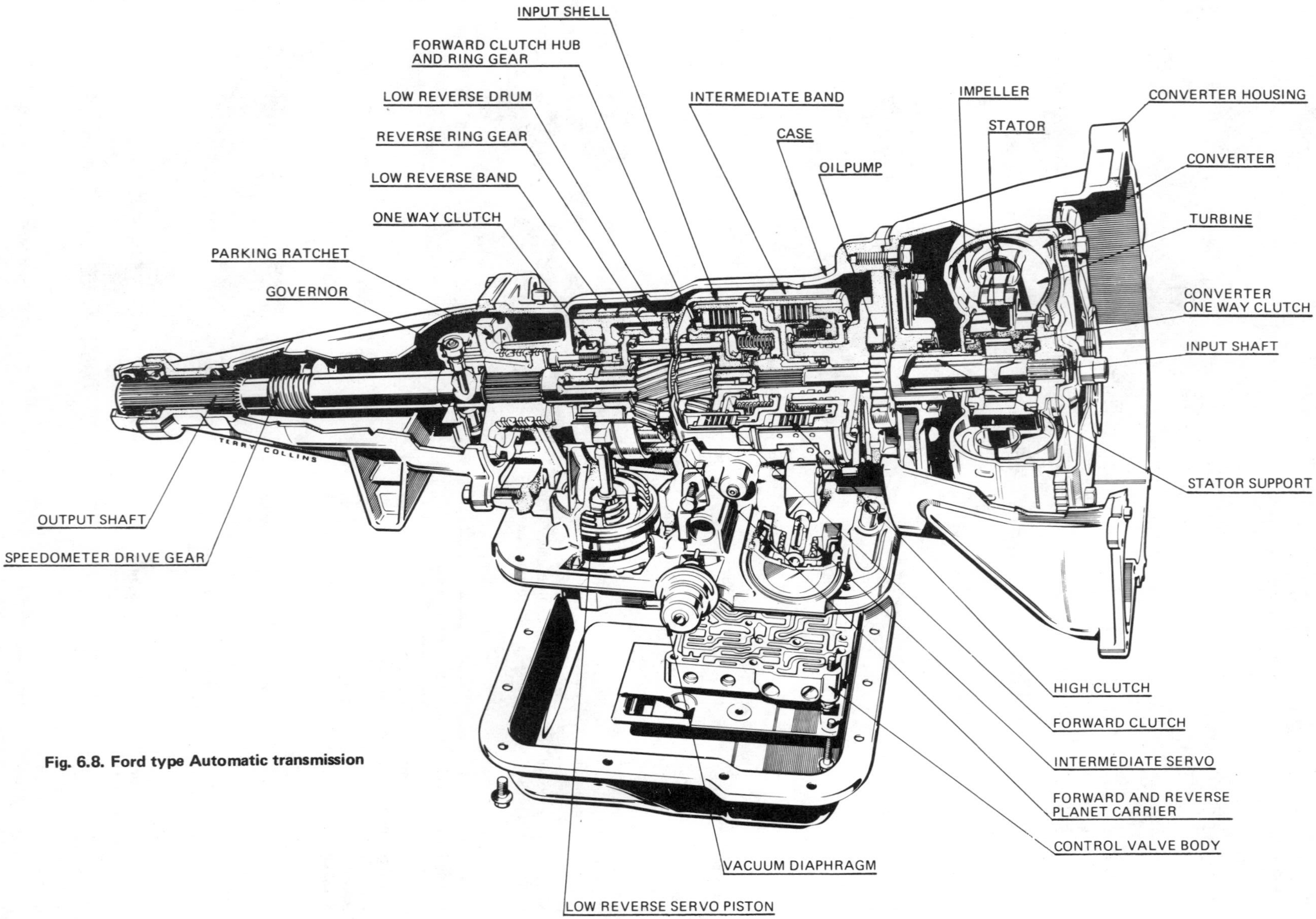

CONVERTER HOUSING

CONVERTER

TURBINE

CONVERTER ONE WAY CLUTCH

INPUT SHAFT

STATOR SUPPORT

HIGH CLUTCH

FORWARD CLUTCH

INTERMEDIATE SERVO

FORWARD AND REVERSE PLANET CARRIER

CONTROL VALVE BODY

IMPELLER

STATOR

INTERMEDIATE BAND

OILPUMP

CASE

VACUUM DIAPHRAGM

LOW REVERSE SERVO PISTON

INPUT SHELL

FORWARD CLUTCH HUB AND RING GEAR

LOW REVERSE DRUM

REVERSE RING GEAR

LOW REVERSE BAND

ONE WAY CLUTCH

PARKING RATCHET

GOVERNOR

OUTPUT SHAFT

SPEEDOMETER DRIVE GEAR

TERRY COLLINS

Fig. 6.8. Ford type Automatic transmission

converter housing to the engine. One of these bolts secures the dipstick tube support bracket.

6 Place a container of at least 10 Imp. pints capacity under the transmission fluid pan. Remove the drain plug and drain the fluid. Take extreme care if the car has just been driven as the fluid may be at or near boiling water temperature.

7 Disconnect the 'kick-down' cable from the throttle rod arm (Fig. 6.9).

8 A circlip or alternatively a split pin may be used to retain the 'kick-down' cable clevis pin.

9 Make a note of the electrical cable connections to the reverse inhibitor switch and disconnect the cables from the switch.

10 Using a pair of circlip pliers contract the speedometer drive cable to transmission casing retaining circlip and withdraw the speedometer inner and outer cable.

11 Refer to Chapter 7, and remove the propeller shaft. To stop accidental dirt ingress, wrap some polythene around the end of the automatic transmission unit and secure with string or wire.

12 Disconnect the exhaust front stiffener bracket mounting by undoing and removing the two nuts, bolts, spring and plain washers.

13 Undo and remove the two nuts that secure the exhaust down pipe to the manifold studs. Ease the coupling from the studs, lower the down pipe and recover the sealing cone.

14 Extract the spring clip lock pin from the clevis pin connecting the selector cable to the operating arm on the side of the transmission unit. Withdraw the clevis pin (Fig. 6.10).

15 Unscrew the cable to bracket locknut and slide the nut up the inner cable. Remove the bolt and cable from the bracket.

16 Undo and remove the set bolts and spring washers that secure the torque converter housing cover plate and lift away the cover plate.

17 The torque converter should next be disconnected from the crankshaft driving plate. Rotate the crankshaft until each bolt may be seen through the starter motor aperture. Undo each bolt and turn one at a time until all the bolts are free (Fig. 6.11).

18 Place a piece of soft wood on the saddle of a jack and support the weight across the rear of the engine. Take care to position the jack securely so that it cannot fly out when the automatic transmission unit is being disconnected or reconnected to the rear of the engine.

19 Place an additional jack under the automatic transmission unit and remove the two bolts and spring washers that secure the unit to the crossmember. Also remove the four bolts that locate the crossmember to the underside of the floor panel (Fig. 6.12).

20 Slowly lower the transmission unit and engine jacks until there is sufficient clearance for the dipstick tube to be removed.

21 Withdraw the dipstick and pull the oil filter tube (dipstick tube) sharply from the side of the transmission unit. Recover the 'O' ring.

22 Undo and remove the remaining bolts and spring washers that secure the converter housing to the engine.

23 Continue to lower the jacks until there is sufficient clearance between the top of the converter housing and underside of the floor for the transmission unit to be satisfactorily withdrawn.

24 Check that no cables or securing bolts have been left in position and tuck the speedometer cable out of the way.

25 The assistance of at least one other person is now required

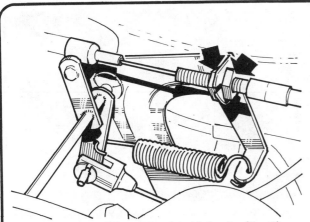

Fig. 6.9. Detachment of throttle cable bracket (Sec. 9)

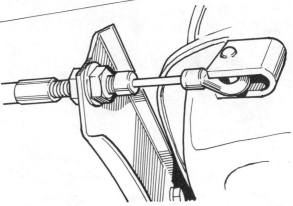

Fig. 6.10. Selector cable and operating arm attachments (Sec. 9)

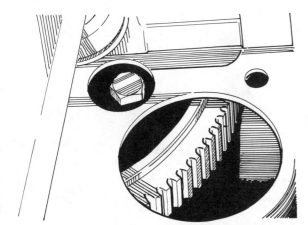

Fig. 6.11. Torque converter securing bolt as seen after removal of starter motor (Sec. 9)

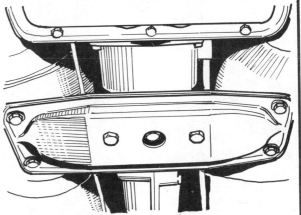

Fig. 6.12. Automatic transmission support and crossmember (Sec. 9)

because of the weight of the complete unit.

26 Carefully pull the unit rearwards and, when possible, hold the converter in place in the housing as it will still be full of hydraulic fluid.

27 Finally withdraw the unit from under the car and place on wooden blocks so that the selector lever is not damaged or bent.

28 To separate the converter housing from the transmission case first lift off the converter from the transmission unit, taking suitable precautions to catch the fluid upon separation. Undo

and remove the six bolts and spring washers that secure the converter housing to the transmission case. Lift away the converter housing.

29 Refitting the automatic transmission unit is the reverse sequence to removal, but there are several additional points which will assist.

30 If the torque converter has been removed, before refitting the transmission unit it will be necessary to align the front drive tangs with the slots in the inner gear and then carefully replace

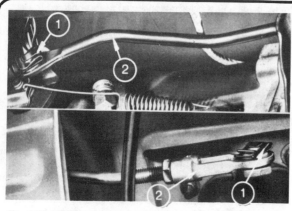

Fig. 6.13. Shift rod and adjustment link (2) and retaining clips (1) Ford Automatic transmission (Sec. 10)

Fig. 6.14. Downshift cable connection (Ford Automatic Transmission) (Sec. 10)

Fig. 6.15. Vacuum pipe connection (Ford Automatic transmission) (Sec. 10)

Fig. 6.16. Starter inhibitor switch (Ford Automatic transmission) (Sec. 10)

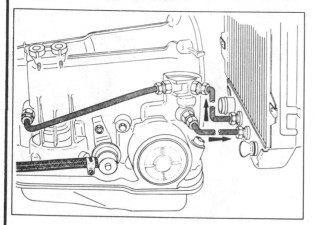

Fig. 6.17. Fluid cooler pipes (Ford Automatic transmission) (Sec. 10)

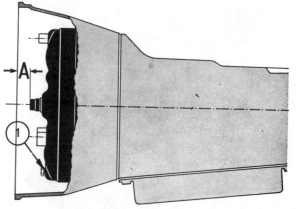

Fig. 6.18. Torque converter drain plug (1) alignment and installation diagram (Ford Automatic transmission) (Sec. 10)

the torque converter. Take extreme precautions not to damage the oil seal.

31 Adjust the selector cable and inhibitor switch as described later in this Chapter.

32 Refill the transmission unit with the specified fluid before starting the engine and check the oil level as described in Section 7.

10 Automatic transmission (Ford) - removal and installation

1 The procedure is similar to that described in the preceding Section, but the following alternative or supplementary operations must be implemented.

2 Remove the shift rod retaining clips and remove the rod (Fig. 6.13).

3 Disconnect the downshift cable from the lever and the holder (Fig. 6.14).

4 Disconnect the vacuum pipe from the transmission end (Fig. 6.15).

5 Disconnect the leads from the starter inhibitor switch (Fig. 6.16).

6 Disconnect the oil cooler pipes from the base of the radiator and plug them (Fig. 6.17).

7 It should be noted that the fluid can only be drained by removing the fluid pan - no drain plug being fitted. When withdrawing the transmission, keep the torque converter pressed firmly against the transmission to prevent loss of fluid.

8 Installation is a reversal of removal but ensure that the torque converter drain plug is in line with the hole in the driveplate. To check that the torque converter is positively engaged, measure the distance 'A' between the converter housing to engine mating face and the end of stub shaft. This should be at least 10 mm. (Fig. 6.18).

9 Fill the unit with specified fluid and check the adjustments, as described in Section 8.

11 Downshift cable (Borg-Warner) - adjustment or renewal

Before the cable is adjusted, it is necessary to confirm that it is the cable that is not correctly adjusted and not some other fault. Generally, if difficulty is experienced in obtaining downshift from 2 to 1 in the 'kick-down' position at just below 31 mph it is an indication that the outer cable is too long.

By means of the outer cable locknuts adjust the cable at the support bracket so that the crimped stop on the inner cable just touches the endface of the outer cable. If a new cable is to be fitted, it will be supplied with the crimped stop loose.

1 Drain the transmission oil, remove the oil pan and fit the new cable to the downshift valve.

2 Refer to Fig. 6.19 and check that the position of the downshift cam is in the idling position as shown in the illustration.

3 Adjust the length of the outer cable so as to remove all the slack from the inner cable.

4 Again refer to Fig. 6.19 and check the position of the downshift cam with the throttle pedal in the 'kick-down' position as shown in the illustration.

5 Refit the sump pan joint, sump pan and retaining bolts with spring washers. Tighten the bolts in diagonal manner.

6 Refill the transmission with correct fluid or use the fluid that was drained originally if it is clean with no streaks showing signs of contamination.

7 Crimp the stop so that it just touches the endface of the outer cable.

12 Downshift cable (Ford) - adjustment

1 Slacken the inner nut on the adjuster right off and then turn the carburettor throttle rod to the fully open position. Disconnect the upper and lower return springs.

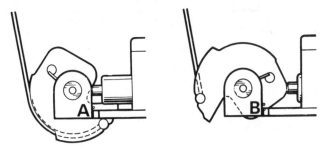

Fig. 6.19. Downshift valve cable adjustment (Borg-Warner)

A   *Idling position*
B   *Kickdown position*

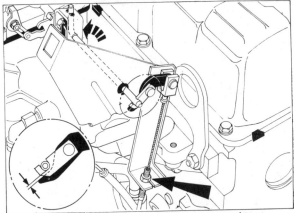

Fig. 6.20. Downshift cable adjustment points (Ford Automatic transmission) (Sec. 12)

2 Move the downshift lever on the transmission to the 'kickdown' position.

3 Adjust the two cable nuts so that the clearance between the throttle valve shaft and the drive lever is between 0.020 and 0.052 in (0.8 mm and 1.3 mm) (Fig. 6.20).

4 Tighten the locknut and reconnect the return springs.

13 Selector linkage (Borg-Warner) - adjustment

1 It is best if this adjustment is carried out with the car placed on ramps. As an alternative the car may be placed on high axle stands.

2 Slacken the locknuts on the outer cable (Fig. 6.10).

3 Move the selector lever to the 'D' position on the lever quadrant.

4 Position the transmission selector lever in the third location forward from the fully rearward positon.

5 Tighten the outer cable locknuts, without moving the selector lever or transmission selector lever.

6 Road test the car and check the six positions of the selector lever.

14 Selector linkage (Ford) - adjustment

1 First check that the selector lever is correctly adjusted. To do this, use feeler gauges to check the end-clearance between the lever pawl and the quadrant notch. This should be between 0.004 and 0.008 in (0.10 and 0.20 mm). If necessary adjust the cable locknut which is accessible after removal of the selector lever housing plug (Fig. 6.21).

2 Disconnect the shift rod from the shift lever at the base of

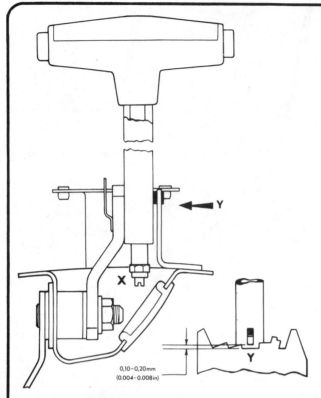

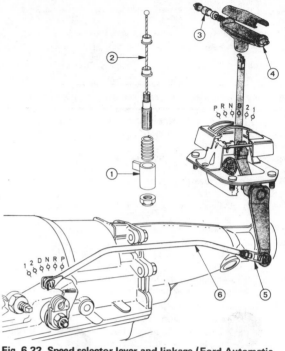

0,10 – 0,20mm
(0.004 – 0.008in)

Fig. 6.21. Hand selector lever adjustment diagram (Ford Automatic transmission) (Sec. 14)

Fig. 6.22. Speed selector lever and linkage (Ford Automatic transmission) (Sec. 14)

1	Pawl	4	Handle
2	Cable	5	Adjusting link
3	Push button	6	Shift rod

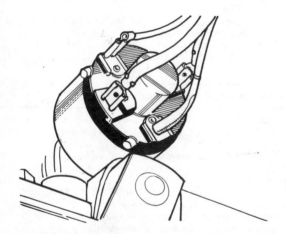

Fig. 6.23. Starter inhibitor and reverse lamp switch (Borg-Warner) (Sec. 15)

Fig. 6.24. Starter/reverse lamp inhibitor switch and actuating mechanism (Ford Automatic transmission) (Sec. 16)

the hand control lever (adjustable end of rod).

3   Place the hand control lever in 'D'.

4   Place the selector lever on the side of the transmission housing in 'D'. This can be determined by counting two 'clicks' back from the fully forward position.

5   Now attempt to reconnect the shift rod to the selector hand control lever by pushing in the clevis pin. The pin should slide in without any side stress at all. If this is not the case, release the locknut on the shift rod and adjust its effective length by screwing the adjusting link in, or out.

15 Starter inhibitor/reverse lamp switch (Borg-Warner) - adjustment

1   Select the 'D', '1' or '2' position. Make a note of the starter inhibitor and reverse lamp switch cable connections and disconnect the cables from the switch (Fig. 6.23).

2   Connect a test lamp and battery across the smaller starter inhibitor terminals and further test lamp and battery across the two larger reverse light terminals.

3   Undo the locknut and screw out the switch about two turns.
Slowly screw in the switch again until the test light connected to
the reverse light terminal goes out. Mark the relative position of
the switch again.
4   Continue screwing in the switch until the test lamp connected
to the starter inhibitor terminals lights. Mark the relative position
of the switch again.
5   Unscrew the switch until it is halfway between the two positions and tighten the locknut.
6   Reconnect the cables and check that the starter motor only
operates when the selector lever is in the 'P' or 'N' position. Also
check that the reverse light only operates with the selector in

the 'R' position. If the switch does not operate correctly it
should be renewed.

16 Starter inhibitor/reverse lamp switch (Ford) - removal and installation

1   This switch is non-adjustable and any malfunction must be
due to a wiring fault, a faulty switch or wear in the internal
actuating cam (Fig. 6.24).
2   When removing and installing the switch, always use a new
'O' ring seal and tighten to specified torque.

17 Fault diagnosis - manual gearbox

Symptom	Reason/s	Remedy
Weak or ineffective synchromesh	Synchronising cones worn, split or damaged	Dismantle and overhaul gearbox. Fit new gear wheels and synchronising cones
	Baulk ring synchromesh dogs worn, or damaged	Dismantle and overhaul gearbox. Fit new baulk ring synchromesh
Jumps out of gear	Broken gearchange fork rod spring	Dismantle and replace spring
	Gearbox coupling dogs badly worn	Dismantle gearbox. Fit new-coupling dogs
	Selector fork rod groove badly worn	Fit new selector fork rod
Excessive noise	Incorrect grade of oil in gearbox or oil level too low	Drain, refill or top up gearbox with correct grade of oil
	Bush or needle roller bearings worn or damaged	Dismantle and overhaul gearbox. Renew bearings
	Gear teeth excessively worn or damaged	Dismantle, overhaul gearbox. Renew gear-wheels
	Countershaft thrust washers worn allowing excessive end play	Dismantle and overhaul gearbox. Renew thrust washers
Excessive difficulty in engaging gear	Clutch cable adjustment incorrect	Adjust clutch cable correctly

18 Fault diagnosis - automatic transmission

Faults in these units are nearly always the result of low fluid level or incorrect adjustment of the selector linkage or downshift cable.
Internal faults should be diagnosed by your main Ford dealer who has the necessary equipment to carry out the work.

Chapter 7 Propeller shaft

Contents

Specifications

Type (1600 manual gearbox)
Single piece type, length ... ...   50.75 inch (1.289 mm)

Type (2000 manual gearbox)
Two piece type, lengths ... ...   20.63/29.27 in (524/743.5 mm)

Type (1600/2000 automatic)
Two piece type, lengths ... ...   22.24/29.27 in (565/743.5 mm)

Single piece type, number of splines   20

Two piece type, number of splines   25

Single piece tube outer diameter ... ...   1.18 - 1.19 in (30.137 - 30.163 mm)

Two piece tube outer diameter
Manual gearbox ... ...   1.37 - 1.38 in (34.915 - 34.941 mm)
Automatic transmission ... ...   1.19 in (30.163 mm)

Depth of splines
1600 manual gearbox ... ...   0.046 - 0.053 in (1.17 - 1.35 mm)
1600 automatic transmission ... ...   0.059 - 0.066 in (1.52 - 1.70 mm)
2000 engine ... ...   0.059 - 0.066 in (1.52 - 1.70 mm)

Universal joints ... ...   Needle roller bearings

Constant velocity joint grease ... ...   S - MIC - 75 - A

Torque wrench settings

	lb f ft	kg f m
Propeller shaft to drive pinion flange	43 - 47	6 - 6.5
Drive shaft centre bearing support bolts	13 - 17	1.8 - 2.3
Constant velocity joint bolts	30	4.1

1 General description

Drive is transmitted from the gearbox to the rear axle by means of a finely balanced tubular propeller shaft. Fitted at each end of the shaft is a universal joint which allows for vertical movement of the rear axle. Each universal joint comprises a four legged centre spider, four needle roller bearings and two yokes.

Fore and aft movement of the rear axle is absorbed by a sliding spline in the front of the propeller shaft which slides over a mating spline on the rear of the gearbox mainshaft. On some models a split propeller shaft is used where a third universal joint is fitted behind the centre bearing. As an alternative to this third universal joint, a constant velocity joint may be encountered.

On some 2000 cc models, a rubber coupling replaces the conventional universal joint at the front splined end.

All models are fitted with the sealed type of universal joint which requires no maintenance.

The propeller shaft assembly is a relatively simple component and therefore reliable in service. Unfortunately it is not possible to obtain spare parts for the conventional universal joints, therefore when these are worn a new assembly must be fitted.

2 Propeller shaft - removal and installation

Single piece propeller shaft

1 Jack-up the rear of the car, or position the rear of the car over a pit or on a ramp.

2 If the rear of the car is jacked-up, supplement the jack with support blocks so that danger is minimised should the jack collapse.

3 If the rear wheels are off the ground place the car in gear and apply the handbrake to ensure that the propeller shaft does not

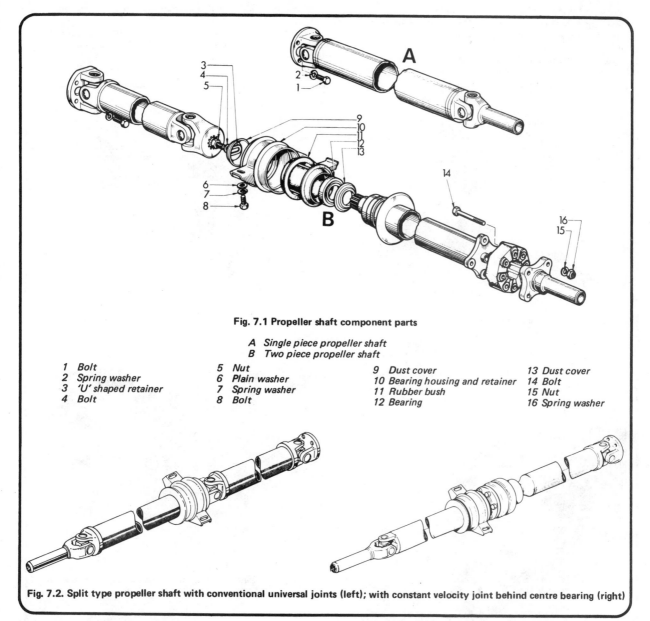

Fig. 7.1 Propeller shaft component parts

A   Single piece propeller shaft
B   Two piece propeller shaft

1 Bolt	5 Nut	9 Dust cover	13 Dust cover
2 Spring washer	6 Plain washer	10 Bearing housing and retainer	14 Bolt
3 'U' shaped retainer	7 Spring washer	11 Rubber bush	15 Nut
4 Bolt	8 Bolt	12 Bearing	16 Spring washer

Fig. 7.2. Split type propeller shaft with conventional universal joints (left); with constant velocity joint behind centre bearing (right)

turn when an attempt is made to loosen the four nuts securing the propeller shaft to the rear axle.

4   The propeller shaft is carefully balanced to fine limits and it is important that it is replaced in exactly the same position it was in prior to removal. Scratch marks on the propeller shaft and rear axle flanges to ensure accurate mating when the time comes for reassembly.

5   Unscrew and remove the four bolts and spring washers which hold the flange on the propeller shaft to the flange on the rear axle.

6   Slightly push the shaft forward to separate the two flanges, and then lower the end of the shaft and pull it rearwards to disengage the gearbox mainshaft splines.

7   Place a large can or a tray under the rear of the gearbox extension to catch any oil which is likely to leak past the oil seal when the propeller shaft is removed.

8   Replacement of the propeller shaft is a reversal of the above procedure. Ensure that the mating marks scratched on the propeller shaft and rear axle flanges line up and always use new spring washers. Check the oil level in the gearbox and top up if necessary.

Split type propeller shaft

9   The removal sequence is basically identical to that for the single piece propeller shaft with the exception that the centre bearing support must be detached from the underside of the body. This should be done before the rear flange securing nuts, bolts and spring washers are removed. Support the centre of the propeller shaft during removal.

10 To detach the centre bearing support, undo and remove the two bolts, spring and plain washers securing it to the underside of the body. Retain any mounting shims, noting their location.

11 Replacement is the reverse sequence to removal.

3   Propeller shaft centre bearing - removal and installation

1   Refer to Section 2 and remove the complete propeller shaft assembly.

2   Using a blunt chisel carefully prise open the centre bearing support retaining bolt locking tab.

3   Slacken the bolt located in the end of the yoke and with a screwdriver ease out the 'U' shaped retainer through the side of

the yoke. These parts are shown in Fig. 7.3.

4   Mark the propeller shaft and yoke for correct refitting. Disconnect the propeller shaft from the yoke and lift off the insulator rubber together with collar from the ball race.

5   Part the insulator rubber from the collar.

6   Refer to Fig. 7.4 and using a universal two leg puller draw

the bearing together with cup from the end of the propeller shaft.

7   To fit a new bearing and cup onto the end of the propeller shaft use a piece of suitable diameter tube and drive into position.

8   With a pair of pliers bend the six metal tongues of the collar

Fig. 7.3. Centre bearing components (Sec. 3)

1 *Rubber bush*	6 *Ball race*
2 *Bearing housing and retainer*	7 *Dust cover*
3 *Washer*	8 *Yoke*
4 *Bolt*	9 *U shaped retainer*
5 *Dust cover*	

'A' shows flange which must be located at top of housing.

Fig. 7.4. Using universal puller to draw off centre bearing (Sec. 3)

Fig. 7.5. Using 'Parrot jaw' pliers to bend over rubber bush locking tabs in housing (Sec. 3)

Fig. 7.6. The centre bearing and 'U' shaped retainer (Sec. 3)
Note the semi circular recess on the periphery of the support

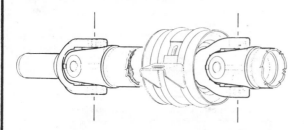

Fig. 7.7. Correct relative positions of the propeller shaft forward and centre yokes (Sec. 3)

Fig. 7.8. Alignment marks made on constant velocity joint and propeller shaft prior to dismantling (Sec. 4)

Fig. 7.9. Removing circlip from front face of constant velocity joint (Sec. 4)

Fig. 7.10. Constant velocity joint and attachments (Sec. 4)

1	Centre bearing support	5	Constant velocity joint
2	Circlip	6	Cup spring
3	Circlip	7	Propeller shaft (rear section)
4	Flange		

slightly outwards and carefully insert the insulator rubber. It is important that the flange of the insulator rubber, when fitted into the support, is uppermost see 'A' (Fig. 7.3).

9   Using a pair of 'parrot jaw' pliers or a chisel bend the metal tongues rearwards over the rubber lip as shown in Fig. 7.5.

10 Next slide the support with the insulator rubber over the ball race. The semi-circular recess in the support periphery must be positioned towards the front end of the car when fitted (Fig. 7.6).

11 Screw in the bolt together with locking tab into the propeller shaft forward end bearing leaving just sufficient space for the 'U' shaped retainer to be inserted.

12 Assemble the two propeller shaft halves in their original positions as denoted by the two previously made marks or by the double tooth (Fig. 7.7).

13 Refit the 'U' shaped retainer with the tagged end towards the splines (Fig. 7.6).

14 Finally tighten the retainer securing bolt and bend over the lockwasher.

4   Constant velocity joint - renewal

Note: *Before starting work, check the availability of a new joint.*

1   Remove the propeller shaft, as previously described.

2   Place alignment marks on the constant velocity joint flange and the rear section of the propeller shaft so that the original balance can be maintained (Fig.7.8).

3   Remove the six bolts and circlip from the front face of the constant velocity joint (Fig. 7.9).

4   Remove the joint from the splined shaft and then extract the cup spring through the opening of the rubber sleeve.

5   No further dismantling should be carried out, but the old joint should be discarded and a new one purchased.

6   Commence reassembly by inserting the cup spring through

the rubber sleeve so that the spring rests against the outer circumference of the constant velocity joint.

7   Attach the joint to the flange with two bolts only, inserted finger-tight.

8   Offer up the propeller shaft (marks made before dismantling in alignment) and engage the splines. Now remove the two bolts, push the joint against the cup spring and fit the circlip.

9   Fill the constant velocity joint with 30 grams of specified grease, once again align the marks and connect the propeller shaft sections. Insert the bolts and tighten to a torque of 30 lb f ft. (4.1 kg f m).

5   Univeral joints - tests for wear

1   Wear in the needle roller bearings is characterised by vibration in the transmission 'clonks' on taking up the drive, and in extreme cases of lack of lubrication, metallic squeaking and ultimately grating and shrieking sounds as the bearings break up.

2   It is easy to check if the needle roller bearings are worn with the propeller shaft in position, by trying to turn the shaft with one hand, the other hand holding the rear axle flange when the rear universal joint is being checked, and the front half coupling when the front universal joint is being checked. Any movement between the propeller shaft and the front and the rear half couplings is indicative of considerable wear. If worn, a new assembly will have to be obtained. Check also by trying to lift the shaft and noticing any movement of the joints.

3   The centre bearing is a little more difficult to test for wear when mounted on the car. Undo and remove the two support securing bolts, spring and plain washers and allow the propeller shaft centre to hang down. Test the centre bearing for wear by grabbing the support and rocking it. If movement is evident the bearing is probably worn and should be renewed, as described in Section 3.

6 Fault diagnosis - propeller shaft

Symptom	Reason/s	Remedy
Vibration when car running on road	Out of balance shaft	Renew
	Wear in splined sleeve	Renew
	Loose flange bolts	Tighten
	Worn shaft joints	Renew joints or exchange complete assembly as appropriate

Chapter 8 Rear axle

Contents

Specifications

Type designation
1600cc	Salisbury, Type A
2000cc	Salisbury, Type B

Axle ratio
1600	3.89 : 1
2000	3.44 : 1 (optional 3.7 : 1)

Number of gearteeth
Crownwheel:
Standard	31
Optional	37

Drive pinion:
Standard	9
Optional	10

Drive pinion bearing preload ... ... 6.8 - 30 lb in (8 - 30 kg cm)

Crownwheel and pinion backlash
Type A	0.004 - 0.008 in (0.10 - 0.20 mm)
Type B	0.0047 - 0.0087 in (0.12 - 0.22 mm)

Number of gears within differential assembly 2

Thickness of thrust washers - differential
Pinions	0.406 - 0.434 in (10.30 - 11.03 mm)
Pinion bearing preload	0.0012 - 0.004 in (0.03 - 0.10 mm)

Oil capacity
Type A	1.76 pints (1.0 litre)
Type B	1.94 pints (1.1 litre)

Torque wrench settings
	lb f ft	kg f m
Bearing cap bolts	43 - 49	6 - 6.8
Drive pinion self locking nut	71 - 86	10 - 12
Crownwheel securing bolts	57 - 62	8 - 8.7
Rear axle housing cover	22 - 29	3 - 4
Axle-shaft to side flange retainer plate	29 - 36	4 - 5
Propeller shaft to drive pinion flange	43 - 47	6 - 6.5
Propeller shaft centre bearing securing bolt	13 - 17	1.8 - 2.3

1 General description

The rear axle is of the semi-floating type and held in place by two lower swinging arms which are able to pivot on brackets welded to the chassis. Coil springs are located between the underside of the body and the swinging arms. Longitudinal and diagonal location of the rear axle is also controlled by two upper swinging arms which locate between the underside of the body and the outer ends of the final drive housing.

The differential unit is of the two pinion design and driven by a hypoid crownwheel and pinion. It is mounted in a cast iron differential housing into which the halfshaft and hub outer tubes are pressed.

Until the end of 1974, the pinion was mounted on two taper roller bearings which are specially pre-loaded using a selective length spacer and shim located between the pinion bearings (types A and B). From the beginning of 1975 collapsible type pinion spacers were used in both types of Salisbury rear axles.

The differential cage is also mounted on two taper roller beatings which are pre-loaded by spreading the differential carrier. The drive is taken through two differential side-gears to both axle-shafts. The axle-shafts are splined to the differential side gears and run in ball races at their outer ends. These ball races have integral oil seals.

2 Rear axle - removal and installation

1   Remove the rear wheel trims and slacken the roadwheel nuts. Chock the front wheels, jack-up the rear of the car and place on axle stands located beneath the lower radius arms. Remove the two rear wheels (Fig. 8.2).
2   Support the weight of the rear axle by placing the saddle of a jack (preferably trolley type) under the centre of the rear axle.
3   With a scriber or file mark a line across the propeller shaft and pinion driving flanges so that they may be refitted together in their original positions.
4   Undo and remove the four bolts and spring washers securing the propeller shaft and pinion driving flanges and carefully lower the propeller shaft. For models fitted with the split type propeller shaft, it is necessary to undo and remove the two bolts with spring and plain washers that secure the centre bearing support to the

underside of the body before the propeller shaft can be lowered.
5   Release the handbrake. Undo and remove the two cheese head screws that secure the brake drum to the axle-shaft. Using a soft faced hammer carefully tap outwards on the circumference of each brake drum and lift away the brake drums.
6   Using a screwdriver placed between brake shoe and relay lever, ease the handbrake cable relay lever inwards. Grip the handbrake cable end with a pair of pliers and release it from the relay lever. Pull the handbrake cable through each brake back-plate (Fig. 8.4).

Fig. 8.2. Correct positioning of axle stand under lower radius arm (Sec. 2)

Fig. 8.3. Rear axle attachments to rear suspension (Sec. 2)

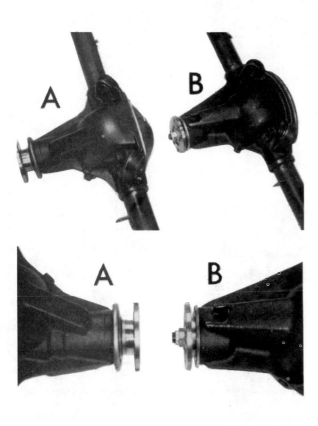

Fig. 8.1. Major differences between Type A and B rear axles (Housing design and drive pinion flange)

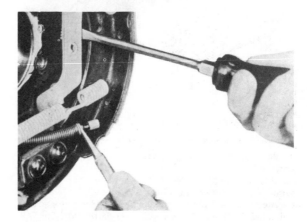

Fig. 8.4. Disconnection of handbrake cable (Sec. 2)

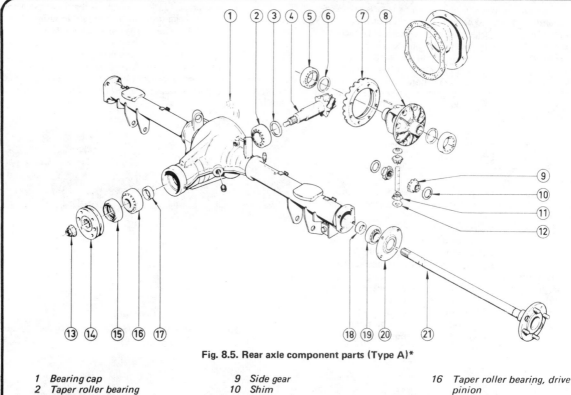

Fig. 8.5. Rear axle component parts (Type A)*

1	Bearing cap	9	Side gear	16	Taper roller bearing, drive pinion
2	Taper roller bearing	10	Shim		
3	Spacer shim, drive pinion	11	Differential pinion	17	Shim, drive pinion
4	Drive pinion gear	12	Thrust washer, differential pinion	18	Locking sleeve
5	Taper roller bearing	13	Self locking nut	19	Ball race, axle-shaft
6	Spacer shim	14	Drive pinion flange	20	Retainer plate
7	Crown wheel	15	Oil seal	21	Axle-shaft
8	Differential case				

*Type B differs in design of pinion flange and axle housing (see Fig. 8.1).

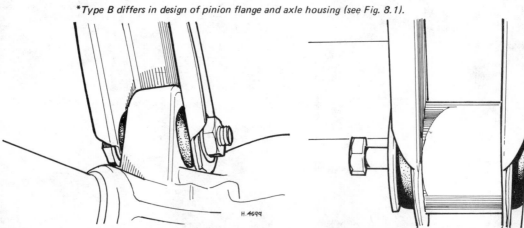

Fig. 8.6 Upper radius arm attachment to axle housing (Sec. 2)

Fig. 8.7. Lower radius arm attachment to rear axle (Sec. 2)

7 Wipe the top of the brake master cylinder reservoir and unscrew the cap. Place a piece of polythene sheeting over the reservoir neck and refit the cap. This is to stop hydraulic fluid syphoning out during subsequent operations.

8 Wipe the area around the brake flexible pipe to metal pipe union just in front of the rear axle and referring to Chapter 9, Section 3, detach the brake flexible hose from the metal pipe.

9 Undo and remove the bolt, nut and plain washer that secures each upper radius arm to the axle housing (Fig. 8.6).

10 Undo and remove the bolt, nut and plain washer that secures each shock absorber to the rear axle. Contract the shock

absorbers.

11 Undo and remove the bolt, nut and plain washer that secures each lower radius arm to the rear axle (Fig. 8.7).

12 Lower the rear axle and remove both coil springs, retaining the upper mounting rubber rings.

13 The complete rear axle assembly may now be withdrawn.

14 Refit the rear axle in the reverse sequence to removal. Re-align the marks on the propeller shaft and pinion flange.

15 For 1972 models onwards, the rear axle drive angle must be checked and adjusted, as described in Section 9, of this Chapter.

16 The lower radius arm mounting bolts must only be tightened

to a torque wrench setting of 42 - 50 lb ft (5.8 - 6.9 kg m) when the roadwheels have been refitted and the car is standing on the ground.

17 The centre bearing retaining bolts should be tightened to a torque wrench setting of 13 - 17 lb ft (1.8 - 2.3 kg m)

18 It will be necessary to bleed the brake hydraulic system as described in Chapter 9, Section 2.

19 Check the amount of oil in the rear axle and top-up if necessary.

3 Drive pinion oil seal (fixed length pinion spacer) - renewal

1 This operation may be performed with the rear axle in position on the bench.

2 With a scriber or file mark a line across the propeller shaft and pinion driving flanges so that they may be refitted together in their original positions.

3 Undo and remove the four bolts and spring washers securing the propeller shaft and pinion driving flanges and carefully lower the propeller shaft. Models fitted with the split type propeller shaft: it is necessary to undo and remove the two bolts and spring and plain washers that secure the centre bearing support to the underside of the body before the propeller shaft can be lowered. Retain any shims.

4 Carefully clean the front of the final drive housing as there will probably be a considerable amount of oil and dirt if the seal has been leaking for a while.

5 Using a mole wrench or large wrench, grip the drive pinion flange and with a socket undo and remove the pinion flange retaining self locking nut. This nut must be discarded and a new one obtained ready for reassembly.

6 Place a container under the front of the final drive housing to catch any oil that may issue once the oil seal has been removed.

7 Using a universal puller and suitable thrust pad pull off the drive pinion flange from the drive pinion.

8 Using a screwdriver or small chisel carefully remove the old oil seal. It will probably be necessary to partially dismantle it. Note which way round it is fitted with the lip facing inwards.

9 Before fitting a new seal apply some grease to the inner face between the two lips of the seal. On the 'B' type axle (see specificiations) this operation is not necessary.

10 Apply a little jointing compound to the outer face of the seal.

11 Using a tubular drift of suitable diameter carefully drive the oil seal into the final drive housing. Make quite sure that it is fitted squarely into the housing.

12 Replace the drive pinion flange and once again hold securely with a mole wrench or large wrench. Fit a new self locking nut and tighten to a torque wrench setting of 71 - 86 lb ft (10 - 12 kg m).

13 Reconnect the propeller shaft aligning the previously made marks on the flanges, and refit the bolts with new spring washers. Tighten to a torque wrench setting of 43 - 47 lb ft (6 - 6.5 kg m).

14 With the split type propeller shaft refit the shims, the centre bearing support securing bolts, spring and plain washers and tighten to a torque wrench setting of 13 - 17 lb ft (1.8 - 2.3 kg m).

15 Finally check the oil level in the rear axle and top-up if necessary.

4 Drive pinion oil seal (collapsible type pinion spacer) - renewal

Note: Renewal of the drive pinion oil seal requires a great deal of care and the use of some special equipment. Without these, the collapsible spacer can be damaged which will require its renewal, and this operation is outside the scope of the do-it-yourself motorist because a special tool is required for removal of the pinion bearing. Whenever the pinion oil seal is renewed, it is essential that the self-locking pinion nut is also renewed.

1 Jack up the rear of the vehicle and support is securely under the bodyframe.

2 Remove the rear roadwheels and brake drums.

3 Disconnect the propeller shaft from the rear axle drive pinion after marking them for correct alignment.

4 Using a spring balance and length of cord wound round the drive pinion flange, determine the torque required to turn the drive pinion and record it. Alternatively, a socket wrench fitted to the pinion nut and a suitable torque wrench may be used.

5 Mark the coupling in relation to the pinion splines to ensure that they are refitted in the same position.

6 Hold the pinion coupling flange by placing two 2 inch long bolts through two opposite holes, bolting them up tight; undo the self-locking nut whilst holding a large screwdriver or tyre lever between the two bolts for leverage. Using a standard two- or three-leg puller, remove the coupling flange from the pinion shaft.

7 Using a hammer and a small chisel or screwdriver, remove the oil seal from the pinion housing. During this operation great care must be taken to ensure that the pinion shaft is not scored in any way. Note that there will be some spillage of the axle oil as the seal is removed.

8 Carefully clean the contact area inside the pinion housing, then apply a film of general purpose grease to this surface and between the lips of the new oil seal. Do not remove the existing grease from the replacement seal.

9 Using a tube of suitable diameter, press in the new seal to its full depth in the pinion housing.

10 Refit the coupling in its correct relative position to the pinion shaft.

11 Using a new self-locking nut, prevent the flange from turning, then carefully and slowly tighten the nut until the same turning torque is achieved as recorded at paragraph 4. Continue tightening until an additional 2 to 3 lbf in (2 to 4 kgf cm) is achieved, to allow for the friction of the new oil seal. After this torque has been obtained, do not tighten the self-locking nut or the collapsible spacer will be damaged (see note at beginning of Section).

12 Remove the two bolts from the coupling flange then refit the propeller shaft taking note of the alignment marks made when removing.

13 Top up the rear axle with the correct grade of oil, then refit the brake drums and roadwheels.

14 Lower the car to the ground.

5 Axle-shaft (halfshaft) - removal and installation

1 Chock the front wheels, remove the rear wheel trim and slacken the wheel nuts. Jack-up the rear of the car and support on firmly based axle stands. Remove the roadwheel and release the handbrake.

2 Undo and remove the two cheese head screws that secure the brake drum to the axle-shaft. Using a soft faced hammer carefully tap outwards on the circumference of the brake drum and lift away the brake drum.

3 Using a socket wrench placed through the holes in the axle shaft flange, undo and remove the four bolts that secure the bearing retainer plate to the axle casing (Fig. 8.8).

4 Place a container under the end of the rear axle to catch any oil that may drain out once the axle-shaft has been removed.

5 The axle-shaft may now be withdrawn from the rear axle.

6 It is possible for the ball races to bind onto the axle-shaft in which case screw in two long bolts through the rear end of the axle tube and thereby ease the axle-shaft assembly out (Fig.8.9).

7 Before refitting the axle-shaft assembly, smear a little grease along the length of the axle-shaft and also on the ball race to prevent corrosion due to moisture.

8 Insert the axle-shaft into the rear axle tube, keep the shaft horizontal until its splines are felt to engage with those of the differential gears.

9 Secure the bearing retainer with the four bolts which should be tightened to a torque wrench setting of 29 - 36 lb ft (4 - 5 kg m).

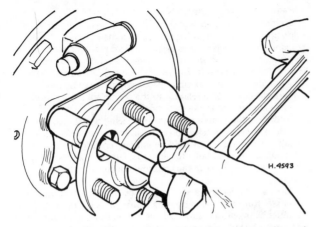

Fig. 8.8. Removal of bearing retainer plate securing bolts (Sec. 5)

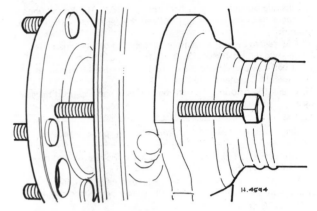

Fig. 8.9. Using long bolts to assist withdrawal of axle-shaft (Sec. 5)

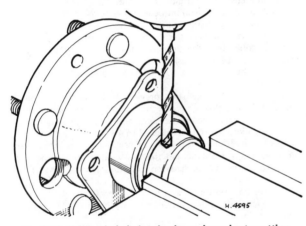

Fig. 8.10. Drilling hole in bearing inner ring prior to cutting with chisel (Sec. 6)

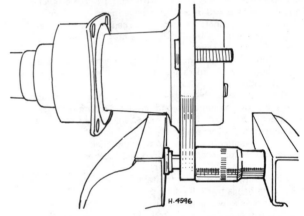

Fig. 8.11. Fitting new wheel stud to axle-shaft flange (Sec. 7)

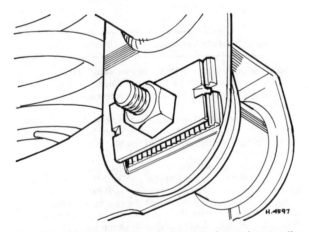

Fig. 8.12. Pinion drive angle adjustment washers at lower radius arm pivot (Sec. 9)

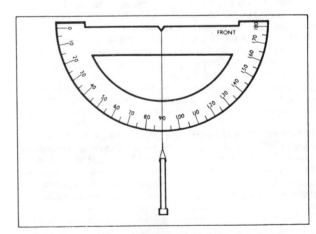

Fig. 8.13. Protractor and plumb line suitable for checking pinion drive angle (Sec. 9)

10 Refit the brake drum and secure with the two cheese head bolts.

11 Refit the roadwheel and lower the car to the ground.

---

6 Axle-shaft (halfshaft) - bearing/oil seal - renewal

1   Remove the axle-shaft, as described in the preceding Section.

2   Secure the axle-shaft in a vice fitted with jaw protectors and

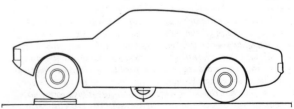

Fig. 8.14. Checking bodyframe side-member for level (Sec. 9)

then carefully drill a hole in the bearing retaining collar. Do not drill right through the collar or the axle-shaft will be damaged. Use a sharp cold chisel and cut the collar from the shaft.

3 A press or suitable bearing extractor will be required to remove the bearing from the shaft. Do not damage the retainer plate during this operation.

4 Commence installation by fitting the retainer plate to the axle-shaft, followed by the bearing (oil seal away from axle-shaft flange) and a new bearing retaining collar.

5 Using a press or two-legged puller, apply pressure to the collar to draw all three components into their correct positions, tight against the axle-shaft end-flange.

6 Apply a little grease to the bearing recess in the end of the axle tube and install the axle-shaft, as described in Section 5.

7 Roadwheel retaining studs - renewal

1 A wheel retaining stud which has broken or whose threads have stripped may be removed and the new one installed using a socket wrench or short piece of tubing as a distance piece in the jaws of a vice (Fig. 8.11).

2 When installing the new stud, make sure that its securing splines are correctly aligned with those in the axle-shaft flange before applying pressure.

8 Rear axle - repair and overhaul

1 It is not recommended that servicing of the rear axle should go beyond the operations described in this Chapter.

2 Special tools and gauges are required to set up the differential, and dismantling and reassembly should be left to your Ford main dealer.

3 The latest trend is in fact for rear axle components not to be supplied individually but the complete factory-built unit only to be supplied as a spare.

4 Reference to the Fault Diagnosis Chart will however assist the home mechanic in eliminating some sources of noise and wear before deciding that it is the rear axle which is undoubtedly due for major overhaul or reconditioning.

9 Pinion drive angle - adjustment

1 Since January 1972, a modified lower radius arm/rear axle mounting is fitted to enable the drive angle to be adjusted. The modified mounting is identified by the serrated washers located behind the radius arm pivot bolts (Fig. 8.12).

2 Position the vehicle on level ground (without any occupants) and using a protractor and plumb line, applied to the centre point of a body frame side-member, raise the front or rear of the vehicle as necessary to ensure that the side-member is perfectly horizontal (Figs. 8.13 and 8.14).

3 Using a right-angled set square located on the rear face of the drive pinion flange, check by means of the protractor and plumb line the inclination of the flange. Where a single piece propeller shaft is installed, the flange should be inclined forward at the top by between 2° and 3° 30'. For a split type propeller shaft, the inclination should be between 0° and 1° 30' forward at the top (Fig. 8.15).

4 Where adjustment is called for, slacken the nuts on the lower radius arm pivot bolts at the axle casing sufficiently to permit the serrated washers to slide over each other (Fig. 8.16).

5 Jack-up the differential carrier until (again using the protractor) the specified pinion drive angle is achieved (Fig 8.17).

6 Engage the serrated washers on both sides of the axle bracket so that identical serrations on the plates with the elongated holes engage with similar ones on the plates with the circular bolt holes.

7 Tighten the pivot bolt nuts finger-tight and then lower the vehicle to the ground and re-check the drive angle. If it is correct, tighten the radius arm pivot bolts to the specified torque with

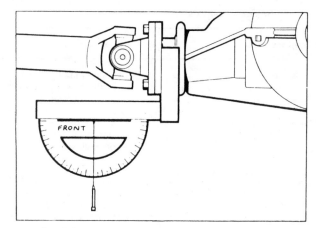
Fig. 8.15. Checking pinion drive flange angle (Sec. 9)

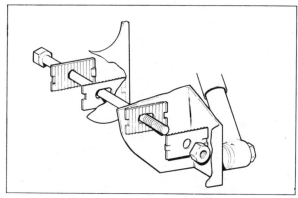
Fig. 8.16. Exploded view of lower radius arm pivot and serrated plates (Sec. 9)

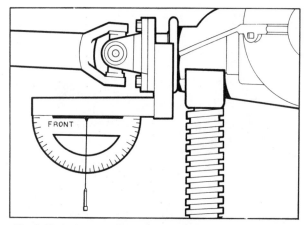
Fig. 8.17. Jacking-up differential carrier to adjust drive pinion angle (Sec. 9)

the normal weight of the vehicle on the roadwheels.

8 When the drive angle is correctly adjusted, the distance between the rear end of the propeller shaft and the underside of the floor should be in accordance with the following measurements.

Single piece propeller shaft	*4.1 in (106.0 mm)*
Split propeller shaft	*5.1 in (130.0 mm)*

10 Fault diagnosis - rear axle

Symptom	Reason/s	Remedy
Oil leakage	Faulty pinion oil seal	Renew
	Faulty axle-shaft oil seals	Renew
	Defective cover gasket	Renew
Noise	Lack of oil	Top-up
	Worn bearings	Renew
	General wear	Have assembly reconditioned or purchase new unit
'Clonk' on taking up drive and excessive backlash	Incorrectly tightened pinion nut	Check (see Sections 3 or 4)
	Worn components	Renew or recondition unit
	Worn axle-shaft splines	Renew unit
	Elongated roadwheel bolt holes	Renew wheels

Chapter 9 Braking system

Contents

Specifications

System type	Hydraulic on all four wheels
Front	Dual line disc, self adjusting
Rear	Dual line drum, self adjusting
Handbrake	Mechanical, on rear wheels only

Front brakes

Disc diameter	9.74 in (247.5 mm)
Pad swept area	191.87 sq in (1254.9 sq cm)
Max. disc runout	0.002 in (0.05 mm)
Cylinder diameter	2.13 in (54.0 mm)
Minimum pad thickness	0.06 - 0.12 in (1.5 - 3 mm)

Rear brakes

	1600 GT and 2000	1600
Drum diameter	9.0 in (228.6 mm)	8.0 in (203.2 mm)
Shoe swept area	97.63 sq in (638.5 sq cm)	74.39 sq in (486.5 mm)
Wheel cylinder diameter	0.70 in (17.78 mm)	0.816 in (20.64 mm)
Minimum lining thickness (all models)	0.06 in (1.52 mm)	

Vacuum servo unit

Type	38
Boost ratio	2.2 : 1

Torque wrench settings

	lb f ft	kg f m
Brake caliper to front suspension	45 - 50	6.22 - 6.91
Brake disc to hub	30 - 34	4.15 - 4.70
Rear brake backplate to axle housing	15 - 18	2.07 - 2.49
Hydraulic pipe union	9 - 11	1.2 - 1.5
Bleed screw	5 - 7	0.70 - 1
Master cylinder - tipping valve securing nut	35 - 45	4.8 - 6.22
Master cylinder to servo	17	2.3

1 General description

Disc brakes are fitted to the front wheels and drum brakes to the rear. All are operated from the brake pedal, this being connected to the master cylinder and servo assembly (when fitted), mounted on the bulkhead.

The hydraulic system is of the dual line principle whereby the front disc brake calipers have a separate hydraulic system to that of the rear drum brake wheel cylinders so that if failure of the hydraulic pipes to the front or rear brakes occurs half the braking system is still operative. Servo assistance in this condition is still available.

The front brake disc is secured to the hub flange and the caliper mounted on the steering knuckle and wheel stub, so that the disc is able to rotate in between the two halves of the calipers. Inside each half of the caliper is a hydraulic cylinder this being interconnected by a drilling which allows hydraulic fluid pressure to be transmitted to both halves. A piston operates in each cylinder, and is in contact with the outer face of the brake pad. By depressing the brake pedal, hydraulic fluid pressure is increased by the servo unit and transmitted to the caliper by a system of metal and flexible hoses whereupon the pistons are moved outwards so pushing the pads onto the face of the disc so slowing down the rotational speed of the disc.

The rear drum brakes have one cylinder operating two shoes. When the brake pedal is depressed hydraulic fluid pressure, increased by the servo unit, is transmitted to the rear brake wheel cylinders by a system of metal and flexible pipes. The pressure moves the pistons outwards so pushing the shoe linings into contact with the inside circumference of the brake drum and slowing down the rotational speed of the drum.

The handbrake provides an independent means of rear brake application.

Also, attached to each of the brake units is an automatic adjuster which operates in conjunction with the handbrake mechanism (up to 1974) or the footbrake (after 1974).

Whenever it is necessary to obtain spare parts for the braking system great care must be taken to ensure that the correct parts are obtained because of the varying types of braking components fitted to the Cortina Mk III range of cars.

2 Bleeding the hydraulic system

1   Removal of all the air from the hydraulic system is essential to the correct working of the braking system, and before undertaking this, examine the fluid reservoir cap to ensure that the vent hole is clear. Check the level of fluid in the reservoir and top-up if required.
2   Check all brake line unions and connections for possible seepage, and at the same time check the condition of the rubber hoses which may be perished.
3   If the condition of the caliper or wheel cylinders is in doubt, check   for possible signs of fluid leakage.
4   If there is any possibility that incorrect fluid has been used in the system, drain all the fluid out and flush through with methylated spirits. Renew all piston seals and cups since they will be affected and could possibly fail under pressure.
5   Gather together a clean jam jar, a 12 inch (300 mm) length of tubing which fits tightly over the bleed screws and a tin of the correct brake fluid.
6   To bleed the system, clean the area around the bleed valves and start on the front right-hand bleed screw by first removing the rubber cup over the end of the bleed screw (Fig. 9.1).
7   Place the end of the tube in a clean jar which should contain sufficient fluid to keep the end of the tube underneath during the operation.
8   Open the bleed screw ¼ turn with a spanner and depress the brake pedal. After slowly releasing the pedal, pause for a moment to allow the fluid to recoup in the master cylinder and then depress it again. This will force air from the system. Continue until no more air bubbles can be seen coming from the tube. At intervals make certain that the reservoir is kept topped-up, otherwise air will enter at this point again.
9   Finally press the pedal down fully and hold it there whilst the bleed screw is tightened. To ensure correct seating it should be tightened to a torque wrench setting of 5 - 7 lb ft (0.70 - 1.0 kg m).
10 Repeat this operation on the second front brake, and then the rear brakes, starting with the right-hand brake unit.
11 When completed check the level of the fluid in the reservoir and then check the feel of the brake pedal, which should be firm and free from any 'spongy' action, which is normally associated with air in the system.

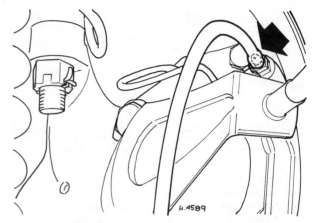

Fig. 9.1. Bleed tube on front disc brake caliper bleed screw (Sec. 2)

12 It will be noticed that during the bleeding operation the effort required to depress the pedal the full stroke will increase because of the loss of vacuum assistance as it is destroyed by repeated operation of the servo unit. Although the servo unit will be inoperative as far as assistance is concerned it does not affect the brake bleed operation.

3 Flexible hose - inspection, removal and refitting

1   Inspect the condition of the flexible hydraulic hoses leading to each of the front disc brake calipers and also the one at the front of the rear axle. If they are swollen, damaged or chafed, they must be renewed.
2   Wipe the top of the brake master cylinder reservoir and unscrew the cap. Place a piece of polythene sheet over the top of the reservoir and refit the cap. This is to stop hydraulic fluid syphoning out during subsequent operations.
3   To remove a front flexible hose, wipe the union and brackets free of dust and undo the union nuts from the metal pipe ends.
4   Undo and remove the locknuts and plain washers securing each flexible hose end to the bracket and lift away the flexible hose.
5   To remove the rear flexible hose follow the instructions for the front flexible hose.
6   Refitting in both cases is the reverse sequence to removal. It will be necessary to bleed the brake hydraulic system as described in Section 2. If one hose has been removed it is only necessary to bleed either the front or rear brake hydraulic system.

4 Front brake pads - inspection, removal and refitting

1   Apply the handbrake, remove the front wheel trim, slacken the wheel nuts, jack-up the front of the car and place on firmly based axle stands. Remove the front wheel.
2   Inspect the amount of friction material left on the pads. The pads must be renewed when the thickness has been reduced to a minimum of 0.12 inch (3.0 mm).
3   If the fluid level in the master cylinder reservoir is high, when the pistons are moved into their respective bores to accommodate new pads the level could rise sufficiently for the fluid to overflow. Place absorbent cloth around the reservoir or syphon a little fluid out so preventing paintwork damage caused by being in contact with the hydraulic fluid.
4   Using a pair of long nosed pliers extract the two small circlips that hold the main retaining pins in place.
5   Remove the main retaining pins which run through the caliper and the metal backing of the pads and the shims (photo).
6   The friction pads can now be removed from the caliper. If they prove difficult to remove by hand a pair of long nosed

4.5 Removing a disc pad retaining pin

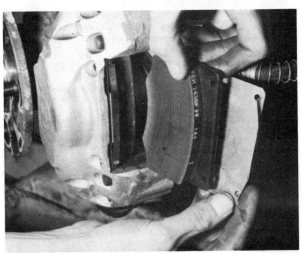

4.6 Disc pad and shim removal

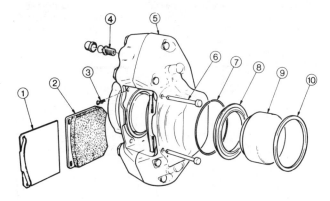

Fig. 9.2. Front disc brake caliper component parts

1 Pad shim	6 Pad retainer	
2 Brake pad	7 Piston bellows retainer	
3 Pad retainer clip	8 Piston bellows	
4 Bleed nipple	9 Piston	
5 Caliper body	10 Piston seal	

pliers can be used. Lift away the shims (photo).

7 Carefully clean the recesses in the caliper in which the friction pads and shims lie, and the exposed faces of each piston from all traces of dust or rust.

8 Using a piece of wood carefully retract the pistons.

9 Fit the new friction pads and shims (the latter can be fitted either way up) and insert the main pad retaining pins. Secure the pins with the small wire clips.

10 Refit the roadwheel and lower the car. Tighten the wheel nuts securely and replace the wheel trim.

11 To correctly seat the pistons pump the brake pedal several times and finally top-up the hydraulic fluid level in the master cylinder reservoir as necessary.

5 Front brake caliper - removal and refitting

1 Apply the handbrake, remove the front wheel trim, slacken the wheel nuts, jack-up the front of the car and place on firmly based axle stands. Remove the front wheel.

2 Wipe the top of the brake master cylinder reservoir and unscrew the cap. Place a piece of polythene sheet over the top of the reservoir and refit the cap. This is to stop hydraulic fluid syphoning out during subsequent operations.

3 Remove the friction pads, as described in Section 4.

4 If it is intended to fit new caliper pistons and/or the seals, depress the brake pedal to bring the pistons into contact with the disc and so assist subsequent removal of the pistons.

5 Wipe the area clean around the flexible hose bracket and detach the pipe as described in Section 3. Tape up the end of the pipe to stop the possibility of dirt ingress.

6 Using a screwdriver or chisel, bend back the tabs on the locking plate and undo the two caliper body mounting bolts. Lift away the caliper from its mounting flange on the steering knuckle and wheel stub.

7 To refit the caliper, position it over the disc and move it until the mounting bolt holes are in line with the two front holes in the steering knuckle and wheel stub mounting flange.

8 Fit the caliper retaining bolts through the two holes in a new locking plate and insert the bolts through the caliper body. Tighten the bolts to a torque wrench setting of 45 - 50 lb ft (6.22 - 6.91 kg m).

9 Using a screwdriver, pliers or chisel, bend up the locking plate tabs so as to lock the bolts.

10 Remove the tape from the end of the flexible hydraulic pipe and reconnect it to the union on the hose bracket. Be careful not to cross thread the union nut during the initial turns. The union nut should be tightened securely, if possible using a torque wrench and special slotted end ring spanner attachment set to 5 - 7 lb ft (0.70 - 1.00 kg m).

11 Push the pistons into their respective bores so as to accommodate the pads. Watch the level of hydraulic fluid in the master cylinder reservoir as it can overflow if too high whilst the pistons are being retracted. Place absorbent cloth around the reservoir or syphon a little fluid out so preventing paintwork damage caused by being in contact with the hydraulic fluid.

12 If the old pads are being re-used, refit them into their respective original positions. If new pads are being used it does not matter which side they are fitted. Replace the shims.

13 Insert the two pad and shim retaining pins and secure in position with the spring clips.

14 Bleed the hydraulic system as described in Section 2. Replace the roadwheel and lower the car.

6 Front brake caliper - dismantling and reassembly

1 The pistons should be removed first. To do this, half withdraw one piston from its bore in the caliper body. (See Fig. 9.2 for the location of the various parts.

2 Carefully remove the securing circlip and extract the sealing bellows from their location in the lower part of the piston skirt. Completely remove the piston.

3 If difficulty is experienced in withdrawing the piston use a
jet of compressed air or a foot pump to move it out of its bore.
4 Remove the sealing bellows from their location in the annular
ring which is machined in the cylinder bore.
5 Remove the piston sealing ring from the cylinder bore using
a small screwdriver but do take care not to scratch the fine finish
of the bore.
6 To remove the second piston repeat the operations in
paragraphs 1 - 5 inclusive.
7 It is important that the two halves of the caliper are not
separated under any circumstances. If hydraulic fluid leaks are
evident, from the joint, the caliper must be renewed.
8 Thoroughly wash all parts in methylated spirits or clean
hydraulic fluid. During reassembly new rubber seals must be fitted and these should be well lubricated with clean hydraulic
fluid.
9 Inspect the pistons and bores for signs of wear, score marks
or damage, and if evident, new parts should be obtained ready
for fitting or a new caliper obtained.
10 To reassemble, fit one of the piston seals into the annular
groove in the cylinder bore.
11 Fit the rubber bellows to the cylinder bore groove so that the
lip is turned outwards.
12 Lubricate the seal and rubber bellows with clean hydraulic
fluid. Push the piston, crown first, through the rubber sealing
bellows and then into the cylinder bore. Take care as it is easy
for the piston to damage the rubber bellows.
13 With the piston half inserted into the cylinder bore fit the
inner edge of the bellows into the annular groove that is in the
piston skirt.
14 Push the piston down the bore as far as it will go. Secure the
rubber bellows to the caliper with the circlip.
15 Repeat the operations in paragraphs 10 to 14 inclusive for
the second piston.
16 The caliper is now ready for refitting. It is recommended
that the hydraulic pipe end is temporarily plugged to stop any
dirt ingress whilst being refitted, before the pipe connection is
made.

7 Front brake disc and hub - removal and installation

1 After jacking-up the car and removing the front wheel, remove
the caliper as described in Section 5.
2 By judicious tapping and levering remove the dust cap from
the centre of the hub.
3 Remove the split pin from the nut retainer and lift away the
adjusting nut retainer.
4 Unscrew the adjusting nut and lift away the thrust washer and
outer tapered bearing.
5 Pull off the complete hub and disc assembly from the stub
axle (Fig. 9.3).

6 From the back of the hub assembly carefully prise out the
grease seal and lift away the inner tapered bearing.
7 Carefully clean out the hub and wash the bearings with
petrol making sure that no grease or oil is allowed to get onto the
brake disc.
8 Should it be necessary to separate the disc from the hub for
renewal or regrinding, first bend back the locking tabs and undo
the four securing bolts. With a scriber mark the relative positions
of the hub and disc to ensure refitting in their original positions
and separate the disc from the hub.
9 Thoroughly clean the disc and inspect for signs of deep scoring
or excessive corrosion. If these are evident, the disc may be reground but no more than a maximum total of 0.060 inch
(1.524 mm) may be removed. It is, however, desirable to fit a
new disc if at all possible.
10 To reassemble make quite sure that the mating faces of the
disc and hub are very clean and place the disc on the hub, lining
up any previously made marks.
11 Fit the four securing bolts and two new tab washers and
tighten the bolts in a progressive and diagonal manner to a final
torque wrench setting of 30 - 34 lb ft (4.15 - 4.70 kg m). Bend
up the locking tabs.
12 Work some grease well into the bearing, fully pack the bearing cages and rollers. **Note**: leave the hub and grease seal empty
to allow for subsequent expansion of the grease.
13 To reassemble the hub, first fit the inner bearing and then
gently tap the grease seal back into the hub. A new seal must
always be fitted as during removal it was   probably damaged. The
lip must face inwards to the hub.
14 Replace the hub and disc assembly on the stub axle and slide
on the outer bearing and thrust washer.
15 Refit the adjusting nut and tighten it to a torque wrench
setting of 27 lb ft (3.7 kg m) whilst rotating the hub and disc
to ensure free movement and centralisation of the bearings.
Slacken the nut back by 90º which will give the required endfloat of 0.001 - 0.005 inch (0.03 - 0.13 mm). Fit the nut retainer
and a new split pin but at this stage do not   lock the split pin.
16 If a dial indicator gauge is available, it is advisable to check
the disc for run out. The measurement should be taken as near to
the edge of the worn yet smooth part of the disc as possible,
and must not exceed 0.002 inch (0.05 mm). If the figure obtained is found to be excessive, check the mating surfaces of the disc
and hub for dirt or damage and also check the bearings and cups
for excessive wear or damage.
17 If a dial indicator gauge is not available the runout can be
checked by means of a feeler gauge placed between the casting
of the caliper and the disc (Fig. 9.4). Establish a reasonably
tight fit with the feeler gauge between the top of the casting
and the disc and rotate the disc and hub. Any high or low spot
will immediately become obvious by extra tightness or looseness
of the fit of the feeler gauge. The amount of runout can be checked by adding or subtracting feeler gauges as necessary. It is only

**Fig. 9.3. Removing the hub and disc assembly from the stub axle
(Sec. 7)**

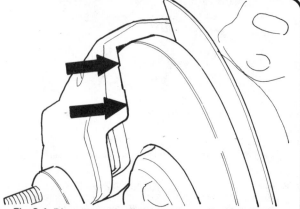

**Fig. 9.4. Disc runout check points when using feeler gauges
(Sec. 7)**

fair to point out that this method is not as accurate as when using a dial indicator gauge owing to the rough nature of the caliper casting.

18 Once the disc runout has been checked and found to be correct bend the ends of the split pin back and replace the dust cap.

19 Reconnect the brake hydraulic pipe and bleed the brakes as described in Section 2 of this Chapter.

8 Drum brake shoes (up to 1974) - inspection, removal and refitting

After high mileages, it will be necessary to fit replacement shoes with new linings. Refitting new brake linings to shoes is not considered economic, or possible without the use of special equipment. However, if the services of a local garage or workshop having brake re-lining equipment are available then there is no reason why the original shoes should not be successfully relined. Ensure that the correct specification linings are fitted to the shoes.

1 Chock the front wheels, jack-up the rear of the car and place on firmly based axle stands. Remove the roadwheel.

2 Release the handbrake, remove the brake drum retaining screw, and using a soft faced hammer on the outer circumference of the brake drum remove the brake drum.

3 Should the situation exist whereby the shoes foul the drum making removal impossible, the shoes must be collapsed by detaching the handbrake cable from the body mounted brackets and then the plunger assembly removed from the backplate. Whenever the plunger is removed it must be discarded and a new one obtained.

4 The brake linings should be renewed if they are so worn that the rivet heads are flush with the surface of the lining. If bonded linings are fitted, they must be renewed when the lining material has worn down to 0.6 inch (1.52 mm) at its thinnest part.

5 Depress each shoe holding down spring and rotate the spring retaining washer through 90° to disengage it from the pin secured to the backplate. Lift away the washer and spring.

6 Ease each shoe from its location slot in the fixed pivot and then detach the other end of each shoe from the wheel cylinder.

7 Note which way round and into which holes in the shoes the two retracting springs fit and detach the retracting springs.

8 Lift away the front shoe followed by the self adjusting push-rod and ratchet assembly.

9 Completely remove the handbrake cable from the body mounted brackets and disconnect the cable from the relay lever (photo).

10 Lift away the rear shoe together with the self adjusting mechanism.

11 If the shoes are to be left off for a while, place a warning on the steering wheel as accidental depression of the brake pedal will eject the pistons from the wheel cylinder.

12 To remove the relay lever assembly, using a screwdriver prise open the 'U' clip on the rear brake shoe and lift away the relay lever assembly. The 'U' clip must be discarded and a new one obtained ready for reassembly.

13 Thoroughly clean all traces of dust from the shoes, backplates and brake drums using a stiff brush. It is recommended that compressed air is **not** used as it blows up dust which should not be inhaled. Brake dust can cause judder or squeal and, therefore, it is important to clean out as described.

14 Check that the pistons are free in the cylinder, that the rubber dust covers are undamaged and in position, and that there are no hydraulic fluid leaks.

15 Prior to reassembly smear a trace of brake grease on the shoe support pads, brake shoe pivots and on the ratchet wheel face and threads.

16 To reassemble first fit the relay lever assembly to the rear brake shoe and retain in position using a new 'U' clip. Using a pair of pliers close up the ends of the clip.

17 Fit the retracting springs to the shoe webs in the same position as was noted during removal. Replace the adjusting

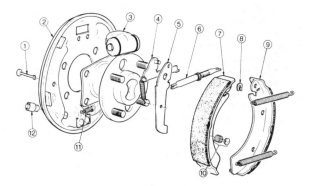

Fig. 9.5 Rear drum brake component parts (up to 1974)

1	Shoe hold down pin	9	Trailing shoe
2	Backplate	10	Hold down spring and washer
3	Wheel cylinder		
4	Self-adjusting lever	11	Handbrake cable retracting spring
5	Handbrake relay lever		
6	Pushrod and ratchet	12	Handbrake adjustment plunger
7	Leading shoe		
8	'U' clip		

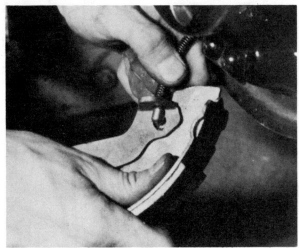

8.9 Disconnection of handbrake cable from relay lever (drum brakes up to 1974)

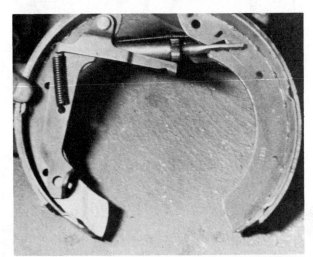

8.17 Refitting adjusting pushrod and retracting springs (drum brakes up to 1974)

pushrod (photo).

18 Position the rear brake shoe on the fixed pivot and wheel cylinder piston extension and using a screwdriver ease the front shoe into position on the brake backplate and wheel cylinder piston extension.

19 Reconnect the handbrake cable to the relay lever taking care to ensure that it does not foul the adjustment plunger.

20 Refit the handbrake cable to the body mounted brackets.

21 Place each shoe holding down clip on its pin followed by the washer, dished face inwards. Depress and turn the washer through 90° to lock in position. Make sure that each shoe is firmly seated on the backplate.

22 Rotate each adjuster pushrod ratchet until all slack in the pushrod is removed. Check that the adjusting arm positively locates in the ratchet wheel   serrations.

23 Refit the brake drum and push it up the studs as far as it will go.

24 The shoes must next be centralised by the brake pedal being depressed firmly several times.

25 Pull on and then release the handbrake lever several times until it is no longer possible to   hear the clicking noise of the ratchet being turned by the adjusting arm.

26 Refit the roadwheel   and lower the car. Road test to ensure correct operation of the rear brakes.

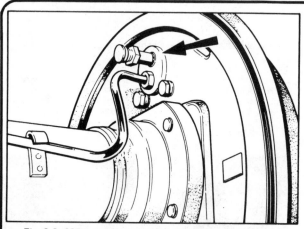

Fig. 9.6. 1974 onwards rear brake identification (Sec. 9)

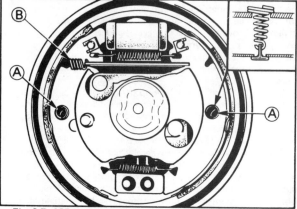

Fig. 9.7. 1974 onwards rear brake internal identification. A hold down springs, B return spring (Sec. 9)

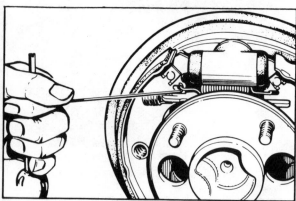

Fig. 9.8. Disconnecting shoe return spring (1974 onwards) (Sec. 9)

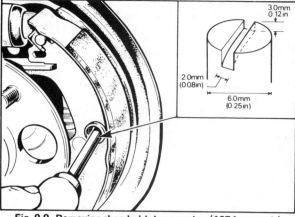

Fig. 9.9. Removing shoe hold down spring (1974 onwards) (Sec. 9)

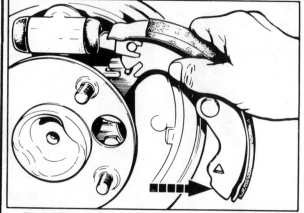

Fig. 9.10. Removing front shoe (1974 onwards) (Sec. 9)

Fig. 9.11. Disconnecting handbrake cable (1974 onwards) (Sec. 9)

9 Drum brake shoes (1974 onwards) - inspection, removal and refitting

1   These brakes are of the self-adjusting type but the adjusting mechanism is actuated by the footbrake not the handbrake as with earlier designs.

2   The brakes may be identified by the round shape of the wheel cylinder which engages in the cut-out in the brake backplate (Fig. 9.6).

3   With the brake drum removed, points of identification are the shoe hold-down springs and the handbrake lever return spring (Fig. 9.7).

4   Using a hooked piece of wire, disconnect both brake shoe return springs (Fig. 9.8).

5   Release and remove the shoe hold-down springs. A rod or old screwdriver, slotted at the end is useful to first depress and then unhook the spring from its retaining bracket (Fig. 9.9).

6   Pull the bottom of the front brake shoe towards the front of the vehicle. This will actuate the self-adjust mechanism to the point where the two ratchets slip out of engagement. Now twist the brake shoe to release it from the spacer strut and remove it (Fig. 9.10).

7   Move the rear shoe away from and below the backplate and at the same time disconnect the handbrake operating cable from the shoe lever (Fig. 9.11).

8   The rear brake shoe can be dismantled by removing the clip from the pivot pin and extracting the pin. Lever the strut from the shoe and detach the lever return spring (Figs. 9.12 and 9.13).

9   The front brake shoe can be dismantled by removing the clip and separating the longer ratchet lever from the shoe. Remove and discard the spring washer and then separate the shorter ratchet lever and spring from the shoe (Fig. 9.14).

10 Reassembly of the new shoes is a reversal of removal and dismantling, but note the following points:

(i)   No lubricant must be supplied to the components.

(ii)   When assembling the smaller ratchet, spring and pivot pin to the front brake shoe, slide two 0.008 in (0.2 mm) feeler blades between the shoe and the ratchet before installing a new spring washer. This will provide the necessary rotational clearance. Make sure that the retaining tabs are correctly positioned as shown in Fig. 9.15.

(iii) Having fitted the longer ratchet and securing clip, arrange the engagement of both ratchets to provide an overlap of 4 or 5 teeth (Fig. 9.16).

(iv)   The spring loaded ratchet lever must be pulled down with a hooked piece of wire so that the second ratchet can be pushed forward to the minimum adjustment position (Fig. 9.17).

(v)   The larger shoe return spring is located at the top of the brake assembly.

11 Once the brake drum has been installed, apply the foot brake pedal several times to adjust the shoes to their minimum drum clearance position.

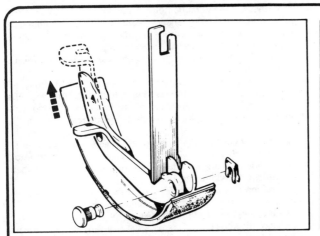

Fig. 9.12. Rear shoe components (1974 onwards) (Sec. 9)

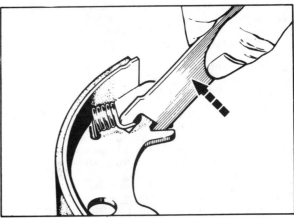

Fig. 9.13. Dismantling rear shoe (1974 onwards) (Sec. 9)

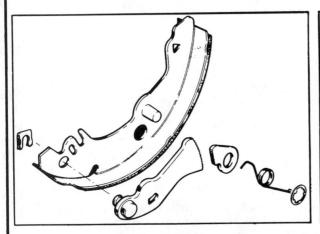

Fig. 9.14. Dismantling front shoe (1974 onwards) (Sec. 9)

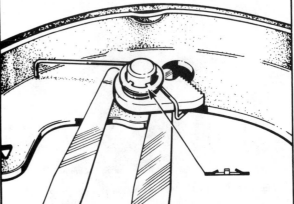

Fig. 9.15. Reassembling shoe smaller ratchet, spring and washer (1974 onwards) (Sec. 9)

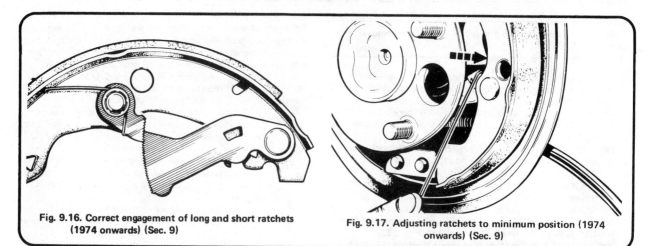

Fig. 9.16. Correct engagement of long and short ratchets (1974 onwards) (Sec. 9)

Fig. 9.17. Adjusting ratchets to minimum position (1974 onwards) (Sec. 9)

10 Drum brake wheel cylinder - removal, inspection and overhaul

If hydraulic fluid is leaking from the brake wheel cylinder, it will be necessary to dismantle it and replace the seals. Should brake fluid be found running down the side of the wheel, or if it is noticed that a pool of liquid forms alongside one wheel or the level in the master cylinder drops it is also indicative of failed seals.

1   Refer to Sections 8 or 9 and remove the brake drum and shoes. Clean down the rear of the backplate using a stiff brush. Place a quantity of rag under the backplate to catch any hydraulic fluid that may issue from the open pipe or wheel cylinder.

2   Wipe the top of the brake master cylinder reservoir and unscrew the cap. Place a piece of polythene sheet over the top of the reservoir and replace the cap. This is to stop hydraulic fluid syphoning out.

3   Using an open ended spanner, carefully unscrew the hydraulic pipe connection union/s to the rear of the wheel cylinder. Note that on the left-hand wheel cylinder two pipes are attached to the wheel cylinder. Note the location of each pipe as these must not be interchanged. To prevent dirt ingress tape over the pipe ends (Fig. 9.18).

4   Undo and remove the two bolts and washers that secure the wheel   cylinder to the brake backplate.

5   Withdraw the wheel cylinder from the front of the brake backplate (Fig. 9.18).

6   To dismantle the wheel cylinder first ease off each rubber dust cover retaining ring and lift away each rubber dust cover.

7   Carefully lift out each piston together with seal from the wheel cylinder bore. Recover the return spring.

8   Using the fingers only, remove the piston seal from each piston, noting which way round it is fitted (Fig. 9.19). Do not use a metal screwdriver as this could scratch the piston.

9   Inspect the inside of the cylinder for score marks caused by impurities in the hydraulic fluid. If any are found, the cylinder and pistons will require renewal. **Note:** if the wheel cylinder requires renewal always ensure that the replacement is exactly similar to the one removed.

10 If the cylinder is sound, thoroughly clean it out with fresh hydraulic fluid.

11 The old rubber seals will probably be swollen and visibly worn. Smear the new rubber seals with hydraulic fluid and refit to the pistons making sure they are the correct way round with the flap face of the seal adjacent to the piston rear shoulder (Fig. 9.19).

12 Wet the cylinder bore with clean hydraulic fluid and insert the return spring. Carefully insert the piston seal end first into the cylinder, making sure that the seals do not roll over as they are initially fitted into the bore.

13 Position the rubber boots on each end of the wheel cylinder and secure in position with the retaining rings.

14 Fit a new ring seal onto the rear of the wheel cylinder and position this in its slot in the backplate. Secure in position with the two bolts and washers.

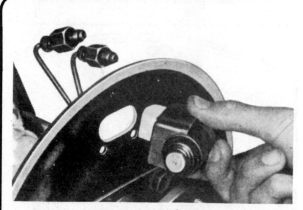

Fig. 9.18. Removal of wheel cylinder from brake backplate (Sec. 10)
(Left-hand wheel with double hydraulic pipe connection)

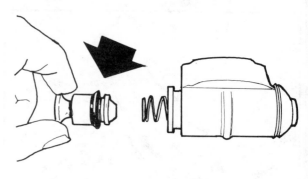

Fig. 9.19. Dismantling wheel cylinder (Sec. 10)
Note which way round seal is fitted

15 Reconnect the brake pipe(s) to the rear of the wheel cylinder, taking care not to cross thread the union nuts. On the left-hand wheel cylinder make sure the pipes are connected the correct way round as was noted during removal.

16 Refit the brake shoes and drum as described in Section 8 or 9.

17 Refer to Section 2 and bleed the brake hydraulic system.

11 Drum brake backplate - removal and refitting

1   To remove the backplate refer to Chapter 8, Section 5 and remove the axle-shaft (halfshaft).

2   Detach the handbrake cable from the handbrake relay lever.

3   Wipe the top of the brake master cylinder reservoir and unscrew the cap. Place a piece of polythene sheet over the top of the reservoir and replace the cap. This is to stop hydraulic fluid syphoning out.

4   Using an open ended spanner, carefully unscrew the hydraulic pipe connection union(s) to the rear of the wheel cylinder. Note that on the left-hand wheel cylinder two pipes are attached to the wheel cylinder. Note the location of each pipe as these must not be interchanged. To prevent dirt ingress tape over the pipe ends.

5   The brake backplate may now be lifted away.

6   Refitting is the reverse sequence to removal. It will be necessary to bleed the brake hydraulic system as described in Section 2.

12 Handbrake - adjustment

1   It is important to check that lack of adjustment is not caused by the cable becoming detached from the body mounted clips, that the equaliser bracket and pivot points are adequately lubricated and that the rear shoe linings have not worn excessively.

2   Chock the front wheels. Jack-up the rear of the car and support on firmly based axle stands located under the rear axle. Release the handbrake.

3   Check the adjustment of the handbrake by measuring the amount of movement of the adjustment plungers located in the brake backplate (Fig. 9.20). This should be 0.02 to 0.04 inch (0.5 to 1.0 mm). If the results obtained differ on one side compared with the other it may be equalised by gripping the handbrake cable at the equaliser bracket and adjusting the position of the cable.

4   If the movement of the adjustment plungers is correct pull on and then release the handbrake lever several times until it is no longer possible to hear the clicking noise of the ratchet being turned by the adjusting arm.

5   If the movement of the adjustment plungers is incorrect the cable may then be adjusted as described in the following paragraphs.

6   Make sure that the handbrake is in the fully off position.

7   Remove all free movement of the adjustment plungers by slackening off the cable as necessary at the right-hand cables to body abutment bracket (Fig. 9.21). The relay levers in the rear brake units will automatically return to the fully off position.

8   Now adjust the cable at the right-hand cable to body abutment bracket so as to give a plunger free movement of 0.02 to 0.04 in (0.5 to 1.0 mm) on each brake backplate.

9   Equalise the movement of the plungers by gripping the handbrake cable at the equaliser bracket and adjusting the position of the cable.

10 Should adjustment of the cable not alter the plunger free movement, it is an indication that the cable is binding or the automatic brake adjuster is not operating correctly - usually due to seizure of the moving parts within the brake unit. It could also be that the adjustment plungers have seized in their locations in the backplate. Further investigation will therefore be necessary.

11 When adjustment is correct tighten the adjuster locknuts.

12 Pull on and then release the handbrake lever several times until it is no longer possible to hear the clicking noise of the

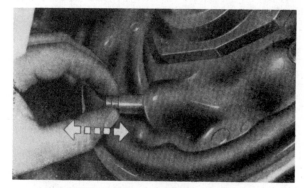

Fig. 9.20. Checking movement of adjustment plungers (Sec. 12)

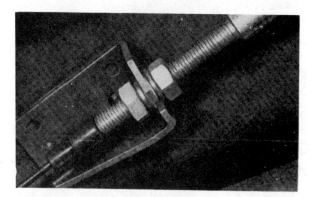

Fig. 9.21. Handbrake cable adjustment location on body mounted bracket (Sec. 12)

Fig. 9.22. Handbrake lever clevis pin (later vehicles) (Sec. 13)

ratchet being turned by the adjuster arm. On 1974 onwards vehicles, apply the footbrake several times.

13 Remove the axle stands and lower the car to the ground.

13 Handbrake cable - removal and refitting

1   Chock the front wheels, jack-up the rear of the car and support on firmly based axle stands located under the rear axle. Release the handbrake. Remove the two rear wheels.

2   *On early vehicles,* remove the centre console and using a pair of pliers, remove the spring clip and withdraw the clevis pin and wave washer that secures the handbrake primary rod to the handbrake lever. Detach the cable from the handbrake lever.

On later vehicles, the clevis pin is accessible from beneath the vehicle (Fig. 9.22).

3 Undo the cable adjuster nuts and then detach the cable from
the clips located under the body and on the radius arms. Using
a pair of pliers withdraw the retaining 'U' shaped clip at the
adjuster bracket.
4 Remove the brake drums. If they are tight they may be removed using a soft faced hammer on the outer drum circumference and tapping outwards.
5 Detach the brake cable from each brake unit relay lever and
pull the cable rearwards through the rear of the backplate.
6 Detach the cable from the equaliser.
7 To refit the cable first feed the cable ends through the rear
of the backplate and reconnect to the relay levers. Replace the
brake drums.
8 Attach the cable to the underbody brackets and clips on the
radius arms. Take care to make sure that the adjuster is correctly
located in its bracket.
9 Engage the cable within the groove of the equaliser and then
connect the primary rod to the handbrake lever.
10 Refit the rear wheels and referring to Section 12 adjust the
handbrake cable.
11 Remove the axle stands and lower the car to the ground.

14 Brake master cylinder - removal and refitting

1 Apply the handbrake and chock the frontwheels. Drain the
fluid from the master cylinder reservoir and master cylinder by
attaching a plastic bleed tube to one of the brake bleed screws.
Undo the screw one turn and then pump the fluid out into a
clean glass container by means of the brake pedal. Hold the brake
pedal against the floor at the end of each stroke and tighten the
bleed screw. When the pedal has returned to its normal position
loosen the bleed screw and repeat the process until the reservoir
is empty.
2 Wipe the area around the two union nuts on the side of the
master cylinder body and using an open ended spanner undo the
two union nuts. Tape over the ends of the pipes to stop dirt
ingress.
3 Undo and remove the two nuts and spring washers that secure
the master cylinder to the rear of the servo unit. Lift away the
master cylinder taking care that no hydraulic fluid is allowed to
drip onto the paintwork.
4 Refitting is the reverse sequence to removal. Always start the
union nuts before finally tightening the master cylinder nuts. It
will be necessary to bleed the hydraulic system: full details will
be found in Section 2.

15 Brake master cylinder - dismantling, examination and re-assembly

If a replacement master cylinder is to be fitted, it will be necessary to lubricate the seals before fitting to the car as they have
a protective coating when originally assembled. Remove the
blanking plugs from the hydraulic pipe union seatings. Inject
clean hydraulic fluid into the master cylinder and operate the
primary piston several times so that the fluid spreads over all the
internal working surfaces.
If the master cylinder is to be dismantled after removal proceed as follows:
1 Undo and remove the two screws and spring washers holding
the reservoir to the master cylinder body. Lift away the reservoir.
Using a suitable sized Allen key, or wrench, unscrew the tipping
valve nut and lift away the seal. Using a suitable diameter rod

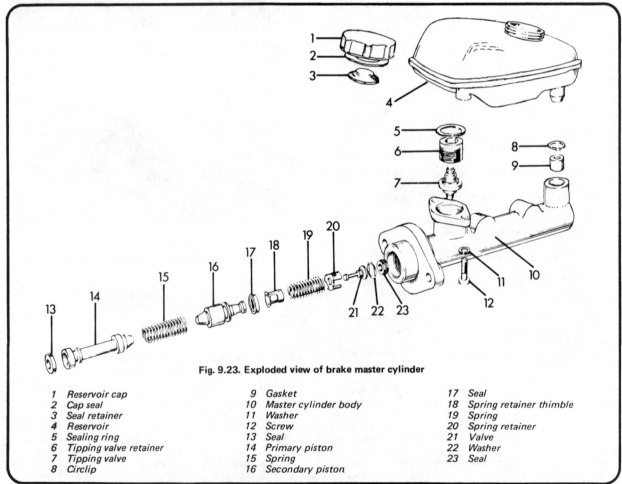

Fig. 9.23. Exploded view of brake master cylinder

1	Reservoir cap	9	Gasket	17	Seal
2	Cap seal	10	Master cylinder body	18	Spring retainer thimble
3	Seal retainer	11	Washer	19	Spring
4	Reservoir	12	Screw	20	Spring retainer
5	Sealing ring	13	Seal	21	Valve
6	Tipping valve retainer	14	Primary piston	22	Washer
7	Tipping valve	15	Spring	23	Seal
8	Circlip	16	Secondary piston		

push the primary plunger down the bore, this operation enabling the tipping valve to be withdrawn.

2   Using a compressed air jet, very carefully applied to the rear outlet connection, blow out all the master cylinder internal components. Alternatively, shake out the parts. Take care that adequate precautions are taken to ensure all parts are caught as they emerge.

3   Separate the primary and secondary plungers from the inter-mediate spring. Use the fingers to remove the gland seal from the primary plunger.

4   The secondary plunger assembly should be separated by lift-ing the thimble leaf over the shouldered end of the plunger. Using the fingers, remove the seal from the secondary plunger.

5   Depress the secondary spring, allowing the valve stem to slide through the keyhole in the thimble, thus releasing the tension on the spring.

6   Detach the valve spacer, taking care of the spring washer which will be found located under the valve head.

7   Examine the bore of the cylinder carefully for any signs of scores or ridges. If this is found to be smooth all over new seals can be fitted. If, however, there is any doubt of the condition of the bore, then a new cylinder must be fitted.

8   If examination of the seals shows them to be apparently over-size, or swollen, or very loose on the plungers, suspect oil conta-mination in the system. Oil will swell these rubber seals, and if one is found to be swollen, it is reasonable to assume that all seals in the braking system will need attention.

9   Thoroughly clean all parts in clean hydraulic fluid or methy-lated spirits. Ensure that the bypass ports are clear.

10 All components should be assembled wet by dipping in clean brake fluid. Using fingers only, fit new seals to the primary and secondary plungers ensuring that they are the correct way round.

Note that the seal on the primary plunger is chamfered and must be fitted with its wide end into the cylinder and its small end towards the pedal pushrod.

Place the dished washer with the dome against the underside of the valve seat. Hold it in position with the valve spacer ensuring that the legs face towards the valve seal.

11 Replace the plunger return spring centrally on the spacer, insert the thimble into the spring, and depress until the valve stem engages in the keyhole of the thimble.

12 Insert the reduced end of the plunger into the thimble, until the thimble engages under the shoulder of the plunger, and press home the thimble leaf. Replace the intermediate spring between the primary and secondary plungers.

13 Check that the master cylinder bore is clean and smear with clean brake fluid. With the complete assembly suitably wetted with brake fluid, carefully insert the assembly into the bore. Ease the lips of the piston seals into the bore taking care that they do not roll over. Push the assembly fully home.

14 Refit the tipping valve assembly, and seal, to the cylinder bore and tighten the securing nut to a torque wrench setting of 27 - 35 lb ft (4.8 - 6.22 kg m).

15 Using a clean screwdriver push the primary piston in and out checking that the recuperating valve opens when the screwdriver is withdrawn and closes again when it is pushed in.

16 Check the condition of the front and rear reservoir gaskets and if there is any doubt as to their condition they must be replaced.

17 Replace the hydraulic fluid reservoir and tighten the two retaining screws.

18 The master cylinder is now ready for refitting to the servo unit. Bleed the complete hydraulic system and road test the car.

---

16 Brake pedal - removal and refitting

1   Open the bonnet and for safety reasons disconnect the battery.

2   Undo and remove the screw and annulus that holds the two halves of the steering column shroud together. Using a knife, split the two halves of the column shroud and lift away.

3   Undo and remove the crosshead screws that secure the facia

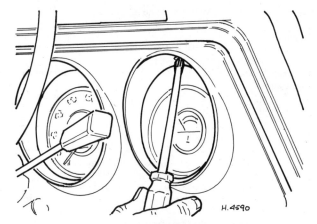

Fig. 9.24. Removing facia panel (Sec. 16)

Fig. 9.25. Instrument cluster drawn forwards giving access to speedometer cable and wiring loom multi-pin connector (Sec. 16)

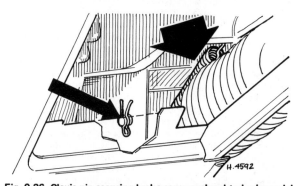

Fig. 9.26. Clevis pin securing brake servo pushrod to brake pedal and brake pedal return spring (Sec. 16)

panel to the instrument panel. Lift away the facia panel (Fig. 9.24).

4   Undo and remove the screws that secure the instrument cluster to the instrument panel. Draw the cluster away from the instrument panel by a sufficient amount to give access to the rear. Detach the wiring loom multi plug connector and the speedo-meter drive cable. Lift away the instrument cluster (Fig. 9.25).

5   Detach and lift away the demister duct.

6   Withdraw the spring clip from the brake servo pushrod to brake pedal clevis pin. Lift away the clevis pin and the bushes (Fig. 9.26).

7   Detach the brake pedal return spring from the brake pedal bracket (Fig. 9.26).

8   Remove the circlips that secure the pedal shaft to the pedal
shaft bracket and carefully push the shaft through the bracket
and pedal (Fig. 9.27).
9   Lift away the brake pedal and split bushes. Remove the half
bushes from each side of the brake pedal.
10 Inspect the bushes for signs of wear and, if evident, they must
be renewed.
11 Refitting the brake pedal is the reverse sequence to removal.
Lubricate all moving parts with engine oil.

17 Handbrake lever - removal and refitting

1   If a centre console is fitted it must first be removed. It is
attached to the transmission cover panels by self-tapping screws.
2   Undo and remove the self-tapping screws that secure the
handbrake lever rubber gaiter to the floor. Slide the gaiter up the
handbrake lever.
3   Lift away the carpeting from around the handbrake area.
4   *On early models,* disconnect the primary rod from the handbrake lever by working inside the vehicle.
    On later models, access to these components is obtained
from beneath the car.
5   Undo and remove the two bolts and spring washers that
secure the handbrake lever to the floor. The handbrake lever
assembly may be lifted away from its location on the floor.
6   Refitting is the reverse sequence to removal. Smear the clevis
pin with a little grease. *On later vehicles,* the handbrake lever
seal must be installed with the paintspot uppermost.

18 Vacuum servo unit - description

1   A vacuum servo unit is fitted into the brake hydraulic circuit
in series with the master cylinder, to provide assistance to the
driver when the brake pedal is depressed. This reduces the effort
required by the driver to operate the brakes under all braking
conditions.
2   The unit operates by vacuum obtained from the induction
manifold and comprises basically a booster diaphragm and check
valve. The servo unit and hydraulic master cylinder are connected
together so that the servo unit piston rod acts as the master
cylinder pushrod. The driver's effort is transmitted through
another pushrod to the servo unit piston and its built-in control
system. The servo unit piston does not fit tightly into the
cylinder, but has a strong diaphragm to keep its edges in constant
contact with the cylinder wall, so assuring an air tight seal
between the two parts. The forward chamber is held under
vacuum conditions created in the inlet manifold of the engine
and, during periods when the brake pedal is not in use, the
controls open a passage to the rear chamber so placing it under
vacuum conditions as well. When the brake pedal is depressed,
the vacuum passage to the rear chamber is cut off and the
chamber opened to atmospheric pressure. The consequent rush
of air pushes the servo piston forward in the vacuum chamber
and operates the main pushrod to the master cylinder.
3   The controls are designed so that assistance is given under all
conditions and, when the brakes are not required, vacuum in the
rear chamber is established when the brake pedal is released. All
air from the atmosphere entering the rear chamber is passed
through a small air filter.
4   Under normal operating conditions the vacuum servo unit is
very reliable and does not require overhaul except at very high
mileages. In this case it is far better to obtain a service exchange
unit, rather than repair the original unit.

19 Vacuum servo unit - removal and installation

1   Slacken the clip securing the vacuum hose to the servo unit
and carefully draw the hose from its union.
2   Refer to Section 14 and remove the master cylinder.
3   Using a pair of pliers remove the spring clip in the end of the

Fig. 9.27. Pedal shaft and pedal retaining clips (Sec. 16)

**Fig. 9.28. Removal of servo unit mounting bracket securing
nuts (Sec. 19)**

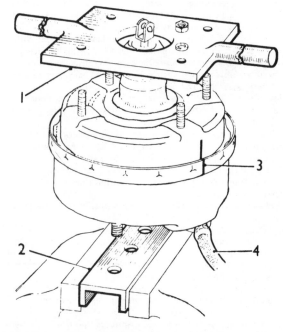

Fig. 9.29. Special tools required to dismantle servo unit (Sec. 20)

1 *Lever* 2 *Base plate*   3 *Scribe line*   4 *Vacuum applied*

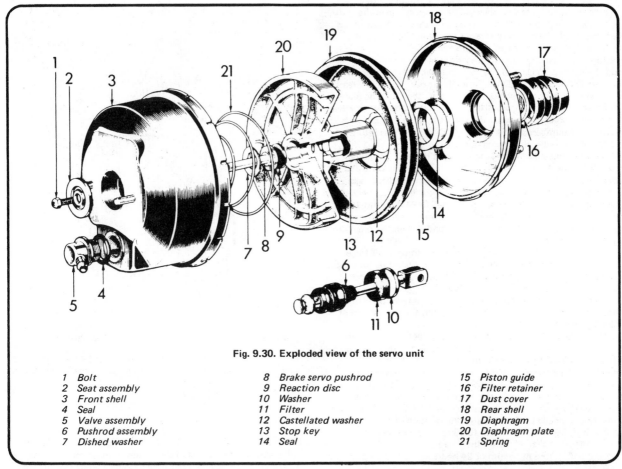

Fig. 9.30. Exploded view of the servo unit

1 Bolt	8 Brake servo pushrod	15 Piston guide
2 Seat assembly	9 Reaction disc	16 Filter retainer
3 Front shell	10 Washer	17 Dust cover
4 Seal	11 Filter	18 Rear shell
5 Valve assembly	12 Castellated washer	19 Diaphragm
6 Pushrod assembly	13 Stop key	20 Diaphragm plate
7 Dished washer	14 Seal	21 Spring

brake pedal to pushrod clevis pin. Lift away the clevis pin and the bushes.

4 Undo and remove the nuts and spring washers that secure the servo unit mounting bracket to the bulkhead. Lift away the servo unit and bracket (Fig. 9.28).

5 Undo and remove the four nuts and spring washers that secure the bracket to the servo unit.

6 Refitting the servo unit is the reverse sequence to removal. It will be necessary to bleed the brake hydraulic system as described in Section 2.

20 Vacuum servo unit - dismantling, inspection and reassembly

Note: *Before dismantling the brake servo for major repair, ensure that service parts are available from your Ford dealer.*

Thoroughly clean the outside of the unit using a stiff brush and wipe with a non-fluffy rag. It cannot be too strongly emphasised that cleanliness is important when working on the servo. Before any attempt is made to dismantle, refer to Fig. 9.29. where it will be seen that two items of equipment are required. Firstly, a base plate must be made to enable the unit to be safely held in a vice. Secondly, a lever must be made similar to the form shown. Without these items it is impossible to dismantle satisfactorily.

To dismantle the unit proceed as follows:

1 Refer to Fig. 9.29 and, using a file or scriber, make a line across the two halves of the unit to act as a datum for alignment.

2 Fit the previously made base plate into a firm vice and attach the unit to the plate using the master cylinder studs.

3 Fit the lever to the four studs on the rear shell as shown in Fig. 9.29.

4 Use a piece of long rubber hose and connect one end to the adaptor on the engine inlet manifold and the other end to the non-return valve. Start the engine and this will create a vacuum in the unit so drawing the two halves together.

5 Rotate the lever in an anti-clockwise direction until the front shell indentations are in line with the recesses in the rim of the rear shell. Then press the lever assembly down firmly whilst an assistant stops the engine and quickly removes the vacuum pipe from the inlet manifold connector. Depress the operating rod so as to release the vacuum, whereupon the front and rear halves should part. If necessary, use a soft faced hammer and lightly tap the front half to break the bond.

6 Lift away the rear shell followed by the diaphragm return spring, the dust cap, end cap and the filter. Also withdraw the diaphragm. Press down the valve rod and shake out the valve retaining plate. Then separate the valve rod assembly from the diaphragm plate.

7 Gently ease the spring washer from the diaphragm plate and withdraw the pushrod and reaction disc.

8 The seal and plate assembly in the end of the front shell are a press fit. It is recommended that, unless the seal is to be renewed, they be left in situ.

9 Thoroughly clean all parts. Inspect all parts for signs of damage, stripped threads etc., and obtain new parts as necessary. All seals should be renewed and for this a 'Major Repair Kit' should be purchased. This kit will also contain two separate greases which must be used as directed and not interchanged.

10 To reassemble first smear the seal and bearing with Ford grease numbered 64949008 EM-1C-14 and refit the rear shell positioning it such that the flat face of the seal is towards the bearing. Press into position and refit the retainer.

11 Lightly smear the disc and hydraulic pushrod with Ford grease number 64949008 EM-1C-14. Refit the reaction disc and pushrod to the diaphragm plate and press in the large spring washer. The small spring washer supplied in the 'Major Repair

Kit' is not required. It is important that the length of the push-rod is not altered in any way and any attempt to move the abutment bolt will strip the threads. If a new hydraulic pushrod has been required, the length will have to be reset. Details of this operation are given at the end of this Section.

12 Lightly smear the outer diameter of the diaphragm plate neck and the bearing surfaces of the valve plunger with Ford grease number 64949008 EM-1C-14. Carefully fit the valve rod assembly into the neck of the diaphragm and fix with the retaining plate.

13 Fit the diaphragm into position and also the non-return valve to the front shell. Next smear the seal and plate assembly with Ford grease numbered 64949008 EM-1C-15 and press into the front shell with the plate facing inwards.

14 Fit the front shell to the baseplate and the lever to the rear shell. Reconnect the vacuum hose to the non-return valve and the adaptor on the engine inlet manifold. Position the diaphragm return spring in the front shell. Lightly smear the outer head of the diaphragm with Ford grease numbered 64949008 EM-1C-14 and locate the diaphragm assembly in the rear shell. Position the rear shell assembly on the return spring and line up the previously made scribe marks.

15 The assistant should start the engine. Watching one's fingers very carefully, press the two halves of the unit together and, using the lever tool, turn clockwise to lock the two halves together. Stop the engine and disconnect the hose.

16 Press a new filter into the neck of the diaphragm plate, refit the end cap and position the dust cover onto the special lugs of the rear shell.

17 Hydraulic pushrod adjustment only applies if a new pushrod has been fitted. It will be seen from Fig. 9.30 that there is a bolt (1) screwed into the end of the pushrod. The amount of protrusion has to be adjusted in the following manner: Remove the bolt and coat the threaded portion with Loctite Grade B. Reconnect the vacuum hose to the adaptor on the inlet valve and non-return valve. Start the engine and screw the prepared bolt into the end of the pushrod. Adjust the position of the bolt head so that it is 0.011 to 0.016 inch (0.28 to 0.40 mm) below the face of the front shell as shown by dimension A in Fig. 9.31. Leave the unit for a minimum of 24 hours to allow the Loctite to set hard.

18 Refit the servo unit to the car as described in the previous Section. To test the servo unit for correct operation after overhaul, first start the engine and run for a minimum period of two minutes and then switch off. Wait for ten minutes and apply the footbrake very carefully, listening to hear the rush of air into the servo unit. This will indicate that vacuum was retained and, therefore, operating correctly.

---

21 Stop light switch - removal and replacement

Up to 1973 models

1   Open the bonnet; for safety reasons disconnect the battery.
2   Undo and remove the screw and annulus that holds the two

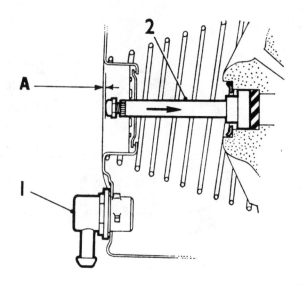

Fig. 9.31. The correct pushrod setting (Sec. 20)

A   *Pushrod setting to 0.011 - 0.016 in. (0.28 - 0.40 mm)*
1   *Vacuum applied   2   Pushrod against reaction disc*

halves of the steering column shroud together. Using a sharp knife split the two halves of the column shroud and lift away.

3   Undo and remove the crosshead screws that secure the facia panel to the instrument panel. Lift away the facia panel.

4   Undo and remove the screws that secure the instrument cluster to the instrument panel by a sufficient amount to give access to the rear. Detach the wiring loom multi-pin connector and the speedometer drive cable. Lift away the instrument cluster.

5   Detach the electric cables from the switch. Undo and remove the switch locknut and remove the switch.

6   Refitting the switch is the reverse sequence to removal.

Post 1973 models

7   The facia need not be removed from these models as the switch can be reached from underneath the dashboard.

22 Fault diagnosis - braking system

Symptom	Cause	Remedy
Pedal travels almost to floor before brakes operate	Brake fluid level too low	Top up master cylinder reservoir. Check for leaks
	Caliper leaking	Dismantle caliper, clean, fit new seals and bleed brakes
	Master cylinder leaking (bubbles in master cylinder fluid)	Dismantle master cylinder, clean and fit new seals. Bleed brakes
	Brake flexible hose leaking	Examine and fit new hose if old hose leaking Bleed brakes
	Brake line fractured	Replace with new brake pipe. Bleed brakes
	Brake system unions loose	Check all unions in brake system and tighten as necessary. Bleed brakes
	Pad or shoe linings over 75% worn	Fit replacement pads or shoes
Brake pedal feels springy	New linings not yet bedded-in	Use brakes gently until springy pedal feeling disappears
	Brake discs or drums badly worn or cracked	Fit new brake discs or drums
	Master cylinder securing nuts loose	Tighten master cylinder securing nuts. Ensure spring washers are fitted
Brake pedal feels spongy and soggy	Caliper or wheel cylinder leaking	Dismantle caliper or wheel cylinder, clean, fit new seals and bleed brakes
	Master cylinder leaking (bubbles in master cylinder reservoir)	Dismantle master cylinder, clean and fit new seals and bleed brakes. Replace cylinder if internal walls scored
	Brake pipe line or flexible hose leaking	Fit new pipeline or hose
	Unions in brake system loose	Examine for leaks, tighten as necessary
Excessive effort required to brake car	Pad or shoe linings badly worn	Fit replacement brake shoes and linings
	New pads or shoes recently fitted - not yet bedded-in	Use brakes gently until braking effort normal
	Harder linings fitted than standard causing increase in pedal pressure	Remove pads or shoes and replace with normal units
	Linings and brake drums contaminated with oil, grease or hydraulic fluid	Rectify source of leak, clean brake drums, fit new linings
Brakes uneven and pulling to one side	Linings and discs or drums contaminated with oil, grease or hydraulic fluid	Ascertain and rectify source of leak, clean discs or drums, fit new pads or shoes
	Tyre pressures unequal	Check and inflate as necessary
	Radial ply tyres fitted at one end of the car only	Fit radial ply tyres of the same make to all four wheels
	Brake caliper loose	Tighten backplate securing nuts and bolts
	Brake pads or shoes fitted incorrectly	Remove and fit correct way round
	Different type of linings fitted at each wheel	Fit the pads or shoes specified by the manufacturer all round
	Anchorages for front suspension or rear suspension loose	Tighten front and rear suspension pick-up points
	Brake discs or drums badly worn, cracked or distorted	Fit new brake discs or drums

Chapter 10 Electrical system

Contents

Specifications

Battery

Type	Lead acid 12 volt, negative (−) earth

	Capacity at 20 hr. rate	Plates per cell
Standard (a)	38 amp/hr	9
Optional (b)	44 amp/hr	9
(c)	55 amp/hr	11
(d)	66 amp/hr	13
Specific gravity charged	1.270 - 1.290 at temperature of 25°C (77°F)	

Starter motor

Type	Pre-engaged
Model:	
C	Lucas M 35 G
D	Lucas M 35 J
E and F	Lucas M 100

	M 35 G	M 100 and M 35 J
Number of brushes	4	4
Brush material	Carbon	Carbon
Min. brush length	0.35 in (9.0 mm)	0.38 in (9.5 mm)
Brushes spring pressure	30 oz (850 gm)	17 oz (480 gm)
Commutator min. diameter	1.338 in (34 mm)	—
Armature endfloat	0.004 - 0.012 in (0.1 - 0.3 mm)	0.004 - 0.012 in (0.1 - 0.3 mm)
Type of drive	Solenoid	Solenoid
Number of pinion gear teeth	10	10
Number of flywheel ring teeth	135	135
Direction of rotation	Clockwise	Clockwise
Maximum output	650 watts	750 watts (M 100); 700w (M 35 J)
Voltage	12	12

Alternator

Type	Lucas type 15 ACR or 17 ACR or Bosch type 28 GI or 35A-KI	
	Lucas 15 ACR	**Lucas 17 ACR**
Rotation	Clockwise	
Output (6000 rpm)	34 amps	36 amps
No. of poles	12	
Stator phases	3	
Max. continuous speed (rpm)	12500	
Stator winding resistance (ohms)	0.133	
Rotor winding resistance (ohms @ 20°C)	4.33 ± 5%	4.165 ± 5%
Slip ring end brushes (length)	½ in (13 mm)	
Regulating voltage	14.0 to 14.4 volts	
	Bosch 28 GI	**Bosch 35A - KI**
Rotation	Clockwise	
Minimum length of brushes	9/16 in (14.0 mm)	
Minimum diameter of slip rings	1 ¼ in (31.5 mm)	
Maximum current	28 amp	35 amp
Speed (ratio to engine)	1 : 1.9	

Torque wrench settings

	lb f ft	kg f m
Alternator pulley nut	29	4.0

1 General description

The electrical system is of the 12 volt negative earth type and the major components comprise a 12 volt battery of which the negative terminal is earthed, an alternator which is driven from the crankshaft pulley, and a starter motor.

The battery supplies a steady amount of current for the ignition, lighting and other electrical circuits and provides a reserve of electricity when the current consumed by the electrical equipment exceeds that being produced by the alternator.

The alternator has its own integral regulator which ensures a high output if the battery is in a low state of charge or the demand from the electrical equipment is high, and a low output if the battery is fully charged and there is little demand for the electrical equipment.

When fitting electrical accessories to cars with a negative earth system it is important, if they contain silicone diodes or transistors, that they are connected correctly, otherwise serious damage may result to the components concerned. Items such as radios, tape players, electronic ignition systems, electronic tachometer, automatic dipping etc, should all be checked for correct polarity.

It is important that the battery positive lead is always disconnected if the battery is to be boost charged, also if body repairs are to be carried out using electric arc welding equipment - the alternator must be disconnected otherwise serious damage can be caused to the more delicate instruments. Whenever the battery has to be disconnected it must always be reconnected with the negative terminal earthed.

2 Battery - removal and refitting

1 The battery is on a carrier fitted to the left-hand wing valance of the engine compartment. It should be removed once every three months for cleaning and testing. Disconnect the positive and then the negative leads from the battery terminals by undoing and removing the plated nuts and bolts (photo). Note that two cables are attached to the positive terminal.

2 Unscrew and remove the bolt, and plain washer that secures the battery clamp plate to the carrier. Lift away the clamp plate. Carefully lift the battery from its carrier and hold it vertically to ensure that none of the electrolyte is spilled.

3 Replacement is a direct reversal of this procedure. **Note:** Replace the negative lead before the positive lead and smear the terminals with petroleum jelly to prevent corrosion. **Never use**

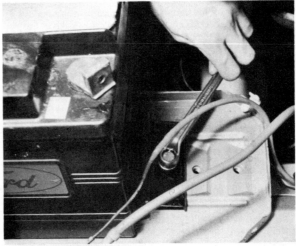

2.1 Removing battery clamp plate

an ordinary grease.

3   Battery - maintenance and inspection

1   Normal weekly battery maintenace consists of checking the electrolyte level of each cell to ensure that the separators are covered by ¼ inch (6 mm) of electrolyte. If the level has fallen, top-up the battery using distilled water only. Do not overfill. If a battery is overfilled or any electrolyte spilled, immediately wipe away the excess as electrolyte attacks and corrodes any metal it comes into contact with very rapidly.
2   If the battery has the 'Auto-fil' device as fitted on original production of the car, a special topping-up sequence is required. The white balls in the Auto-fil battery are part of the automatic topping-up device which ensures correct electrolyte level. The vent chamber should remain in position at all times except when topping-up or taking specific gravity readings. If the electrolyte level in any of the cells is below the bottom of the filling tube top up as follows:

  a) *Lift off the vent chamber cover.*
  b) *With the battery level, pour distilled water into the trough until all the filling tubes and trough are full.*
  c) *Immediately replace the cover to allow the water in the trough and tubes to flow into the cells. Each cell will automatically receive the correct amount of water.*

3   As well as keeping the terminals clean and covered with petroleum jelly, the top of the battery, and especially the top of the cells, should be kept clean and dry. This helps prevent corrosion and ensures that the battery does not become partially discharged by leakage through dampness and dirt.
4   Once every three months remove the battery and inspect the battery securing bolts, the battery clamp plate, tray and battery leads for corrosion (white fluffy deposits on the metal which are brittle to touch). If any corrosion is found clean off the deposit with ammonia and paint over the clean metal with an anti-rust/anti-acid paint.
5   At the same time inspect the battery case for cracks. If a crack is found, clean and plug it with one of the proprietary compounds marketed by such firms as Holts for this purpose. If leakage through the crack has been excessive then it will be necessary to refill the appropriate cell with fresh electrolyte as detailed later. Cracks are frequently caused to the top of the battery case by pouring in distilled water in the middle of winter *after* instead of *before* a run. This gives the water no chance to mix with the electrolyte and so the former freezes and splits the battery case.
6   If topping up the battery becomes excessive and the case has been inspected for cracks that could cause leakage, but none are found, the battery is being overcharged.
7   With the battery on the bench at the three monthly interval check, measure the specific gravity with a hydrometer to determine the state of charge and condition of the electrolyte. There should be very little variation between the different cells and, if a variation in excess of 0.025 is present it will be due to either:

  a) *Loss of electrolyte from the battery at some time caused by spillage or a leak, resulting in a drop in the specific gravity of the electrolyte when the deficiency was replaced with distilled water instead of fresh electrolyte.*
  b) *An internal short circuit caused by buckling of the plates or similar malady pointing to the likelihood of total battery failure in the near future.*

8   The specific gravity of the electrolyte for fully charged conditions, at the electrolyte temperature indicated, is listed in Table A. The specific gravity of a fully discharged battery at different temperatures of the electrolyte is given in Table B.

Table A - Specific gravity - battery fully charged

1.268 at 100°F or 38°C electrolyte temperature
1.272 at 90°F or 32°C electrolyte temperature
1.276 at 80°F or 27°C electrolyte temperature
1.280 at 70°F or 21°C electrolyte temperature
1.284 at 60°F or 16°C electrolyte temperature
1.288 at 50°F or 10°C electrolyte temperature
1.292 at 40°F or 4°C electrolyte temperature
1.296 at 30°F or -1.5°C electrolyte temperature

Table B - Specific gravity - battery fully discharged

1.098 at 100°F or 38°C electrolyte temperature
1.102 at 90°F or 32°C electrolyte temperature
1.106 at 80°F or 27°C electrolyte temperature
1.110 at 70°F or 21°C electrolyte temperature
1.114 at 60°F or 16°C electrolyte temperature
1.118 at 50°F or 10°C electrolyte temperature
1.122 at 40°F or 4°C electrolyte temperature
1.126 at 30°F or -1.5°C electrolyte temperature

4   Battery - electrolyte replenishment

1   If the battery is in a fully charged state and one of the cells maintains a specific gravity reading which is 0.025 or more lower than the others and a check of each cell has been made with a voltage meter to check for short circuits (a four to seven second test should give a steady reading of between 1.2 and 1.8 volts), then it is likely that electrolyte has been lost from the cell with the low reading at some time.
2   Top-up the cell with a solution of 1 part sulphuric acid to 2.5 parts of water. If the cell is already fully topped-up draw some electrolyte out of it with a pipette.

5   Battery   charging

1   In winter time when heavy demand is placed upon the battery, such as when starting from cold and much electrical equipment is continually in use, it is a good idea to occasionally have the battery fully charged from an external source at the rate of 3.5 to 4 amps.
2   Continue to charge the battery at this rate until no further rise in specific gravity is noted over a four hour period.
3   Alternatively, a trickle charger charging at the rate of 1.5 amps can be safety used overnight.
4   Specially rapid 'boost' charges which are claimed to restore the power of the battery in 1 to 2 hours are most dangerous as they can cause serious damage to the battery plates through overheating.
5   While charging the battery note that the temperature of the electrolyte should never exceed 100°F (37.8°C).

6   Alternator - general description

The main advantage of an alternator lies in its ability to provide a high charge at low revolutions. Driving slowly in heavy traffic with a dynamo invariably means no charge is reaching the battery. In similar conditons even with the wiper, heater, lights and perhaps radio switched on the alternator will ensure a charge reaches the battery.
An important feature of the Lucas alternator is a built in output control regulator, based on 'thick film' hybrid integrated micro-circuit technique, which results in the alternator being a self contained generating and control unit.
The system provides for direct connection of a charge indicator light, and eliminates the need for a field switching relay or warning light control unit, necessary with former systems.
The alternator is of rotating field, ventilated design. It comprises, principally, a laminated stator on which is wound a star

connected 3-phase output winding; a twelve pole rotor carrying the field windings - each end of the rotor shaft runs in ball race bearings which are lubricated for life; natural finish aluminium die cast end brackets, incorporating the mounting lugs; a rectifier pack for converting the AC output of the machine to DC for battery charging; and an output control regulator.

The rotor is belt driven from the engine through a pulley keyed to the rotor shaft. A pressed steel fan adjacent to the pulley draws cooling air through the machine. This fan forms an integral part of the alternator specification. It has been designed to provide adequate air flow with a minimum of noise, and to withstand the high stresses associated with the maximum speed. Rotation is clockwise viewed on the drive end. Maximum continuous rotor speed is 12500 rpm.

Recitification of an alternator output is achieved by six silicone diodes housed in a rectifier pack and connected as a 3-phase full wave bridge. The rectifier pack is attached to the outer face of the slip ring end bracket and contains also three

'field' diodes; at normal operating speeds, rectified current from the stator output windings flow through these diodes to provide the self excitation of the rotor field, via brushes bearing on face type slip rings.

The slip rings are carried on a small diameter moulded drum attached to the rotor shaft outboard of the slip ring end bearing. The inner ring is centred on the rotor shaft axle, while the outer ring has a mean diameter of ¾ inch approximately. By keeping the mean diameter of the slip rings to a minimum relative speeds between brushes and rings, and hence wear, are also minimal. The slip rings are connected to the rotor field winding by wires carried in grooves in the rotor shaft.

The brush gear is housed in a moulding screwed to the outside of the slip ring and bracket. This moulding thus encloses the slip ring and brush gear assembly, and together with the shielded bearing, protects the assembly against the entry of dust and moisture.

The regulator is set during manufacture and requires no

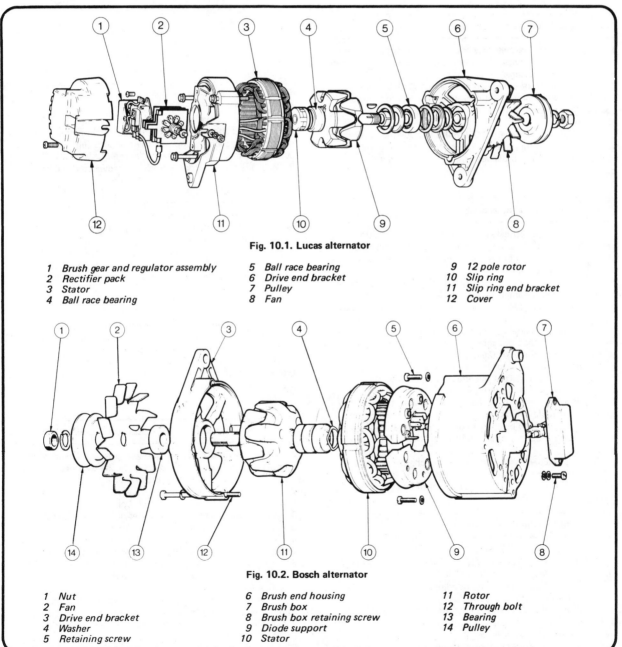

Fig. 10.1. Lucas alternator

1 Brush gear and regulator assembly	5 Ball race bearing	9 12 pole rotor
2 Rectifier pack	6 Drive end bracket	10 Slip ring
3 Stator	7 Pulley	11 Slip ring end bracket
4 Ball race bearing	8 Fan	12 Cover

Fig. 10.2. Bosch alternator

1 Nut	6 Brush end housing	11 Rotor
2 Fan	7 Brush box	12 Through bolt
3 Drive end bracket	8 Brush box retaining screw	13 Bearing
4 Washer	9 Diode support	14 Pulley
5 Retaining screw	10 Stator	

further attention. Briefly, the 'thick film' regulator comprises resistors and conductors screen printed onto a 1 inch square alumina substrate. Mounted on the substrate are Lucas semiconductor dice consisting of three transistors, a voltage reference diode and a field recirculation diode, and also two capacitors. The internal connections between these components and the substrate are made by special Lucas patented connectors. The whole assembly is 0.0625 inch (1.588 mm) thick, and is housed in a recess in an aluminium heat sink, which is attached to the slip ring and bracket. Complete hermetic sealing is achived by a silicone rubber encapsulant to provide environmental protection.

Electrical connections to external circuits are brought out to Lucar connector blades, these being grouped to accept a moulded connector socket which ensures correct connection.

The Bosch alternator operates on the same principles as the Lucas alternator and only differs in design as may be seen when Fig. 10.1 and Fig. 10.2 are compared.

7 Alternator - routine maintenance

1   The equipment has been designed for the minimum amount of maintenance in service, the only items subject to wear being the brushes and bearings.
2   Brushes should be examined after about 75,000 miles (120,000 km) and renewed if necessary. The bearings are prepacked with grease for life, and should not require further attention.
3   Check the fan belt every 3,000 miles (5,000 km) for correct adjustment which should be 0.5 inch (13 mm) total movement at the centre of the run between the alternator and water pump pulleys.

8 Alternator - special procedures

Whenever the electrical system of the car is being attended to or external means of starting the engine are used, there are certain precautions that must be taken otherwise serious and expensive damage can result.
1   Always make sure that the negative terminal of the battery is earthed. If the terminal connections are accidentally reversed or if the battery has been reverse charged the alternator diodes will burn out.
2   The output terminal on the alternator marked 'BAT' or B+ must never be earthed but should always be connected directly to the positive terminal of the battery.
3   Whenever the alternator is to be removed or when disconnecting the terminals of the alternator circuit always disconnect the battery earth terminal first.
4   The alternator must never be operated without the battery to alternator cable connected.
5   If the battery is to be charged by external means always disconnect both battery cables before the external charge is connected.
6   Should it be necessary to use a booster charger or booster battery to start the engine always double check that the negative cable is connected to negative terminal and the positive cable to positive terminal.

9 Alternator - removal and refitting

1   Disconnect the battery leads.
2   Note the terminal connections at the rear of the alternator and disconnect the plug or multi pin connector.
3   Undo and remove the alternator adjustment arm bolt, slacken the alternator mounting bolts and push the alternator inwards towards the engine. Lift away the fan belt from the pulley.
4   Remove the remaining two mounting bolts and carefully lift the alternator away from the car.
5   Take care not to knock or drop the alternator otherwise this

can cause irreparable damage.
6   Refitting the alternator is the reverse sequence to removal. Adjust the fan belt so that it has 0.5 inch (13 mm) total movement at the centre of the run between the alternator and water pump pulleys.

10 Alternator - fault finding and repair

Due to the specialist knowledge and equipment required to test or service an alternator it is recommended that if the performance is suspect, the car be taken to an automobile electrician who will have the facilities for such work. Because of this recommendation, information is limited to the inspection and renewal of the brushes. Should the alternator not charge or the system be suspect the following points may be checked before seeking further assistance:
1   Check the fan belt tension, as described in Section 7.
2   Check the battery, as described in Section 3.
3   Check all electrical cable connections for cleanliness and security.

11 Alternator brushes (Lucas) - inspection, removal and refitting

1   Refer to Fig. 10.1 and undo and remove the two screws that hold on the end cover. Lift away the end cover.
2   To inspect the brushes correctly the brush holder moulding should be removed by undoing the two securing bolts and disconnecting the 'Lucar' connector to the diode plates.
3   With the brush holder moulding removed and the brush assemblies still in position check that they protrude from the face of the moulding by at least 0.2 inch (5 mm). Also check that when depressed, the spring pressure is 7 - 10 oz (198 -283 gms) when the end of the brush is flush with the face of the brush moulding. To be done with any accuracy this requires a push type spring scale.
4   Should either of the foregoing requirements not be fulfilled the spring assemblies must be renewed. This can be done by simply removing the holding screws of each assembly and replacing them.
5   With the brush holder moulding removed the slip rings on the face end of the rotor are exposed. These can be cleaned with a petrol soaked cloth and any signs of burning may be removed very carefully with fine glass paper. On no account should any other abrasive be used or any attempt at machining be made.
6   Reassemble in the reverse order of dismantling. Make sure that leads which may have been connected to any of the screws are reconnected correctly.

12 Alternator brushes (Bosch) - inspection, removal and refitting

1   Undo and remove the two screws, spring and plain washers that secure the brush box to the rear of the brush end housing (see Fig. 10.2). Lift away the brush box.
2   Check that the carbon brushes are able to slide smoothly in their guides without any sign of binding.
3   Measure the length of the brushes and if they have worn down to 0.35 inch (9 mm) or less, they must be renewed.
4   Hold the brush wire with a pair of engineer's pliers and unsolder it from the brush box. Lift away the two brushes.
5   Insert the new brushes and check to make sure that they are free to move in their guides. If they bind, lightly polish with a very fine file.
6   Solder the brush wire ends to the brush box taking care that solder is allowed to pass to the stranded wire.
7   Whenever new brushes are fitted new springs should be fitted.
8   Refitting the brush box is the reverse sequence to removal.

13 Starter motor - general description

The starter motor fitted to engines covered by this manual is of the pre-engaged type and of Lucas manufacture.

The 'C' type as shown in Fig. 10.3 is a series parallel wound four pole, four brush motor fitted with a pre-engagement solenoid. Incorporated in the pinion assembly is a roller clutch which is able to transmit torque from the starter motor to the engine but not in the reverse direction thereby ensuring that the armature is not driven by the engine at any time.

The solenoid comprises a soft iron plunger, starter switch contacts, main closing winding (series winding) and a hold on (short winding). When the starter ignition switch is operated both the coils are energised in parallel but the closing winding is shorted out by the starter switch contacts when they are closed.

The 'D' type starter motor is basically identical to the 'C' type. The operating position of the engaging lever in the drive end bracket is pre-set and cannot be altered. This eliminates the adjustment of setting the pinion position to obtain the correct operation of the actuating solenoid. The lever pivots on a non-adjustable pivot pin which is retained in the drive end bracket by a special type of retaining ring which is a spring fit into a groove in the pin.

The 'E' type starter motor is basically identical to the 'D' type with the exception that the solenoid is slightly larger and a different commutator end plate is fitted.

14 Starter motor - testing on engine

1 If the starter motor fails to operate then check the condition of the battery by turning on the headlamps. If they glow brightly for several seconds and then gradually dim the battery is in an uncharged condition.

2 If the headlights continue to glow brightly and it is obvious that the battery is in good condition, then check the tightness of the battery wiring connections (and in particular the earth lead from the battery terminal to its connection on the body frame). If the positive terminal on the battery becomes hot when an attempt is made to work the starter this is a sure sign of a poor connection on the battery terminal. To rectify remove the terminal, clean the mating faces thoroughly and reconnect. Check the connections on the starter solenoid. Check the wiring with a voltmeter or test lamp for breaks or shorts.

3 Test the continuity of the solenoid windings by connecting a test lamp circuit comprising a 12 volt battery and low wattage bulb between the 'STA' terminal and the solenoid body. If the two windings are in order the lamp will light. Next connect the test lamp (fitted with a high wattage bulb) between the solenoid main terminals. Energise the solenoid by applying a 12 volt supply between the unmarked 'Lucar' terminal and the solenoid body. The solenoid should be heard to operate and the test bulb light. This indicates full closure of the solenoid contacts.

4 If the battery is fully charged, the wiring in order, and the starter/ignition switch working and the starter motor still fails to operate then it will have to be removed from the car for examination. Before this is done ensure that the starter motor pinion has not jammed in mesh with the flywheel by engaging a gear (not automatic) and rocking the car to-and-fro. This should free the pinion if it is stuck in mesh with the flywheel teeth.

15 Starter motor - removal and installation

1 Disconnect the positive and negative terminals from the battery.

2 Make a note of the cable connections to the front of the solenoid and detach the cables.

3 Undo and remove the starter motor securing nuts, bolts and

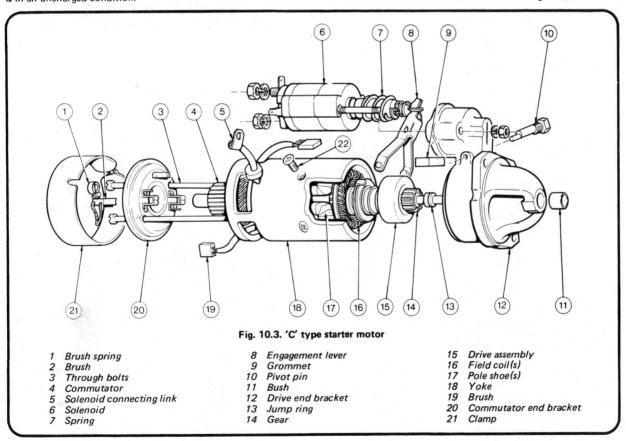

Fig. 10.3. 'C' type starter motor

1	Brush spring	8	Engagement lever	15	Drive assembly
2	Brush	9	Grommet	16	Field coil(s)
3	Through bolts	10	Pivot pin	17	Pole shoe(s)
4	Commutator	11	Bush	18	Yoke
5	Solenoid connecting link	12	Drive end bracket	19	Brush
6	Solenoid	13	Jump ring	20	Commutator end bracket
7	Spring	14	Gear	21	Clamp

spring washers and lift away the starter motor.

4   Refitting is the reverse sequence to removal.

16 Starter motor (Type C) - dismantling and reassembly

1   With the starter motor on the bench, loosen the screw on the cover band and slip the cover band off (Fig. 10.3). With a piece of bent wire in the shape of a hook lift back each of the brush springs in turn and check the movement of the brushes in their holders by pulling on the flexible connectors. If the brushes are so worn that their faces do not rest against the commutator or if the ends of the brush leads are exposed on their working faces they must be renewed.

2   If any of the brushes tend to stick in their holders then wipe them with a petrol moistened cloth and if necessary, lightly polish the sides of the brushes with a very fine file, until the brushes move quite freely in their holders.

3   Undo the large nut holding the heavy duty cable to the lower solenoid terminal (marked STA). Remove the nut, spring washer and cable connector.

4   Undo and remove the nuts and spring washers that secure the solenoid to the drive end bracket. Carefully withdraw the solenoid from its mounting. It will be observed that the plunger will be left attached to the engagement lever.

5   Lift the plunger return spring from the plunger and put it in a safe place. Disengage the end of the plunger from the top of the engagement lever.

6   Undo the locknut securing the eccentric pivot pin to the starter motor body. This will be found towards the top of the drive end bracket. Unscrew the eccentric pivot pin.

7   Unscrew and remove the two through bolts and spring washers from the rear of the commutator end bracket which will release the yoke from the end bracket. With a scriber mark the relative position of the drive end bracket and yoke. To separate the two parts, using a soft faced hammer tap on the end bracket whilst holding the yoke.

8   Pull the commutator end bracket off the rear of the yoke. Lift off the steel thrust washer and fibre thrust washer from the spigot on the end of the commutator (if these washers are fitted). Also lift away the rubber grommet located at the top of the yoke and commutator end bracket.

9   Carefully withdraw the armature with the drive pinion assembly and engagement lever from the fixing bracket.

10   If it is necessary to dismantle the starter pinion drive, place the armature between soft faces in a bench vice and using a universal puller draw the jump ring from the armature.

11   Tap down the circlip retaining cover and remove the washer, circlip and cover. The pinion assembly may now be removed.

12   Draw the actuating bush towards the pinion so as to expose the circlip and remove the circlip, bush, spring and large washer. It is very important that the one way clutch is not gripped in the vice at the point adjacent to the pinion whilst this is being carried out otherwise the clutch will be damaged.

13   The drive pinion and one way clutch are serviced as a complete assembly so if one part is worn or damaged a new assembly must be obtained.

14   At this stage if the brushes are to be renewed, their flexible connectors must be cut leaving 0.25 inch (7 mm) attached to the field coils. Discard the old brushes. Solder new brushes to the flexible connector stubs. Check that the new brushes move freely in their holders as described in paragraph 2.

15   If cleaning the commutator with petrol fails to remove all the burnt areas and spots, then wrap a piece of glass paper round the commutator and rotate the armature.

16   If the commutator is very badly worn remove the drive gear, (if still in place on the armature), and mount the armature in a lathe. With the lathe turning at high speed take a very fine cut-out of the commutator and finish the surface by polishing with glass paper. **Do not undercut the mica insulators between the commutator segments.**

17   With the starter motor dismantled test the four field coils for

an open circuit. Connect a 12 volt battery with a 12 volt bulb in one of the leads between the field terminal post and the tapping point of the field coils to which the brushes are connected. An open circuit is proved by the bulb not lighting.

18   If the bulb lights, it does not necessarily mean that the field coils are in order, as there is a possibility that one of the coils will be earthed to the starter yoke or pole shoes. To check this, remove the lead from the brush connector and place it against a clean portion of the starter yoke. If the bulb lights then the field coils are earthing. Replacement of the field coils calls for the use of a wheel operated screwdriver, a soldering iron, caulking and riveting operations and is beyond the scope of the majority of owners. The starter yoke should be taken to a reputable electrical engineering works for new field coils to be fitted. Alternatively purchase an exchange Lucas starter motor.

19   If the armature is damaged this will be evident after visual inspection. Look for signs of burning, discoloration, and for conductors that have lifted away from the commutator.

20   Reassembly is the reverse sequence to dismantling but it will be necessary to adjust the pinion movement.

21   Once the starter motor has been completely reassembled, test for correct operation by securing it in a vice and connecting a heavy gauge cable between the starter motor solenoid lower terminal and a 12 volt battery. Connect the cable from the other battery terminal to earth on the starter motor body. If the motor turns at high speed it is in good order.

22   Disconnect the heavy duty cable from the lower terminal marked 'STS' and by referring to Fig. 10.4 connect a 12 volt battery to the starter motor as shown. Do not make the final battery connection yet.

23   Undo but do not remove the eccentric pin locknut on the side of the fixing bracket. Then screw the eccentric pin fully.

24   Connect the final battery connection so energising the solenoid pull in winding and hold in winding which will, via the engaging lever, move the pinion to its engagement position.

25   Refer to Fig. 10.4 and locate a feeler gauge between the pinion and thrust washer. With the fingers gently press the pinion towards the motor, so that any lost motion in the linkage may be taken up.

26   With a screwdriver rotate the eccentric pin until the gap is between 0.005 - 0.150 inch (0.13 - 3.8 mm). Finally tighten the eccentric pin locknut.

17 Starter motor bushes (Type C) - inspection, removal and refitting

1   With the starter motor stripped down check the condition of the bushes. They should be renewed when they are sufficiently worn to allow visible side movement of the armature shaft.

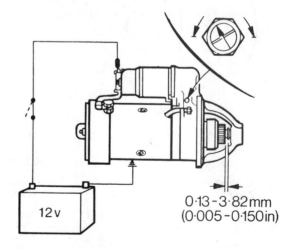

12v   0.13 - 3.82mm (0.005 - 0.150in)

Fig. 10.4. Setting eccentric pin (Sec. 16)

2 The old bushes are simply driven out with a suitable drift and the new bushes inserted by the same method. As the bushes are of the phosphor bronze type it is essential that they are allowed to stand in engine oil for at least 24 hours before fitment. If times does not allow, place the bushes in oil at 100°C (212°F) for 2 hours.

18 Starter motor (Type D) - dismantling and reassembly

Due to the fact this starter motor uses a face commutator on which the brushes make contact end on, a certain amount of thrust is created on the armature at the commutator end. A

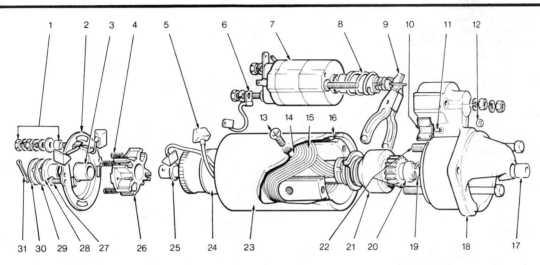

Fig. 10.5. 'D' type starter motor (Sec. 18)

1	Terminal nuts and washers	9	Engagement lever	17	Bush	25	Thrust washer
2	Commutator end bracket	10	Sleeve	18	Drive end bracket	26	Brush box moulding
3	Bush	11	Pivot pin	19	Jump ring	27	Screw
4	Spring	12	Washer	20	Collar	28	Thrust collar
5	Brush	13	Pole piece screw	21	Drive assembly	29	Washer (shim)
6	Terminal lead	14	Screw location	22	Bolts	30	Washer (plate)
7	Solenoid	15	Field coil	23	Yoke	31	Split pin
8	Return spring	16	Pole shoe	24	Commutator		

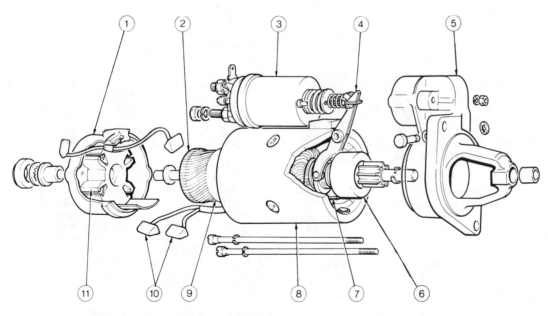

Fig. 10.6. 'E' and 'F' type starter motors (Sec. 19)

1	Commutator end bracket	5	Drive end bracket	9	Armature
2	Commutator	6	Drive assembly	10	Brush
3	Solenoid	7	Pole shoe	11	Brush box moulding
4	Engagement lever	8	Yoke		

thrust bearing is therefore incorporated at the commutator end. Dismantling, overhaul and reassembly is basically identical to that of the type 'C' as described in Section 16, but the following operations should be borne in mind during dismantling:

1   Remove the split pin from the rear end of the armature shaft and slide off the shims, washer and thrust plate (Fig. 10.5).
2   Remove the two screws which retain the end plate and pull off the end plate complete with brush holders and brushes.
3   Should the brushes have to be renewed because they have worn, follow the instructions given in Section 16, paragraph 14 with the exception that the brush flexible connectors must be unsoldered and not cut.
4   To remove the armature, long through bolts are not used to hold the commutator end bracket and drive end bracket to the yoke. Short bolts which screw into the yoke are used at each end.
5   Reassembling this starter motor is the reverse sequence to dismantling. The armature endfloat should be measured and if more than 0.010 inch (0.254 mm) with an 8 volt current activating the solenoid it must be corrected by fitting an appropriate size shim or shims between the thrust plate and split pin. Always fit a new split pin.
6   The engagement lever movement is not adjustable but is located by a straight pivot pin.

19 Starter motor (Types E and F) - dismantling and reassembly

Follow the instructions given in Sections 16 and 18 as these starter motors are basically identical to the 'D' type with the exception of the commutator end bracket and a larger solenoid. An exploded view of these motors is shown in Fig. 10.6.

20 Flasher circuit - fault tracing and rectification

1   The actual flasher unit consists of a small alloy container positioned at the rear of the instrument panel (Fig. 10.7).
2   If the flasher unit works twice as fast as usual when indicating either right or left turns, this is an indication that there is a broken filament in the front or rear indicator bulb on the side operating too quickly.
3   If the external flashers are working but the internal flasher warning light has ceased to function, check the filament of the warning bulb and replace as necessary.
4   With the aid of the wiring diagram check all the flasher circuit connections if a flasher bulb is sound but does not work.
5   With the ignition switched on check that the current is reaching the flasher unit by connecting a voltmeter between the 'plug' terminal and earth. If it is found that current is reaching the unit, connect the two flasher unit terminals together and operate the direction indicator switch. If one of the flasher warning lights comes on this proves that the flasher unit itself is at fault and must be replaced as it is not possible to dismantle and repair it.

21 Windscreen wiper mechanism - maintenance

1   Renew the windscreen wiper blades at intervals of 12,000 miles (20,000 km) or 12 months, or more frequently if found necessary.
2   The washer round the wheelbox spindle can be lubricated with several drops of glycerine every 6,000 miles (10,000 km). The windscreen wiper linkage pivots may be lubricated with a little engine oil.

22 Windscreen wiper blades - removal and refitting

1   Lift the wiper arm away from the windscreen and remove the old blade by turning it in towards the arm and then disengage the arm from the slot in the blade.

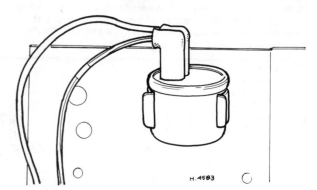

Fig. 10.7. Location of direction indicator flasher unit (Sec. 20)

2   To fit a new blade, slide the end of the wiper arm into the slotted spring fastening in the centre of the blade. Push the blade firmly onto the arm until the raised portion of the arm is fully home in the hole in the blade.

23 Windscreen wiper arms - removal and refitting

1   Before removing a wiper arm, turn the windscreen wiper switch on and off to ensure the arms are in their normal parked position parallel with the bottom of the windscreen.
2   To remove the arm, pivot the arm back and pull the wiper arm head off the splined drive. If the arm proves difficult to remove, a screwdriver with a long blade can be used to lever the wiper arm head off the splines. Care must be taken not to damage the splines.
3   When replacing an arm, position it so it is in the correct relative parked position and then press the arm head onto the splined drive until it is fully home on the splines.

24 Windscreen wiper mechanism - fault diagnosis and rectification

1   Should the windscreen wipers fail, or work very slowly, then check the terminals on the motor for loose connections and make sure the insulation of all wiring has not been damaged thus causing a short circuit. If this is in order then check the current the motor is taking by connecting an ammeter in the circuit and turning on the wiper switch. Consumption should be between 2.3 and 3.1 amps.
2   If no current is passing through the motor, check that the switch is operating correctly.
3   If the wiper motor takes a very high current check the wiper blades for freedom of movement. If this is satisfactory check the gearbox cover and gear assembly for damage.
4   If the motor takes a very low current ensure tha the battery is fully charged. Check the brush gear and ensure the brushes are bearing on the commutator. If not, check the brushes for freedom of movement and, if necessary, renew the tension springs. If the brushes are very worn, they should be replaced with new ones. Check the armature by substitution if this part is suspect.

25 Windscreen wiper linkage - removal and installation

1   For safety reasons disconnect the battery. Undo and remove the fixing screw and unclip the plastic wiper motor cover. Lift away the cover. (photo)
2   Undo and remove the bolts that secure the wiper assembly

mounting bracket to the scuttle panel; note that one of the bolts retains the earth wire terminal. Detach the multi-pin plug from the motor.

3   Carefully lever off the wiper system linkage from the windscreen wiper motor. Undo and remove the three bolts and spring washers that secure the motor to the bracket assembly (Fig. 10.8).

4   Undo and remove the bolts that secure the heater unit and draw the heater unit box to one side just sufficient for the wiper motor and bracket assembly to be withdrawn.

5   Refer to Section 23, and remove the wiper arms and blades.

6   Carefully unscrew the spindle nuts and washers and working within the engine compartment lift away the wiper linkage.

7   Refitting is the reverse sequence to removal. Lubricate all moving parts with the exception of the wiper spindles with engine oil. Lubricate the wiper spindles with three drops of glycerine.

26 Windscreen wiper motor - removal and refitting

1   Refer to Section 25 and follow the sequence described in paragraphs 1 to 3 inclusive.

2   Undo and remove the bolts that secure the heater hose and pull the heater box to one side. Lift away the windscreen wiper

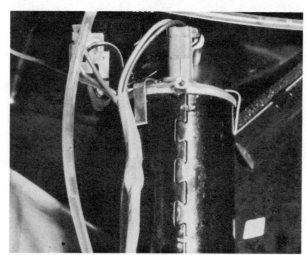

25.1 Windscreen wiper motor with plastic cover removed

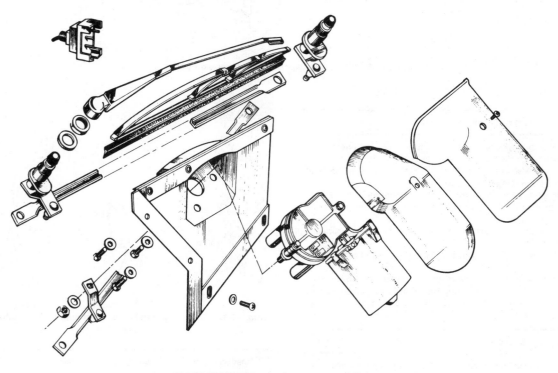

Fig. 10.8. Windscreen wiper motor and linkage

motor from the mounting bracket and the operating arm from the motor.

3   Refitting the windscreen wiper motor is the reverse sequence to removal.

27 Windscreen wiper motor - dismantling, inspection and reassembly

1   Refer to Fig. 10.9 and undo and remove the two crosshead screws that secure the gearbox cover plate to the gearbox.

2   Undo and remove the nut that secures the operating arm to the gear shaft. Lift away the operating arm, wave and plain

washers.

3   Release the spring clips that secure the case and armature to the gearbox. Lift away the case and armature.

4   Wipe away all the grease from inside the gearbox and using a pair of circlip pliers remove the circlip that secures the gear to the shaft. Separate the gear from the shaft.

5   Undo and remove the screw that secures the brush mounting plate, detach the wiring loom plug and remove the brushes.

6   Clean all parts and then inspect the gears and brushes for wear or damage. Refit the spindle and check for wear in its bush in the gearbox body. Obtain new parts as necessary.

7   Reassembly is the reverse sequence to dismantling. Pack the gearbox with grease.

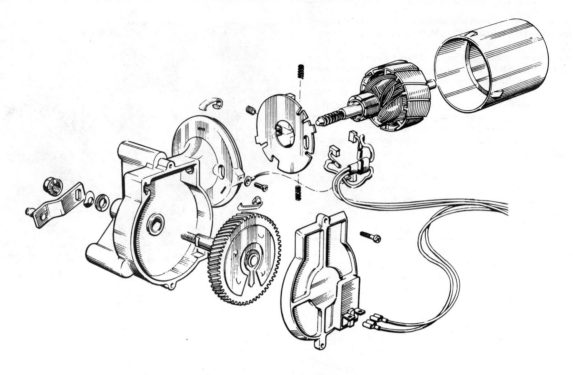

Fig. 10.9. Windscreen wiper motor component parts

28 Horn - fault tracing and rectification

1   If the horn works badly or fails completely, first check the
wiring leading to the horn for short circuits and loose
connections. Also check that the horn is firmly secured and that
there is nothing lying on the horn body.
2   Using a test lamp check the wiring to the number 5 fuse on
the fuse box located in the engine compartment. Check that the
fuse has not blown.
3   If the fault is an internal one it will be necessary to obtain a
replacement horn.
4   To remove the horn, disconnect the battery and remove the
radiator.
5   Detach the lead at the rear of the horn and then undo and
remove the retaining bolt, spring, horn bracket and star-washer.
6   Refitting the horn is the reverse sequence to removal.

29 Headlight assembly (circular type) - removal and refitting

1   Open the bonnet and for safety reasons disconnect the
battery.
2   Undo and remove the nine crosshead screws that secure the
radiator grille to the front body panels. Lift away the radiator
grille.
3   **Sealed beam unit:** Undo and remove the three inner bezel
retaining screws that secure the sealed beam unit to the backplate.
4   Carefully lift away the bezel and sealed beam unit. Detach
the plug from the rear of the sealed beam unit. Note the plug
also carries the side light bulb.
5   Fit the plug to the new sealed beam unit and refit the unit
and radiator grille, this being the reverse sequence to removal.
6   **Semi-sealed beam unit:** Detach the bulb holder from the lens
by rotating in an anticlockwise direction and pulling away the
bulb holder. Lift away the bulb (Fig. 10.10).
7   Refitting the new bulb and the radiator grille is the reverse
sequence to removal.

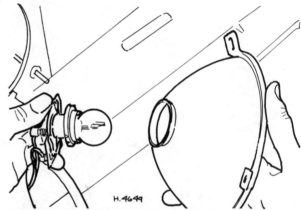

Fig. 10.10. Removing bulb holder from semi-sealed headlamp
(Sec. 29)

30 Headlight assembly (rectangular type) - removal and refitting

1   Open the bonnet, disconnect the battery leads and remove
the radiator grille.
2   Remove the single screw which secures the headlight unit to
the body (Fig. 10.11).
3   Pull the headlamp far enough forward to enable the bulb and
its holder to be detached from the rear of the reflector.
4   Refitting is a reversal of removal.

31 Headlight alignment

1   It is always advisable to have the headlights aligned using
special optical beam setting equipment but if this is not available
the following procedure may be used for single headlight units.
Models fitted with twin headlight units must be taken to the

Fig. 10.11. Rectangular type headlamp securing screw (Sec. 30)

Fig. 10.12. Removing rectangular type headlamp (Sec. 30)

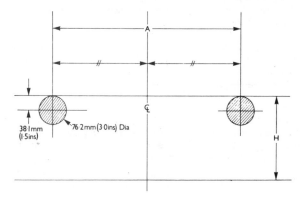

Fig. 10.13. Headlamp alignment (Sec. 31)

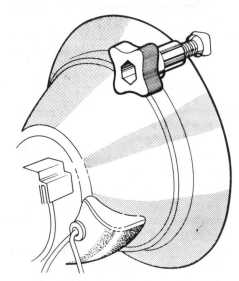

Fig. 10.14. Headlamp adjusters (Sec. 31)

local Ford garage.

2   Position the car on level ground, 10 ft (3 m) in front of a
dark wall or board. The wall or board must be at right angles to
the centre-line of the car.

3   Draw a vertical line on the board in line with the centre-line
of the car (Fig. 10.13).

4   Bounce the car on its suspension to ensure correct settlement
and then measure the height between the ground and the centre
of the headlights.

5   Draw a horizontal line across the board at this measured
height. On this horizontal line mark a cross either side of the
vertical centre line equal to half of the distance between the
centres of the two headlights. Switch the headlights on to main
beam.

6   By careful adjustment of the two plastic adjusters at the rear
of the headlight assembly and accessible from within the engine
compartment set the centres of each beam onto the crosses
which have been previously marked on the board or wall.

7   Bounce the car once more and recheck the setting. Now
lower the beams by about 1.5 inch (38.1 mm) on vehicles
equipped with circular headlights or 1.75 in (45.0 mm) on
vehicles equipped with rectangular headlights, so as not to
dazzle other road users and to compensate for those occasions
when there is weight in the back of the car.

---

32 Sidelight bulb - removal and refitting

---

1   Models fitted with 'sealed beam' type headlights have the
sidelight bulb mounted on the connecting plug at the rear of the
sealed beam unit. To remove the bulb is a simple matter of
pulling away from the connecting plug once the headlight unit
has been removed as described in Section 29. Refitting is a
reversal of removal.

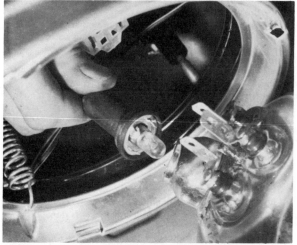

32.2 Sidelight bulb holder and sealed beam unit connector

2   Models fitted with 'semi-sealed' type headlights have the sidelight bulb inserted in the rear of the outer reflector and lens
assembly. To remove the bulb refer to Section 29 and remove
the headlight unit and then detach the bulb holder from the
reflector (photo). Press in and turn the bulb in an anticlockwise

direction to release the bayonet fixing and lift away the bulb. Refitting is a reversal of the removal procedure.

33 Front direction indicator light assembly and bulb - removal and refitting

1   Working under the wheel arch disconnect the electric cable to the light assembly.
2   Undo and remove the retaining nut and push the light assembly forwards away from its location in the front wing.
3   Refitting is the reverse sequence to removal.
4   If it is necessary to remove the bulb, undo and remove the two crosshead screws that secure the lens to the light body. Lift away the lens (Fig. 10.16).
5   To detach the bulb press in and turn in an anticlockwise direction to release the bayonet fixing and lift away the bulb. Refitting the bulb and lens is the reverse sequence to removal. Make sure that the lens gasket is correctly fitted to prevent dirt and water ingress.

34 Rear direction indicator, stop and tail light assembly and bulbs - removal and refitting

1   Open the luggage compartment and detach the cables from the rear of the unit noting the location of the cables.
2   Undo and remove the nuts that secure the rear light assembly to the rear wing. Lift away the rear light assembly.
3   Refitting is the reverse sequence to removal.
4   Should it be necessary to fit a new bulb undo and remove the four crosshead screws that secure the lens to the light body. Lift away the lens and its sealing washer.
5   Remove the applicable bulb by pressing and turning in an anticlockwise direction. (photo)
6   Refitting the bulb and lens is the reverse sequence to removal. Take care to ensure that the lens sealing washer is correctly fitted to prevent dirt and water ingress.

35 Rear number plate light assembly and bulb - removal and refitting

1   Undo and remove the two crosshead screws that secure the light assembly to the bumper. Detach the electric cables and lift away the lamp.
2   Undo and remove the two crosshead screws that fasten the lens to the assembly. Lift away the lens and sealing washer.
3   To remove the bulb press and turn in an anticlockwise direction.
4   Refitting the bulb, lens and assembly is the reverse sequence to removal. Take care to ensure that the lens sealing washer is correctly fitted to prevent dirt and water ingress.

36 Interior light - removal and refitting

1   Very carefully pull the interior light assembly from its location in the roof panel (Fig. 10.17).
2   Disconnect the wires from the terminal connectors and lift away the light unit.
3   If the bulb requires renewal either lift the bulb from its clips (festoon type) or press and turn in an anticlockwise direction (bayonet cap type).
4   Refitting the interior light is the reverse sequence to removal.

37 Instrument cluster and printed circuit (up to 1973) - removal and installation

1   Open the bonnet, and for safety reasons disconnect the battery.
2   If a manual choke control is fitted pull off the choke control knob.
3   Undo and remove the screw and annulus that holds the two halves of the steering column shroud together. Using a knife split the two halves of the column shroud and lift away.
4   Undo and remove the crosshead screws that secure the facia panel to the instrument panel. Lift away the facia panel (Fig. 10.18).
5   Undo and remove the screws that secure the instrument cluster to the instrument panel. Draw the cluster away from the instrument panel by a sufficient amount to give access to the rear. Detach the wiring loom multi pin connector and also the speedometer drive cable by depressing the knurled pad on the speedometer cable ferrule and pull the cable from the speedometer head. Lift away the instrument cluster.
6   Remove the eight illuminating bulbs and voltage regulator unit (retained by one crosshead screw) from the rear of the instrument cluster.
7   Undo and remove the instrument securing nuts and very carefully detach the printed circuit.
8   Refitting the instrument cluster and facia is the reverse sequence to removal.

38 Instrument cluster glass or bulb (up to 1973) - removal and installation

Glass
Refer to Section 37 and remove the instrument cluster as described in paragraphs 1 to 5 inclusive. The glass many now be removed once the screws have been removed. If a clock is fitted the control knob must be removed. Refitting the glass is the reverse sequence to removal.

Bulb
Refer to Section 37 and remove the instrument cluster, as described in paragraphs 1 to 5 inclusive. Refitting is the reverse sequence to removal.

39 Instrument voltage regulator (up to 1973) - removal and refitting

1   Refer to Section 37 and remove the instrument cluster as described in paragraphs 1 to 5 inclusive. Undo and remove the crosshead screw that secures the voltage regulator to the cluster and lift away the regulator (Fig. 10.19).
2   Refitting the voltage regulator is the reverse sequence to removal.

40 Instrument cluster and printed circuit (1973 onwards) - removal and installation

1   Open the bonnet and disconnect the battery leads.
2   Unscrew the lower shroud from the steering column and remove it; then unclip the upper half (Fig. 10.20).
3   Pull off the instrument panel light switch knob and the two radio control knobs.
4   Remove the six countersunk screws which retain the instrument cluster and its bezel.
5   Holding the bezel assembly square to the dashpanel, pull it forward far enough to allow disconnection of the two multi-connectors at the back of the instruments, also the leads from the cigar lighter, the hazard flasher switch and the heated rear window switch (Fig. 10.21).
6   Disconnect the speedometer cable from the speedometer head and then remove the instrument cluster and bezel.
7   The instruments, the warning light bulbs and their holders and the printed circuit can now all be removed from the instrument assembly.
8   Refitting is a reversal of removal.

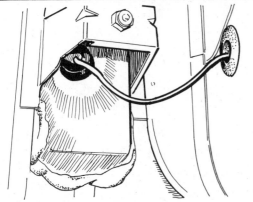

Fig. 10.15. Rear view of front direction indicator lamp (Sec. 33)

Fig. 10.16. Removing a front indicator lens (Sec. 33)

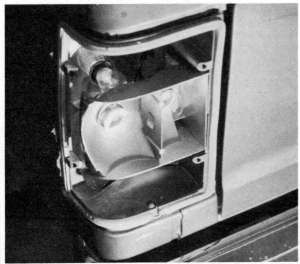

34.5 Three bulbs, light baffles and sealing washer of rear light cluster

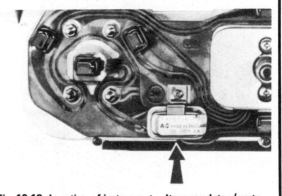

Fig. 10.17. Withdrawing interior lamp assembly (Sec. 36)

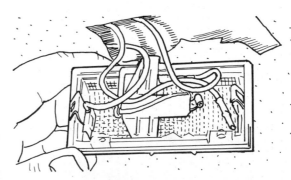

Fig. 10.19. Location of instrument voltage regulator (up to 1973) (Sec. 39)

Fig. 10.18. Withdrawing instrument facia (up to 1973) (Sec. 37)

Fig. 10.20. Removing steering column shroud (Sec. 40)

Fig. 10.21. Withdrawing instrument panel bezel (Sec. 40)

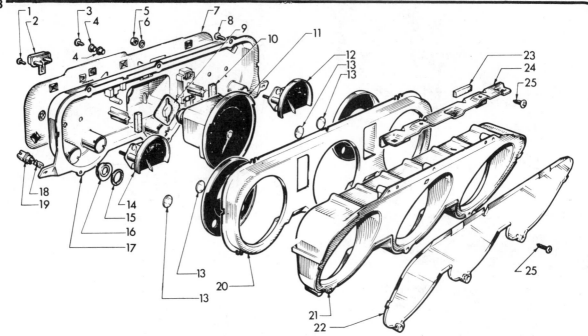

Fig. 10.22. Instrument cluster - basic and L models (up to 1973)

1	Screw	7	Printed circuit	13	Lens	19	Bulb holder
2	Voltage regulator	8	Screw	14	Fuel gauge	20	Cluster front cover
3	Screw	9	Gasket	15	Washer	21	Cluster frontice
4	Shaped bush	10	Foam pad	16	Light holder	22	Cluster glass
5	Nut	11	Speedometer	17	Cluster body	23	Packing
6	Spring washer	12	Temperature gauge	18	Bulb capless type	24	Cluster top rail
						25	Screw

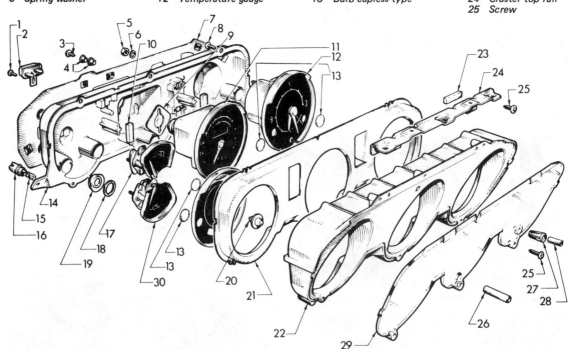

Fig. 10.23. Instrument cluster - XL models (up to 1973)

1	Screw	9	Gasket	17	Fuel gauge	25	Screw
2	Voltage regulator	10	Foam pad	18	Washer	26	Trip reset knob
3	Screw	11	Speedometer	19	Light holder	27	Tapered insert
4	Shaped bush	12	Clock	20	Shaped clip	28	Clock winder knob
5	Nut	13	Lens	21	Cluster front cover	29	Cluster glass
6	Spring washer	14	Cluster body	22	Cluster frontice	30	Temperature gauge
7	Printed circuit	15	Bulb - capless type	23	Packing		
8	Screw	16	Bulb holder	24	Cluster top rail		

41 Instrument voltage regulator (1973 onwards) - removal and refitting

1   Remove the instrument panel, as described in the preceding Section.
2   Unscrew and remove the single screw which secures the voltage regulator to the printed circuit and withdraw it (Fig. 10.24).

42 Speedometer head - removal and refitting

1   Refer to Section 37 and remove the instrument cluster, as described in paragraphs 1 to 5 inclusive.
2   Undo and remove the crosshead screws that secure the speedometer head, to the instrument cluster. Lift away the speedometer head.
3   Refitting the speedometer head is the reverse sequence to removal.

43 Speedometer inner and outer cable - removal and refitting

1   *Manual gearbox:* Working under the car using a pair of circlip pliers remove the circlip that secures the speedometer cable to the gearbox extension housing and withdraw the speedometer cable.
   Automatic transmission: Undo and remove the bolt, and spring washer that secures the forked plate to the extension housing. Lift away the forked plate and withdraw the speedometer cable (Fig. 10.25).
2   Remove the clip that secures the speedometer outer cable to the bulkhead.
3   Working under the facia depress the knurled pad on the speedometer cable ferrule and pull the cable from the speedometer head.
4   Remove the grommet that seals the cable at the bulkhead. Withdraw the speedometer cable.
5   Refitting the speedometer cable is the reverse sequence to removal.
6   It is possible to remove the inner cable from the outer cable whilst still attached to the car. Follow the instructions in paragraphs 1 and 3 and pull the inner cable from the outer cable.

44 Fuel tank indicator unit - removal and installation

1   With the level of petrol in the tank lower than the bottom of the indicator unit wipe the area around the unit free of dirt.
2   Detach the fuel tank indicator unit cable from its terminal (photo).
3   Using two crossed screwdrivers in the slots of the indicator unit body or a soft metal drift carefully unlock the indicator unit. Lift away the indicator unit and sealing ring.
4   Refitting the indicator unit is the reverse sequence to removal. Always fit a new seal in the recess in the tank to ensure no leaks develop.

45 Light switch - removal and refitting

1   Disconnect the battery. Pull the knob from the switch stalk and using a pair of pliers unscrew the bezel.
2   Working under the dash panel pull the wiring loom from its retaining clips.
3   Pull the light switch rearwards from its location and detach the wiring loom plug from the back of the switch.
4   Refitting the light switch is the reverse sequence to removal.

Fig. 10.24. Location of instrument voltage regulator (1973 onwards) (Sec. 41)

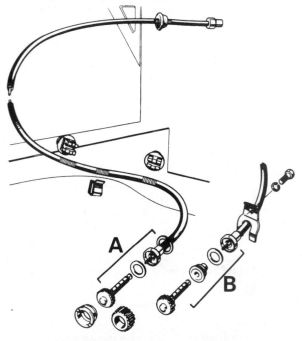

Fig. 10.25. Speedometer cable and driven gear

A   *Manual and Automatic transmission*
B   *Alternative Automatic transmission type*

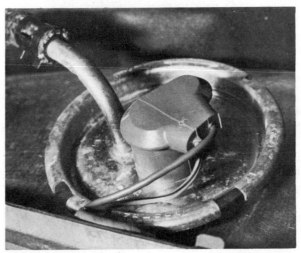

44.2 Fuel tank sender unit

46 Direction indicator switch - removal and refitting

1 Open the bonnet and for safety reasons disconnect the battery.
2 If a manual choke control is fitted pull off the choke control knob.
3 Undo and remove the screw and annulus that holds the two halves of the steering column shroud together. Using a knife split the two halves of the column shroud and lift away.
4 Detach the multi pin plug from the underside of the switch.
5 Undo and remove the two screws and shakeproof washers located on lever side of the switch and detach the switch assembly from the steering column (Fig. 10.26).
6 Refitting the direction indicator switch is the reverse sequence to removal. Before the shroud is refitted check that the switch and self cancel system operates correctly; for this the battery will have to be reconnected.

47 Ignition switch and lock (up to 1973) - removal and refitting

1 Open the bonnet and for safety reasons disconnect the battery.
2 Make a careful note of the cable connections to the ignition switch and lock body. Detach these cables.
3 Carefully unscrew the chrome bezel that secures the lock to the switch panel.
4 Using a suitable diameter drill remove the headless bolts that clamp the lock to the steering column. An alternative method of removal is to use a centre punch and unscrew the bolts. Lift away the complete assembly. **Note:** new shear bolts will be required during reassembly (Fig. 10.27).
5 To refit, place the lock assembly with the key in the lock onto the steering column. Withdraw the lock so as to allow the pawl to enter the steering shaft.
6 Position the loose half of the clamp on the lock and engage new shear bolts in their tapped holes. Tighten the bolts a turn at a time until the heads shear off. Whilst the bolts are being tightened continually check that operation of the pawl is smooth and free.
7 Refitting is now the reverse sequence to removal.

48 Ignition switch and lock (1973 onwards) - removal and refitting

1 Remove the instrument cluster and bezel, as described in Section 40.
2 Unscrew and remove the dash lower insulation panel.
3 Remove the two bolts which secure the wiper switch and light switch in position. Unplug the multi-connector and detach the switch assembly.
4 Pull off the section of air duct which passes across the steering column.
5 Remove the wiring harness block from the base of the ignition switch (two screws).
6 Unscrew and remove the clamp bolts from the steering column brackets both at the instrument panel and the foot pedal support. Allow the steering column to be lowered until it is supported by the steering wheel resting on the front seat squab.
7 Working within the engine compartment, bend back the locking tabs on the flexible coupling clamp plate. Slacken both bolts and then remove one of them and swing the clamp plate to one side.
8 Withdraw the steering column completely into the vehicle interior and then remove it.
9 Secure the steering column in a vice fitted with jaw protectors and drill out the two shear bolts which retain the two halves of the steering column lock to the column.
10 Commence reassembly by fitting the new lock to the steering column so that the lock tongue engages in the cut-out in the column. Tighten the bolts slightly more than finger-tight and

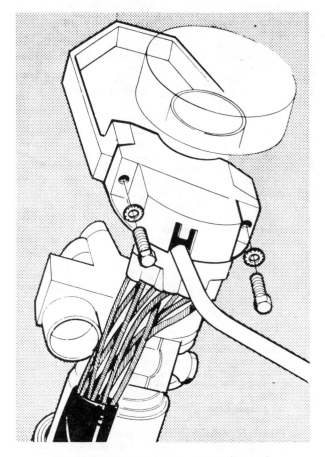

Fig. 10.26. Direction indicator switch (Sec. 46)

Fig. 10.27. Ignition switch and lock removal (Sec. 47)

check the operation of the lock by inserting the ignition key. Move the lock assembly fractionally if necessary to ensure smooth and positive engagement when the key is turned.
11 Fully tighten the bolts until the heads shear.
12 Refit the steering column, applying brake fluid to the lower floor pan seal if necessary to ease installation.
13 Before tightening the column clamp securing bolts move the steering column to achieve the dimension illustrated in Fig. 10.28. Tighten the bracket bolts to 15 lb ft (2.1 kg m).
14 Position the flexible coupling on the shaft, swing the plate into position and insert the bolt which was removed and then tighten both coupling bolts only finger-tight.
15 Check that the whole of the sealing plug in the end of the

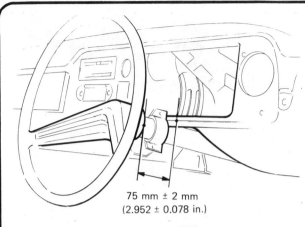

Fig. 10.28. Steering column setting dimension (Sec. 48)

75 mm ± 2 mm
(2.952 ± 0.078 in.)

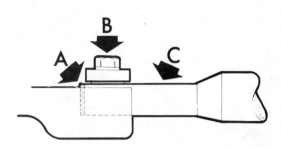

Fig. 10.29. Location of steering column shaft sealing plug
in relation to lower clamp plate (Sec. 48)

A Sealing plug   B Clamp plate   C Steering column shaft

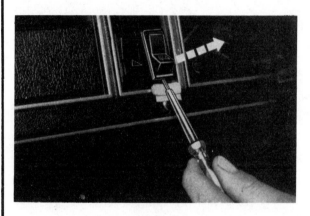

Fig. 10.30. Removing heated rear window switch (Sec. 50)

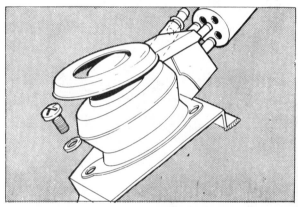

Fig. 10.31. Foot-operated washer/wiper switch (Sec. 51)

steering column shaft is exposed beyond the end of the lower
clamp plate. Tighten the flexible coupling bolts and the clamp
plate bolts to a torque of 15 lb ft (2.1 kg m). Bend up the
clamp plate locking tabs (Fig. 10.29).
16 Refit all switches and other components.

49 Windscreen wiper switch - removal and refitting

1 Pull the heater control knobs from their respective operating
levers. It will be necessary to tap out the dowel pin of the lower
knob: take care not to bend the operating lever.
2 Working under the dashboard carefully press out the
operating levers bezel.
3 Remove the radio switch bezel (if fitted).
4 Pull the windscreen wiper switch knob from the switch stalk
and unscrew the bezel. Detach the plug from the rear of the
switch and finally remove the switch.
5 Refitting the switch is the reverse sequence to removal.

50 Hazard warning and heated rear window switches - removal and installation

1 Both switches are removed from the instrument panel by
inserting a screwdriver at their lower edge and then levering
them from their locations (Fig. 10.30).

2 Withdraw the switch far enough to permit the multi-plug to
be disconnected.

51 Windscreen washer/wiper foot-operated switch - removal and installation

1 Disconnect the battery and peel back the carpet from
around the switch.
2 Disconnect the leads, the water pipe and remove the securing
screws from the switch (Fig. 10.31).
3 Installation is a reversal of removal.

52 Fuses

1 On vehicles built up to 1972, the fuses are located on a block
which is mounted on the engine compartment inner wing panel
and upon inspection it will be seen that there are seven fuses.
Their function is shown on the plastic cover. (photo)
    There are three unused connections, these being 1, 2 and 7
and these may be used for the fitment of accessories. Fuses
numbered 2 and 7 are connected via the ignition switch whilst
fuse 1 is connected to a direction current supply and is live all
the time.
    There are two additional fuses mounted on the inner wing
panel, these being integral with the headlamp relay. All fuses
have an 8 amp rating.

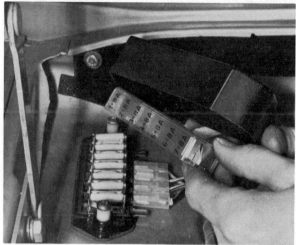

52 Fuse block with outer and inner covers removed

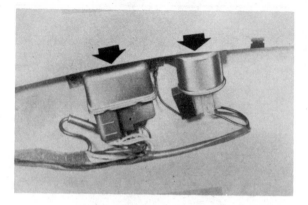

Fig. 10.32. Location of headlamp flasher relay (A) and horn relay (B) (Sec. 53)

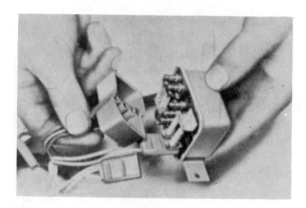

Fig. 10.33. Removing multi-plug connector from headlamp flasher relay (Sec. 53)

Fig. 10.34. Horn relay earth connection (Sec. 53)

Fuse	Function
1	Interior lights, warning indicator system, clock, cigar lighter, glove box lamp
2	Rear number plate light, instrument panel lights, switching stage indicator light
3	Tail light RH, side light RH
4	Tail light LH, side light LH
5	Horn, heater blower motor, current control heated rear window
6	Windscreen wiper motor, foot operated windscreen wiper motor, reverse light
7	Flasher system, stop light, voltage divider
8	Main beam RH and LH
9	Dipped beam RH and LH.

Fig. 10.35. Location of heated rear window relay (Sec. 53)

2   On vehicles built after 1972, the fuse circuits are shown on the relevant wiring diagram at the end of this Chapter.
3   Before any fuse that has blown is renewed, it is important to find the cause of the trouble and for it to be rectified, as a fuse acts as a safety device and protects the electrical system against expensive damage should a fault occur.

53 Relays - renewal

1   Three relays are incorporated in the electrical system: headlamp flasher, heated rear window and horn.

Headlamp flasher relay

2   This is located together with the horn relay on the side apron within the engine compartment (Fig. 10.32).
3   The relay can be removed after disconnecting the multi-plug and two other connectors and unscrewing the relay securing screws (Fig. 10.33).

Horn relay

4   The horn relay is removed in a similar manner to that described for the flasher relay (Fig. 10.32).
5   When installing the new unit, ensure that the earth lead is

secured under the relay securing screw (Fig. 10.34).

Heated rear window relay

6   This relay is located on the support bracket for the bonnet release lever which is located under the instrument panel (Fig. 10.35).
7   Access to the relay can be facilitated if the parcels tray and the instrument panel lower insulation panel are first removed and the flasher unit extracted from its securing clip.

54 Radios and tape players - installation

A radio or tape player is an expensive item to buy; and will only give its best performance if fitted properly. It is useless to expect concert hall performance from a unit that is suspended from the dashpanel by string with its speaker resting on the back seat or parcel shelf! If you do not wish to do the installation yourself there are many in-car entertainment specialists who can do the fitting for you.

Make sure the unit purchased is of the same polarity as the vehicle. Ensure that units with adjustable polarity are correctly set before commencing installation.

It is difficult to give specific information with regard to fitting, as final positioning of the radio/tape player, speakers and aerial is entirely a matter of personal preference. However, the following paragraphs give guidelines to follow, which are relevant to all installations.

Radios

Most radios are a standardised size of 7 inches wide, by 2 inches deep - this ensures that they will fit into the radio aperture provided in most cars. If your car does not have such an aperture, then the radio must be fitted in a suitable position either in, or beneath, the dashpanel. Alternatively, a special console can be purchased which will fit between the dashpanel and the floor, or on the transmission tunnel. These consoles can also be used for additional switches and instrumentation if required. Where no radio aperture is provided, the following points should be borne in mind before deciding exactly where to fit the unit.

a) *The unit must be within easy reach of the driver wearing a seat belt.*
b) *The unit must not be mounted in close proximity to an electric tachometer, the ignition switch and its wiring, or the flasher unit and associated wiring.*
c) *The unit must be mounted within reach of the aerial lead, and in such a place that the aerial lead will not have to be routed near the components detailed in the preceding paragraph 'b'.*
d) *The unit should not be positioned in a place where it might cause injury to the car occupants in an accident; for instance, under the dashpanel above the driver's or passenger's legs.*
e) *The unit must be fitted really securely.*

Some radios will have mounting brackets provided together with instructions: others will need to be fitted using drilled and slotted metal strips, bent to form mounting brackets - these strips are available from most accessory stores. The unit must be properly earthed, by fitting a separate earth lead between the casing of the radio and the vehicle frame.

Use the radio manufacturer's instructions when wiring the radio into the vehicle's electrical system. If no instructions are available refer to the relevant wiring diagram to find the location of the radio 'feed' connection in the vehicle's wiring circuit. A 1-2 amp 'in-line' fuse must be fitted in the radio's 'feed' wire - a choke may also be necessary (see next Section).

The type of aerial used, and its fitted position is a matter of personal preference. In general the taller the aerial, the better the reception. It is best to fit a fully retractable aerial - especially, if a mechanical car-wash is used or if you live in an area where cars tend to be vandalised. In this respect electric aerials which are raised and lowered automatically when switching the radio on or off are convenient, but are more likely to give trouble than the manual type.

When choosing a site for the aerial the following points should be considered:

a) *The aerial lead should be as short as possible,- this means that the aerial should be mounted at the front of the vehicle.*
b) *The aerial must be mounted as far away from the distributor and HT leads as possible.*
c) *The part of the aerial which protrudes beneath the mounting point must not foul the roadwheels, or anything else.*
d) *If possible the aerial should be positioned so that the coaxial lead does not have to be routed through the engine compartment.*
e) *The plane of the panel on which the aerial is mounted should not be so steeply angled that the aerial cannot be mounted vertically (in relation to the 'end-on' aspect of the vehicle). Most aerials have a small amount of adjustment available.*

Having decided on a mounting position, a relatively large hole will have to be made in the panel. The exact size of the hole will depend upon the specific aerial being fitted, although, generally, the hole required is of ¾ inch diameter. On metal bodied cars, a 'tank-cutter' of the relevant diameter is the best tool to be used for making the hole. This tool needs a small diameter pilot hole drilled through the panel, through which, the tool clamping bolt is inserted. On GRP bodied cars, a 'hole saw' is the best tool to use. Again, this tool will require the drilling of a small pilot hole. When the hole has been made the raw edges should be de-burred with a file and then painted, to prevent corrosion.

Fit the aerial according to the manufacturer's instructions. If the aerial is very tall, or if it protrudes beneath the mounting panel for a considerable distance it is a good idea to fit a stay between the aerial and the vehicle frame. This stay can be manufactured from the slotted and drilled metal strips previously mentioned. The stay should be securely screwed or bolted in place. For best reception it is advisable to fit an earth lead between the aerial body and the vehicle frame - this is essential on fibre glass bodied vehicles.

It will probably be necessary to drill one, or two holes through bodywork panels in order to feed the aerial lead into the interior of the car. Where this is the case ensure that the holes are fitted with rubber grommets to protect the cable, and to stop possible entry of water.

Positioning and fitting of the speaker depends mainly on its type. Generally, the speaker is designed to fit directly into the aperture already provided in the car (usually in the shelf behind the rear seats, or in the top of the dashpanel). Where this is the case, fitting the speaker is just a matter of removing the protective grille from the aperture and screwing or bolting the speaker in place. Take great care not to damage the speaker diaphragm whilst doing this. It is a good idea to fit a 'gasket' between the speaker frame and the mounting panel in order to prevent vibration - some speakers will already have such a gasket fitted.

If a 'pod' type speaker was supplied with the radio, the best acoustic results will normally be obtained by mounting it on the shelf behind the rear seat. The pod can be secured to the mounting panel with self-tapping screws.

When connecting a rear mounted speaker to the radio, the wires should be routed through the vehicle beneath the carpets or floor mats - preferably through the middle, or along the side of the floorpan, where they will not be trodden on by passengers. Make the relevant connections as directed by the radio manufacturer.

By now you will have several yards of additional wiring in the car; use PVC tape to secure this wiring out of harm's way. Do not leave electrical leads dangling. Ensure that all new electrical connections are properly made (wires twisted together will not do) and completely secure.

The radio should now be working, but before you pack away your tools it will be necessary to 'trim' the radio to the aerial. Follow the radio manufacturer's instructions regarding this adjustment.

Tape players

Fitting instructions for both cartridge and cassette stereo tape players are the same and in general the same rules apply as when fitting a radio. Tape players are not usually prone to electrical interference like radio - although it can occur - so positioning is not so critical. If possible the player should be mounted on an 'even-keel'. Also, it must be possible for a driver wearing a seat belt to reach the unit in order to change, or turn over, tapes.

For the best results from speakers designed to be recessed into a panel, mount them so that the back of the speaker pro-trudes into an enclosed chamber within the vehicle (eg; door interiors or the boot cavity).

To fit recessed type speakers in the front doors first check that there is sufficient room to mount the speaker in each door without it fouling the latch or window winding mechanism. Hold the speaker against the skin of the door, and draw a line, around the periphery of the speaker. With the speaker removed draw a second 'cutting' line, within the first, to allow enough room for the entry of the speaker back, but at the same time providing a broad seat for the speaker flange. When you are sure that the 'cutting-line' is correct, drill a series of holes around its periphery. Pass a hacksaw blade through one of the holes and then cut through the metal between the holes until the centre section of the panel falls out.

De-burr the edges of the hole and then paint the raw metal to prevent corrosion. Cut a corresponding hole in the door trim panel - ensuring that it will be completely covered by the speaker grille. Now drill a hole in the door edge and a corresponding hole in the door surround. These holes are to feed the speaker leads through - so fit grommets. Pass the speaker leads through the door trim, door skin and out through the holes in the side of the door and door surround. Refit the door trim panel and then secure the speaker to the door using self-tapping screws. Note: if the speaker is fitted with a shield to prevent water dripping on it, ensure that this shield is at the top.

'Pod' type speakers can be fastened to the shelf behind the rear seat, or anywhere else offering a corresponding mounting point on each side of the car. If the 'pod' speakers are mounted on each side of the shelf behind the rear seat, it is a good idea to drill several large diameter holes through to the trunk cavity beneath each speaker - this will improve the sound reproduction. 'Pod' speakers sometimes offer a better reproduction quality if they face the rear window - which then acts as a reflector - so it is worthwhile experimenting before finally fixing the speakers.

55 Radios and tape players - suppression of interference (general)

To eliminate buzzes, and other unwanted noises, costs very little and is not as difficult as sometimes thought. With a modicum of common sense and patience and following the instructions in the following paragraphs, interference can be virtually eliminated.

The first cause for concern is the generator. The noise this makes over the radio is like an electric mixer and the noise speeds up when you rev up the engine (if you wish to prove the point, you can remove the fanbelt and try it). The remedy for this is simple; connect a 1.0 mf - 3.0 mf capacitor between earth, probably the bolt that holds down the generator base, and the *large* terminal on the alternator. This is most important, for if you connect it to the small terminal, you will probably damage the generator permanently (see Fig. 10.36).

A second common cause of electrical interference is the ignition system. Here a 1.0 mf capacitor must be connected

between earth and the SW or + terminal on the coil (see Fig. 10.37). This may stop the tick-tick-tick sound that comes over the speaker. Next comes the spark itself.

There are several ways of curing interference from the ignition HT system. One is the use of carbon-cored HT leads as original equipment. Where copper cable is susbstituted then you must use resistive spark plug caps (see Fig. 10.38) of about 10,000 ohm to 15,000 ohm resistance. If, due to lack of room, these cannot be used, an alternative is to use 'in-line' suppressors - if the interference is not too bad, you may get away with only one suppressor in the coil to distributor line. If the interference does continue (a "clacking" noise) then modify all HT leads.

At this stage it is advisable to check that the radio is well earthed, also the aerial and to see that the aerial plug is pushed well into the set and that the radio is properly trimmed (see preceding Section). In addition, check that the wire which supplies the power to the set is as short as possible and does not wander all over the car. At this stage it is a good idea to check that the fuse is of the correct rating. For most sets this will be about 1 to 2 amps.

At this point the more usual causes of interference have been suppressed. If the problem still exists, a look at the causes of interference may help to pinpoint the component generating the stray electrical discharges.

The radio picks up electromagnetic waves in the air; now some are made by regular broadcasters, and some, which we do not want, are made by the car itself. The home made signals are produced by stray electrical discharges floating around in the car. Common producers of these signals are electric motors, ie, the windscreen wipers, electric screen washers, electric window winders, heater fan or an electric aerial if fitted. Other sources of interference are flashing turn signal and instruments. The remedy for these cases is shown in Fig. 10.39 for an electric motor whose interference is not too bad and Fig. 10.40 for instrument suppression. Turn signals are not normally suppressed. In recent years, radio manufacturers have included in the line (live) of the radio, in addition to the fuse, an 'in-line' choke. If your circuit lacks one of these, put one in as shown in Fig. 10.41.

All the foregoing components are available from radio stores or accessory stores. If you have an electric clock fitted this should be suppressed by connecting a 0.5 mf capacitor directly across it as shown for a motor in Fig. 10.39.

If after all this, you are still experiencing radio interference, first assess how bad it is, for the human ear can filter out un-obtrusive unwanted noises quite easily. But if you are still adamant about eradicating the noise, then continue.

As a first step, a few "experts" seem to favour a screen between the radio and the engine. This is OK as far as it goes - literally! - for the whole set is screened anyway and if inter-ference can get past that then a small piece of aluminium is not going to stop it.

A more sensible way of screening is to discover if interference is coming down the wires. First, take the live lead; interference can get between the set and the choke (hence the reason for keeping the wires short). One remedy here is to screen the wire and this is done by buying screened wire and fitting that. The loudspeaker lead could be screened also to prevent "pick-up" getting back to the radio although this is unlikely.

Without doubt, the worst source of radio interference comes from the ignition HT leads, even if they have been suppressed. The ideal way of suppressing these is to slide screening tubes over the leads themselves. As this is impractical, we can place an aluminium shield over the majority of the lead areas. In a vee- or twin-cam engine this is relatively easy but for a straight engine, the results are not particularly good.

Now for the really impossible cases, here are a few tips to try out. Where metal comes into contact with metal, an electrical disturbance is caused which is why good clean connections are essential. To remove interference due to overlapping or butting panels you must bridge the join with a wide braided earth strap (like that from the frame to the engine/transmission). The most common moving parts that could create noise and should be

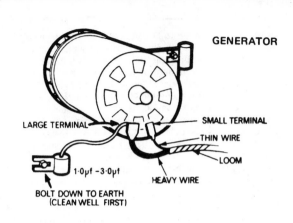

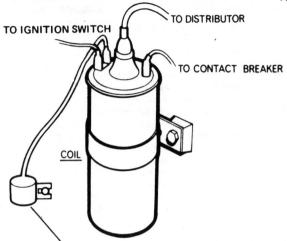

Fig. 10.36. The correct way to connect a capacitor to the generator

Fig. 10.37. The capacitor must be connected to the ignition switch side of the coil

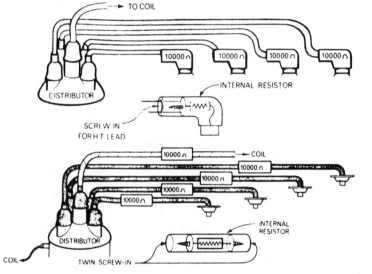

Fig. 10.38. Ignition HT lead suppressors

Resistive spark plug caps (top left)
'In-line' suppressors (bottom left)

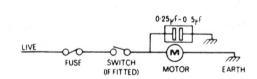

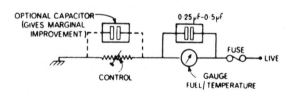

Fig. 10.39. Correct method of suppressing electric motors

Fig. 10.40. Method of suppressing gauges and their control units

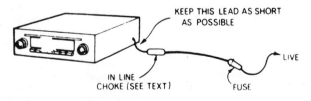

Fig. 10.41. An 'in-line' choke should be fitted into the live supply lead as close to the unit as possible

strapped are, in order of importance:
> (a) *Silencer to frame.*
> (b) *Exhaust pipe to engine block and frame.*
> (c) *Air cleaner to frame.*
> (d) *Front and rear bumpers to frame.*
> (e) *Steering column to frame.*
> (f) *Bonnet and boot lids to frame.*
> (g) *Hood frame to bodyframe on soft tops.*

These faults are most pronounced when (1) the engine is idling, (2) labouring under load. Although the moving parts are already connected with nuts, bolts, etc, these do tend to rust and corrode, thus creating a high resistance interference source.

If you have a "ragged" sounding pulse when mobile, this could be wheel or tyre static. This can be cured by buying some anti-static powder and sprinkling it liberally inside the tyres.

If the interference takes the shape of a high pitched screeching noise that changes its note when the car is in motion and only comes now and then, this could be related to the aerial, especially if it is of the telescopic or whip type. This source can be cured quite simply by pushing a small rubber ball on top of the aerial as this breaks the electric field before it can form; but

it would be much better to buy yourself a new aerial of a reputable brand. If, on the other hand, you are getting a loud rushing sound every time you brake, then this is brake static. This effect is most prominent on hot dry days and is cured only by fitting a special kit, which is quite expensive.

In conclusion, it is pointed out that it is relatively easy, and therefore cheap, to eliminate 95 per cent of all noise, but to eliminate the final 5 per cent is time and money consuming. It is up to the individual to decide if it is worth it. Please remember also, that you cannot get a concert hall performance out of a cheap radio.

Finally, players and eight track players are not usually affected by car noise but in a very bad case, the best remedies are the first three suggestions plus using a 3 - 5 amp choke in the "live" line and in incurable cases screen the live and speaker wires.

Note: if your car is fitted with electronic ignition, then it is not recommended that either the spark plug resistors or the ignition coil capacitor be fitted as these may damage the system. Most electronic ignition units have built-in suppression and should, therfore, not cause interference.

56 Fault diagnosis - electrical system

Symptom	Cause	Remedy
Starter motor fails to turn engine	Battery discharged	Charge battery
	Battery defective internally	Fit new battery
	Battery terminal leads loose or earth lead not securely attached to body	Check and tighten leads
	Loose or broken connections in starter motor circuit	Check all connections and tighten any that are loose
	Starter motor switch or solenoid faulty	Test and replace faulty components with new
	Starter brushes badly worn, sticking, or brush wires loose	Examine brushes, replace as necessary, tighten down brush wires
	Commutator dirty, worn or burnt	Clean commutator, recut if badly burnt
	Starter motor armature faulty	Overhaul starter motor, fit new armature
	Field coils earthed	Overhaul starter motor
Starter motor turns engine very slowly	Battery in discharged condition	Charge battery
	Starter brushes badly worn, sticking, or brush wire loose	Examine brushes, replace as necessary, tighten down brush wires
	Loose wires in starter motor circuit	Check wiring and tighten as necessary
Starter motor operates without turning engine	Starter motor pinion sticking on the screwed sleeve	Remove starter motor, clean starter motor
	Pinion or flywheel gear teeth broken or worn	Fit new gear ring to flywheel, and new pinion to starter motor drive
Starter motor noisy or excessively rough engagement	Pinion or flywheel gear teeth broken or worn	Fit new gear teeth ot flywheel, or new pinion to starter motor drive
	Starter motor retaining bolts loose	Tighten starter motor securing bolts. Fit new spring washer if necessary
Battery will not hold charge for more than a few days	Battery defective internally	Remove and fit new battery
	Electrolyte level too low or electrolyte too weak due to leakage	Top up electrolyte level to just above plates
	Plate separators no longer fully effective	Remove and fit new battery
	Battery plates severely sulphated	Remove and fit new battery
	Fan/alternator belt slipping	Check belt for wear, replace if necessary, and tighten
	Battery terminal connections loose or corroded	Check terminals for tightness, and remove all corrosion
	Alternator not charging properly	Take car to specialist
	Short in lighting circuit causing continual battery drain	Trace and rectify
Ignition light fails to go out, battery runs flat in a few days	Fan belt loose and slipping or broken	Check, replace and tighten as necessary
	Alternator faulty	Take car to specialist

Failure of individual electrical equipment to function correctly is dealt with alphabetically, item-by-item, under the headings listed below.

Fuel gauge gives no reading	Fuel tank empty!	Fill fuel tank
	Electric cable between tank sender unit and gauge earthed or loose	Check cable for earthing and joints for tightness
	Fuel gauge case not earthed	Ensure case is well earthed
	Fuel gauge supply cable interrupted	Check and replace cable if necessary
	Fuel gauge unit broken	Replace fuel gauge
Fuel gauge registers full all the time	Electric cable between tank unit and gauge broken or disconnected	Check over cable and repair as necessary
Horn operates all the time	Horn push either earthed or stuck down	Disconnect battery earth. Check and rectify source of trouble
	Horn cable to horn push earthed	Disconnect battery earth. Check and recitfy source of trouble
Horn fails to operate	Blown fuse	Check and renew if broken. Ascertain cause
	Cable or cable connection loose, broken or disconnected	Check all connections for tightness and cables for breaks
	Horn has an internal fault	Remove and overhaul horn
Horn emits intermittent or unsatisfactory noise	Cable connections loose	Check and tighten all connections
	Horn incorrectly adjusted	Adjust horn until best note obtained
Lights do not come on	If engine not running, battery discharged	Push-start car and charge battery (not automatics)
	Light bulb filament burnt out or bulbs broken	
	Wire connections loose, disconnected or broken	Check all connections for tightness and wire cable for breaks
	Light switch shorting or otherwise faulty	By-pass light switch to ascertain if faulty is in switch and fit new switch as appropriate
Lights come on but fade out	If engine not running battery discharged	Push-start car and charge battery (not automatics)
Lights give very poor illumination	Lamp glasses dirty	Clean glasses
	Reflector tarnished or dirty	Fit new reflectors
	Lamps badly out of adjustment	Adjust lamps correctly
	Incorrect bulb with too low wattage fitted	Remove bulb and replace with correct grade
	Existing bulbs old and badly discoloured	Renew bulb units
	Electrical wiring too thin not allowing full current to pass	Re-wire lighting system
Lights work erratically - flashing on and off, especially over bumps	Battery terminals or earth connection loose	Tighten battery terminals and earth connection
	Lights not earthing properly	Examine and rectify
	Contacts in light switch faulty	By-pass light switch to ascertain if fault is in switch and fit new switch as appropriate
Wiper motor fails to work	Blown fuse	Check and replace fuse if necessary
	Wire connections loose, disconnected or broken	Check wiper wiring. Tighten loose connections
	Brushes badly worn	Remove and fit new brushes
	Armature worn or faulty	If electricity at wiper motor remove and overhaul and fit replacement armature
	Field coils faulty	Purchase reconditoned wiper motor
Wiper motor works very slowly and takes excessive current	Commutator dirty, greasy or burnt	Clean commutator thoroughly
	Drive to wheelboxes bent or unlubricated	Examine drive and straighten out severe curvature. Lubricate
	Wheelbox spindle binding or damaged	Remove, overhaul, or fit replacement
	Armature bearings dry or unaligned	Replace with new bearings correctly aligned
	Armature badly worn or faulty	Remove, overhaul, or fit replacement armature
Wiper motor works slowly and takes little current	Brushes badly worn	Remove and fit new brushes
	Commutator dirty, greasy, or burnt	Clean commutator thoroughly
	Armature badly worn or faulty	Remove and overhaul armature or fit replacement
Wiper motor works but wiper blades remain static	Wheelbox gear and spindle damaged or worn	Examine and if faulty, replace
	Wiper motor gearbox parts baldy worn	Overhaul or fit new gearbox

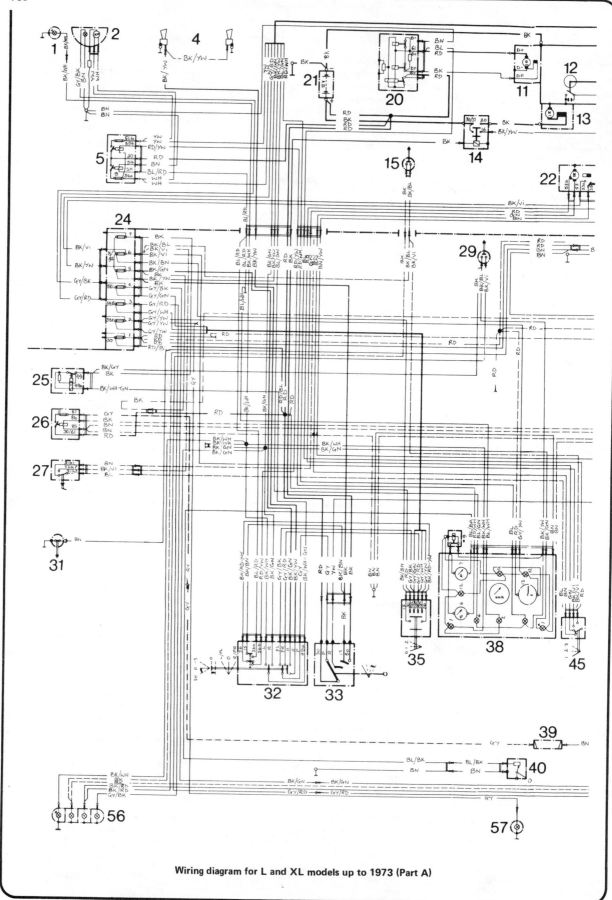

Wiring diagram for L and XL models up to 1973 (Part A)

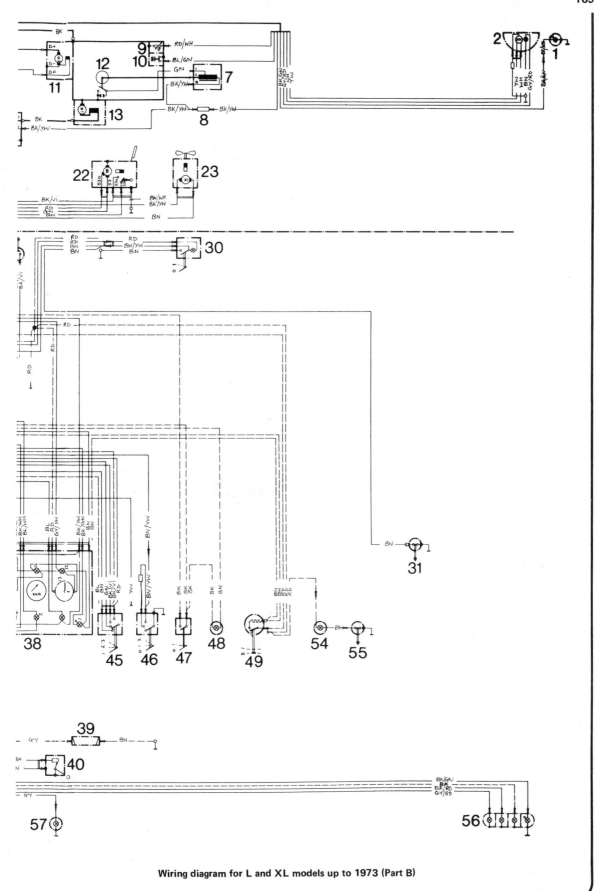

Wiring diagram for L and XL models up to 1973 (Part B)

Key to wiring diagram for L and XL models up to 1973

1	Front indicator	32	Indicator switch
2	Headlamp	33	Steering lock/Ignition switch
4	Horn	35	Light switch
5	Headlamp relay	38	Instrument cluster
7	Ignition coil		1 Indicator warning light (red)
8	Series resistance — coil		2 Main beam warning light (blue)
9	Temperature gauge sender unit		3 Ignition warning light (red)
10	Oil pressure switch		4 Oil pressure warning light (amber)
11	Generator		6 Temperature gauge
12	Distributor		7 Fuel gauge
13	Starter motor		9 Voltage regulator
14	Starter solenoid		12 Instrument lights
15	Reversing lamp switch		13 Electric clock
20	Regulator	39	Heated rear window
21	Battery	40	Fuel gauge sender unit
22	Wiper motor	45	Wiper motor switch
23	Heater motor	46	Heater blower switch
24	Fuse block	47	Switch — heated rear window
25	Flasher unit	48	Heated rear window warning light
26	Relay — heated rear window	49	Cigarette lighter
27	Wiper motor foot switch	54	Glove box lamp
29	Stop light switch	55	Glove box lamp switch
30	Interior light	56	Rear lamp assembly
31	Courtesy light	57	Number plate lamp

Fuses

1	Cigarette lighter, electric clock, interior light, glove box light	6	Wiper motor, reversing lamps
2	Instrument lights, number plate light	7	Voltage regulator, indicator lamps, brake lights
3	Rear light RH, side light RH	8	Dipped beam
4	Rear light LH, side light LH	9	Main beam
5	Heater blower motor, horn, heated rear window (control current)	10	Heated rear window (operating current)

All unmarked fuses are 8 amps

Colour Codes

BK	=	Black	PK	=	Pink	YW	=	Yellow	GY	=	Grey
WH	=	White	GN	=	Green	BL	=	Blue	BN	=	Brown
RD	=	Red							VI	=	Violet

————————————— Standard wire
— — — — — — — — — Standard wire for L only
— · — · — · — · — Standard wire for XL only

Key to wiring diagram for GT and GXL models up to 1973

1	Front indicator		38	Instrument cluster
2	Headlamp			1 Indicator warning light (red)
4	Horn			2 Main beam warning light (blue)
5	Headlamp relay			3 Ignition warning light (red)
7	Ignition coil			9 Voltage regulator
8	Series resistance — coil			11 Tachometer
9	Temperature gauge sender unit			12 Instrument lights
12	Distributor			13 Electric clock
13	Starter motor		39	Heated rear window
15	Reversing lamp switch		40	Fuel gauge sender unit
19	Alternator with regulator		43	Console
20	Battery sensing wire			5 Oil pressure gauge
21	Battery			6 Temperature gauge
22	Wiper motor			7 Fuel gauge
23	Heater motor			10 Ammeter
24	Fuse block			12 Instrument lights
25	Flasher unit		45	Wiper motor switch
26	Relay — heated rear window		46	Heater blower switch
27	Wiper motor foot switch		47	Heated rear window switch
29	Stop light switch		48	Heated rear window warning light
30	Interior light		49	Cigarette lighter
31	Courtesy light switch		54	Glove box lamp
32	Indicator warning light		55	Glove box lamp switch
33	Steering lock/Ignition switch		56	Rear lamp assembly
35	Light switch		57	Number plate lamp

Fuses

1	Cigarette lighter, electric clock, interior light		6	Wiper motor, reversing lamps
2	Instrument lights, number plate light		7	Voltage regulator, indicator lamps, brake lights
3	Rear light RH, side light RH		8	Dipped beam
4	Rear light LH, side light LH		9	Main beam
5	Heater blower motor, horn, heater blower motor (control current)		10	Heated rear window (operating current)

All unmarked fuses are 8 amps

Colour codes

BK	=	Black	PK	=	Pink	YW	=	Yellow	GY = Grey
WH	=	White	GN	=	Green	BL	=	Blue	BN = Brown
RD	=	Red							VI = Violet

—.—.—.—.—.—.—. For GXL Export only

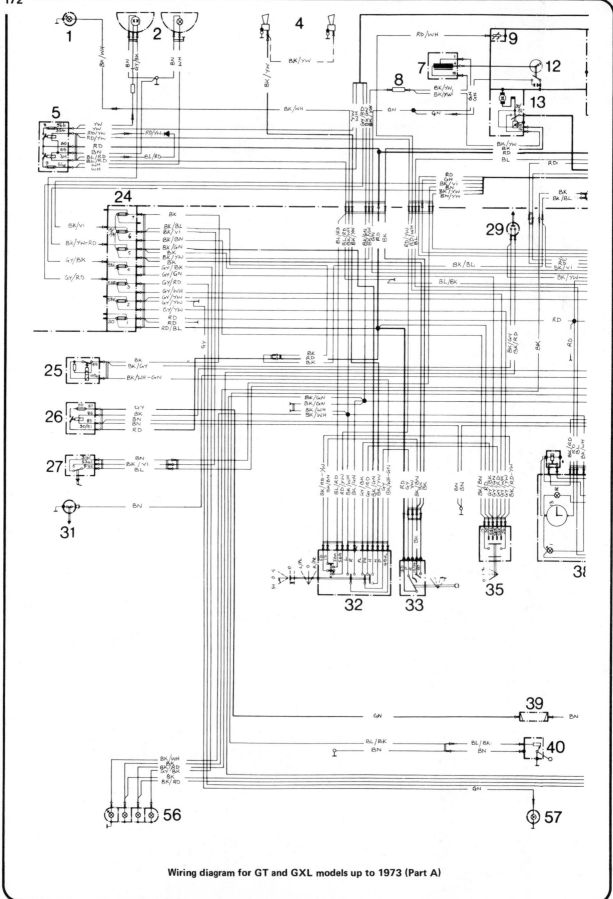

Wiring diagram for GT and GXL models up to 1973 (Part A)

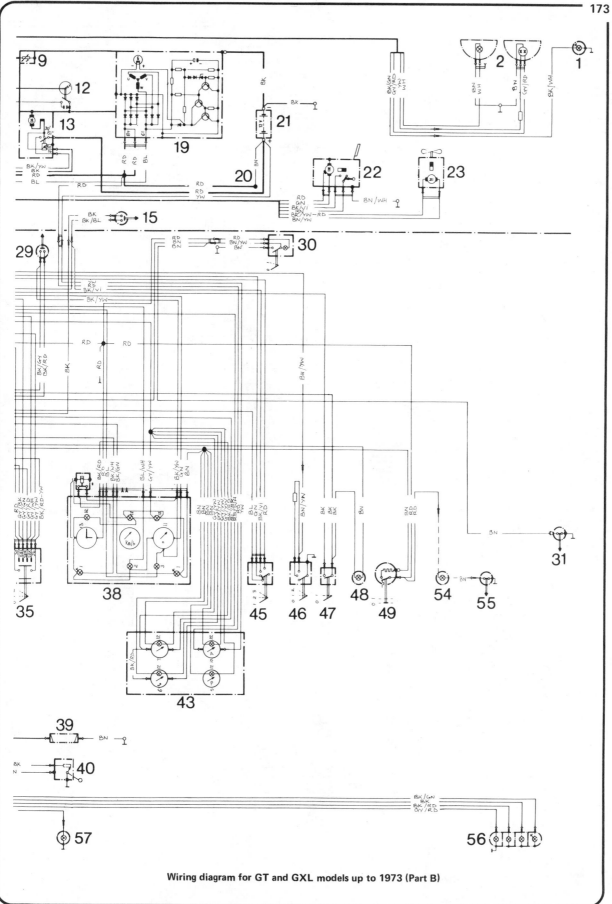

Wiring diagram for GT and GXL models up to 1973 (Part B)

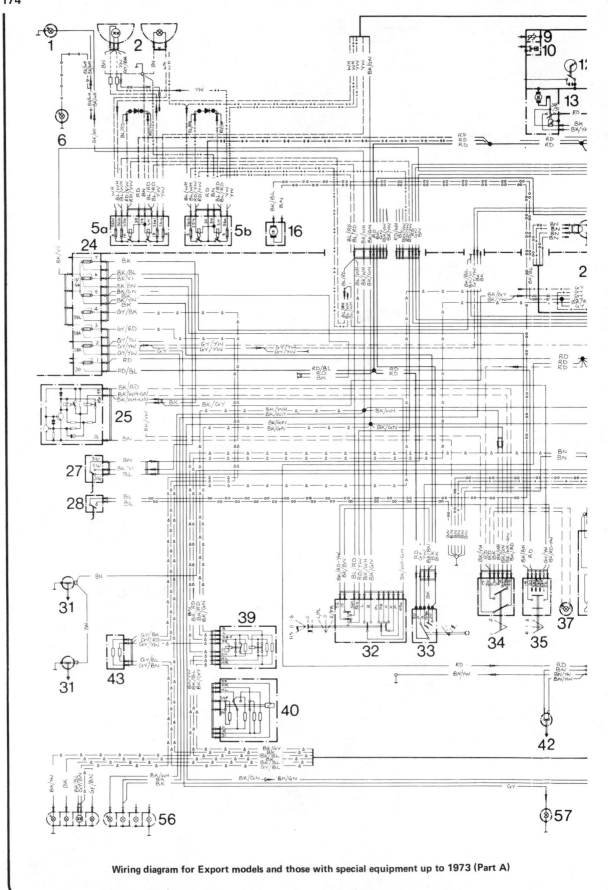

Wiring diagram for Export models and those with special equipment up to 1973 (Part A)

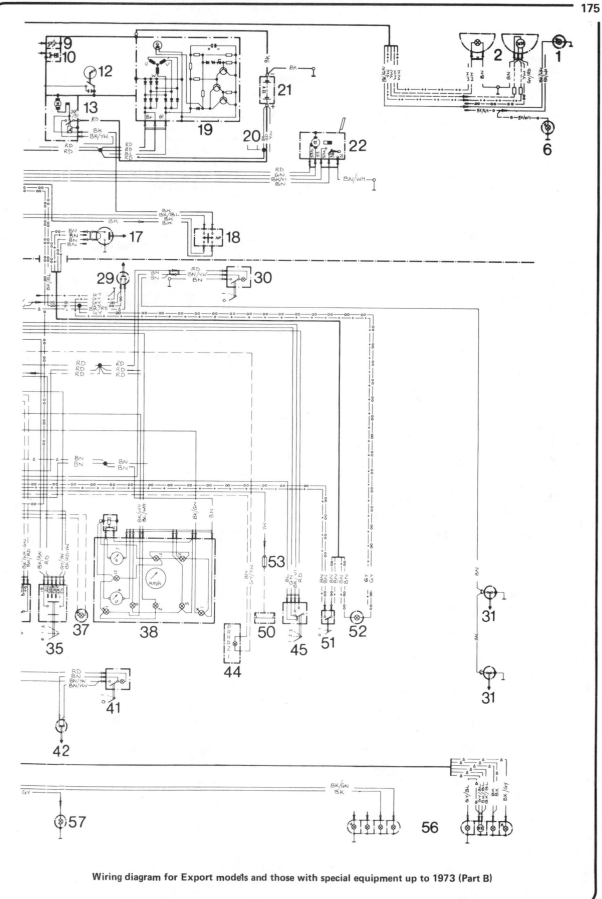

Wiring diagram for Export models and those with special equipment up to 1973 (Part B)

Key to wiring diagram for Export models and those with special equipment up to 1973

1	Front indicator	34	Hazard flasher unit
2	Headlamp	35	Light switch
5a	Headlamp relay (Italy only)	37	Hazard flasher warning light
5b	Headlamp relay (France only)	38	Instrument cluster
6	Front side repeater lamp		1 Indicator warning light (red)
9	Temperature gauge sender unit		2 Main beam warning light (blue)
10	Oil pressure switch		3 Ignition warning light (red)
12	Distributor		4 Oil pressure warning light (amber)
13	Starter motor		6 Temperature gauge
16	Windshield washer motor		7 Fuel gauge
17	Dual brake warning light switch		9 Voltage regulator
18	Inhibitor switch (auto trans)		12 Instrument lights
19	Alternator with regulator	39)	Relay for dual intensity rear lamps (RPO Great
20	Battery sensing wire	40)	Britain)
21	Battery	41	Luggage compartment lamp
22	Wiper motor	42	Luggage compartment lamp switch
24	Fuse block	43	Resistor dual intensity rear lamps
25	Flasher unit	44	Auto trans quadrant illumination
27	Wiper motor foot switch	45	Wiper motor switch
28	Windshield washer motor foot switch	50	Radio
29	Stop light switch	51	Dual brake warning light test switch
30	Interior light	52	Dual brake warning light
31	Courtesy light	53	Fuse — radio
32	Indicator warning light	56	Rear lamp assembly
33	Steering lock/Ignition switch	57	Number plate lamp

Fuses

1	Luggage compartment light, hazard flasher warning light, interior light	8	Dipped beam — RH/LH
		8a	(Italy and France only)
2	Instrument lights, number plate light, auto trans quadrant lamp, reversing lamps (Italy only)	9	Main beam — RH/LH
		9a	(Italy and France only)
6	Wiper motor, reversing lamps		
7	Indicator lamps, windshield washer motor, dual brake warning light		

All unmarked fuses are 8 amps

Colour codes

BK	=	Black	PK	=	Pink	YW	=	Yellow	GY	=	Grey
WH	=	White	GN	=	Green	BL	=	Blue	BN	=	Brown
RD	=	Red							VI	=	Violet

————————————	Standard wiring
– – – – – – – – – – – –	For Italy
– △ — △ — △ — △ —	For Great Britain
–o–o–o–o–o–o–o–o–o	For Denmark, Italy and Norway
–oo––oo––oo––oo––oo––oo–	For Sweden
–+–+–+–+–+–+–+–+	For Switzerland and Norway
–++–++–++–++–++–++	For France
—— · —— · —— · —— · ——	Special wiring

Wire SH1 BL/RD is broken at the front bulkhead multi-plug for Austria only

Chapter 11 Suspension and steering

Contents

Specifications

Front suspension

Type	Independent, coil spring, long and short swinging arms. Double acting, hydraulic, telescopic shock absorbers

	Up to Aug. 1973	Aug. 1973 onwards
Springs:		
Number of coils	7.2 or 7.5	7.5 or 8.08
Identification	Coded with different paint colours. For replacement use spring of same colour coding.	
Toe-in - checking	0 to 0.28 in (0 to 7 mm)	0.08 in toe out to 0.16 in toe in (2 mm toe out to 4 mm toe in)
- adjusting	0.16 in ± 0.04 in (4 mm ± 1 mm)	0.04 in ± 0.04 in (1mm ± 1 mm)
Castor	3° 09' ± 1°	2° 45' ± 1°
Camber	0° 37' ± 0° 45'	0° 18' ± 0° 45'
Steering axis inclination	3° 35' ± 0° 30'	3° 35' ± 0° 30'
Toe-out on turns	20° back lock, front lock 19°	20° back lock, front lock 18° 40'
	35° back lock, front lock 32° 18'	35° back lock, front lock 31° 50'

Rear suspension

Type	Radius arms, coil springs. Double acting, hydraulic, telescopic shock absorbers

Saloon models	1600	1600 GT and 2000
Spring wire diameter	0.516 in (13.1 mm)	0.528 in (13.4 mm)
Coil inside diameter	4.047 in (102.8 mm)	4.024 in (102.2 mm)
Number of turns	6.3	6.0
Free-height of spring:		
Standard	11.0 in (279 mm)	10.75 in (273 mm)
Heavy duty	10.9 in (277 mm)	10.9 in (277 mm)
Installed height:		
Standard	8.49 in (215.7 mm)	8.54 in (217 mm)
Heavy duty	8.47 in (215.2 mm)	8.47 in (215.2 mm)
Spring rate (mm/100 kg)	26.6	23.2

Estate car (1600)

	Standard	Heavy duty
Spring wire diameter	0.516 in (13.1 mm)	0.563 in (14.3 mm)
Coil inside diameter	4.05 in (102.8 mm)	3.95 in (100.4 mm)
Number of turns	6.3	6.8
Freespring height	11.4 in (290 mm)	
Fitted height	8.488 in (215.6 mm)	9.192 in (233.5 mm)
Spring rate	26.6 mm/100kg	19.95 mm/100kg

Estate car (2000)

	Standard	Heavy duty
Spring wire diameter	0.528 in (13.4 mm)	0.563 in (14.3 mm)
Coil inside diameter	4.02 in (102.2 mm)	3.95 in (100.4 mm)
Number of turns	6.0	6.8
Free spring height	11.4 in (290 mm)	
Fitted height	8.5 in (215.9 mm)	9.19 in (233.5 mm)
Spring rate	23.2 mm/100 kg	19.95/100 kg

Steering

Type	Rack and pinion
Steering wheel diameter	15.51 x 14.53 in (394 x 369 mm)
Turns (lock-to-lock)	3.7
Steering ratio	18.7 : 1
Steering gear adjustment	Shims

	Up to 1973	1973 onwards
Minimum turning circle diameter	31ft 10 in (9.7 m)	32ft. 8 in (9.9 m)
Maximum turning angle:		
Outer wheel	38° 48'	35° 28'
Inner wheel	35° 36'	38° 47'
Lubricant capacity	0.25 pint (0.14 litre)	38° 47'

Wheels and tyres

Wheel size:	
Standard	4½J x 13
Optional and GT and 2000	5½J x 13

Tyre pressures - kg sq cm (lb sq in):

	Tyre size	Normally laden*		Fully laden**	
		Front	Rear	Front	Rear
Saloon:	6.00 — 13 4PR	1.6 (23)	1.7 (24)	1.8 (26)	2.1 (30)
	6.95 — S13 4PR	1.6 (23)	1.6 (23)	1.8 (26)	2.0 (28)
	165 — SR13	1.8 (26)	1.8 (26)	2.0 (28)	2.5 (36)
	185/70 HR13	1.6 (23)	1.6 (23)	1.8 (26)	2.1 (30)
Estate car:	6.95 — S13 4PR	1.6 (23)	1.7 (24)	1.8 (26)	2.4 (34)
	165 — SR13	1.8 (26)	1.8 (26)	2.0 (28)	2.8 (40)
	185/70 — HR13	1.6 (23)	1.7 (24)	1.8 (26)	2.3 (33)

*Up to three people, plus luggage
**Four or five people, plus luggage

Torque wrench settings

Front suspension

	lb f ft	kg f m
¼ in - 20 UNC	5 - 7	0.69 - 0.97
5/16 in - 18 UNC	12 - 15	1.66 - 2.07
5/16 in - 24 UNF	12 - 15	1.66 - 2.07
3/8 in - 16 UNC	17 - 22	2.35 - 3.04
3/8 in - 24 UNF	22 - 27	3.04 - 3.73
7/16 in - 14 UNC	30 - 35	4.15 - 4.84
7/16 in - 20 UNF	40 - 45	5.53 - 6.22
½ in - 13 UNC	45 - 50	6.22 - 6.91
½ in - 20 UNF	50 - 60	6.91 - 8.29
9/16 in - 12 UNC	60 - 70	8.29 - 9.67
9/16 in - 18 UNF	65 - 75	9.98 - 10.37
5/8 in - 11 UNC	75 - 85	10.37 - 11.75
5/8 in - 18 UNF	100 - 110	13.82 - 15.20

Rear suspension

	lb f ft	kg f m
Upper radius arm to body*	42 - 50	5.8 - 6.9
Upper radius arm to axle*	42 - 50	5.8 - 6.9
Lower radius arm to body*	42 - 50	5.8 - 6.9
Lower radius arm to axle*	42 - 50	5.8 - 6.9
Coil spring to bottom plate	28 - 34	3.9 - 4.8

*These bolts must be tightened after the vehicle has been lowered to the ground.

Torque wrench settings

Steering						lb f ft	kg fm
Steering gear to crossmember ...	...	...	...	...		15 - 18	2.1 - 2.4
Track rod end to steering arm ...	...	...	...	...		18 - 22	2.5 - 3.0
Coupling to pinion spline	...	...	...	...		12 - 15	1.7 - 2.1
Universal joint to steering shaft spline		...	...	...		12 - 15	1.7 - 2.1
Steering wheel to steering shaft	...	...	...			20 - 25	2.8 - 3.4
Track rod end locknut ...	...	...	...	...		40 - 45	5.5 - 6.3
Track rod end ball housing	...	...	...	...		33 - 37	4.6 - 5.2
Pinion pre-load cover	...	...	...	...	...	6 - 8	0.9 - 1.1
Rack slipper cover	...	...	...	...	...	6 - 8	0.9 - 1.1
Pinion turning torque	...	...	...	...	...	5 - 15 (lb in)	6 - 17 (kg cm)
Wheel nuts	...	...	...	...	...	50 - 55	7.0 - 7.7

1 General description

The independent front suspension comprises short and long swinging arms with coil springs and hydraulic double acting shock absorbers which operate on the lower swinging arms. The main suspension framework is located on the underbody side members and acts as a mounting point for the wishbone type upper and single lower swinging arms. Attached to the upper frame are rubber bump stops to absorb excessive swinging arm movement. The suspension arms are mounted on rubber bushes and carry the stub axle balljoints at their outer ends.

Located on each axle stub are two taper roller bearings and these run in cups which are pressed into the wheel hubs. To keep the grease in the hub is a spring loaded neoprene seal located in the inner end of the hub. The wheel studs are splined and pressed into the hub flange.

Bolted to the lower arm are rubber mounted tie bars which control the suspension castor angle. The tie bars are connected to a stabilizer bar via a bolt and spacer and bushed at its connection points. It is mounted in split bushes which are clipped to brackets which are bolted to the body side members.

The rear suspension comprises lower and upper radius arms and coil spring. The two lower radius arms are in position in the axial direction of the vehicle and the two upper radius arms are in a diagonal position so as to absorb any forces created during cornering. All four radius arms are mounted in insulated rubber blocks. Fitted between the rear axle casing and underside of the body are rubber mounted double acting hydraulic telescopic shock absorbers.

The coil springs are mounted on the lower radius arms and locate on a rubber ring between the spring and underside of the body.

The steering gear is of the rack and pinion type and is located on the front crossmember by two 'U' shaped clamps, the pinion connected to the steering column by a flexible coupling. Above the flexible coupling the steering column is split by a universal joint that is designed to collapse on impact thus minimising injury to the driver in the event of an accident.

Turning the steering wheel causes the rack to move in a lateral direction and the track rods attached to either end of the rack pass this movement to the steering arms on the stub axle assemblies thereby moving the roadwheels.

Two adjustments are possible on the steering gear, namely rack slipper bearing adjustment and pinion bearing pre-load adjustment, but the steering gear must be removed from the car to carry out these adjustments. Both adjustments are made by varying the thickness of shim packs.

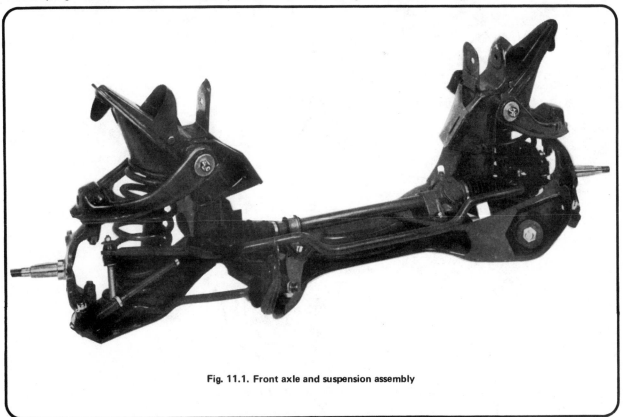

Fig. 11.1. Front axle and suspension assembly

Fig. 11.2. Rear axle and suspension assembly (late 1973 onwards)

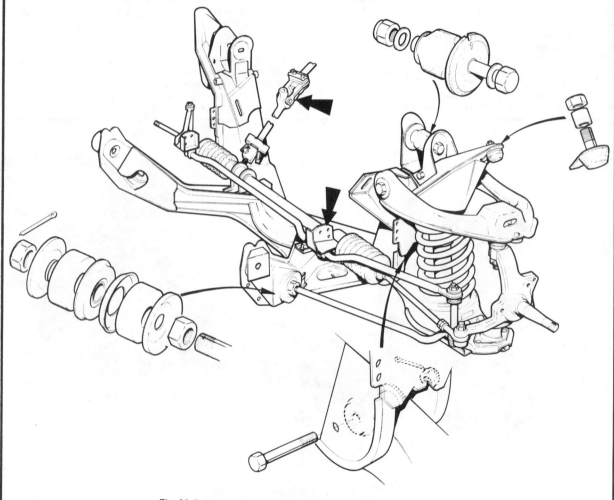

Fig. 11.3. Front suspension components (July 1973 onwards)

The two trackrods are adjustable in length to allow adjustment of the toe-in setting and to ensure the wheel lock angles are correct. Lock stops are built in to the steering gear and are not adjustable.

Vehicles built after early 1972 have modified rear axle mountings to permit adjustment of the pinion drive angle (see Chapter 8).

From late 1973, a stabilizer bar is fitted to the rear suspension and changes to components of the front suspension have been carried out. These include the following:

(i)   *Front subframe to body insulators of increased diameter.*
(ii)   *Front brake lines no longer located on crossmember.*
(iii) *Re-designed lower arm inner pivot bush and bolt.*
(iv)   *Re-designed front tie-bar mountings.*
(v)   *Re-designed stabilizer bar mounting brackets.*
(vi)   *Bolt-on type bump stop rubber cushions.*

---

2 Front hub bearings - removal and refitting

---

1   Refer to Chapter 9, Section 5, paragraphs 1, 2, 3, 5 and 6 and remove the disc brake caliper.
2   By judicious tapping and levering remove the dust cap from the centre of the hub.
3   Remove the split pin from the nut retainer and lift away the adjusting nut retainer.
4   Unscrew the adjusting nut and lift away the thrust washer and outer tapered bearing (Fig. 11.4A).
5   Pull off the complete hub and disc assembly from the stub axle.
6   From the back of the hub assembly carefully prise out the grease seal noting which way round it is fitted. Lift away the inner tapered bearing.
7   Carefully clean out the hub and wash the bearings with petrol making sure that no grease or oil is allowed to get onto the brake disc.
8   Using a soft metal drift carefully remove the inner and outer bearing cups.
9   To fit new cups make sure they are the right way round and using metal tubes of suitable size carefully drift them into position.
10 Pack the cone and roller assembly with grease working the grease well into the cage and rollers. **Note:** Leave the hub and

grease seal empty to allow for subsequent expansion of the grease.
11 To reassemble the hub first fit the inner bearing and then gently tap the grease seal back into the hub. A new seal must always be fitted as during removal it was probably damaged. The lip must face inwards to the hub.
12 Replace the hub and disc assembly on the stub axle and slide on the outer bearing and thrust washer.
13 Refit the adjusting nut and tighten it to a torque wrench setting of 27 lb ft (3.7 kg m) whilst rotating the hub and disc to ensure free movement and centralisation of the bearings (Fig. 11.4). Slacken the nut back by 90° which will give the required endfloat of 0.001 - 0.005 inch (0.03 - 0.13 mm). Fit the nut retainer and new split pin. Bend over the ears of the split pin.
14 Refit the dust cap to the centre of the hub.
15 Refit the caliper as described in Chapter 9, Section 5.

---

3 Front hub bearings - adjustment

---

1   To check the condition of the hub bearings, jack-up the front of the car and support on firmly based stands. Grasp the roadwheel at two opposite points to check for any rocking movement

Fig. 11.4. Tightening the front hub adjusting nut (Sec. 3)

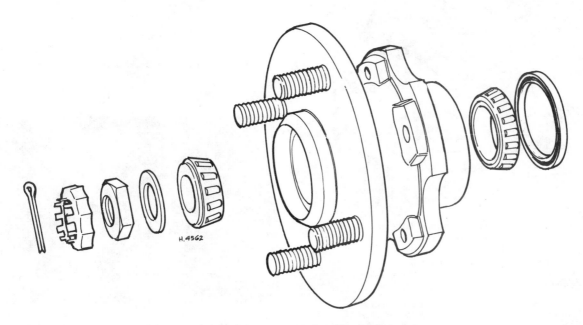

H.4562

Fig. 11.4A. Front hub and bearings

in the wheel hub. Watch carefully for any movement in the steering gear which can easily be mistaken for hub movement.

2   If a front wheel hub has excessive movement, this is adjusted by removing the hub cap and then tapping and levering the dust cap from the centre of the hub.

3   Remove the split pin from the nut retainer and lift away the adjusting nut retainer.

4   If a torque wrench is available tighten the centre adjusting nut to a torque wrench setting of 27 lb ft (3.73 kg m) as shown in Fig. 11.4 and then slacken the nut back by 120° (two flats of the nut). Replace the nut retainer and lock with a new split pin.

5   Assuming a torque wrench is not available however, tighten the centre adjusting nut until a slight drag is felt on rotating the wheel. Then loosen the nut very slowly until the wheel turns freely again and there is   just a perceptible endfloat. Refit the nut retainer and lock with a new split pin.

6   Refit the dust cap to the centre of the hub.

4   Front hub - removal and installation

1   Follow the instructions given in Section 2 of this Chapter up to and including paragraph 5.

2   Bend back the locking tab and undo the four bolts holding the hub to the brake disc.

3   If a new hub assembly is being fitted it is supplied complete with new cups and bearings. The bearing cups will already be fitted in the hub. It is essential to check that the cups and bearings are of the same manufacture, this can be done by reading the name on the bearings and by looking at the initial letter stamped on the hub, 'T' stands for Timken and 'S' for Skefco.

4   Clean with scrupulous care the mating surfaces of the hub and check for blemishes or damage. Any dirt or blemishes will almost certainly give rise to disc run-out. Using new locking tabs bolt the

disc and hub together and tighten the bolts to a torque wrench setting of 30 - 34 lb ft (4.15 - 4.70 kg m).

5   To grease and reassemble the hub assembly follow the instructions given in Section 2, paragraphs 10 onwards.

5   Front axle assembly - removal and installation

1   Chock the rear wheels, jack-up the vehicle and support the body on firmly based axle stands. Remove the front wheels.

2   Using a garage crane or overhead hoist support the weight of the engine.

3   Wipe the top of the brake master cylinder reservoir and unscrew the cap. Place a piece of polythene sheet over the top of the reservoir and refit the cap. This is to stop hydraulic fluid syphoning out during subsequent operations.

4   *On vehicles built before July 1973:* Wipe the area around the 3 way union on the axle frame and detach the main feed pipe to the union. Place some tape over the end of the pipe and open union to stop dirt ingress.

5   *On vehicles built after July 1973:* Disconnect the flexible brake hoses at the body support brackets (Fig. 11.6).

6   Slacken the steering column clamp plate and carefully withdraw the column.

7   Undo and remove the engine mounting securing nuts at the underside of the mounting. There is one nut to each mounting as shown in Fig. 11.7.

8   Using a garage hydraulic jack or blocks support the weight of the front axle sub-assembly.

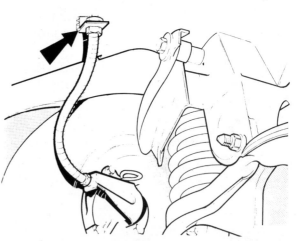

Fig. 11.6. A front flexible brake hose (July 1973 onwards) (Sec. 7)

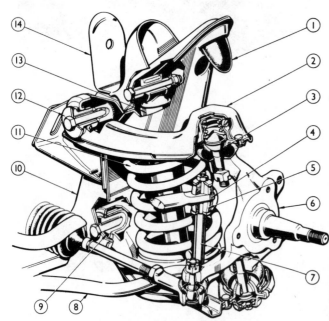

Fig. 11.5. Component parts of left-hand front suspension assembly

1 *Bump stop*	8 *Tie bar*
2 *Upper arm*	9 *Lower arm bush*
3 *Balljoint*	10 *Frame*
4 *Stabiliser*	11 *Spring*
5 *Stabiliser bar bush*	12 *Upper arm bush*
6 *Stub axle*	13 *Shock absorber*
7 *Connecting link*	14 *Frame to body mounting*

Fig. 11.7. Engine mounting securing nut (Sec. 5)

9 Undo and remove the bolts which secure the front axle sub-assembly to the body sidemembers as shown in Fig. 11.7. Carefully lower the complete assembly and draw forwards from under the front of the vehicle.

10 Refitting the front axle sub-assembly is the reverse sequence to removal. It will be necessary to bleed the brake hydraulic system as described in Chapter 9, Section 2.

6 Front axle assembly - overhaul

After high mileage it may be considered necessary to overhaul the complete front axle assembly. It is far better to remove the complete unit as described in Section 5 and dismantle it rather than to work on it still mounted on the car. Then proceed as follows:

1 Refer to Chapter 9, Section 5 and remove the caliper.

2 Prise off the hub dust cap and withdraw the split pin and nut retainer. Undo and remove the nut (Fig. 11.4A).

3 Carefully pull the hub and disc assembly from the axle stub.

4 Undo and remove the ball stud securing nuts and then using a universal balljoint separator release the balljoint taper pins from their stub axle locations.

5 Next remove the trackrod-ends from their locations on the stub axles and remove the stub axle assembly as shown in Fig. 11.9

6 Withdraw the long bolt that secures the upper arm to the axle frame and lift away the upper arm.

7 It is necessary to compress the spring. For this either make up a spring compressor tool comprising two parts as shown in Fig. 11.10 or borrow one from the local Ford garage. Do not attempt to use any makeshift tools as this can be very dangerous.

8 Using the spring compressors, contract the spring by at least 2 inches (51 mm).

9 Undo and remove the upper and lower shock absorber retaining nuts (lower fixing) and bolt (upper fixing). The shock absorber may now be lifted away through the coil spring and lower arm aperture.

10 Undo and remove the bolts that secure the tie bar to the lower arm. The lower arm should now be pulled down until there is sufficient clearance for the coil spring to be lifted away.

11 Bend back the lock tabs and unscrew and remove the four bolts that secure the steering 'U' shaped rack brackets to the front axle frame. Lift away the steering rack assembly.

12 Undo and remove the nut and bolt that secures the lower arm to the front axle frame. Lift away the lower arm.

13 Using a suitable diameter drift or long bolt, piece of metal tube, packing washers and nut, remove the lower arm bush.

14 The operations described in paragraphs 1 - 13 should now be repeated for the second front suspension assembly. It will be necessary to release the coil spring compressor.

15 Undo and remove the nuts that secure the tie bars to the axle frame. Lift away the connecting link, tie bar and stabilizer bar assembly.

16 Undo and remove the nuts and washers from each of the connecting links and part the stabilizer bar from the tie bars.

17 It is now beneficial to cut away the bushes in the tie bar and stabilizer which will make removal far easier.

18 Pull out the two bump stop rubbers from the axle frame.

19 *On vehicles built before July 1973.* Undo and remove the three way union retaining nut, release the brake pipe from its mounting clips and lift away the complete brake pipe assembly.

20 Dismantling is now complete. Wash all parts and wipe dry ready for inspection. Inspect all bushes for signs of wear and all parts for any damage or excessive corrosion: if evident, new parts must be obtained. If one coil spring requires renewal the second one must also be renewed as it will have settled over a period of time. If the brake pipe has corroded now is the time to obtain a new one.

21 During reassembly it is important that none of the rubber mounted bolts are fully tightened until the weight of the vehicle is taken on the front wheels.

22 *On early models:* Position the three way union and brake

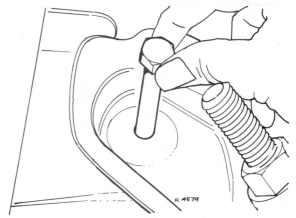

Fig. 11.8. Front axle securing bolts to body side member (Sec. 5)

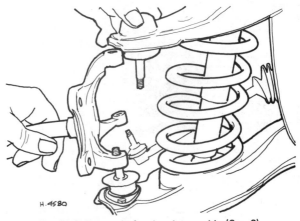

Fig. 11.9. Removal of stub axle assembly (Sec. 6)

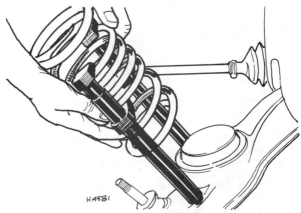

Fig. 11.10. Front coil spring with compressor fitted (Sec. 6)

pipe on the front axle frame and secure in position with the nut and clips.

23 Replace the rubber bump stops. If they are difficult to insert in their locations smear with a little washing up liquid. On later models, the bump stops are bolted in position.

24 *On all models:* Fit new end bushes to the stabilizer and tie bar and then locate the connecting links in the stabilizer.

25 Next locate the connecting links in the tie bar and stabilizer bar bushes. Secure with their nut and washers.

26 Screw the nuts on the tie bar ends and follow with the washer together with the bush. Locate the tie bars in their respective

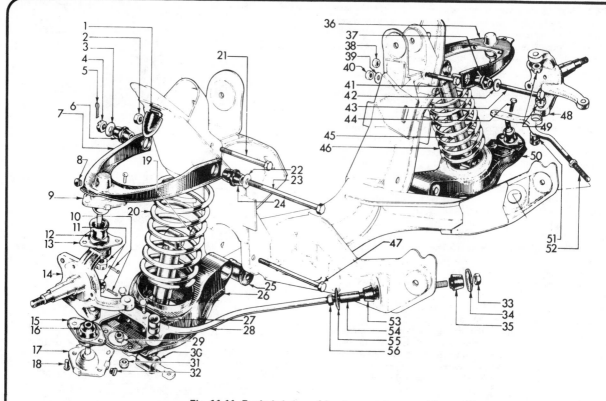

Fig. 11.11. Exploded view of front suspension assembly

1 *Bump rubber*	15 *Retaining plate*	29 *Nut*	43 *Bolt*
2 *Nut*	16 *Rubber boot*	30 *Shock absorber*	44 *Bolt*
3 *Plain washer*	17 *Balljoint*	31 *Nut*	45 *Shock absorber*
4 *Castellated nut*	18 *Rivet*	32 *Rubber plug*	46 *Coil spring*
5 *Split pin*	19 *Nut*	33 *Nut*	47 *Bolt*
6 *Bush*	20 *Coil spring*	34 *Dished washer*	48 *Stub axle*
7 *Upper arm*	21 *Bolt*	35 *Bush*	49 *Castellated nut*
8 *Rubber plug*	22 *Plain washer*	36 *Upper arm*	50 *Lower suspension arm*
9 *Balljoint*	23 *Bolt*	37 *Bush*	51 *Bush*
10 *Split pin*	24 *Bush*	38 *Nut*	52 *Tie bar*
11 *Castellated nut*	25 *Bush*	39 *Plain washer*	53 *Bush*
12 *Rubber boot*	26 *Lower suspension arm*	40 *Nut*	54 *Spacer*
13 *Retaining plate*	27 *Bush*	41 *Bolt*	55 *Dished washer*
14 *Stub axle*	28 *Tie bar*	42 *Plain washer*	56 *Nut*

positions on the frame and loosely refit the spacer, bush, nut and washer.

27 Using a bench vice and suitable diameter tube fit a new bush to the lower arm. On later models, the lower arm pivot bolt is fitted with a nyloc nut and split pin. Tighten the nut to 55 lb ft (7.6 kg m).

28 Locate the lower arm in the frame and line up the holes with a screwdriver. Refit the pivot bolt and washers making sure that bolt head is towards the front of the axle frame.

29 Refit the tie bar to the lower suspension arm and retain with the two nuts and bolts.

30 Place the coil spring between the frame and lower arm. Insert the shock absorber through the lower arm and spring and secure the shock absorber in position with the bolt (upper fixing) and nuts (lower fixing).

31 Unscrew the spring compressor and repeat the operations in paragraphs 24 to 30 for the second front suspension assembly.

32 Check the condition of the steering rack mounting rubbers and renew if necessary. Position the steering rack on the axle frame and secure to the mounting brackets with the 'U' clamps. Always use new locking plate under the bolt heads. Tighten the bolts to a torque wrench setting of 15 - 18 lb ft (2.1 - 2.4 kg m),

and bend up the locking plate.

33 Place the upper suspension arm on the axle frame, insert the pivot bolt through the arm and frame holes so that the head is towards the front of the axle frame. Secure with the washer and nut. Repeat this operation for the second upper suspension arm.

34 Connect the stub axle assembly to the suspension arm balljoints, locate the trackrod ends in the stub axle, and tighten all the nuts. The trackrod end to steering arm nuts should be tightened to a torque wrench setting of 18 - 22 lb ft (2.5 - 3 kg m).

35 Refer to Section 4 and refit the hub and disc assemblies.

36 The complete front axle assembly may now be refitted to the car, as described in Section 5.

37 Check the wheel alignment and steering angles (Section 22).

7 Front axle mounting bushes - removal and refitting

1 Refer to Section 5, and remove the front axle assembly.

2 Using a piece of tube about 4 inches (101.6 mm) long and suitable diameter, a long bolt and nut and packing washers draw the bushes from the side member (Fig. 11.13).

3 New bushes may now be fitted using the reverse procedure as was used for removal.

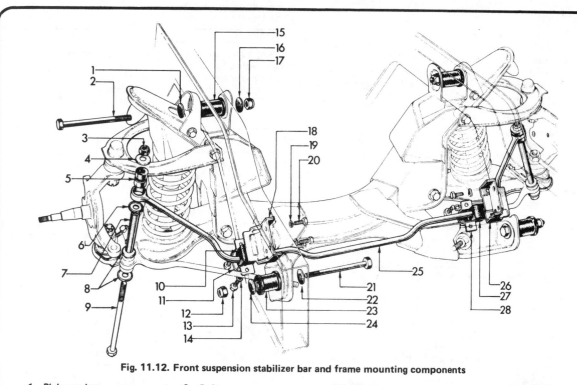

Fig. 11.12. Front suspension stabilizer bar and frame mounting components

1	Plain washer	9	Bolt	17	Nut	25	Stabilizer bar
2	Bolt	10	Rubber bush	18	Bracket	26	Bracket
3	Nut	11	Bracket	19	Spring washer	27	Rubber bush
4	Dished washer	12	Nut	20	Bolt	28	Bracket
5	Bush	13	Bolt	21	Bolt		
6	Dished washer	14	Spring washer	22	Plain washer		
7	Spacer	15	Bush	23	Bush		
8	Dished washer	16	Plain washer	24	Plain washer		

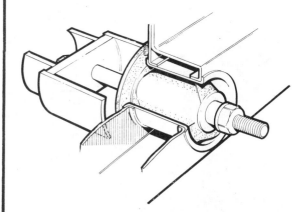

Fig. 11.13. Removing a front axle mounting bush (Sec. 7)

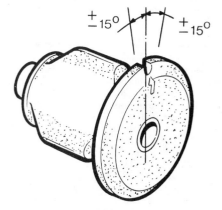

Fig. 11.14. Front axle mounting bush alignment mark (July 1973 onwards) (Sec. 7)

4   Refit the front assembly, as described in Section 5.
5   On vehicles built after July 1973, the new bushes must be installed so that the arrows are in alignment with the indentation in the bodyframe. The flange position of the bushes must be: **front bush**, flange located **inside** sidemember; **rear bush**, flange located **outside** sidemember (Fig. 11.14).

8   Stub axle - removal and installation

1   Refer to Section 2 and remove the front hub and disc

assembly.
2   Undo and remove the three bolts and spring washers that secure the brake disc splash shield to the stub axle.
3   Extract the split pins and then undo and remove the castellated nuts that secure the three balljoint pins to the stub axle.
4   Using a universal balljoint separator, separate the balljoint pins from the stub axle. Lift away the stub axle.
5   Refitting the stub axle is the reverse sequence to removal. The trackrod end to steering arm retaining nut must be tightened to a torque wrench setting of 18 - 22 lb ft (2.5 - 3.0 kg m).
6   If a new stub axle has been fitted it is recommended that the

steering geometry and front wheel toe-in be checked. Further information may be found in Section 22.

9 Lower suspension arm - removal and installation

1 Chock the rear wheels, jack-up the front of the car and place on firmly based axle stands. Remove the roadwheel.
2 Undo and remove the bolt that secures the brake pipe bracket and carefully push the pipes to one side.
3 It is now necessary to compress the spring. For this either make up a spring compressor tool comprising two parts as shown in Fig. 11.10 or borrow one from the local Ford garage. Do not attempt to use any makeshift tools as this can be very dangerous.
4 Using the spring compressor, contract the spring by at least 2 inches (51 mm).
5 Undo and remove the upper and lower shock absorber retaining nuts (lower fixing) and bolt (upper fixing). The shock absorber may now be lifted away through the coil spring and lower arm aperture.
6 Withdraw the split pin, undo and remove the castellated nut that secures the lower wishbone balljoint pin to the stub axle. Using a universal balljoint separator separate the balljoint pin from the stub axle.
7 The lower suspension arm may now be parted and the coil spring removed.
8 Undo the tie bar locknut and remove the two bolts and nuts that secure the tie bar to the lower arm.
9 Undo and remove the bolt that secures the lower arm to the front axle frame. The low suspension arm can now be lifted rearwards and downwards away from the front axle frame.
10 To fit a new bush first remove the old bush by using a piece of tube about 4 inches (101.6 mm) long and suitable diameter, a long bolt and nut and packing washer, draw the bush from the lower suspension arm. Fitting a new bush is the reverse sequence to removal.
11 Refitting the lower suspension arm is the reverse sequence to removal. The lower arm retaining bolts must be tightened once the car has been lowered to the ground.
12 If a new lower steering arm has been fitted it is recommended that the steering geometry and front wheel toe-in be checked. Further information may be found in Section 22.

10 Stabilizer bar - removal and installation

1 Undo and remove the bolt that secures each stabilizer bar mounting bush clip to the stabilizer bar mounting bracket.
2 Release the clips and then undo and remove the three bolts and spring washers that secure each mounting bracket to the body sidemember (Fig. 11.15).
3 Undo and remove the two nuts, dished washers and upper bushes and detach the connecting links from their locations in the stabilizer bar. The stabilizer bar may now be lifted away from the underside of the car.
4 Refitting the stabilizer bar is the reverse sequence to removal.
5 After 1973, new type stabilizer bar brackets are fitted to clear the crossmember.

11 Stabilizer bar mounting bushes - removal and installation

1 Undo and remove the bolt that secures each stabilizer bar mounting bush clip to the stabilizer bar mounting brackets.
2 Using a metal bar such as a tyre lever carefully ease the stabilizer bar downwards and push the split mounting bushes and washers clear   of their locations.
3 Push the new bushes and washers onto the bar in their approximate positions and then align the bushes with the stabilizer bar mounting brackets and refit the retaining clips and bolts.

12 Stabilizer bar connecting link bush - removal and refitting

1 Refer to Section 10 and remove the stabilizer bar.
2 Using a sharp knife or hacksaw blade cut the cone ends off the connecting link bushes and discard the bushes.
3 Using a bench vice, a piece of tube of suitable diameter and a socket fit the new connecting link bushes.
4 Refit the stabilizer bar as described in Section 10.

13 Front shock absorber - removal and refitting

1 Chock the rear wheels, jack-up the front of the car and place on firmly based stands. Remove the roadwheel.
2 Locate a small jack under the lower suspension arm and partially compress the coil spring.
3 Undo and remove the shock absorber top mounting bolt.
4 Undo and remove the two nuts that secure the shock absorber lower mounting. The shock absorber may now   be lifted away through the coil spring and lower arm aperture.
5 Examine the shock absorber for signs of damage to the body,

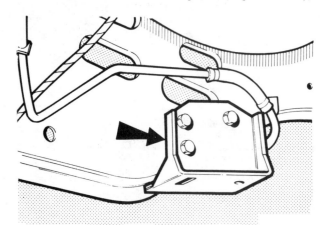

Fig. 11.15. Front stabilizer bar brackets (July 1973 onwards) (Sec. 10)

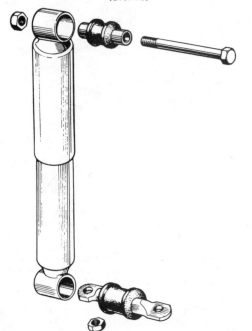

Fig. 11.16. Front shock absorber and mountings (Sec. 13)

distorted piston rod, loose mounting or hydraulic fluid leakage which, if evident, means a new unit should be fitted.

6   To test for shock absorber efficiency, hold the unit in the vertical position and gradually extend and contract the unit between its maximum and minimum limit ten times. It should be apparent that there is equal resistance on both directions of movement. If this is not   apparent a new unit should be fitted - always renew the shock absorbers in pairs.

7   Refitting the shock absorbers is the reverse sequence to removal.

14 Tie bar - removal and refitting

1   Chock the rear wheels, jack-up the front of   the car and place on firmly based axle stands. Remove the roadwheel.

2   Undo and remove the bolts that secure the tie bar to the lower suspension arm.

3   Extract the split pin from the end of   the bar. Undo and remove the forward of the two nuts that secure the tie bar to the chassis frame member.

4   Where fitted disconnect the stabilizer bar connecting link.

5   Remove the bush and spacer assembly from the threaded end of the tie bar. Lift away the tie bar (Fig. 11.17).

6   If it is necessary to fit new bushes, use a sharp knife or hacksaw blade and cut the cone ends from the tie bar bush. Discard the old bush.

7   Using a tube of suitable diameter, a socket and bench vice,

fit a new tie bar end bush.

8   Refitting   the tie bar is the reverse sequence to removal. It is recommended that the steering geometry and front wheel toe-in be checked. Further information will be found in Section 22.

15 Rear suspension and rear axle - removal and installation

1   Chock the front wheels, jack-up the rear of the car and support the body on firmly based stands. Remove the rear wheels.

2   Unscrew the two cheese-head screws that secure the brake

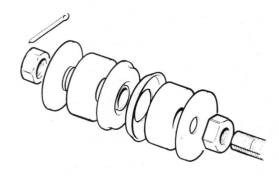

Fig. 11.17. Tie bar connection detail (July 1973 onwards) (Sec. 14)

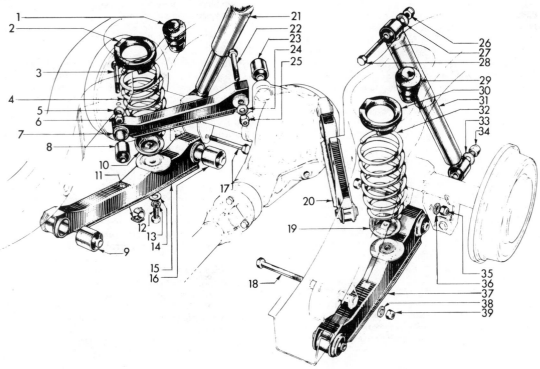

Fig. 11.18. Rear suspension components

1	Rebound rubber	11	Cable clip	21	Shock absorber	31	Shock absorber
2	Spring seat rubber	12	Bolt	22	Bolt	32	Coil spring
3	Bolt	13	Spring washer	23	Bush	33	Plain washer
4	Coil spring	14	Plain washer	24	Plain washer	34	Nut
5	Plain washer	15	Lower radius arm	25	Nut	35	Nut
6	Nut	16	Bush	26	Nut	36	Plain washer
7	Upper radius arm	17	Bolt	27	Plain washer	37	Lower radius arm
8	Bush	18	Bolt	28	Bolt	38	Plain washer
9	Bush	19	Spring seat metal	29	Rebound rubber	39	Nut
10	Spring seat metal	20	Upper radius arm	30	Spring seat rubber		

drum to the hub.

3   Release the handbrake and remove the brake drum, using a soft faced hammer on the outer circumference.

4   Should the situation exist whereby the shoes foul the drum making removal impossible the shoes must be collapsed by detaching the handbrake cable from the body mounted brackets and   then the plunger assembly removed from the backplate. Whenever the plunger is removed it must be discarded and a new one obtained.

5   Completely remove the handbrake cable from the body mounted brackets and disconnect the cable from the relay lever inwards. Grip the handbrake cable end with a pair of pliers and release it from the end of the relay lever. Pull the handbrake cable through each brake backplate.

6   With a scriber or file mark a line across the propeller shaft and pinion driving flanges so that they may be refitted together in their original positions.

7   Undo and remove the four bolts and spring washers securing the propeller shaft driving flanges and carefully lower the propeller shaft. *Models fitted with the split type propeller shaft:* it is necessary to undo and remove the two bolts with spring and plain washers that secure the centre bearing support to the underside of the body before the propeller shaft can be removed. Wipe the top of the brake master cylinder reservoir and unscrew the cap. Place a piece of polythene sheeting over the reservoir neck and refit the cap. This is to stop hydraulic fluid syphoning out during subsequent operations.

8   Wipe the area around the brake flexible pipe to metal pipe union just in front of the rear axle and referring to Chapter 9, Section 3, detach the flexible hose from the metal pipe.

9   Slacken the nuts which secure the lower radius arms to the rear axle casing. Carefully position a jack under one radius arm and very slightly compress the spring. Remove the nut and bolt from the front mounting. Now lower the jack so allowing the spring to extend. When the spring is fully extended lift it away and recover the rubber ring from the upper spring mounting.

10 Support the weight of the rear axle by placing the saddle of a jack (preferably trolley type) under the centre of the rear axle.

11 Undo and remove the nut and bolt securing the top of the shock absorber to the body mounted bracket.

12 Undo and remove the nut and bolt that secures the radius arm to the underside of the body.

13 Repeat the operations in paragraphs 11 and 12 for the second side of the rear suspension assembly.

14 The rear suspension and axle assembly may now be withdrawn from under the rear of the car.

15 Refitting the rear suspension and axle assembly is the reverse sequence to removal. The two marks previously made on the propeller shaft and pinion flanges should be correctly aligned.

16 The lower radius   arm mounting bolts must only be tightened to a torque wrench setting of 42 - 50 lb ft (5.8 - 6.9 kg m), when the roadwheels have been refitted and the car is standing on the ground.

17 It will be necessary to bleed the brake hydraulic system, as described in Chapter 9, Section 3.

18 The brake shoes must be centralised by the brake pedal being depressed firmly several times. Pull on and then release the handbrake lever until it is no longer possible to hear the clicking noise of the ratchet being turned by the adjusting arm.

19 On vehicles built after July 1973, check and adjust the pinion drive angle, as described in Chapter 8.

---

16 Rear suspension upper radius arm - removal and installation

1   Chock the front wheels, jack-up the rear of the car and support the body on firmly based stands. Remove the rear wheels.

Vehicles built before July 1973

2   Support the weight of the rear axle and then undo and remove the nut and bolt securing the radius arm. Should it be found that the bolt is trapped by a spring coil, undo and remove the shock absorber lower mounting nut and bolt. This will enable the rear

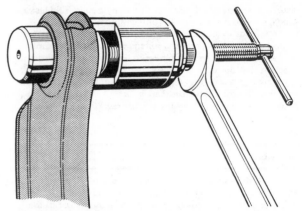

Fig. 11.19. Extracting a rear suspension radius arm bush (Sec. 16)

axle to drop slightly, thereby extending the spring enough for the through bolt to be removed through the spring coils.

3   Lift away the upper radius arm.

Vehicles built after July 1973

4   Disconnect the stabilizer bar from the radius arm which is being removed and swing it to one side.

5   Jack-up the rear axle so that the shock absorber can be disconnected from the axle mounting.

6   Lower the jack and press the coil spring from its upper retainer. Now twist the spring from its lower retainer.

7   Again jack-up the rear axle and having relieved the radius arm bolts of any strain, remove the bolts and withdraw the radius arm.

All models

8   Should it be necessary to fit new mounting insulator bushes the bushes may be removed using a piece of tube about 4 inches (101.6 mm) long and suitable diameter, a long bolt and nut and packing washers and drawing out the old bushes (Fig. 11.19).

9   Fitting new bushes is the reverse procedure as was used for removal.

10 Refitting is the reverse sequence to removal. The upper radius arm attachments to the body and axle must be tightened to a torque wrench setting of 42 - 50 lb ft (5.8 - 6.9 kg m), when the car has been lowered to the ground.

---

17 Rear suspension lower radius arm - removal and refitting

1   Chock the front wheels, jack-up the rear of the car and support the body on firmly based axle stands. Remove the rear wheels.

On vehicles built before July 1973

2   Support the weight of the rear axle and then undo and remove the two radius arm mounting through bolt nuts. Remove the front mounting through bolt and carefully lower the jack. This will remove the load from the rear coil spring.

3   Remove the radius arm rear mounting through bolt and lift away the radius arm and coil spring. Recover the upper spring rubber bush. Finally detach the spring from the radius arm.

On vehicles built after July 1973

4   Disconnect the stabilizer bar from the radius arm and swing it to one side.

5   Jack-up the rear axle and disconnect the shock absorber lower mounting.

6   Lower the jack and press the coil spring from the upper retainer. Twist the spring from the lower retainer.

7   Remove the radius arm pivot bolts and withdraw the arm.

All models

8   Should it be necessary to fit new mounting insulator bushes,

the bushes may be removed using a piece of tube about 4 inches (101.6 mm) long and suitable diameter, a long bolt and nut and packing washers and drawing out the old bushes.

9   Fitting new bushes is the reverse procedure as was used for removal. **Note:** the two bushes are of different diameters.

10 Refitting the lower radius arm is the reverse sequence to removal. The upper spring rubber bush **must** be refitted correctly. The attachments to the body and axle must be tightened to a torque wrench setting of 42 - 50 lb ft (5.8 - 6.9 kg m), after the car has been lowered to the ground.

18 Rear suspension bump rubber - removal and refitting

Removal of a bump rubber is simply a matter of pulling it downwards from its mushroom shaped mounting stud. Refitting is a reversal of the removal procedure.

19 Rear shock absorber - removal and refitting

1   Chock the front wheels, jack-up the rear of the car and support the axle on firmly based stands. Remove the rear wheel.

2   Undo and remove the shock absorber upper   and lower mounting   nuts and bolts. Lift away the shock absorbers.

3   Should it be necessary to fit new rubber bushes, use a suitable diameter drift and drive out the spacer sleeve and then the rubber bushes. Refitting new bushes is the reversal of the removal sequence.

4   Examine the shock absorber for signs of damage to the body, distorted piston rod or hydraulic leakage which, if evident, means a new unit should be fitted.

5   To test for damper efficiency hold the unit in the vertical position and gradually extend and contract the unit between its maximum and minimum limits ten times. It should be apparent that there is equal resistance in both directions of movement. If this is not apparent a new unit should be fitted; always renew shock absorbers in pairs.

6   Refitting the shock absorber is the reverse sequence to removal.

20 Rear stabilizer bar - removal and installation

1   Remove   the bolts which secure each end of the stabilizer bar to the radius arms.

2   Unscrew the self-locking nuts and withdraw the front and rear mounting brackets together with the insulating bushes.

3   Bushes are renewed in a similar manner to those for the shock absorbers, by first removing the metal spacer. The use of a little brake fluid will facilitate installation of the rubber bush.

21 Steering - lubrication

1   Lubrication of the rack and pinion during normal service operation is not necessary, the lubricant is contained in the assembly   by rubber gaiters. However, should a loss occur due to a leak from the rack housing or rubber gaiters then the correct amount of oil should be inserted using an oil can. Obviously before replenishment is carried out the source of leak must be found and rectified.

2   To top-up the oil in the rack and pinion assembly, remove the clip from the rubber gaiter on the right-hand end of the steering rack housing and rotate the steering wheel until the rack is in the normal straight ahead position. Allow any remaining oil to seep out so that it is not overfilled. Using an oil can filled with Hypoy 90 type gear oil insert the nozzle into the end of the rack housing and refill with not more than 0.25 pint (0.14 litre) of oil.

3   Reposition the gaiter and tighten the clip quickly to ensure minimum loss of oil and then move the steering wheel from lock to lock very slowly to distribute the oil in the housing.

Fig. 11.20. Rear shock absorber and mountings (Sec. 19)

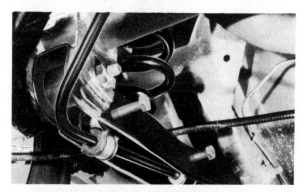

Fig. 11.21. Rear stabilizer bar to lower radius arm mounting (Sec. 20)

Fig. 11.22. Rear stabilizer bar mounting components (Sec. 20)

Important: If at any time the car is raised from the ground and the front wheels are clear and suspended, do not use any excessive force or rapid movement when moving the wheels, especially from one lock to the other, otherwise damage could occur to the steering mechanism.

22 Front wheel - alignment and steering angles

1   Accurate front wheel alignment is essential to prevent excessive steering and tyre wear. Before considering the steering/ suspension geometry, check that the tyres are correctly inflated, that the front wheels are not buckled, the hub bearings are not worn or incorrectly adjusted and that the steering linkage is in good order, without slackness or wear at the joints.

2   Wheel alignment consists of four factors:

Camber, which is the angle at which the front wheels are set from the vertical when viewed from the front of the car. Positive camber is the amount (in degrees) that the wheels are tilted outwards at the top from the vertical (Fig. 11.23).

Castor, is the angle between the steering axis and a vertical line when viewed from each side of the car. Positive castor is when the steering axis is inclined rearward (Fig. 11.24).

Steering axis inclination, is the angle, when viewed from the front of the car between the vertical and an imaginary line drawn between the upper and lower suspension control arm balljoints (Fig. 11.25).

Toe-in, is the amount by which the distance between the front inside edges of the roadwheels (measured at hub height) is less than the diametrically opposite distance measured between the rear inside edges of the front roadwheels (Fig. 11.26).

3   Due to the need for special gauges it is not normally within the scope of the home mechanic to check and adjust any steering angle except toe-in. Where suitable equipment can be borrowed however, adjustment can be carried out in the following way, setting the tolerances to those given in **Specifications.**

4   Before carrying out any adjustment, place the vehicle on level ground, tyres correctly inflated and the front roadwheels set in the 'straight-ahead' position. Make sure that all suspension and

steering components are securely attached and without wear in the moving parts.

The camber and steering axis inclination angles are set in production and they cannot be altered or adjusted. Any deviation from the angles specified must therefore be due to collision damage or gross wear in the components.

5   *To adjust the castor angle,* release the tie bar nuts and screw

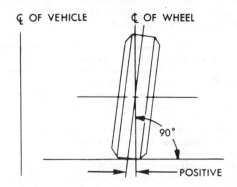

Fig. 11.23. Camber diagram (Sec. 22)

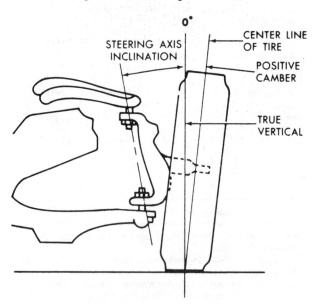

Fig. 11.25. Steering axis inclination diagram (Sec. 22)

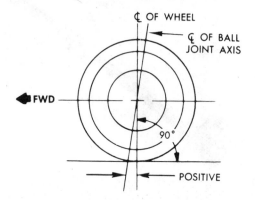

Fig. 11.24. Castor diagram (Sec. 22)

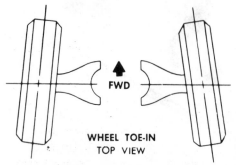

Fig. 11.26. Toe-in diagram (Sec. 22)

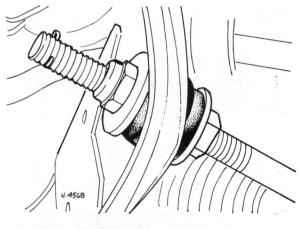

Fig. 11.27. Tie-bar nuts (Sec. 22)

them in, or out, as necessary (Fig. 11.27).

6 *To adjust the toe-in* (which must always be carried out after adjustment of the castor angle - where required), make or obtain a toe-in gauge. One can be made up from a length of tubing or bar, cranked to clear the sump, clutch or torque converter bell-housing and having a screw and locknut at one end.

7 Use the gauge to measure the distance between the two inner wheel rims (at hub height and at the rear of the roadwheels).

8 Push or pull the vehicle to rotate the roadwheels through 180° (half a turn) and then measure the distance between the inner wheel rims (at hub height and at the front of the roadwheels). This last measurement will be less than the first by the amount of toe-in specified in the Specifications Section according to vehicle year of production. This represents the correct toe-in of the front wheels.

9 Where the toe-in is found to be incorrect, loosen the locknuts on both the trackrod ends, also release the screws on the steering bellow clips (Fig. 11.28).

10 Turn each trackrod in opposite directions by not more than one quarter turn at a time and then recheck the toe-in. When the adjustment is correct, tighten the locknuts without moving the trackrods and make sure that the trackrod ends are in their correct plane (centre position of arc of travel).

11 Tighten the steering bellows clips making sure that the bellows have not twisted during the adjustment operations.

12 It is important to always adjust each trackrod equally. Where new components have been fitted, adjust the height of each trackrod so that they are equal and the front roadwheels in approximately the 'straight-ahead' position, before commencing final setting with the toe-in gauge.

23 Steering wheel - removal and refitting

1 If a steering wheel embellishment is fitted, undo and remove the two crosshead screws that secure it to the spokes. The screw heads will be found on the underside of the spokes. Lift away the embellishment.

2 With the front wheels in the straight-ahead position note the position of the spokes of the steering wheel and mark the hub of the steering wheel and inner shaft to ensure correct positioning upon refitting.

3 Using a socket or box spanner of correct size slacken and remove the steering wheel nut. Remove the wheel by thumping the rear of the rim adjacent to the spokes with the palms of the hands which should loosen the hub splines from the steering shaft spline. Lift away the steering wheel.

4 Replacement is the reverse procedure to removal. Correctly align the two marks previously made to ensure correct positioning of the spikes. Do not thump the steering wheel when refitting as it could cause the inner shaft to collapse. Refit the nut and tighten to a torque wrench setting of 20 - 25 lb ft (2.8 - 3.4 kg m).

24 Steering column assembly (up to July 1973) - removal and installation

1 Bend back the lockwasher tabs and undo and remove the two bolts that secure the clamp bar to the upper universal joint assembly. Lift away the lockwasher and clamp bar.

2 Undo and remove the nut, spring washer and long bolt that holds the two halves of the column shroud. Lift away the annulus from the top of the shroud. Pull off the choke control knob (if a manual choke is fitted). Using a knife separate the two halves of the shroud and lift away.

3 Slacken the choke control locknut on the bracket positioned at the side of the steering column. Release the choke outer cable from the bracket by sliding it through the slot in the bracket.

4 Locate the ignition switch wiring loom multi pin connector located half way down the column and detach the connector and two single connectors.

5 Undo and remove the two bolts and shakeproof washers that

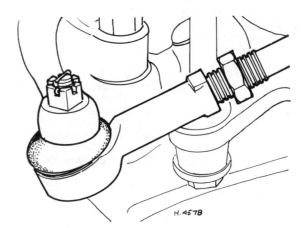

Fig. 11.28. Trackrod-end locknut (Sec. 22)

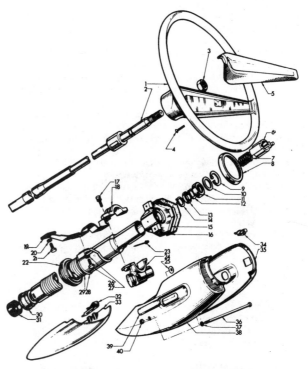

Fig. 11.29. Steering wheel and column assembly

1	Steering wheel	22	Rubber grommet
2	Steering shaft	23	Rivet
3	Nut	24	Bracket
4	Screw	25	Clip
5	Embellisher	26	Bolt
6	Self cancel cam	27	Spring washer
7	Spring	28	Outer tube
8	Annulus	29	Collapsible outer tube
9	Circlip	30	Lower bearing
10	Plain washer	31	Bearing cover
11	Bearing cover	32	Spire nut
12	Circlip	33	Column shroud half (alternative)
13	Upper bearing		
14	Circlip	34	Clip
15	Bracket	35	Column shroud half
16	Bracket surround	36	Bolt
17	Bolt	37	Spring washer
18	Bracket end cap	38	Column shroud half
19	Bracket - lower	39	Chrome finisher (automatic choke only)
20	Spring washer		
21	Bolt	40	Nut

secure the direction indicator switch. Lift away the switch.
6   Remove the steering wheel as described in Section 23.
7   Lift away the direction indicator self cancel cam and spring
from the inner shaft.
8   Detach the brake pedal return spring from the pedal assembly.
9   Undo and remove the bolts and spring washers that secure the
steering column mounting bolts to the underside of the dash
panel.
10 Pull the column assembly into the car and lift away. Take care
not to touch the headlining or trim with the column.
11 To refit the steering column locate it in its approximate
position making sure that the grommets located at the bottom of
the assembly locate in the dash panel. The triangular shaft
locates in the universal joint clamp.
12 Refitting is now the reverse sequence to removal. Make sure
that the ear on the self cancel cam is adjacent to the cancelling
lever of the indicator switch when the front wheels are in the
atraight-ahead position. When refitting the steering wheel do not
thump it as the inner shaft could collapse. Finally before the
steering wheel nut is replaced check that direction indicators self
cancel operate correctly.

Fig. 11.30. Dash lower insulation panel securing screws (Sec. 25)

25 Steering column assembly (after July 1973) - removal and installation

1   Disconnect the battery and then working within the engine
compartment, bend back the locktabs on the flexible coupling
clamp plate. Slacken both bolts, extract one and swing the clamp
plate to one side.
2   Unscrew and remove the steering column lower shroud and
remove it, then unclip the upper shroud.
3   Pull off the instrument panel light switch knob and the radio
control knobs.
4   Remove the six screws which retain the instrument cluster
and bezel. Pull the bezel far enough forward to enable the multi-
pin connectors to be disconnected at the rear of the instruments.
Also disconnect the leads from the cigar lighter, the hazard
warning switch and the heated rear window switch and the
speedometer cable.
5   Unscrew and remove the dash lower insulation panel.
6   Remove the two bolts which secure the wiper and light
switch, disconnect the multi-pin connector and remove the
switch.
7   Remove the section of air duct which passes over the steering
column.
8   Remove the two screws which secure the wiring harness plug
to the bottom of the ignition switch.
9   Remove the upper and lower steering column bracket bolts,
lower the column and then withdraw it through the vehicle
interior.
10 Installation is a reversal of removal but great care must be
taken to align the column, as described in Chapter 10, Section
48.

26 Steering column shaft (up to July 1973) - removal and refitting

1   Refer to Section 24 and remove the steering column assembly.
2   Lift away the lower bearing cover. Using a pointed chisel
carefully prise open the staking and ease out the lower bearing.
3   With a pair of circlip pliers contract and withdraw the circlip
and plain washer from the top end of the shaft.
4   Again with the circlip pliers remove the upper bearing top
retaining circlip.
5   Using a soft faced hammer carefully tap the shaft down
through the outer tube and then remove the top bearing together
with its cover.
6   The shaft may now be completely removed from the outer
tube. Finally remove the upper bearing lower retaining circlip.
7   Inspect the shaft for signs of collapse. The total length of the
shaft must be 31.12 ± 0.02 inch (790.5 ± 0.5 mm) and if it is

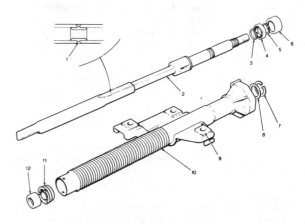

Fig. 11.31. Steering column and shaft assembly

1	'Deirin' insert	7	Column retaining circlip
2	Steering shaft	8	Plain washer
3	Upper bearing lower circlip	9	Mounting bracket
4	Upper bearing	10	Collapsible outer tube
5	Upper bearing top circlip	11	Lower bearing
6	Upper bearing cover	12	Lower bearing cover

shorter it may be carefully pulled back to the optimum length.
Grasp both ends and try twisting. If backlash is evident a new
shaft must be obtained. Check that the steering wheel location
splines are in good order and not worn.
8   To reassemble first fit a new upper bearing lower retainer
circlip. Insert the shaft into the outer tube and slide the upper
bearing onto the shaft until it locates on its splines in front of the
circlip.
9   Fit the upper bearing cover and push the shaft into its final
fitted position in the outer tube. Locate and fit a new upper bearing top retaining circlip.
10 Next fit the plain washer and secure the assembly with a new
shaft retaining circlip.
11 Fit a new lower bearing and secure it in position by staking it
in the place provided. Refit the lower bearing cover.

27 Steering column shaft (after July 1973) - removal and refitting

1   It is not recommended that the steering column is dismantled:
in the event of wear occurring, a new column assembly should be
fitted.

28 Steering column flexible coupling and universal joint assembly - removal and refitting

1   Undo and remove the nut, clamp bolt and spring washer that secures the flexible coupling bottom half to the pinion shaft.
2   Bend back the locktabs and undo and remove the two bolts securing the universal joint lock bar to the lower steering shaft. Lift away the tab washer and lock bar.
3   The lower steering shaft may now be lifted away.
4   To refit place the lower steering shaft in its approximate fitted position and align the master splines on the shaft and pinion. Connect the shaft to the pinion.
5   Position the triangular clamp on the bottom of the steering column and secure with the clamp bar bolts and tab washer. Tighten the bolts fully and lock by bending up the tabs.
6   Refit the flexible coupling bottom half clamp bolt spring washer and nut. Tighten to a torque wrench setting of 12 - 15 lb ft (1.7 - 2.1 kg m).
7   On vehicles built after July 1973, the flexible coupling is larger and of different design but the removal and installation procedure is the same as for earlier units.

29 Rack and pinion steering gear - removal and installation

1   Before starting this operation set the steering wheel to the straight-ahead position.
2   Jack-up the front of the car and place blocks under the wheels. Lower the car slightly so that the track rods are in a near horizontal position.
3   Undo and remove the nut, bolt and spring washer that secures the flexible coupling bottom half clamp to the pinion shaft.
4   Bend back the lock tabs and then undo and remove the bolts that secure the steering gear assembly to the mountings on the front axle frame. Lift away the bolts, lock washers and 'U' shaped clamps.
5   Withdraw the split pins and undo and remove the castellated nuts from the ends of each trackrod where they join the steering arms. Using a universal balljoint separator, separate the trackrod ball pins from the steering arms and lower the steering gear assembly downwards out of the car.
6   Before replacing the steering gear assembly make sure the wheels have remained in the straight-ahead position. Also check the condition of the mounting rubbers round the housing and if they appear worn or damaged they must be renewed.
7   Check that the steering rack is also in the straight-ahead position. This can be done by ensuring that the distances between the ends of both trackrods and the rack housing on both sides are the same.
8   Place the steering gear assembly in its location on the front axle frame and at the same time mate up the splines on the pinion shaft with the splines   in the clamp on the steering column flexible column. There is a master spline so make sure these are in line.
9   Replace the two 'U' shaped clamps using new locking tabs under the bolts, tighten the bolts to a torque wrench setting of 12 - 15 lb ft (1.7 - 2.0 kg m). Bend up the locking tabs.
10 Refit the trackrod ends into the steering arms, replace the castellated nuts and tighten them to a torque wrench setting of 18 - 22 lb ft (2.5 - 3.0 kg m). Use new split pins to lock the nuts.
11 Tighten the clamp bolt on the steering column flexible coupling to a torque wrench setting of 12 - 15 lb ft (1.7 - 2.1 kg m), having first double checked that the pinion is correctly located in on the splines.
12 Jack-up the car, remove the blocks from under the wheels and lower the car to the ground. The toe-in must now be checked and further information will be found in Section 22.

30 Rack and pinion steering gear - adjustments

1   For the steering gear to function correctly, two adjustments

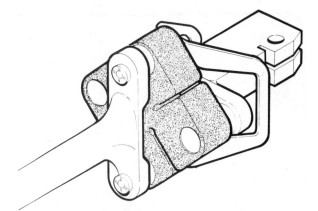

Fig. 11.32. Steering column flexible coupling (July 1973 onwards) (Sec. 28)

are necessary. These are pinion bearing pre-load and rack damper adjustment. Care must be taken not to overtighten otherwise seizure may take place. Double check all readings.
2   To carry out these adjustments, remove the steering gear from the car as described in Section 29, then mount the steering gear assembly in a soft jawed vice so that the pinion is in a horizontal position and the rack damper cover plate to the top.
3   Remove the rack damper cover plate by undoing and removing the two retaining bolts and spring washers. Lift away the cover plate, gasket and shims. Also remove the small   spring and the recessed yoke, which bears onto the rack. These parts are shown in Fig. 11.33.
4   Now remove the pinion bearing pre-load cover plate from the base of the pinion, by undoing and removing the two bolts and spring washers. Lift away the cover plate, gasket and shims.
5   To set the pinion bearing pre-load replace the cover plate with the shim pack (0.093 in. shim uppermost). Tighten the bolts down evenly, and firmly until the cover plate makes contact. Leave out the gasket at this stage.
6   Measure the gap between the cover plate and pinion housing. This gap should be 0.011 - 0.013 in. (0.28 - 0.33 mm). Take several readings near each bolt to ensure the inner plate is parallel. Note the final reading.
7   Build up a shim pack to the required thickness and use at least two shims in addition to the 0.093 in. shim which must always be fitted next to the cover BUT subtract 0.001 inch from your final reading before doing so. Select your shims from those given in a shim pack and make it   within 0 to plus 0.025 of this figure. For example,   if the final reading was 0.028 in. the shim pile selected should be within 0.027 to 0.0295 when measured with a micrometer. Shim thicknesses available are given below.

Part No.	Material	Thickness
71BB - 3K544 - AA	Steel	0.005 in (0.13 mm)
71BB - 3K544 - BA	Steel	0.007 in (0.19 mm)
71BB - 3K544 - CA	Steel	0.010 in (0.25 mm)
71BB - 3K544 - DA	Steel	0.092 in (2.35 mm)
71BB - 3K544 - LA	Steel	0.002 in (0.05 mm)
71BB - 3581 - AA	Buna coated flexoid	0.01 in (0.254 mm)

8   With the cover plate removed, make sure that the pinion grease seal is packed with grease. Smear jointing compound onto the cover plate mating face and refit the cover plate.
9   Smear a little Loctite or similar sealer on the threads of the bolts and tighten them down to a torque wrench setting of 6 - 8 lb ft (0.9 - 1.1 kg m).
10 To reset the rack damper adjustment, replace the yoke in its location on the rack and make sure it is fully home. Using a straight edge and feeler gauges, measure the distance between the top of the slipper and the surface of the pinion housing. Make a note of this dimension.
11 Assemble a shim pack including the gasket whose thickness is

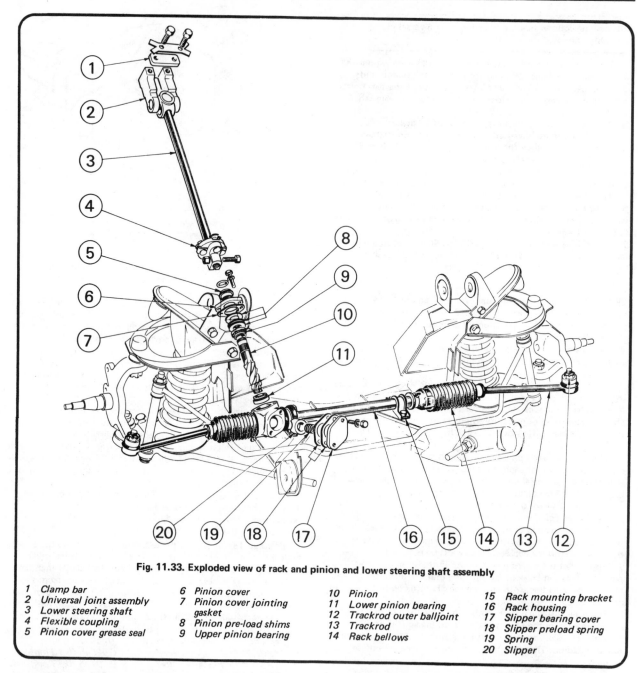

Fig. 11.33. Exploded view of rack and pinion and lower steering shaft assembly

1 Clamp bar	6 Pinion cover
2 Universal joint assembly	7 Pinion cover jointing
3 Lower steering shaft	gasket
4 Flexible coupling	8 Pinion pre-load shims
5 Pinion cover grease seal	9 Upper pinion bearing

10 Pinion	15 Rack mounting bracket
11 Lower pinion bearing	16 Rack housing
12 Trackrod outer balljoint	17 Slipper bearing cover
13 Trackrod	18 Slipper preload spring
14 Rack bellows	19 Spring
	20 Slipper

greater than the measurement obtained in paragraph 10, by
between 0.006 - 0.0005 in. (0.152 - 0.013 mm). Shim thicknesses
available are listed below:

Part No.	Material	Thickness
71BB - 3N597 - AA	Steel	0.005 in (0.127 mm)
71BB - 3N597 - BA	Steel	0.007 in (0.19 mm)
71BB - 3N597 - CA	Steel	0.010 in (0.25 mm)
71BB - 3N597 - DA	Steel	0.015 in (0.38 mm)
71BB - 3N597 - EA	Steel	0.020 in (0.50 mm)
71BB - 3N597 - FA	Steel	0.060 in (1.5 mm)
71BB - 3N598 - AA	Buna coated flexoid	0.010 in (0.25 mm)

12 Fit the spring into the recess in the yoke. Place the shim pack
so that the gasket will be next to the cover plate and refit the
cover plate. Apply a little Loctite or similar sealing compound to
the bolt threads. Tighten down the bolts to a torque wrench
setting of 6 - 8 lb ft (0.9 - 1.1 kg m).

31 Rack and pinion steering gear - dismantling and reassembly

1   Remove the steering gear assembly from the car as described
in Section 29.
2   Undo the trackrod balljoint locknuts and unscrew the balljoints. Lift away the plain washer and remove the locknut. To
assist in obtaining an approximate correct setting for trackrod
adjustment mark the threads or count the number of turns
required to undo the balljoint.
3   Slacken off the clips securing the rubber gaiter to each track
rod and rack housing end. Carefully pull off the gaiters. Have a
quantity of rag handy to catch the oil which will escape when
the gaiters are removed. **Note:** on some steering gear assemblies
soft iron wire is used instead of clips. Always secure the gaiter
with clips.
4   To dismantle the steering gear assembly it is only necessary

to remove the trackrod which is furthest away from the pinion.

5   To remove the trackrod place the steering gear assembly in a soft jawed vice. Working on the trackrod balljoint carefully drill out the pin that locks the ball housing to the locknut. Great care must be taken not to drill too deeply or the rack will be irreparably damaged. The hole should be about 0.375 in. (9.525 mm) deep.

6   Hold the locknut with a spanner, then grip the ball housing with a mole wrench and undo it from the threads on the rack.

7   Take out the spring and ball seat from the recess in the end of the rack and then unscrew the locknut from the threads on the rack. The spring and ball seat must be renewed during reassembly.

8   Carefully prise out the pinion dust seal and then withdraw the pinion together with the bearing assembly nearest the flexible coupling. As the bearings utilise bearing tracks and loose balls (14 in each bearing) care must be taken not to lose any of the balls or drop them into the steering gear on reassembly.

9   Undo and remove the two bolts and spring washers that secure the rack damper cover. Lift away the cover, gasket shims, springs and yoke.

10 With the pinion removed, withdraw the complete rack assembly with one trackrod still attached from the pinion end of the casing.

11 The remaining pinion bearing assembly may now be removed from the rack housing.

12 It is always advisable to withdraw the rack from the pinion end of the rack housing. This avoids passing the rack teeth through the bush at the other end of   the casing and causing possible damage.

13 Carefully examine all parts for signs of wear or damage. Check the condition of the rack support bush at the opposite end of the casing from the pinion. If this is worn renew it. If the rack or pinion teeth are in any way damaged a new rack and pinion will have to be obtained.

14 Take the pinion seal off the top of the casing and replace it with a new seal.

15 To commence reassembly fit the lower pinion bearing and thrust washer into their recess in the casing. The loose balls can be held in place by a small amount of grease.

16 Replace the rack in the housing from the pinion end and position it in the straight-ahead position by equalising the amount it protrudes at either end of the casing.

17 Replace the remaining pinion bearing and thrust washer onto the pinion and fit the pinion into its housing so that the larger masterspline on the pinion shaft is parallel to the rack and on the right-hand side of the pinion.

18 Replace the rack damper yoke, springs, shims, gasket and cover plate.

19 To replace the track rod that has been removed, start by fitting a new spring and ball seat to the recess in the end of the rack shaft and replace the locknut onto the threads of the rack.

20 Lubricate the ball, ball seat and ballhousing with a small amount of Hypoy 90 type gear oil. Then slide the ballhousing over the trackrod and screw the housing onto the rack threads keeping the trackrod in the horizontal position until the trackrod starts to become stiff to move.

21 Using a normal spring balance hook it round the trackrod 0.5 in. (12.70 mm) from the end and check the effort required to move it from the horizontal position.

22 By adjusting the tightness of the ballhousing on the rack threads the effort required to move the trackrod must be set at 5 lb (2.8 kg).

23 Tighten the locknut up to the housing and then recheck that the effort required to move the trackrod is still correct at 5 lb (2.8 kg).

24 On the line where the locknut and ballhousing met, drill a 0.125 in. (3.175 mm) diameter hole which must be 0.375 in. (9.525 mm) deep. Even if the two halves of the old hole previously drilled out align, a new hole must be drilled.

25 Tap a new retaining pin into the hole and peen the end over to secure it.

26 Refit the rubber gaiters and trackrod ends ensuring that they

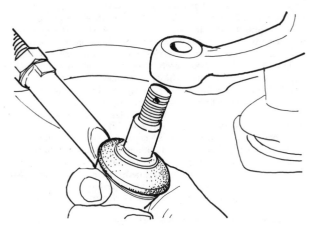

Fig. 11.34. Disconnecting a trackrod-end from steering arm (Sec. 32)

are replaced in exactly the same position from which they were removed.

27 Remove the rack damper cover plate and pour in 0.25 pint (0.15 litre, of Hypoy 90 type gear oil. Then carry out both steering gear adjustments as described in Section 30.

28 After the steering gear has been refitted to the car the toe-in must be checked. Further information will be found in Section 22.

32 Steering rack rubber gaiter - removal and refitting

1   Jack-up the front of the car and place blocks under the wheels. Lower the car slightly so that the trackrods are in a near horizontal position.

2   Withdraw the split pin and undo the castellated nut holding the balljoint taper pin to the steering arm. Using a universal balljoint separator part the taper pin from the steering arm.

3   Undo the trackrod balljoint locknut and unscrew the balljoint. To assist in obtaining an approximate correct setting for trackrod adjustment mark the threads or count the number of turns required to undo the balljoint.

4   Slacken off the clips securing the rubber gaiter to the trackrod and rack housing end. Carefully pull off the gaiter. Have a quantity of rag handy to catch the oil which will escape when the gaiters are removed. **Note:** on some steering gear assemblies soft iron wire is used instead of clips. Always secure the gaiter with clips.

5   Fitting a new rubber gaiter is now the reverse sequence to removal. It will be necessary to refill the steering gear assembly with Hypoy 90 type gear oil. Full information will be found in Section 22.

6   It is recommended that the toe-in be checked by the local Ford garage at the earliest opportunity. Further information will be found in Section 22.

33 Trackrod end - removal and refitting

Full information will be found in Section 32, omitting paragraphs 4 and 5.

34 Wheels and tyres

1   The roadwheels are of pressed steel type and the tyres may be crossply or radial construction. Never mix tyres of different construction on the same axle.

2   Check the tyre pressures weekly (including the spare).

3   The roadwheel nuts should be tightened to a torque of between 50 and 70 lb ft (6.91 and 9.67 kg m) and it is an

advantage if a smear of grease is applied to the wheel stud threads.

4   Every 6,000 miles (10,000 km) the roadwheels should be moved round the vehicle (this does not apply where the wheels have been balanced on the vehicle) in order to even out the tyre tread wear (this procedure is not recommended for fabric belted radials). To do this, remove each wheel in turn, clean it thoroughly (both sides) and remove any flints which may be embedded in the tread). Check the tread wear pattern which will indicate any mechanical or adjustment faults in the suspension or steering components. Examine the wheel bolt holes for elongation or wear. If such conditions are found, renew the wheel.

5   Renewal of the tyres should be carried out when the thickness of the tread pattern is worn to a minimum of 1/16 inch or the wear indicators (if incorporated) are visible.

6   The method of moving the tyres depends on whether the spare (5th) wheel is brought into the rotational pattern. Always adjust the front and rear tyre pressures after moving the wheels round

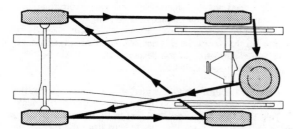

Fig. 11.35. Tyre rotational pattern (crossply or steel belted radials) (Sec. 34)

as previously described.

7   Have all wheels balanced initially and again halfway through the useful life of the tyres.

35 Fault diagnosis - suspension and steering

Symptom	Cause	Remedy
Steering feels vague, car wanders and floats at speed	Tyre pressures uneven	Check pressures and adjust as necessary
	Dampers worn	Test, and replace if worn
	Spring broken	Renew spring
	Steering gear ball joints badly worn	Fit new ball joints
	Suspension geometry incorrect	Check and rectify
	Steering mechanism free play excessive	Adjust or overhaul steering mechanism
	Front suspension and rear axle pickup points out of alignment	Normally caused by poor repair work after a serious accident. Extensive rebuilding necessary
Stiff and heavy steering	Tyre pressure too low	Check pressures and inflate tyres
	No oil in steering gear	Top up steering gear
	Front wheel toe-in incorrect	Check and reset toe-in
	Suspension geometry incorrect	Check and rectify
	Steering gear incorrectly adjusted too tightly	Check and re-adjust steering gear
	Steering column badly misaligned	Determine cause and rectify (usually due to bad repair after severe accident damage and difficult to correct)
Wheel wobble and vibration	Seized ball joints or swivels	Renew
	Wheel nuts loose	Check and tighten as necessary
	Front wheels and tyres out of balance	Balance wheels and tyres and add weights as necessary
	Steering ball joints badly worn	Replace steering gear ball joints
	Hub bearings badly worn	Remove and fit new hub bearings
	Steering gear free play excessive	Adjust and overhaul steering gear
	Front springs weak or broken	Inspect and overhaul as necessary

Chapter 12 Bodywork and fittings

Contents

Specifications

Overall length

Saloon	168.0 in (426.7 cm)
Estate	171.5 in (435.6 cm)

Overall height

Saloon	52.0 in (132.1 cm)
Estate	54.0 in (137.2 cm)

Wheelbase ... ... 101.5 in (258.1 cm)

Track (front) ... ... 56.0 in (142.2 cm)

Track (rear) ... ... 56.0 in (142.2 cm)

Ground clearance ... ... 5.0 in (12.7 cm)

Luggage capacity

Saloon	12 cu. ft (0.34 cu. m)
Estate	33 cu. ft (0.93 cu. m) or seat flat 64 cu. ft (1.81 cu. m)

1 General description

The combined body and underframe is of all steel welded construction. This makes a very strong and torsionally rigid shell.

The Cortina is available in either saloon or estate car versions. There are four forward hinged doors for either version (two door as an option on saloon models) with a seating capacity of five adults. The windscreen is slightly curved and is zone toughened for additional driver and passenger safety. In the event of windscreen shattering this 'zone' breaks into much larger pieces than the rest of the screen thus giving the driver much better vision than would otherwise be possible.

The Aeroflow type of ventilation system is fitted. Air drawn in through a grille on the scuttle can either be heated or pass straight into the car. Used air passes out through a grille below the rear window.

The estate cars have the same engine, technical and general specification as the saloon car except for the air extraction vents on the rear quarter panels and for the counterbalanced tailgate fitted with a lock.

Although the wheelbase for the saloon and estate car versions is the same, the overall length of the estate car is longer.

For additional occupant safety the instruments and controls

are deeply recessed in the facia and thick padding is used to surround the top of the dash panel.

2 Maintenance - bodywork and underframe

1   The condition of your car's bodywork is of considerable importance as it is on this that the second-hand value of the car will mainly depend. It is much more difficult to repair neglected bodywork than to renew mechanical assemblies. The hidden portions of the body, such as the wheel arches, the underframe and the engine compartment are equally important, although obviously not requiring such frequent attention as the immediately visible paintwork.

2   Once a year or every 12,000 miles (20,000 km) it is a sound scheme to visit your local main agent and have the underside of the body steam cleaned. All traces of dirt and oil will be removed and the underside can then be inspected carefully for rust, damaged hydraulic pipes, frayed electrical wiring and similar maladies.

3   At the same time, the engine compartment should be cleaned in a similar manner. If steam cleaning facilities are not available then brush a water soluble cleanser over the whole engine and engine compartment with a stiff paint brush, working it well in where there is an accumulation of oil and dirt. Do not paint the ignition system, and protect it with oily rags when the cleanser is washed off. As the cleanser is washed away it will take with it all traces of oil and dirt, leaving the engine looking clean and bright.

4   The wheel arches should be given particular attention as under sealing can easily come away here and stones and dirt thrown up from the roadwheels can soon cause the paint to chip and flake, and so allow rust to set in. If rust is found, clean down to the bare metal with wet and dry paper, apply an anti-corrosive coating such as zinc primer or red lead, and renew the paintwork and undercoating.

5   The bodywork should be washed once a week or when dirty. Thoroughly wet the car to soften the dirt and then wash the car down with a soft sponge and plenty of clean water. If the surplus dirt is not washed off very gently, in time it will wear paint down as surely as wet and dry paper. It is best to use a hose if this is available. Give the car a final wash down and then dry with a soft chamois leather to prevent the formation of spots.

6   Spots of tar and grease thrown up from the road can be removed by a rag dampened with petrol.

7   Once every six months, or more frequently if wished, give the bodywork and chromium trim a thoroughly good wax polish. If a chromium cleaner is used to remove rust on any of the car's plated parts remember that the cleaner also removes part of the chromium so use sparingly.

3 Maintenance - upholstery and carpets

1   Remove the carpets or mats and thoroughly vacuum clean the interior of the car every three months or more frequently, if necessary.

2   Beat out the carpets and vacuum clean them if they are very dirty. If the upholstery is soiled apply an upholstery cleaner with a damp sponge and wipe off with a clean dry cloth.

4 Maintenance - PVC external roof covering

Under no circumstances try to clean any external PVC roof covering with detergents, caustic soaps or spirit cleaners. Plain soap and water is all that is required, with a soft brush to clean dirt that may be ingrained. Wash the covering as frequently as the rest of the car.

5 Minor body damage - repair

The photo sequence on pages 206 and 207 illustrate the operations detailed in the following sub-sections.

Repair of minor scratches in the car's bodywork

If the scratch is very superficial, and does not penetrate to the metal of the bodywork, repair is very simple. Lightly rub the area of the scratch with a paintwork renovator (eg; T-Cut), or a very fine cutting paste, to remove loose paint from the scratch and to clear the surrounding bodywork of wax polish. Rinse the area with clean water.

Apply touch-up paint to the scratch using a thin paint brush, continue to apply thin layers of paint until the surface of the paint in the scratch is level with the surrounding paintwork. Allow the new paint at least two weeks to harden; then blend it into the surrounding paintwork by rubbing the paintwork, in the scratch area with a paintwork renovator (eg; T-Cut), or a very fine cutting paste. Finally apply wax polish.

An alternative to painting over the scratch is to use Holts "Scratch-Patch". Use the same preparation for the affected area; then simply pick a patch of a suitable size to cover the scratch completely. Hold the patch against the scratch and burnish its backing paper; the patch will adhere to the paintwork, freeing itself from the backing paper at the same time. Polish the affected area to blend the patch into the surrounding paintwork. Where the scratch has penetrated right through to the metal of the bodywork, causing the metal to rust, a different repair technique is required. Remove any loose rust from the bottom of the scratch with a penknife, then apply rust inhibiting paint (eg; Kurust) to prevent the formation of rust in the future. Using a rubber nylon applicator fill the scratch with bodystopper paste. If required, this paste can be mixed with cellulose thinners to provide a very thin paste which is ideal for filling narrow scratches. Before the stopper-paste in the scratch hardens, wrap a piece of smooth cotton rag around the top of a finger. Dip the finger in cellulose thinners and then quickly sweep it across the surface of the stopper-paste in the scratch; this will ensure that the surface of the stopper-paste is slightly hollowed. The scratch can now be painted over as described earlier in this Section.

Repair of dents in the car's bodywork

When deep denting of the car's bodywork has taken place, the first task is to pull the dent out, until the affected bodywork almost attains its original shape. There is little point in trying to restore the original shape completely, as the metal in the damaged area will have stretched on impact and cannot be reshaped fully to its original contour. It is better to bring the level of the dent up to a point which is about 1/8 inch (3 mm) below the level of the surrounding bodywork. In cases where the dent is very shallow anyway, it is not worth trying to pull it out at all.

If the underside of the dent is accessible, it can be hammered out gently from behind, using a mallet with a wooden or plastic head. Whilst doing this, hold a suitable block of wood firmly against the impact from the hammer blows and thus prevent a large area of bodywork from being 'belled-out'.

Should the dent be in a section of the bodywork which has a double skin or some other factor making it inaccessible from behind, a different technique is called for. Drill several small holes through the metal inside the dent area - particularly in the deeper sections. Then screw long self-tapping screws into the holes just sufficiently for them to gain a good purchase in the metal. Now the dent can be pulled out by pulling on the protruding heads of the screws with a pair of pliers.

The next stage of the repair is the removal of the paint from the damaged area, and from an inch or so of the surrounding 'sound' bodywork. This is accomplished most easily by using a wire brush or abrasive pad on a power drill, although it can be done just as effectively by hand using sheets of abrasive paper. To complete the preparations for filling, score the surface of the bare metal with a screwdriver or the tang of a file, or alternatively, drill small holes in the affected area. This will provide a really good 'key' for filler paste.

To complete the repair see the Section on filling and respraying.

Repair of rust holes or gashes in the car's bodywork

Remove all paint from the affected area and from an inch or so of the surrounding 'sound' bodywork, using an abrasive pad or a wire brush on a power drill. If these are not available a few sheets of abrasive paper will do the job just as effectively. With the paint removed you will be able to gauge the severity of the corrosion and therefore decide whether to replace the whole panel (if this is possible) or to repair the affected area. Replacement body panels are not as expensive as most people think and it is often quicker and more satisfactory to fit a new panel than to attempt to repair large areas of corrosion.

Remove all fittings from the affected area except those which will act as a guide to the original shape of the damaged bodywork (eg; headlamp shells etc.). Then, using tin snips or a hacksaw blade, remove all loose metal and any other metal badly affected by corrosion. Hammer the edges of the hole inwards in order to create a slight depression for the filler paste.

Wire brush the affected area to remove the powdery rust from the surface of the remaining metal. Paint the affected area with rust inhibiting paint (eg; Kurust); if the back of the rusted area ia accessible treat this also.

Before filling can take place it will be necessary to block the hole in some way. This can be achieved by the use of one of the following materials: Zinc gauze, Aluminium tape or Polyurethane foam.

Zinc gauze is probably the best material to use for a large hole. Cut a piece to the approximate size and shape of the hole to be filled. Then position it in the hole so that its edges are below the level of the surrounding bodywork. It can be retained in position by several blobs of filler paste around its periphery.

Aluminium tape should be used for small or very narrow holes. Pull a piece off the roll and trim it to the approximate size and shape required, then pull off the backing paper (if used) and stick the tape over the hole; it can be overlapped if the thickness of one piece is insufficient. Burnish down the edges of the tape with the handle of a screwdriver or similar, to ensure that the tape is securely attached to the metal underneath.

Polyurethane foam is best used where the hole is situated in a section of bodywork of complex shape, backed by a small box section (eg; where the sill panel meets the rear wheel arch - most cars). The usual mixing procedure for this foam is as follows: Put equal amounts of fluid from each of the two cans provided in the kit, into one container. Stir until the mixture begins to thicken, then quickly pour this mixture into the hole, and hold a piece of cardboard over the larger apertures. Almost immediately the polyurethane will begin to expand, gushing frantically out of any small holes left unblocked. When the foam hardens it can be cut back to just below the level of the surrounding bodywork with a hacksaw blade.

Bodywork repairs - filling and respraying

Before using this Section, see Section on dent, deep scratch, rust hole, gash repairs.

Many types of bodyfiller are available, but generally speaking those proprietary kits which contain a tin of filler paste and a tube of resin hardener (eg; Holts Cataloy) are best for this type of repair. A wide, flexible plastic or nylon applicator will be found invaluable for imparting a smooth and well contoured finish to the surface of the filler.

Mix up a little filler on a clean piece of card or board - use the hardener sparingly (follow the maker's instructions on the packet) otherwise the filler will set very rapidly.

Using the applicator, apply the filler paste to the prepared area; draw the applicator across the surface of the filler to achieve the correct contour and to level the filler surface. As soon as a contour that approximates to the correct one is achieved, stop working the paste - if you carry on too long the paste will become sticky and begin to 'pick-up' on the applicator.

Continue to add thin layers of filler paste at twenty-minute intervals until the level of the filler is just 'proud' of the surrounding bodywork.

Once the filler has hardened, excess can be removed using a Surform plane or Dreadnought file. From then on, progressively finer grades of abrasive paper should be used, starting with a 40 grade production paper and finishing with 400 grade 'wet-and-dry' paper. Always wrap the abrasive paper around a flat rubber, cork, or wooden block - otherwise the surface of the filler will not be completely flat. During the smoothing of the filler surface the 'wet-and-dry' paper should be periodically rinsed in water. This will ensure that a very smooth finish is imparted to the filler at the final stage.

At this stage the 'dent' should be surrounded by a ring of bare metal, which in turn should be encircled by the finely 'feathered' edge of the good paintwork. Rinse the repair area with clean water, until all of the dust produced by the rubbing-down operation is gone.

Spray the whole repair area with a light coat of grey primer - this will show up any imperfections in the surface of the filler. Repair these imperfections with fresh filler paste or bodystopper, and once more smooth the surface with abrasive paper. If bodystopper is used, it can be mixed with cellulose thinners to form a really thin paste which is ideal for filling small holes. Repeat this spray and repair procedure until you are satisfied that the surface of the filler, and the feathered edge of the paintwork are perfect. Clean the repair area with clean water and allow to dry fully.

The repair area is now ready for spraying. Paint spraying must be carried out in a warm, dry, windless and dust free atmosphere. This condition can be created artificially if you have access to a large indoor working area, but if you are forced to work in the open, you will have to pick your day very carefully. If you are working indoors, dousing the floor in the work area with water will 'lay' the dust which would otherwise be in the atmosphere. If the repair area is confined to one body panel, mask off the surrounding panels; this will help to minimise the effects of a slight mis-match in paint colours. Bodywork fittings (eg; chrome strips, door handles etc.,) will also need to be masked off. Use genuine masking tape and several thicknesses of newspaper for the masking operation.

Before commencing to spray, agitate the aerosol can, thoroughly, then spray a test area (an old tin, or similar) until the technique is mastered. Cover the repair area with a thick coat of primer; the thickness should be built up using several thin layers of paint rather than one thick one. Using 400 grade 'wet-and-dry' paper, rub down the surface of the primer until it is really smooth. While doing this, the work area should be thoroughly doused with water, and the 'wet-and-dry' paper periodically rinsed in water. Allow to dry before spraying on more paint.

Spray on the top coat, again building up the thickness by using several thin layers of paint. Start spraying in the centre of the repair area and then, using a circular motion, work outwards until the whole repair area and about 2 inches of the surrounding original paintwork is covered. Remove all masking material 10 to 15 minutes after spraying on the final coat of paint.

Allow the new paint at least 2 weeks to harden fully; then, using a paintwork renovator (eg; T-Cut) or a very fine cutting paste, blend the edges of the new paint into the existing paintwork. Finally apply wax polish.

6 Major body damage - repair

1 Because the body is built on the monocoque principle and is integral with the underframe, major damage must be repaired by competent mechanics with the necessary welding and hydraulic straightening equipment.
2 If the damage has been serious it is vital that the body is checked for correct alignment as otherwise the handling of the car will suffer and many other faults such as excessive tyre wear and wear in the transmission and steering may occur.

3 There is a special body jig which most large body repair shops have and to ensure that all is correct it is important that this jig be used for all major repair work.

7 Maintenance - hinges and locks

Once every 3000 miles (5000 km) or 3 months, the door, bonnet and boot or tailgate hinges and locks should be given a few drops of oil from an oil can. The door striker plates can be given a thin smear of grease to reduce wear and to ensure free movement.

8 Front bumper - removal and installation

1 Open the bonnet and remove the radiator grille, as described in Section 33.
2 Undo and remove the nut, washer and spacer assemblies that secure the wrap round ends of the bumper bar. Then unscrew the crosshead screws that secure the under-riders to the body (Fig. 12.1).
3 The front bumper assembly may now be lifted away taking care not to scratch the paintwork on the front wings.
4 If it is necessary to detach the under-riders from the bumper bar, undo and remove the nut and washers that secure the bracket and under-rider to the bumper bar.
5 Refitting the bumper bar and under-riders is the reverse sequence to removal. Do not fully tighten the fixings until the bumper bar is perfectly straight and correctly located.

9 Rear bumper - removal and installation

1 Undo and remove the crosshead screws that secure the number plate light and place to one side.
2 Undo and remove the crosshead screws that secure the under-riders to the body.
3 Open the luggage compartment lid and roll back the matting. Undo and remove the bolts and washers that secure the bumper bar brackets to the body (Fig. 12.2).
4 The rear bumper may now be lifted away taking care not to scratch the paintwork on the rear wings.
5 If it is necessary to detach the under-riders and brackets undo and remove the bolts, spring and plain washers.
6 Refitting the bumper bar and under-riders is the reverse sequence to removal. Do not fully tighten the fixings until the bumper bar is perfectly straight and correctly located.

10 Windscreen glass - removal and installation

1 If you are unfortunate enough to have a windscreen shatter, or should you wish to renew your present windscreen, fitting replacement is one of the few jobs which the average owner is advised to leave to a professional. For the owner who wishes to attempt the job himself the following instructions are given.
2 Cover the bonnet with a blanket or cloth to prevent accidental damage and remove the windscreen wiper blades and arms as detailed in Chapter 10.
3 Put on a pair of lightweight shoes and get onto one of the front seats. An assistant should be ready to catch the glass as it is released from the body aperture.
4 Place a piece of soft cloth between the soles of your shoes and the windscreen glass and with both feet on one top corner of the windscreen push firmly.
5 When the weatherstrip has freed itself from the body aperture flange in that area repeat the process at frequent intervals along the top edge of the windscreen until from outside the car the glass and weatherstrip can be removed together.
6 If you are having to replace your windscreen due to a shattered screen, remove all traces of sealing compound from the weather-strip and body flange.
7 Now is the time to remove all pieces of glass if the screen has shattered. Use a vacuum cleaner to extract as much as possible. Switch on the heater boost motor and adjust the screen controls to 'screen defrost' but watch out for flying pieces of glass which might have blown out of the ducting.
8 Carefully inspect the rubber moulding for signs of splitting or deterioration.
9 To refit the glass first fit the weatherstrip onto the glass with the joint at the lower edge.
10 Insert a piece of thick cord into the channel of the weatherstrip with the two ends protruding by at least 12 inches (300 mm) at the top centre of the weatherstrip.
11 Mix a concentrated soap and water solution and apply to the flange of the windscreen aperture.
12 Offer up the screen to the aperture and with an   assistant to press the rubber surround hard against one end of the cord moving round the windscreen and so drawing the lip over the windscreen flange of the body. Keep the   draw cord parallel to the windscreen. Using the palms of the hands, thump on the glass from the outside to assist the lip in passing over the flange and to seat the screen correctly onto the aperture.
13 To ensure a good watertight joint apply some Seelastik SR51 between the weatherstrip and the body and press the weather-strip against the body to give a good seal.
14 Any excess Seelastik may be removed with a petrol moistened

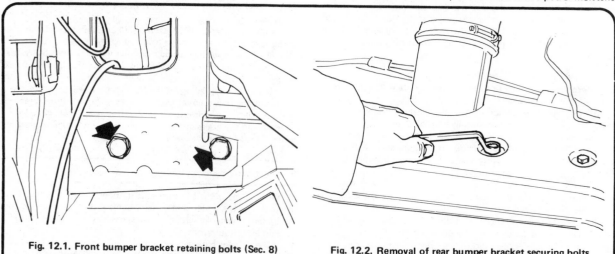

Fig. 12.1. Front bumper bracket retaining bolts (Sec. 8)   Fig. 12.2. Removal of rear bumper bracket securing bolts (Sec. 9)

cloth.

15 A special shaped tool is now required to insert the finisher and full details of this are given in Fig. 12.3. A handyman should be able to make up an equivalent using netting wire and a wooden file handle.

16 Fit the eye of the tool into the groove and feed in the finisher strip.

17 Push the tool around the complete length of the moulding, feeding the finisher into the channel as the eyelet opens it.

18 Refit the wiper arms and blades and do not forget the Road Fund Tax disc.

11 Door rattles - tracing and rectification

1 The most common cause of door rattle is a misaligned, loose or worn striker plate; however other causes may be:
   a) Loose door or window winder handles;
   b) Loose or misaligned door lock components;
   c) Loose or worn remote control mechanism.

2 It is quite possible for door rattles to be the result of a combination of the above faults so a careful examination should be made to determine their exact cause.

3 If striker plate wear or misalignment is the cause, the plate should be renewed or adjusted as necessary. The procedure is detailed in Section 13.

4 Should the window winder handle rattle, this can be easily rectified by inserting a rubber washer between the escutcheon and door trim panel.

5 If the rattle is found to be emanating from the door lock it will in all probability mean that the lock is worn and therefore should be replaced with a new lock unit, as described in Section 15.

6 Lastly if it is worn hinge pins causing rattles they should be renewed.

12 Front and rear door - removal and installation

1 Using a pencil, accurately mark the outline of the hinge

relative to the door once the hinges have been released. Remove the two bolts that secure each hinge to the pillar and lift away the complete door.

2 For storage it is best to stand the door on an old blanket and allow it to lean against a wall also suitably padded at the top to stop scratching.

3 Refitting the door is the reverse sequence to removal. If, after refitting, adjustment is necessary, it should be done at the hinges to give correct alignment, or the striker reset if the door either moves up or down on final closing.

13 Door striker plate - removal, refitting and adjustment

1 If it is wished to renew a worn striker plate, mark its position on the door pillar so a new plate can be fitted in the same position.

2 To remove the plate simply undo and remove the four crosshead screws which hold the plate in position. Lift away the plate.

3 Replacement of the door striker plate is the reverse sequence to removal.

4 To adjust the door striker plate slacken the four crosshead screws and move the striker plate in or out as necessary. Make sure that the lock engages fully when the door is flush with the body exterior line. It is very important that the door is not adjusted to be flush with the body in the safety catch position. When the correct position has been found tighten the four crosshead screws firmly.

14 Door trim - removal and refitting

1 Using a knife or thin wide bladed screwdriver, carefully prise the plastic trim from its recesses in the window winder handle. This will expose the handle retaining screw (Fig. 12.5).

2 Wind up the window and note the position of the handle. Undo and remove the crosshead retaining screw and lift away the handle.

3 Undo and remove the two crosshead screws that secure the

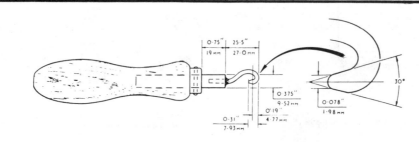

Fig. 12.3. Special tool for inserting **chrome moulding (Sec. 10)**

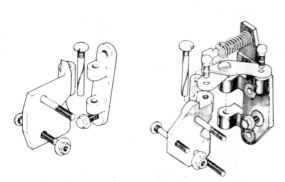

Fig. 12.4. Front and rear door hinges (Sec. 12)

Fig. 12.5. **Detaching window regulator handle plastic insert (Sec. 14)**

door pull. Lift away the door pull. Unscrew the interior lock knob (Fig. 12.6).

4   Using a screwdriver carefully remove the door lock remote control housing bezel by sliding the bezel towards the hinge end of the door. Lift away the bezel (Fig. 12.7).

5   Insert a thin strip of metal with all the sharp edges removed, or a thick knife blade, between the door and the trim panel. This will release one or two of the trim panel retaining clips without damaging the trim. The panel can now be gently eased off by hand.

6   Carefully remove the plastic weatherproof sheeting. Removal is now complete.

7   Replacement is generally a reversal of the removal procedure.

Note: When replacing the panel ensure that each of the trim panel retaining clips is firmly located in its hole by sharply striking the panel in the approximate area of each clip with the palm of the hand. This will make sure the trim is seated fully.

15 Door lock assembly - removal and refitting

1   Refer to Section 14 and remove the door interior trim.
2   Carefully ease out the door lock remote control housing assembly clear of its location in the door inner panel. Unhook the remote control rod and remove the remote control unit.
3   Working inside the door shell carefully prise the two control rods clear of their locations in the lock assembly.
4   Undo and remove the two bolts that secure the door exterior handle to the door outer panel. The exterior handle assembly complete with control rods can now be removed (Fig. 12.8).
5   Undo and remove the three crosshead screws and cup shaped shakeproof washers that secure the lock assembly to the door shell. The lock assembly may now be lifted away from inside the door (Fig. 12.9).
6   Refitting the door lock assembly is the reverse sequence to removal. Lubricate all moving parts with a little grease.

16 Door glass and regulator - removal and refitting

1   Using a screwdriver carefully ease out the door inner and outer weatherstrips from their retaining clips on the door panel.
2   Undo and remove the two bolts that secure the door glass to the window regulator. Tilt the glass and carefully remove it upwards (Fig. 12.10).

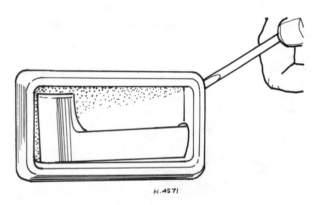

Fig. 12.6. Location of door pull securing screws (Sec. 14)

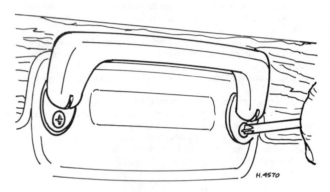

Fig. 12.7. Removing door interior lock bezel (Sec. 14)

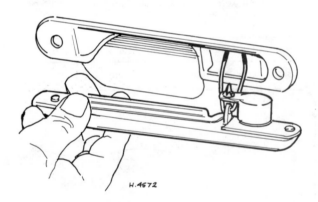

Fig. 12.8. Removing door exterior handle (Sec. 15)

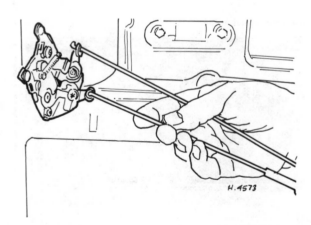

Fig. 12.9. Removing door lock assembly (Sec. 15)

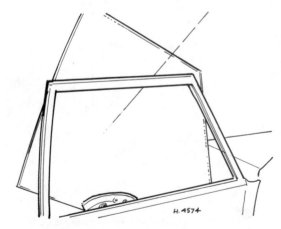

Fig. 12.10. Door glass removal (Sec. 16)

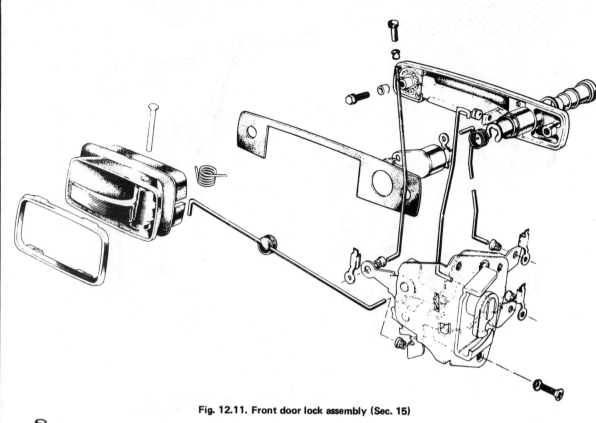

Fig. 12.11. Front door lock assembly (Sec. 15)

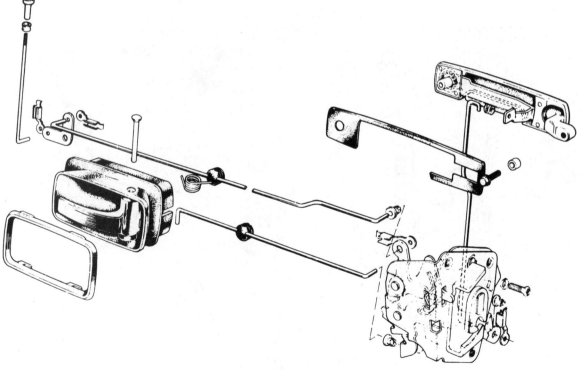

Fig. 12.12. Rear door lock assembly (Sec. 15)

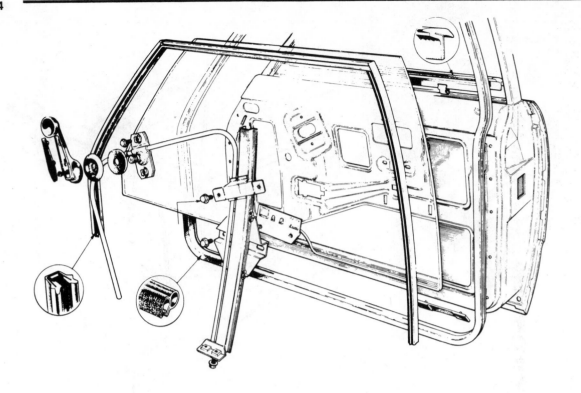

Fig. 12.13. Front door window regulator and seals (Sec. 16)

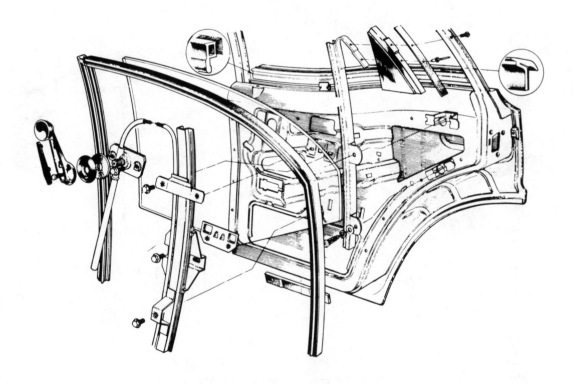

Fig. 12.14. Rear door window regulator and seals (Sec. 16)

3   Undo and remove the bolts that secure the window regulator
to the door inner panel and lift away the regulator mechanism
through the large aperture in the bottom inner panel (Fig. 12.15).
4   Should   it be necessary to remove the glass run channel, start
at the front lower frame end and carefully ease the glass run
channel from its location in the door frame.
5   Refitting the door glass and regulator is the reverse sequence
to removal. Lubricate all moving parts with a little grease. Before
refitting the trim panel check the operation and alignment of the
glass and regulator and adjust if necessary. When all is correct
fully tighten all securing bolts.

17 Door outer belt weatherstrip - removal and refitting

1   Wind the window down to its fullest extent. Carefully prise
its weatherstrip out of the groove in the door outer bright
metal finish moulding.
2   To refit correctly position the weatherstrip over its groove and

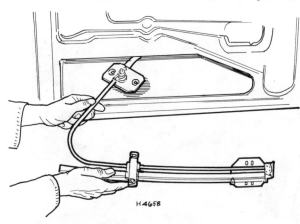

H.4658

Fig. 12.15. Withdrawing window regulator (Sec. 16)

using the thumbs carefully press the strip fully into the groove.
3   Wind the window up and check that the weatherstrip is
correctly fitted.

18 Bonnet - removal and installation

1   Open the bonnet and support it open using   the bonnet stay.
To act as a datum for refitting, mark   the position of the hinges
relative to the bonnet   inner panel.
2   With the assistance of a second person hold the bonnet in the
open position and release the stay.
3   Undo and remove the two bolts, spring and plain washers
that secure each hinge   to the bonnet, and lift away the bonnet
taking care not to scratch the top of the wings.
4   Lean the bonnet up against a wall, suitably padded to stop
scratching the paint.
5   Refitting the bonnet is the reverse sequence to removal. Any
adjustment necessary can be made either at the hinges or the
bonnet catch.

19 Bonnet lock - adjustment

1   Should it be necessary to adjust the bonnet catch first slacken
the locknut securing the shaft in position.
2   Using a wide bladed screwdriver, screw the shaft in, or out,
as necessary until the correct bonnet front height is obtained.
Tighten the locknut.

20 Bonnet release cable (up to July 1973) - removal, refitting and adjustment

1   Detach the operating cable from the bonnet lock spring and
then undo and remove the bolt and clamp that secures the outer
cable to the front panel (Fig. 12.17).
2   Working under the dashboard remove the spring clip securing
the inner cable clevis pin. Withdraw the clevis pin. It may be
found easier if the two bonnet release bracket retaining screws

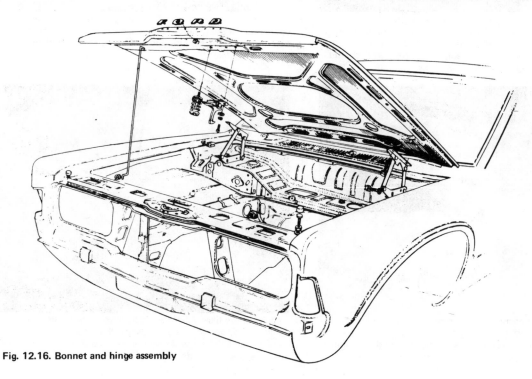

Fig. 12.16. Bonnet and hinge assembly

This sequence of photographs deals with the repair of the dent and paintwork damage shown in this photo. The procedure will be similar for the repair of a hole. It should be noted that the procedures given here are simplified — more explicit instructions will be found in the text

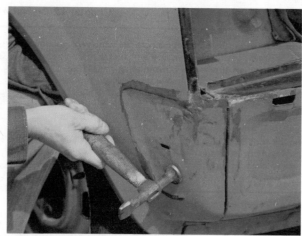

In the case of a dent the first job — after removing surrounding trim — is to hammer out the dent where access is possible. This will minimise filling. Here, the large dent having been hammered out, the damaged area is being made slightly concave

Now all paint must be removed from the damaged area, by rubbing with coarse abrasive paper. Alternatively, a wire brush or abrasive pad can be used in a power drill. Where the repair area meets good paintwork, the edge of the paintwork should be 'feathered', using a finer grade of abrasive paper

In the case of a hole caused by rusting, all damaged sheet-metal should be cut away before proceeding to this stage. Here, the damaged area is being treated with rust remover and inhibitor before being filled

Mix the body filler according to its manufacturer's instructions. In the case of corrosion damage, it will be necessary to block off any large holes before filling — this can be done with aluminium or plastic mesh, or aluminium tape. Make sure the area is absolutely clean before...

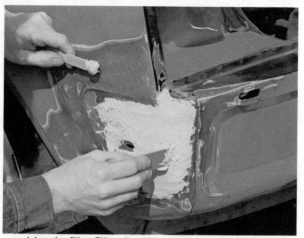

...applying the filler. Filler should be applied with a flexible applicator, as shown, for best results; the wooden spatula being used for confined areas. Apply thin layers of filler at 20-minute intervals, until the surface of the filler is slightly proud of the surrounding bodywork

Initial shaping can be done with a Surform plane or Dread-nought file. Then, using progressively finer grades of wet-and-dry paper, wrapped around a sanding block, and copious amounts of clean water, rub down the filler until really smooth and flat. Again, feather the edges of adjoining paintwork

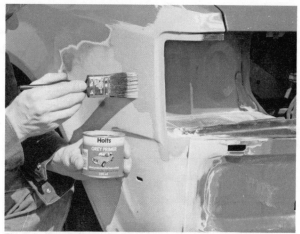

The whole repair area can now be sprayed or brush-painted with primer. If spraying, ensure adjoining areas are protected from over-spray. Note that at least one inch of the surrounding sound paintwork should be coated with primer. Primer has a 'thick' consistency, so will fill small imperfections

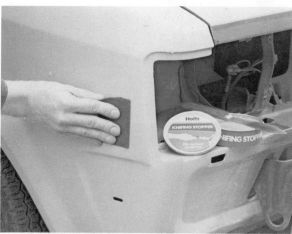

Again, using plenty of water, rub down the primer with a fine grade of wet-and-dry paper (400 grade is probably best) until it is really smooth and well blended into the surrounding paintwork. Any remaining imperfections can now be filled by carefully applied knifing stopper paste

When the stopper has hardened, rub down the repair area again before applying the final coat of primer. Before rubbing down this last coat of primer, ensure the repair area is blemish-free — use more stopper if necessary. To ensure that the surface of the primer is really smooth use some finishing compound

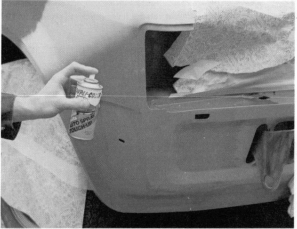

The top coat can now be applied. When working out of doors, pick a dry, warm and wind-free day. Ensure surrounding areas are protected from over-spray. Agitate the aerosol thoroughly, then spray the centre of the repair area, working outwards with a circular motion. Apply the paint as several thin coats

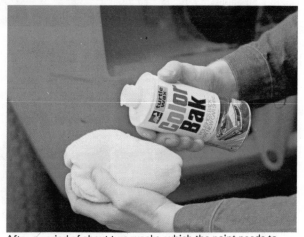

After a period of about two weeks, which the paint needs to harden fully, the surface of the repaired area can be 'cut' with a mild cutting compound prior to wax polishing. When carrying out bodywork repairs, remember that the quality of the finished job is proportional to the time and effort expended

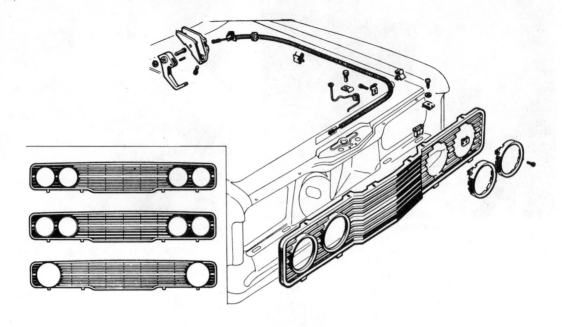

Fig. 12.17. Alternative front grilles and attachments (up to 1973)

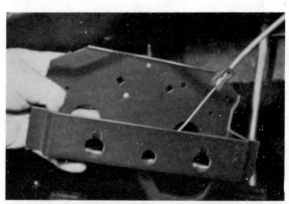

Fig. 12.19. Bonnet release lever bracket (after July 1973) (Sec. 21)

Fig. 12.18. Alternative front grilles (July 1973 onwards) - securing screws arrowed

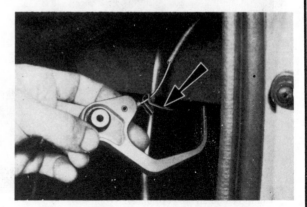

Fig. 12.20. Bonnet release lever (after July 1973) (Sec. 21)

are removed before the clevis pin is withdrawn to give better access.

3   Release the outer cable from its spring clips and withdraw it from the grommet in the bulkhead.

4   Well lubricate the inner and outer cable and then refit which is the reverse sequence to removal.

5   To adjust the cable slacken the bolt that secures the cable clip nearest to the lock assembly. Push or pull the outer cable as necessary to adjust the inner cable tension and secure in its new position by tightening the clamp bolt.

21 Bonnet release cable (after July 1973) - removal, refitting and adjustment

1   Remove the parcels tray.

2   Remove the dash lower instrument panel.

3   Detach the direction indicator flasher unit and the heated rear window relay from their mountings (see Chapter 10).

4   Through the holes in the side of the bonnet release lever bracket, insert a screwdriver and unscrew the bracket securing screws (Fig. 12.19).

5   Remove the bracket and disengage the bonnet release cable.

6   Remove the radiator grille and disconnect the cable from the bonnet lock and extract the cable from its securing clips. With-draw the cable into the vehicle interior.

7   The bonnet release lever is retained by a pivot pin and circlip and the cable is secured to the lever with a tension pin.

8   Installation is a reversal of removal.

22 Boot lid - removal and installation

1   Open the boot lid to its fullest extent. To act as a datum for refitting, mark the position of the hinge relative to the lid inner panel.

2   With the assistance of a second person hold the boot in the open position and then undo and remove the two bolts, spring and plain washers that secure each hinge to the boot lid. Lift away the boot lid taking care not to scratch the top of the rear wings.

3   Lean the boot lid up against a wall, suitably padded to stop

scratching the paint.

4   Refitting the boot lid is the reverse sequence to removal. Any adjustment necessary can be made at the hinge.

23 Boot lid lock - removal and refitting

1   Open the boot lid and carefully withdraw the spring clip located at the end of the lock spindle.

2   Undo and remove the three bolts and spring washers that secure the lock to the boot lid (Fig. 12.21). Lift away the lock assembly.

3   Refitting the lock assembly is the reverse sequence to removal.

24 Boot lid lock striker plate - removal and refitting

1   Open the boot lid and with a pencil mark the outline of the

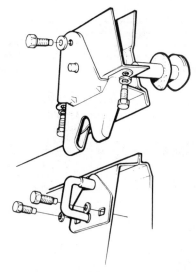

Fig. 12.21. Boot lid lock and striker plate (Sec. 23)

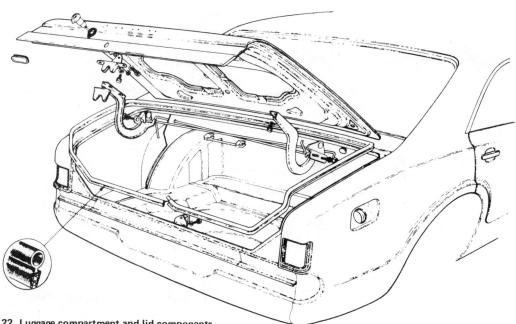

Fig. 12.22. Luggage compartment and lid components

striker plate relative to the inner rear panel to act as a datum for refitting.

2   Undo and remove the two bolts with spring and plain washers that secure the striker plate. Lift away the striker plate.

3   Refitting the striker plate is the reverse sequence to removal. Line up the striker plate with the previously made marks and tighten the securing bolts.

25 Tailgate assembly - removal and installation

1   Open the tailgate and with a pencil mark the outline of the hinges relative to the inner panel.

2   With the assistance of a second person hold the tailgate in position and then undo and remove the bolts, spring and plain washers that secure each hinge to the tailgate. Lift away the tailgate taking care not to scratch the side panels.

3   Refitting the tailgate is the reverse sequence to removal. Any adjustment may be made at the hinges.

26 Tailgate lock - removal and refitting

1   Use a wide bladed screwdriver or a thick knife blade between the tailgate and the trim panel. This will release one or two of the trim panel retaining clips without damaging the trim. The panel can now be gently eased out by hand.

2   Undo and remove the large hexagonal nut that retains the lock cylinder. Lift away the lock cylinder (Fig. 12.23).

3   Undo and remove the lock securing bolts and spring washers and lift away the lock and operating rod assembly.

4   Undo and remove the two nuts, spring and plain washers that secure the tailgate handle. Lift away the tailgate handle and its gasket.

5   To refit the lock assembly is the reverse sequence to removal. Do not tighten the lock and operating rod assembly bolts until the lock cylinder has been refitted and the cylinder keyways connected to the operating rod assembly.

27 Tailgate lock striker plate - removal and refitting

1   Open the tailgate and with a pencil mark the outline of the striker plate relative to the luggage compartment floor.

2   Undo and remove the bolts, spring and plain washers that secure the striker plate and lift away the striker plate.

3   Refitting the striker   plate is the reverse sequence to removal. Line up the striker plate with the previously made mark and tighten the securing bolts.

28 Tailgate hinge and torsion bar - removal and refitting

1   Refer to Section 25 and remove the tailgate assembly.

2   With a pencil mark the outline of the hinge and torsion bar assembly to the body.

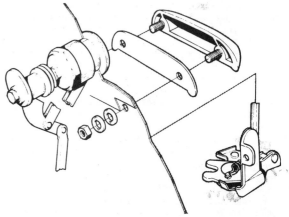

Fig. 12.23. Tailgate lock assembly (Sec. 26)

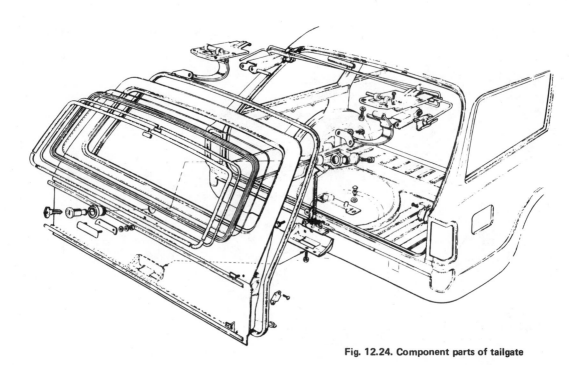

Fig. 12.24. Component parts of tailgate

3   Undo and remove the four bolts, spring and plain washers that secure the hinge and torsion bar assembly to the body and lift away the assembly.

4   Refitting the tailgate hinge and torsion bar assembly is the reverse sequence to removal. Line up the hinge with the previously made mark and tighten the securing bolts.

29 Fixed rear quarter window glass - removal and refitting

1   Using a blunt screwdriver carefully ease the moulding from the weatherstrip.

2   An assistant should now be ready to catch the glass as it is released from the body aperture. Working inside the car push on the glass next to the weatherstrip so releasing it from the aperture flange. Lift away the glass and weatherstrip.

3   Remove the weatherstrip and clean off all traces of sealer. Inspect the weatherstrip for signs of splitting or deterioration and, if evident, a new weatherstrip must be obtained.

4   To refit the glass assembly first fit the moulding to its groove in the weatherstrip and apply a little sealer to the groove in which the glass seats. Fit the glass to the weatherstrip.

5   Fit a draw cord in the weatherstrip to body groove and position the glass to the aperture. Working inside the car, pull on the draw cord whilst the assistant pushes on the glass so drawing the lip over the flange.

6   Apply a little sealer to the weatherstrip to aperture flange. Clean off surplus sealer with a petrol moistened cloth.

30 Opening rear quarter window glass - removal   and refitting

1   Part and remove the window glass moulding halves and then carefully detach the pivot clips from the pivot rubbers in the door pillar (Fig. 12.26). Lift away the glass.

2   Inspect the window aperture weatherstrip for signs of deterioration; If evident, the weatherstrip should be removed from the aperture.

3   Before fitting a new weatherstrip apply a little sealer to the weatherstrip to body groove and then carefully fit the weatherstrip to the body flange.

4   Refitting the glass and moulding is the reverse sequence to removal.

31 Rear window glass - removal and refitting

1   Undo and remove the self-tapping screws that secure the front edge of the rear seat cushion to the heel plate. Lift out the cushion taking care not to damage the upholstery or headlining.

2   Open the boot lid and undo and remove the screws that secure the top of the rear seat backrest to the body. Carefully lift away the backrest.

3   Remove the retainers and bend back the lock tabs securing the rear parcel shelf. Lift away the parcel shelf.

4   Place a blanket over the boot lid so that it is not accidentally scratched and remove the rear window glass using the same

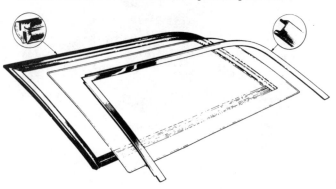

Fig. 12.25. Rear quarter window - Estate

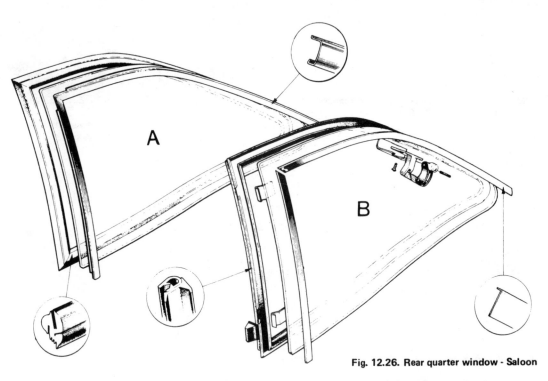

Fig. 12.26. Rear quarter window - Saloon

A Fixed type   B Opening type

procedure as for the front windscreen. Further information will be found in Section 10, paragraphs 3 to 5 inclusive.

5 Refitting the rear window glass is similar to the refitting of the front windscreen. Refer to Section 10, paragraphs 8 to 17 inclusive.

6 Beware if a heated rear window is fitted. To avoid damage have a specialist look at this.

32 Tailgate window glass - removal and refitting

The procedure for removal and replacement of the tailgate window glass is basically identical to that for the rear window glass. Refer to Section 31, paragraphs 4 and 5 for full information.

33.1 Grille tab rubber grommet located in lower panel

Fig. 12.27. Headlamp bezel securing screws (arrowed) on later models (Sec. 33)

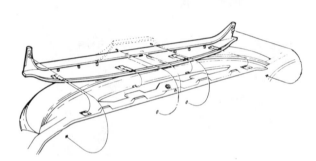

Fig. 12.28. Instrument panel crash padding attachments (up to July 1973) (Sec. 34)

Fig. 12.29. Removing air vent surround (Sec. 35)

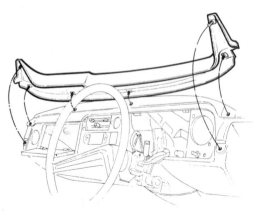

Fig. 12.30. Crash pad securing points on later models (Sec. 35)

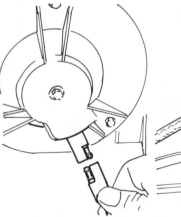

Fig. 12.31. Heater multi-pin plug connector (Sec. 36)

Fig. 12.32. Speedometer cable securing clip (Sec. 36)

33 Radiator grille - removal and installation

1 Open the bonnet and support in the open position. Undo and remove the crosshead screws that secure the radiator grille to the front body panels. Lift away the radiator grille. Refitting is the reverse sequence to removal but take care to locate the grille tabs in their respective slots in the front lower panel (photo).
2 On vehicles built after July 1973 with circular headlamps, the two screws nearest the headlamps, secure the headlamp bezel (Fig. 12.27).

34 Instrument panel crash padding (up to July 1973) - removal and installation

1 Refer to Section 36 and remove the heater control knobs and panel.
2 If there is a radio fitted it must be removed before the crash padding can be removed. The method of removing the radio depends on the type fitted.
3 Undo and remove the small screws that secure the heater and radio bezel and lift away the bezel.
4 Undo and remove the nut that secures the crash pad centre stud. Using a thick knife blade carefully ease the crash padding forwards and upwards so releasing its retaining clips (Fig. 12.28).
5 Refitting the crash padding is the reverse sequence to removal.

35 Instrument panel crash padding (after July 1973) - removal and installation

1 Disconnect the battery.
2 Remove the steering column shroud and pull off   the instrument panel light switch knob.
3 Remove the instrument bezel (six screws) and pull it forward so that all electrical leads, plugs and the speedometer cable can be disconnected. Remove the bezel.
4 Remove the glove compartment lock striker.
5 Remove the glove compartment securing screws, pull the assembly forward, disconnect the lamp leads and remove the assembly.
6 Remove the air vent surround (passenger side) and then remove the two exposed air vent securing screws and pull the vent from the facia so that the hose can be disconnected from it.
7 Access to the crash pad securing nuts can now be obtained through the glove compartment aperture. Installation is a reversal of removal (Fig. 12.30).

36 Heater assembly - removal and installation

1 Refer to Chapter 2 and drain the cooling system.
2 Locate the multi-pin plug connector for the heater unit blower motor and detach the plug from the socket (Fig. 12.31).
   On later models, disconnect the speedometer drive cable from the clip on the heater assembly (Fig. 12.32).
3 Remove the water drain pipe from the air inlet chamber.
4 Slacken the clips that secure the heater water pipes to the heater unit. Note which way round the pipes are fitted and carefully withdraw the two pipes.
5 Undo and remove the self tapping screws that secure the heater unit to the bulkhead. Their locations are shown in Fig. 12.33. Detach the heater control flap operating lever and draw the heater away from the bulkhead.
6 Note that there are three gaskets located between the heater housing flange and if these are damaged they must be renewed (Fig. 12.34).
7 To refit the heater assembly, stick on three new gaskets to the heater joint face. If the original gaskets are to be retained apply some sealer to the free face of the gasket pack.
8 Move the flap located in the centre of the heater housing and the control lever inside the car to either the 'cold' or 'hot'

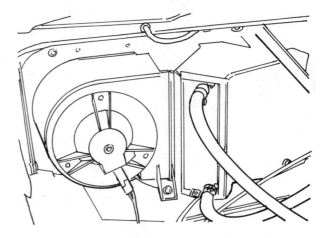

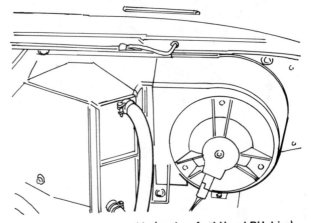

Fig. 12.33. Heater assembly (versions for LH and RH drive) (Sec. 36)

position.
9 Fit the heater to the bulkhead and connect the quadrant of the control valve pivot. Secure the heater with the self tapping screws.
10 Refit the water drain pipe and reconnect the multi-pin plug to the blower motor.
11 Reconnect the two hoses to the heater unit and secure with the clips.
12 Refill the cooling system as described in Chapter 2.

37 Heater assembly - dismantling and   reassembly

1 Refer to Section 36 and remove the heater assembly.
2 Undo and remove the self-tapping screws that secure the heater radiator lower panel to the main casing. Lift away the lower panel (Fig. 12.35).
3 Carefully slide out the heater radiator together with its foam rubber packing.
4 Undo and remove the three bolts that secure the blower motor baseplate and lift away the blower motor assembly (Fig. 12.35).
5 Inspect the heater radiator for signs of leaks which, if evident, may be repaired in a similar manner used for the engine cooling system radiator as described in Chapter 2. It is a good policy to reverse flush the heater radiator to remove any sediment.
6 Reassembling the heater assembly is the reverse sequence to removal.
7 It is possible to remove the heater radiator and the blower motor whilst the heater assembly is still fitted in the car.

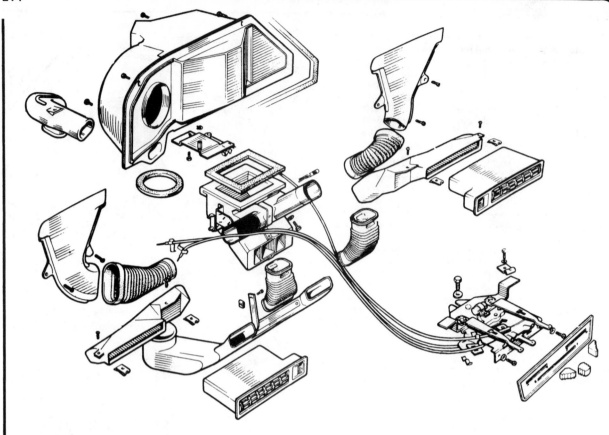

Fig. 12.34. Heater and ventilation system components (Sec. 37)

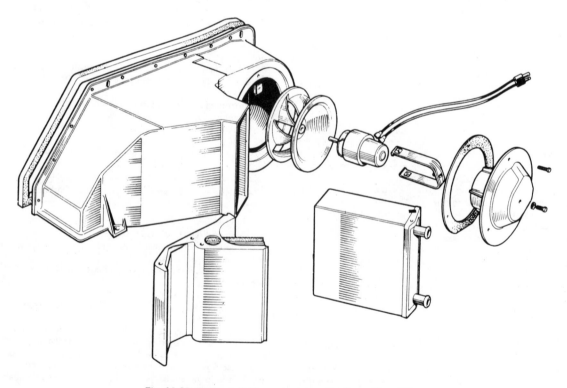

Fig. 12.35. Heater unit blower motor and radiator (Sec. 37)

38 Heater controls (up to 1973) - removal and refitting

Removal

1 Remove the cover plate of the radio recess.
2 Remove the knobs from the control levers (to this effect tap out the dowel pin of the lower knob).
3 From underneath the dashboard, press out the bezel of the control levers.
4 Remove the bezel of the radio switch.
5 Detach both upper control cables from the control unit and withdraw the wire plug connectors.
6 Remove the screws of the control unit and disconnect the lower cable.

Refitting

7 Move the blower control lever to its left-hand stop and lock in this position by pulling the lever out. In this position, connect and adjust the lower control cable.
8 Fit the control switch, reconnect and adjust the upper control cables. Refit the wire plug connectors.
9 Refit the radio switch bezel.
10 Position the control switch bezel and secure.
11 Check operation of heater flaps and blower. Readjust control cables if necessary.
12 Replace the knobs to the levers and press in the dowel pin of the centre knob.
13 Replace the cover plate to the radio recess.

39 Heater controls (1973 onwards) - removal and refitting

1 Disconnect the battery leads.
2 Remove the parcels tray from the transmission tunnel.
3 Remove the cowl trim (five screws) (Fig. 12.36).
4 Remove the steering column shroud.
5 Remove the instrument cluster and bezel (see Chapter 10).
6 Disconnect the now accessible heater controls from the operating levers of the heater unit and then remove the heater control assembly (three screws) (Fig. 12.37).
7 Should the resistance unit be defective, it can be renewed by drilling out the rivets (Fig. 12.38).
8 Installation is a reversal of removal but check for correct operation of the controls before refitting the instrument assembly.

40 Centre console - removal and installation

1 On earlier models, unscrew the console mounted instrument panel and pull it forward so that the instrument connections can be disconnected.
2 Unscrew and remove the securing screws from within the parcels and ashtray wells of the console.
3 On later models, prise out the clock (or the blanking plate) and disconnect the clock leads.
4 Unscrew and remove the two screws accessible through the clock aperture and the two located at the rear sides of the console (Figs. 12.40 and 12.41).

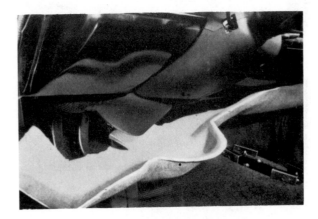

Fig. 12.36. Removing the cowl trim (1973 onwards) (Sec. 39)

Fig. 12.37. Heater control connections (1973 onwards) (Sec. 39)

Fig. 12.38. Location of resistance on heater control (1973 onwards) (Sec. 39)

216

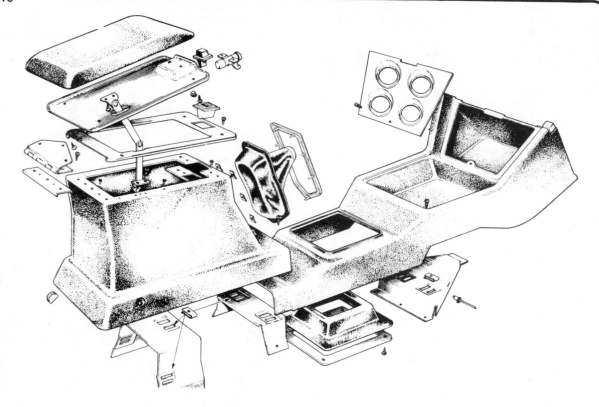

Fig. 12.39. Front passenger compartment console components (up to July 1973) (Sec. 40)

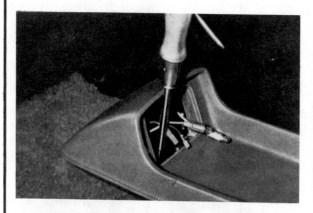

Fig. 12.40. Removing centre console screw through clock aperture (1973 on) (Sec. 40)

Fig. 12.41. Centre console rear securing screw (1973 onwards - Automatic transmission shown) (Sec. 40)

Chapter 13 Supplement

Contents

1 Introduction

The purpose of this Supplement is to provide information on the Lucas M35G inertia-type starter motor fitted to some models, to provide additional information on camshaft/cam follower wear, clutch pilot bearing renewal, dismantling and reassembly procedures for an alternative type of gearbox, and to include supplementary wiring diagrams to cover later models. Information is also included relating to the later type 'bypass (sonic) idle' carburettors and tamperproof carburettors as fitted to models from mid-1975 and mid-1976 respectively. As such, the Supplement should be used in conjunction with the relevant information contained in Chapters 1 to 12.

2 Specifications

Carburation
Motorcraft carburettors
Key to headings
   (a) 1600 cc manual transmission models fitted with manual choke carburettor
   (b) 1600 cc manual transmission models fitted with automatic choke carburettor
   (c) 1600 cc automatic transmission models fitted with automatic choke carburettor
Note that where a specification is centralised under all three columns, it applies to all three carburettor types

	(a)	(b)	(c)
Main jet		135	
Idle speed (rpm)		800 ± 25	
Mixture CO (%)		0.5 ± 0.1	
Fast idle (rpm)	1000 ± 100	2000 ± 100	2200 ± 100
Float level in (mm)		1.14 ± 0.03 (29.0 ± 0.75)	
Choke plate pull down setting in (mm)	0.13 ± 0.01 (3.3 ± 0.25)	0.15 ± 0.01 (3.8 ± 0.25)	0.12 ± 0.01 (3.0 ± 0.25)
Dechoke in (mm)	—	0.21 ± 0.02 (5.3 ± 0.5)	0.21 ± 0.02 (5.3 ± 0.5)
Accelerator pump stroke in (mm)		0.11 ± 0.005 (2.9 ± 0.13)	
Vacuum piston link hole	—	Outer	Outer
Thermostatic spring slot	—	Centre	Centre
'V' mark setting in (mm)	—	0.20 (5.0)	0.18 (4.5)

Weber carburettors
Key to headings
   (a) 1600 cc models with manual transmission
   (b) 1600 cc models with automatic transmission
   (c) 2000 cc models with manual transmission
   (d) 2000 cc models with automatic transmission
Note that where a specification is centralised under two or more columns, it applies to all of those carburettor types

	(a)	(b)	(c)	(d)
Main jet	130/125		137/127	135/127
Idle speed (rpm)	800 ± 20		825 ± 25	
Mixture CO (%)		1.5 ± 0.25		
Fast idle * (rpm)	2000 ± 100		2100 ± 100	
Float level ** in (mm)	1.61 ± 0.02 (41.0 ± 0.5)			
Choke plate pull down setting in (mm)	0.24 (6.0) max		0.28 (7.0) max	
Choke phasing in (mm)	0.09 ± 0.01 (2.25 ± 0.25)			

Automatic choke type set at phase point
** *Figures given apply to brass float. For plastic float this should read 1.39 ± 0.02 in (35.3 ± 0.5 mm)*

Gearbox

Gearbox type reference	Type C
Number of gears	Four forward, one reverse
Type of gears	Helical, constant mesh
Synchromesh	All forward gears
Oil capacity	1.75 Imp pts (1 litre)
Gear ratios	
First	3.65 : 1
Second	1.97 : 1
Third	1.37 : 1
Top	1.00 : 1
Reverse	3.66 : 1

Torque wrench settings	lbf ft	kgf m
Gearbox top cover bolts	15	2.1
Gearbox spigot bearing retainer bolts	15	2.1
Extension housing bolts	25	3.5
Bellhousing bolts	40	5.5
Drain and filler plugs	25	3.5

Electrical system

Starter motor

Type	Lucas M35G inertia

Specifications as for M35G pre-engaged type except for the following items:

Brushes spring pressure	15 oz (420 gm)
Type of drive	Inertia
Number of flywheel ring teeth	110
Maximum output	620 watts

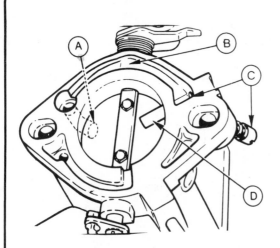

Fig. 13.1. Sonic idle carburettor

A Air entry into bypass system   C Mixture screw
B Air distribution channel   D Sonic discharge tube

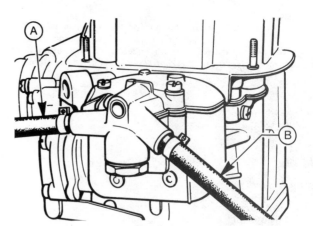

Fig. 13.2. Weber fuel return system

A Fuel return pipe   B Fuel supply pipe

3 Engine

Clutch pilot bearing - renewal

1 During any major engine repair, prise out the clutch pilot bearing from the rear end of the crankshaft; this may require the use of a hook-ended tool to get behind the bearing.

2 Fit the replacement bearing with the seal outwards (where applicable) so that it is just below the surface of the crankshaft flange.

Excessive cam lobe/cam follower wear

3 If excessive cam follower wear is evident (and possibly excessive cam lobe wear), this may be due to a malfunction of the valve drive lubrication tube. If this has occurred, renew the tube and the cam follower. If more than one cam follower is excessively worn, renew the camshaft, all the cam followers and the lubrication tube; this also applies where excessive cam lobe wear is found.

4 During any operation which requires removal of the valve rocker cover, ensure that the oil is being discharged from the lubrication tube nozzles by cranking the engine on the starter motor. During routine maintenance operations this can be done after checking the valve clearances.

4 Carburation

General description - later carburettors

1 The European Economic Community and Economic Commission of Europe have approved legislation to reduce the level of atmospheric pollution from toxic substances emitted by motor vehicles. At present this legislation covers mainly crankcase and exhaust emissions.

2 Regulations agreed by the EEC and ECE require that after a running in period of 1875 miles (3000 km), the level of carbon monoxide present in the exhaust emissions should be below 4.5%. Legislation also requires that from October 1976 onwards, all carburettors fitted by vehicle manufacturers should be of the tamperproof type. This requirement is to discourage indiscriminate adjustments being made without the necessary measuring equipment, which could lead to the vehicle producing CO emissions above the statutory level.

3 The first of these two requirements was initially fulfilled by Ford with the progressive introduction from mid-1975 of the 'bypass (sonic) idle' carburettors. The second requirement was met by the progressive introduction from May 1976 of 'tamperproof' carburettors, the tamperproofing normally being achieved by the use of sealing plugs blanking off certain adjustment screws, in particular that controlling mixture adjustment.

4 General descriptions and adjustment procedures are given in this Section for these later type carburettors, but it should be noted that all other overhaul procedures are basically similar to those described in Chapter 3.

Ford single venturi (IV) sonic idle carburettors - description and adjustment

5 From mid-1975, the Ford bypass (sonic) idle carburettor was progressively introduced on Cortina models. The carburettor idle system differs from the conventional type in that the majority of the idle air flow and all of the idle fuel flow passes through the bypass system. The remaining airflow flows past the carburettor butterfly which is held in a slightly open position.

6 During idle, with the butterfly almost closed, air is drawn into the bypass system (see Fig. 13.1). This air travels along the air distribution channel and mixes with the fuel entering via the mixture screw; the resulting mixture is drawn into the engine via the sonic discharge tube.

7 The sonic idle carburettor may be instantly recognised by the following:

a) Seven screws retaining the upper body, compared with six on previous units

b) The distributor advance/retard vacuum pick-up tube is increased in length from 14 mm (0.52 in) to 35 mm (1.37 in)

c) The idle mixture screw is repositioned to a point just above where the vacuum pick-up tube was previously situated (see Chapter 3)

d) The vacuum pick-up tube is repositioned to a point just above where the idle mixture screw was previously situated

8 Adjustment procedures for the sonic idle carburettor are as given in Chapter 3 (except where a tamperproof carburettor is fitted), and all specification details are given in the Specifications section of this Supplement. It should be remembered that where a sonic idle carburettor is fitted, the following amendments will apply:

a) A revised inlet manifold (which may also be used with earlier single venturi carburettors). The carburettor flange gasket must be fitted with the tab towards the front of the engine

b) A revised initial advance ignition timing of 6º BTDC at 800 rpm for 1600 models except GT, and 8º BTDC at 800 rpm and 825 rpm for 1600 GT models and 2000 models respectively

Weber dual venturi (2V) sonic idle carburettors - description and adjustment

9 The Weber dual venturi carburettor described in Chapter 3 was modified from May 1975 and progressively introduced on the appropriate Cortina models. In addition to the bypass idle characteristic, the modified Weber 2V carburettor includes a fuel return system (Fig.13.2), and on some models (mainly automatic transmission) an anti-stall device.

10 The fuel return system ensures that the temperature of fuel entering the float chamber is maintained at a constant level at all times, and this in turn keeps the quantity of fuel vapour from the float chamber to the engine constant. Previously, if the engine was left idling for long periods, the idle mixture became over-rich.

11 Refer to Fig. 13.3 and observe that, on the Weber bypass idle system, fuel is initially supplied via the float chamber to the secondary main jet (A). Fuel then travels up to the secondary idle jet (B) where air is introduced into the system through the drilling (C). The air/fuel mixture then passes through a restrictor and is atomised as it enters the main bypass air flow (D). The mixture then passes through the fixed discharge channel (F) and the bypass discharge channel (G), the latter being adjustable by the bypass idle screw (E), and thence to the engine.

12 Adjustment of the modified Weber 2V carburettor is similar to that described in Chapter 3, but it should be remembered that the basic idle speed screw (Fig. 13.6) should not be adjusted during normal routine servicing; it should only require adjustment after a carburettor overhaul or if the correct idle speed is impossible to achieve using the bypass idle screw. It is also imperative that an exhaust gas analyser is used to make the adjustment to the mixture screw.

13 The anti-stall device fitted to some models consists of a housing, diaphragm and spring. Engine vacuum is applied by an external tube to one side of the diaphragm which is then pulled back against spring tension. This action draws fuel from the accelerator pump reservoir to the opposite side of the diaphragm. If the engine attempts to stall, there will be an initial drop in engine vacuum and, immediately this occurs, the diaphragm will be released and spring pressure will pump a quantity of fuel through the accelerator pump discharge tube, thus temporarily enriching the mixture and overcoming the stall.

14 Where an anti-stall device is fitted (mainly automatic transmission models) it is important to set the engine idle speed correctly; if it is too slow, the anti-stall device will give an intermittent fuel delivery causing 'hunting'.

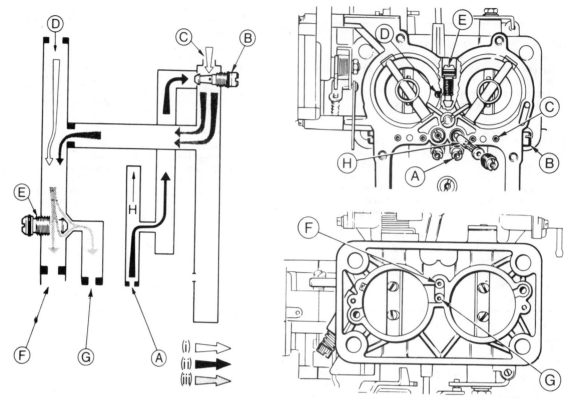

Fig.13.3. Weber bypass idle system

(i) Air supply	A Main jet	E Bypass idle screw
(ii) Fuel supply	B Idle jet	F Fixed discharge channel
(iii) Air/fuel mixture	C Air bleed	G Bypass discharge channel
	D Main air supply	H Secondary emulsion tube

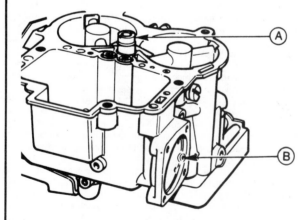

Fig.13.4. Location of anti-stall device (carburettor dismantled)

A Discharge tube
B Fuel entry

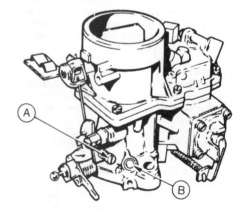

Fig.13.5. Ford single venturi tamperproof carburettor

A Idle speed screw
B Plastic sealing plug over idle mixture screw

Tamperproof carburettors - description and adjustment

15 From May 1976, all carburettors are not only of the sonic idle type, but are also tamperproof in respect of the idle mixture adjustment. This is effected by a plastic plug being installed over the idle mixture adjustment screw, and has been introduced to comply with EEC regulations.

16 The carburettor body is slightly modified to accommodate the recessed idle mixture screw which is beneath a white plastic plug. The carburettor is so designed that after the initial running-in period of a new engine, the percentage of carbon monoxide (CO) in the exhaust gas will be in accordance with a predetermined requirement (this may mean that during running-in, the requirement may not be met). Therefore, in order to comply with the regulations, adjustment should only be made with an exhaust gas analyser coupled to the car exhaust system.

17 Should adjustment be necessary, the white plastic plug may be punctured in its centre using a small screwdriver, and then prised out. Where this adjustment has been found necessary, a blue replacement plug should be pressed in on completion.

18 It is not essential for satisfactory operation of the carburettor to have the plastic plug fitted after any adjustment, but future legislation may (officially) restrict the adjustment procedure and supply of replacement plastic plugs to authorised dealers. Where adjustment is carried out, the exhaust gas CO content at idle speed is given in the Specifications Section.

19 When using an exhaust gas analyser on tamperproof carburettors it is imperative to obtain the correct reading, due to the fine CO percentage limits imposed on them. The engine must be at its normal operating temperature and the CO meter and exhaust gas analyser must be connected to the engine in accordance with the manufacturers' instructions.

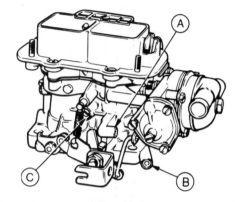

Fig.13.6. Weber twin venturi tamperproof carburettor

    A *Basic idle speed screw*
    B *Mixture screw*
    C *Bypass idle speed screw*

20 Run the engine at 3000 rpm for approximately 30 seconds then allow it to idle. Then, as soon as the meters have stabilised, and within 10 to 30 seconds, record the CO percentage. If it takes longer than 30 seconds to make any adjustment, the engine should be run at 3000 rpm for 30 seconds again.

21 If it is found impossible to adjust the carburettor within the specification limits, the ignition timing, valve clearances, and general engine condition should be checked.

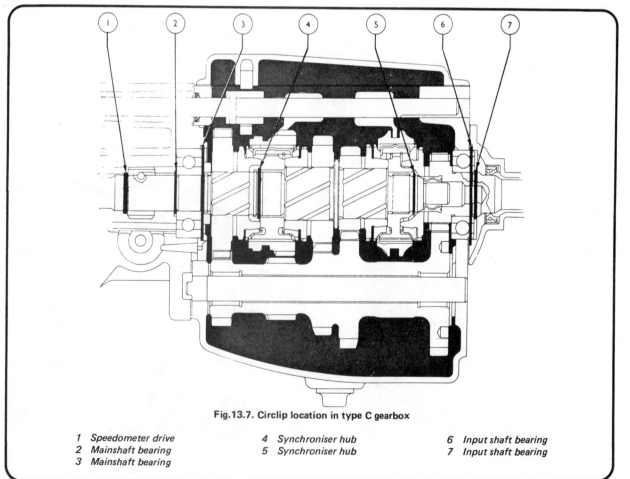

Fig.13.7. Circlip location in type C gearbox

1 *Speedometer drive*	4 *Synchroniser hub*	6 *Input shaft bearing*
2 *Mainshaft bearing*	5 *Synchroniser hub*	7 *Input shaft bearing*
3 *Mainshaft bearing*		

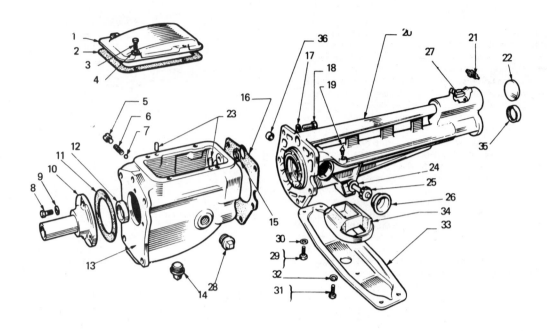

Fig.13.8. Exploded view of the gearbox casing and extension

1 Gearbox cover	13 Gearbox casting	25 Speedometer gear
2 Gasket	14 Drain plug	26 Plug
3 Bolt	15 Selector rod seal	27 Gear lever orifice
4 Washer	16 Gasket	28 Filler/level plug
5 Screw	17 Washer	29 Bolt
6 Spring	18 Bolt	30 Washer
7 Ball	19 Breather	31 Bolt
8 Bolt	20 Gearbox extension	32 Washer
9 Washer	21 Reverse light switch	33 Rear crossmember
10 Bearing retainer	22 Plug	34 Rubber mounting
11 Gasket	23 Dowels	35 Oil seal
12 Oil seal	24 Circlip	36 Seal

5.1 Remove the clutch release bearing

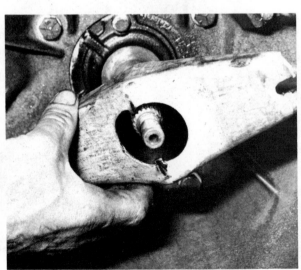

5.2 Lift out the release lever

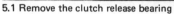

5 Gearbox

This Section provides information on a gearbox which may be fitted to some models covered by this manual. The gearbox is generally as described in Chapter 6, which also includes the procedure for its removal and installation. However, it is important to note that the selective circlips are in different positions as shown in Fig.13.7, and the dismantling and reassembly procedures are as described below.

Gearbox - dismantling
1   Remove the clutch release bearing from the gearbox input shaft (photo).
2   Lift out the clutch release lever (photo).
3   Undo and remove the four bolts holding the bellhousing to the gearbox (photo).
4   Detach the bellhousing from the gearbox (photo).
5   Slightly loosen the gearbox drain plug and mount the gearbox upright in a vice using the drain plug as a pivot. Make sure the vice is firmly gripping the drain plug so the assembly cannot tilt.
6   Referring to Fig.13.8, undo the four bolts holding the gearbox

5.3 Remove the bellhousing retaining bolts

5.4 Detach the bellhousing

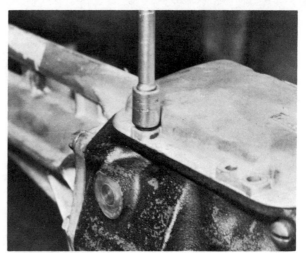
5.6A Undo the bolts . . .

5.6B . . . and remove the top cover

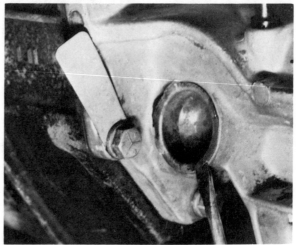
5.7 Prise out the cup-shaped retainer plug

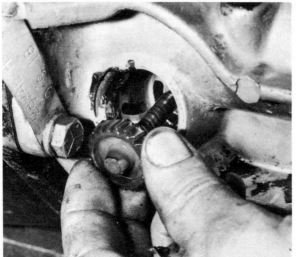
5.8 Remove the speedometer gear

5.9 Drive out the rear extension oil seal

5.10 Remove the plunger screw

5.11 Drive out the selector boss pin

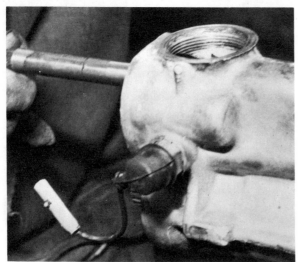
5.12A Withdraw the selector rod . . .

5.12B . . . whilst holding the selector boss and cam

top cover (1) in place (photo A) and remove the cover (photo B). On later gearboxes, the selector spring and detent ball will now be exposed; lift out the spring and remove the ball using a screwdriver with a blob of grease on the end.

7   Prise out the cup-shaped retainer plug (26) on the side of the gearbox extension (photo).

8   From under this seal pull out the speedometer gear (25) (photo). To start it, it may be necessary to tap it from the other end.

9   From where the gear lever enters the extension housing drive out the rear extension oil seal (22) (photo).

10 Remove the plunger screw (5), its spring (6) and the ball (7) from the right-hand side of the gearbox casing (early models only) (photo).

11 Using a small drift drive out the pin holding the selector boss to the selector rod (photo).

12 Now withdraw the selector rod (photo A), at the same time holding onto the selector boss and cam (photo B) to prevent them falling into the gearbox.

13 To remove the selector forks, it is necessary to knock the two synchro hubs towards the front of the gearbox, this can be done with a small drift or a screwdriver. Now lift out the selector forks.

14 Turn now to the gearbox extension (20) (Fig.13.8) and remove the bolts (18) and washers (17) which hold it to the gearbox casing.

15 Knock it slightly rearwards with a soft-headed hammer, then rotate the whole extension until the cut-out on the extension face coincides with the rear end of the layshaft in the lower half of the gearbox casing.

16 Obtain a metal rod to act as a dummy layshaft 6.8 in (173 mm) long with a diameter of 0.625 in (16 mm).

17 Tap the layshaft rearwards with a drift until it is just clear of the front of the gearbox casing, then insert the dummy shaft and drive the layshaft out allowing the laygear cluster to drop out of mesh with the mainshaft gears into the bottom of the casing.

18 Withdraw the mainshaft and extension assembly from the gearbox casing, pushing the 3rd/top synchronizer hub forward slightly to obtain the necessary clearance. A small roller bearing should come away on the nose of the mainshaft, but if it is not there it will be found in its recess in the input shaft and should be removed.

19 Moving to the front of the gearbox remove the bolts (8) (Fig.13.8) and washers (9) holding the input shaft bearing retainer (10) and take it off the shaft.

20 Remove the large circlip now exposed and then tap on the bearing outer race to remove it, and the input shaft, from inside the gearbox.

21 The laygear can now be withdrawn from the rear of the gearbox together with its thrust washers (one at each end).

22 Remove the mainshaft assembly from the gearbox extension by taking out the large circlip (20, Fig.13.10) adjacent to the mainshaft bearing, then tapping the rear of the shaft with a soft-headed hammer. Do not discard the circlip at this stage as it is required for setting-up during reassembly.

23 The reverse idler gear can be removed by screwing a suitable bolt into the end of the shaft and then levering the shaft out

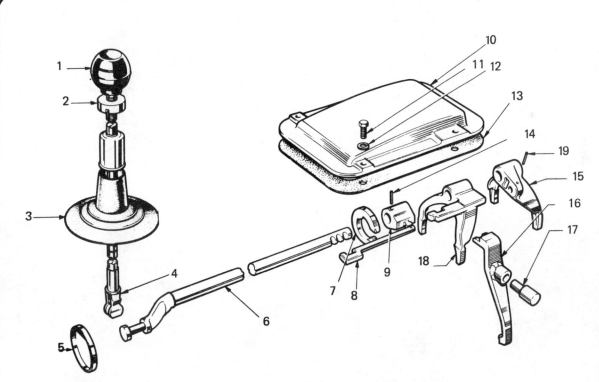

Fig.13.9. Exploded view of the gearchange mechanism

1 Gear lever knob	8 Third and fourth gearchange gate	14 Split locking pin
2 Knob locknut	9 Selector arm	15 First and second gear selector fork
3 Gear lever boot	10 Gearbox cover	16 Reverse gear selector fork
4 Gear lever	11 Bolt	17 Fork pivot
5 Plug	12 Spring washer	18 Third and fourth gear selector fork
6 Gear selector rod	13 Gasket	19 Pin
7 Selector interlock plate		

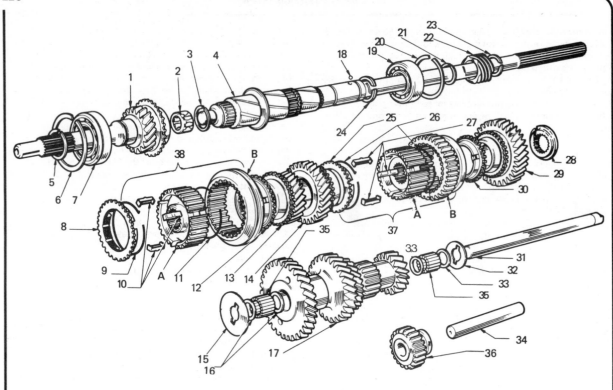

Fig. 13.10. Exploded view of the internal gearbox components

1 Input shaft
2 Caged roller bearing
3 Circlip
4 Mainshaft
5 Small circlip
6 Bearing retaining circlip
7 Bearing
8 Synchroniser ring
9 Spring ring
10 Blocker bars
11 Spring ring

12 Synchroniser ring
13 Third gear
14 Second gear
15 Laygear thrust washer
16 Needle roller bearing thrust washers
17 Laygear
18 Ball
19 Mainshaft bearing
20 Circlip (selective)

21 Circlip (selective)
22 Speedometer drive
23 Circlip
24 Circlip
25 Synchroniser ring
26 Spring rings
27 Blocker bars
28 Thrust washer
29 First gear
30 Synchroniser ring

31 Layshaft
32 Layshaft thrust washer
33 Needle roller bearing thrust washer
34 Reverse gear shaft
35 Needle roller bearings
36 Reverse gear
37 First and second gear synchroniser assembly
38 Third and top gear synchroniser assembly

5.23 Remove the reverse idler shaft

5.35 Remove the large bearing

with the aid of two large open-ended spanners (photo).
24 The gearbox is now completely stripped and must be
thoroughly cleaned. If there is a quantity of metal chips and
fragments in the bottom of the gearbox casing then it is obvious
that several items will be found to be badly worn. The component
parts of the gearbox and laygear should be examined for wear.
The input shaft and mainshaft assemblies can be dismantled
further as described in the following paragraphs.

Input shaft
25 The only reason for dismantling the input shaft is to fit a
new bearing assembly or, if the input shaft is being renewed
and the old bearing is in excellent condition, the fitting of a
new shaft to an old bearing.
26 With a pair of expanding circlip pliers remove the circlip (5),
(Fig.13.10) from the input shaft.
27 With a soft-headed hammer gently tap the bearing forward
and then remove it from the shaft.

Mainshaft
28 The mainshaft has to be dismantled before some of the
synchroniser rings can be inspected. For dismantling purposes
it is best to mount the plain portion of the shaft between two
pieces of wood in a vice.
29 From the forward end of the mainshaft pull off the caged
roller bearing (2) and the synchro ring (8) (Fig.13.10).
30 With a pair of circlip pliers remove the circlip (3) which holds
the third/fourth gear synchroniser hub in place.
31 Ease the hub (38) and third gear (13) forward by gentle
leverage with a pair of long nosed pliers.
32 The hub (38) and synchro ring (12) are then removed from
the mainshaft.
33 Then slide off third gear. Nothing else can be removed from
this end of the mainshaft because of the raised lip on the shaft.
34 Move to the other end of the mainshaft and remove the small
circlip (23), then slide off the speedometer drive taking care not
to lose the ball (18) which is located in a groove in the gear and
a small recess in the mainshaft.
35 Remove the circlip (21) and then gently lever off the large
bearing with the aid of two tyre levers as shown in the photo.
36 The bearing (19), followed by the large thrust washer (28),
can then be pulled off. Follow these items by pulling off first
gear (29) and the synchroniser ring (30).
37 With a pair of circlip pliers remove the circlip (24) which
retains the first and second gear synchroniser assembly (37) in
place.
38 The first and second gear synchroniser, followed by second
gear (14), are then simply slid off the mainshaft. The mainshaft
is now completely dismantled.

Gearbox - inspection
39 Carefully clean and then examine all the component parts for
general wear, distortion, slackness of fit, and damage to machined
faces and threads.
40 Examine the gearwheels for excessive wear and chipping of
teeth. Renew them as necessary.
41 Examine the layshaft for signs of wear, particularly in the
areas where the layshaft needle roller bearings run. If a small
ridge can be felt at either end of the shaft it will be necessary to
renew it.
42 The four synchroniser rings (8, 12, 25, 30) (Fig.13.10) are
bound to be worn and it is false economy not to renew them.
New rings will improve the smoothness and speed of the gearchange considerably.
43 The needle roller bearing and cage (2) located between the
nose of the mainshaft and the annulus in the rear of the input
shaft is also liable to wear, and should be renewed.
44 Examine the condition of the two bearing assemblies, one
on the input shaft (7) and the other on the mainshaft (19).
Check them for noisy operation, looseness between the inner
and outer races, and for general wear. Normally they should be
renewed on a gearbox that is being rebuilt.
45 If either of the synchroniser units (37, 38) are worn it will be

necessary to buy a complete assembly as the parts are not sold
individually.
46 Examine the ends of the selector forks where they rub
against the channels in the periphery of the synchroniser units.
If possible compare the selector forks with new units to help
determine the wear that has occurred. Renew them if necessary.
47 If the bush bearing in the extension is badly worn it is best to
take the extension to your local Ford dealer to have a new one
fitted.
48 The rear oil seal (35, Fig.13.8) should be renewed as a
matter of course. Drive out the old seal with the aid of a drift
or broad screwdriver. It will be found that the seal comes out
quite easily.
49 With a piece of wood to spread the load evenly, carefully
tap a new seal into place ensuring that it enters the bore in the
extension squarely.
50 The only point on the mainshaft that is likely to be worn is
the nose where it enters the input shaft. However, examine it
thoroughly for any signs of scoring, picking-up, or flats, and if
damage is apparent renew it.

Gearbox - reassembly
Mainshaft
51 If a new synchroniser assembly is being fitted it is necessary
to take it to pieces first to clean off all the preservative. These
instructions are also pertinent in instances where the outer
sleeve has come off the hub accidentally during dismantling.
52 To dismantle an assembly for cleaning slide the synchroniser
sleeve off the splined hub and clean all the preservative from the
blocker bars (10, 27) (Fig.13.10), spring rings (9, 11, 26), the hub
itself (A), and the sleeve (B).
53 Oil the components lightly and then fit the sleeve (B) to the
hub (A) so the lines marked on them (see Fig.13.11) are in line.
Note the three slots in the hub and fit a blocker bar in each.
54 Fit the two springs; one on the front face and one on the
rear face of the inside of the synchroniser sleeve under the
blocker bars, with the tagged end of each spring locating in the
'U' section of the same bar. One spring must be put on anticlockwise and one clockwise when viewed face on from one side
(see Fig.13.12). When either side of the assembly is viewed face on
the direction of rotation of the springs should then appear the
same.
55 Prior to reassembling the mainshaft read paragraphs 61 and
63 of this Section, to ensure that the correct thickness of
selective circlips can be obtained. Reassembly commences by
fitting second gear (14) (Fig.13.10), with its gear teeth facing
the raised lip, and its synchroniser ring (25) on the rear portion
of the mainshaft (photo).

5.55 Refit the second gear and synchroniser ring

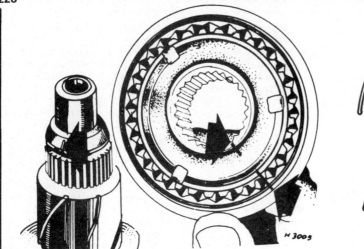

Fig.13.11. The synchroniser assembly alignment marks

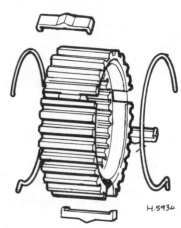

Fig.13.12. The synchroniser hub springs must be put on as shown in this illustration

5.56A Slide on the first and second gear synchroniser assembly . . .

5.56B . . . and ensure that the synchro ring fits over the blocker bars

5.57 Refit the circlip

5.59 Slide on the first gear

56 Next slide on the first and second gear synchroniser assembly (37), (photo A) *and ensure* that the cut-outs in the synchroniser ring fit over the blocker bars in the synchroniser hub (photo B); that the marks on the mainshaft and hub are in line (where made); and that the reverse gear teeth cut on the synchroniser sleeve periphery are adjacent to second gear.

57 Refit the circlip (24) which holds the synchroniser hub in place (photo).

58 Then fit the other synchroniser ring (30), again ensuring that the cut-outs in the ring fit over the blocker bars in the synchroniser hub.

59 Next slide on first gear (29) so the synchronising cone portion lies inside the synchronising ring just fitted (photo).

60 Fit the splined thrust washer (28) to the front of first gear (photo).

61 If a new mainshaft bearing (19) or a new gearbox extension is being used, it will now be necessary to select a new large circlip to eliminate endfloat of the mainshaft. To do this, first fit the original circlip in its groove in the gearbox extension and draw it outwards (ie away from the rear of the extension). Now accurately measure the dimension from the base of the bearing housing to the outer edge of the circlip and record the figure. Also accurately measure the thickness of the bearing outer track and subtract the figure from the depth already recorded. This will give the required shim thickness to give zero endfloat.

62 Loosely fit the selected circlip, lubricate the bearing contact surfaces, then press it onto the shaft. To press the bearing home, close the jaws of the vice until they are not quite touching the mainshaft and, with the bearing resting squarely against the side of the vice jaws, draw the bearing on by tapping the end of the shaft with a soft-headed hammer (photo).

63 Refit the small circlip retaining the main bearing in place. This is also a selective circlip and must be such that all endfloat between the bearing inner track and the circlip edge is eliminated (photo).

64 Refit the small ball (18) that retains the speedometer drive in its recess in the mainshaft (photo).

65 Slide on the speedometer drive (22) noting that it can only be fitted one way round as the groove in which the ball fits does not run the whole length of the drive (photo).

66 Now fit the circlip (23) to retain the speedometer drive (photo). Assembly of this end of the mainshaft is now complete.

67 Moving to the short end of the mainshaft slide on third gear (13) so that the machined gear teeth lie adjacent to second gear, then slide on the synchroniser ring (12) (photo).

68 Fit the third and fourth gear synchroniser assembly (38) (photo) again ensuring that the cut-outs on the ring line up with the blocker bars.

5.60 Refit the splined thrust washer

5.62 Drive the bearing home

5.63 Refit the main bearing selective circlip

5.64 Place the speedometer drive retaining ball in its recess

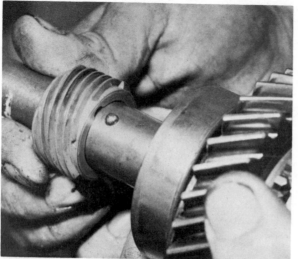

5.65 Slide on the speedometer drive gear

5.66 Refit the circlip

5.67 Slide on the third gear and synchroniser ring

5.68 Refit the third and fourth gear synchroniser assembly

5.69 Drive the synchroniser fully home

5.70 Refit the securing circlip

5.77 Position the laygear needle rollers carefully . . .

5.78 . . . and fit the external washers

5.79 Slide in the dummy layshaft

5.81 Place the smaller thrust washer at the rear

5.82 Position the laygear carefully

5.83A Slide in the input shaft assembly . . .

5.83B . . . and drive the bearing into place

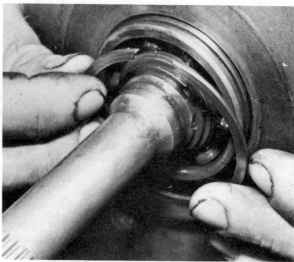

5.84 Refit the securing circlip

5.85 Apply sealing compound to the bearing retainer

5.86A Refit the input shaft bearing retainer . . .

5.86B . . . and tighten the bolts

5.87 Slide in the mainshaft assembly

69 With a suitable piece of metal tube over the mainshaft, tap the synchroniser fully home onto the mainshaft (photo).
70 Then fit the securing circlip (3) in place (photo). Apart from the needle roller bearing race which rests on the nose of the mainshaft this completes mainshaft reassembly.

Input shaft

71 When fitting the new input shaft bearing (7) ensure that the groove cut in the outer periphery faces away from the gear. If the bearing is fitted the wrong way round it will not be possible to fit the large circlip which retains the bearing in the housing.
72 Using the jaws of a vice as a support behind the bearing tap the bearing squarely into place by hitting the rear of the input shaft with a soft-headed hammer.
73 Refit the circlip (5) which holds the bearing to the input shaft.

Gearbox main assembly

74 If removed refit the reverse idler gear and selector lever in the gearbox, by tapping in the shaft (34). Once it is through the casing fit the gearwheel (36) so that its teeth are facing in towards the main gearbox area.
75 Fit the reverse selector lever in the groove in the idler gear then drive the shaft home with a soft-headed hammer until it is flush with the gearbox casing.
76 Slide a retaining washer (16, 33) into each end of the laygear (17) so that they abut the internal machined shoulder.
77 Smear thick grease on the laygear needle roller bearing surface and fit the needle rollers (35) one at a time (photo) until all are in place. The grease will hold the needle rollers in position. Build up the needle roller bearings in the other end of the laygear in a similar fashion. There should be 20 at each end.
78 Fit the external washer to each end of the laygear, taking care not to dislodge the needle roller bearings (photo).
79 Carefully slide in the dummy layshaft used previously for driving out the layshaft (photo).
80 Grease the two thrust washers (15 and 32) and position the larger of the two (15) in the front of the gearbox so that the tongues fit into the machined recesses.
81 Fit the smaller of the thrust washers (32) to the rear of the gearbox in the same way (photo).
82 Fit the laygear complete with dummy layshaft in the bottom of the casing taking care not to dislodge the thrust washers (photo).
83 From inside the gearbox slide in the input shaft assembly (1) (photo A), and drive the bearing into place with a suitable drift (photo B).
84 Secure the bearing in position by refitting the circlip (6) (photo).
85 Fit a new gasket to the bearing retainer and smear on a proprietary sealing compound (photo).
86 Refit the bearing retainer on the input shaft (photo A) ensuring that the oil drain hole is towards the bottom of the gearbox, and tighten the bolts (photo B).
87 Submerge the gearbox end of the extension housing in hot water for a few minutes, then mount it in a vice and slide in the mainshaft assembly. Take care that the splines do not damage the oil seal (photo).
88 Secure the mainshaft to the gearbox extension by locating the circlip already placed loosely behind the main bearing into its groove in the extension (photo A). Photo B shows the circlip correctly located.
89 Fit a new gasket to the extension housing and then refit the small roller bearing on the nose of the mainshaft. Lubricate the roller bearing with gearbox oil (photo).
90 Slide the combined mainshaft and housing assembly into the rear of the gearbox and mate up the nose of the mainshaft with the rear of the input shaft (photo).
91 Completely invert the gearbox so that the laygear falls into mesh with the mainshaft gears.
92 Turn the extension housing round until the cut-out on it coincides with the hole for the layshaft (photo). It may be necessary to trim the gasket.

5.88A Locate the circlip in the groove in the extension

5.88B The circlip correctly located

5.89 Locate the mainshaft roller bearing

5.90 Slide the mainshaft and extension housing into the gearbox casing

5.92 Turn the extension to align the cut-out with the hole for the layshaft

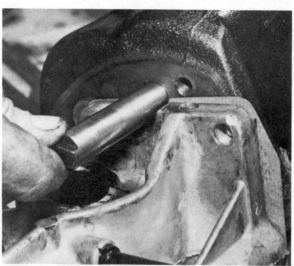

5.93 Push in the layshaft

5.94 Ensure that the cut-out in the end of the layshaft is in the horizontal position

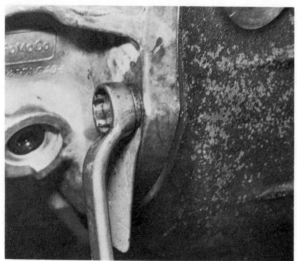

5.95 Secure the extension housing to the gearbox casing

5.96A Push both synchroniser hubs . . .

93 Push the layshaft into its hole from the rear thereby driving out the dummy shaft at the same time (photo).
94 Tap the layshaft into position until its front end is flush with the gearbox casing and ensure that the cut-out on the rear end is in the horizontal position so it will fit into its recess in the extension housing flange (photo).
95 Turn the gearbox the right way up again; correctly line up the extension housing, and secure it to the gearbox. Apply a non-setting gasket sealant to the bolt threads before fitting them (photo).
96 The selector forks cannot be refitted until the two synchroniser hubs are pushed, by means of a screwdriver or drift, to their most forward positions (photos A and B).
97 Now lower the selector forks into position (photo A) and it will be found that they will now drop in quite easily (photo B). Now return the synchroniser hubs to their original positions.
98 Slide the gearchange selector rod into place from the rear of the extension and as it comes into the gearbox housing, slide onto it the selector boss and 'C' cam, having just made sure that the cam locates in the cut-outs in the selector fork extension arms.
99 Push the selector rod through the boss and the selector forks until the pin holes on the boss and rail align. Tap the pin into place thereby securing the boss to the selector rod. During this operation ensure that the cut-out on the gearbox end of the selector rail faces to the right.
100 Refit the ball, spring and retaining screw in the top right-hand side of the gearbox casing (early gearboxes only).
101 Apply a small amount of sealer to the blanking plug and gently tap it into position in the rear of the extension housing behind the selector rail. Peen it with a centre punch in 3 or 4 places to retain it.
102 Insert the detent ball and spring into the drilling on the gearbox top flange (later gearboxes only).
103 Place a new gasket on the gearbox top cover plate, then refit the top cover and tighten down its four retaining bolts.
104 Refit the speedometer gear in the extension, smear the edges of its retaining cup with sealing compound and tap the cup into place. Remove the gearbox from the vice and tighten the drain plug.
105 Refit the bellhousing onto the gearbox, apply a non-setting jointing compound to the bolt threads.
106 Refit the clutch release fork and bearing.

---

6 Electrical system

Lucas M35G inertia starter motor - general description

1 The starter motors fitted to engines covered by this manual are of Lucas manufacture and are of either inertial or pre-engaged type, details of the latter appearing in Chapter 10.
2 The M35G inertia type is a series parallel wound four pole, four brush motor fitted with an inertia starter drive pinion mounted on a barrel unit. The screwed sleeve which carries the barrel unit is free to move along the splined armature shaft extension, but is retained in its static position by an internal spring. When the starter motor is energised the inertia of the barrel unit causes the pinion to move along the armature shaft and into mesh with the flywheel ring gear, so rotating the engine. As soon as the engine starts, the starter pinion is made to rotate at a faster speed than the armature and this action causes the pinion to disengage from the ring gear and return to its static position.

Lucas M35G inertia starter motor - removal and refitting

3 Removing and refitting this type of starter motor is similar to the procedure described in Chapter 10, Section 15. However, note that the cable connection is on the front of the starter motor body.

5.96B . . . fully forward . . .

5.97A . . . then lower the selector forks . . .

5.97B . . . into position

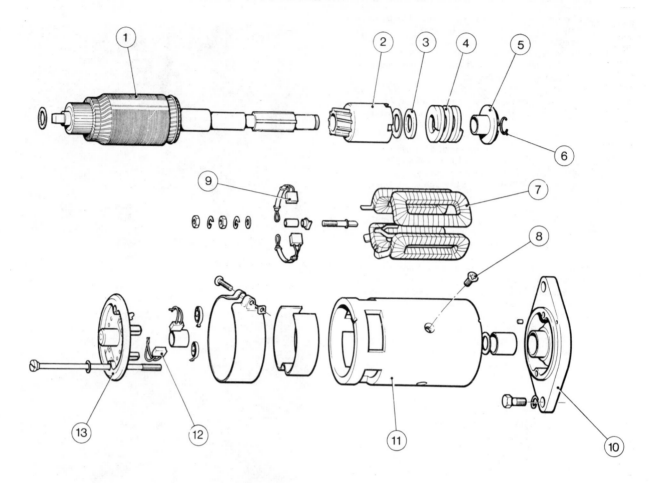

Fig.13.13. Lucas M35G inertia type starter motor

1   Armature
2   Barrel and pinion
3   Washer
4   Spring
5   Sleeve nut

6   Circlip
7   Field coils
8   Screw
9   Field brushes

10 Drive end bracket
11 Yoke
12 Brushes
13 Commutator end bracket

Lucas M35G inertia starter motor - dismantling and reassembly

4   With the starter motor on the bench, loosen the screw on the cover band and slip the cover band off. With a piece of wire bent into the shape of a hook, lift back each of the brush springs in turn and check the movement of the brushes in their holders by pulling on the flexible connectors. If the brushes are so worn that their faces do not rest against the commutator, or if the ends of the brush leads are exposed on their working face, they must be renewed.

5   If any of the brushes tend to stick in their holders, then wash them with a fuel moistened cloth, and if necessary, lightly polish the sides of the brush with a very fine file, until the brushes move quite freely in their holders.

6   If the surface of the commutator is dirty or blackened, clean it with a fuel dampened rag. Secure the starter motor in a vice and check it by connecting a heavy gauge cable between the starter motor terminal and a 12 volt battery.

7   Connect the cable from the other battery terminal to earth on the starter motor body. If the motor turns at high speed it is in good order.

8   If the starter motor still fails to function, or if it is wished to renew the brushes, it is necessary to further dismantle the motor.

9   Lift the brush springs with the wire hook and lift all four brushes out of their holders one at a time.

10 Unscrew and remove the starter through-bolts and carefully withdraw the armature together with the drive endplate.

11 At this stage, if the brushes are to be renewed, unsolder the brush leads connected to the earthed holders and cut the brushes from the field coils leaving 0.25 in (7.0 mm) of copper wire clear for attaching the new brush leads.

12 Check the endplate bushes for wear and renew them if necessary. The old bushes are simply driven out with a suitable drift and the new bushes inserted by the same method, but, before installing them, new bushes should be allowed to stand in engine oil for at least 24 hours, or alternatively soaked in engine oil at 100°C (212°F) for 2 hours.

13 Solder new brushes into position and check that they move freely in their holders as detailed above.

14 If cleaning the commutator with fuel fails to remove all the burnt areas and spots, then wrap a piece of fine glass paper round the commutator and rotate the armature. If the commutator is very badly worn, mount the armature in a lathe and, with the lathe turning at high speed, take a very fine cut out of the commutator and finish the surface by polishing with fine glass paper. **Do not undercut the mica insulators between the commutator segments.**

15 With the starter motor dismantled, test the four field coils

for an open circuit. Connect a 12 volt battery with a 12 volt bulb in one of the leads between the field terminal post and the tapping point of the field coils to which the brushes are connected. An open circuit is proved by the bulb not lighting.

16 If the bulb lights, it does not necessarily mean that the field coils are in order, as there is a possibility that one of the coils will be earthing to the starter yoke or pole shoes. To check this, remove the lead from the brush connector and place it against a clean portion of the starter yoke. If the bulb lights, the field coils are earthing. Renewal of the field coils calls for the use of a wheel operated screwdriver, a soldering iron, caulking and riveting operations and is beyond the scope of the majority of owners. The starter yoke should be taken to a reputable electrical engineering works for new field coils to be fitted. Alternatively,

purchase an exchange starter motor.

17 If the armature is damaged, this will be evident after visual inspection. Look for signs of burning, discolouration, and for conductors that have lifted away from the commutator.

18 To remove the starter motor drive unit, the spring must be compressed by using a proprietary compressor (available from most accessory stores) so that the circlip can be extracted from the armature shaft. Once removed, examine the pinion and barrel assembly and renew them if they are worn or chipped.

19 Reassembly of the starter motor is a straightforward reversal of the dismantling procedure but when refitting the drive unit, ensure that the teeth are towards the starter body and lubricate the unit with a little thin oil.

Key to wiring diagram for L models 1973 onwards (Export only)

1	Direction indicator, LH front		16	Inhibitor switch, automatic transmission
1a	Direction indicator, RH front		17	Relay, automatic transmission
2	Headlamp, LH		18	Test switch, dual-circuit brake warning system
2a	Headlamp, RH		19	Fuse box
3	Direction indicator, LH side		20	Flasher unit
3a	Direction indicator, RH side		21	Foot switch, headlights washer system
4	Dipping relay		22	Fuse holder
5	Wiper motor, headlights		23	Door switch, luggage compartment lamp
6	Windscreen and headlights washer motor		24	Steering/ignition/starter lock
7	Transmitter, water temperature gauge		25	Instrument cluster
8	Oil pressure warning light		26	Luggage compartment lamp
9	Distributor		27	Selector dial
10	Starter motor		28	Fuse holder
11	Alternator		29	Radio
12	Fuse link wire		30	Switch, dual-circuit brake warning system
13	Battery		31	Tail lamp cluster, LH
14	Battery		31a	Tail lamp cluster, RH
15	Regulator			

Fuses (fuse box)

1	Luggage compartment lamp (cluster)
2	Reversing lamps, selector dial illumination
3	Tail light, RH rear
4	Tail light, LH rear
7	Flasher unit

All unmarked fuses are 8 amps

Fuses (dipping relay)

8) 9)	Main beam (LH/RH) _
10) 11)	Dipped beam (LH/RH) _
12	Headlamp washer system
13	Radio

Colour codes

BK	=	Black	PK	=	Pink	YW	=	Yellow	GY	=	Grey
WH	=	White	GN	=	Green	BL	=	Blue	BN	=	Brown
RD	=	Red							VI	=	Violet

────────────	Option
─ ─ ─ ─ ─ ─ ─ ─ ─ ─	Standard wire
─+─+─+─+─+─+─+─+─	Specified for particular countries

238

Wiring diagram for L models 1973 onwards (Export only — Part A)

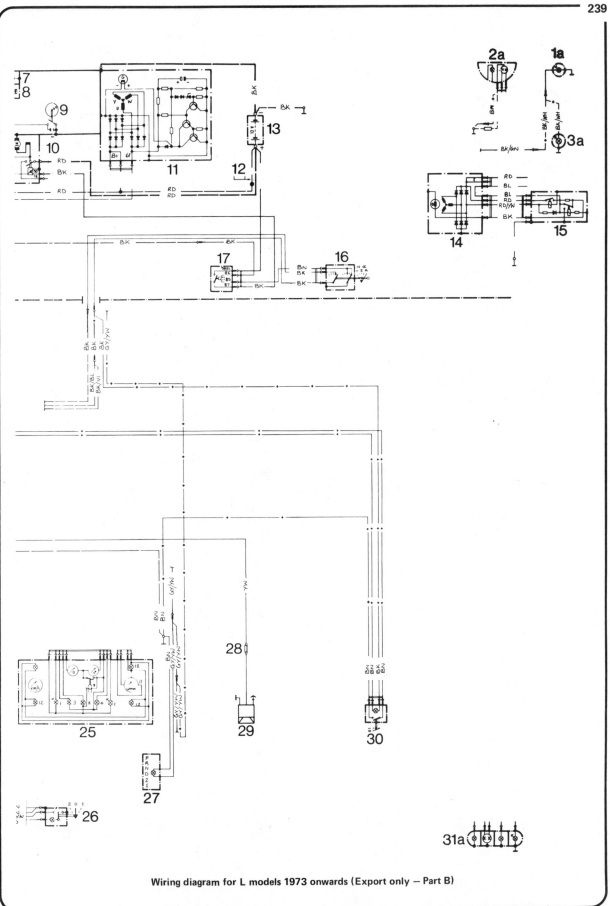

Wiring diagram for L models 1973 onwards (Export only – Part B)

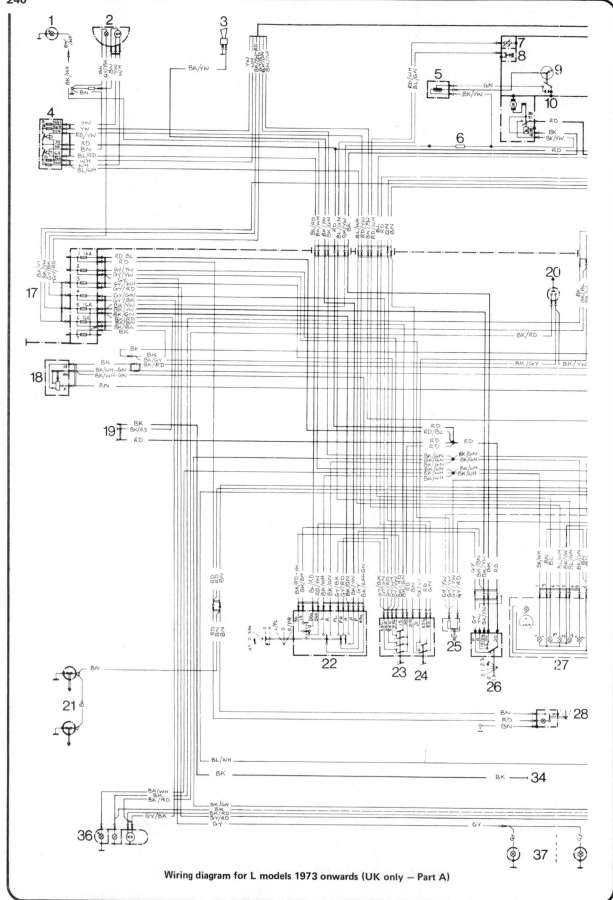

Wiring diagram for L models 1973 onwards (UK only – Part A)

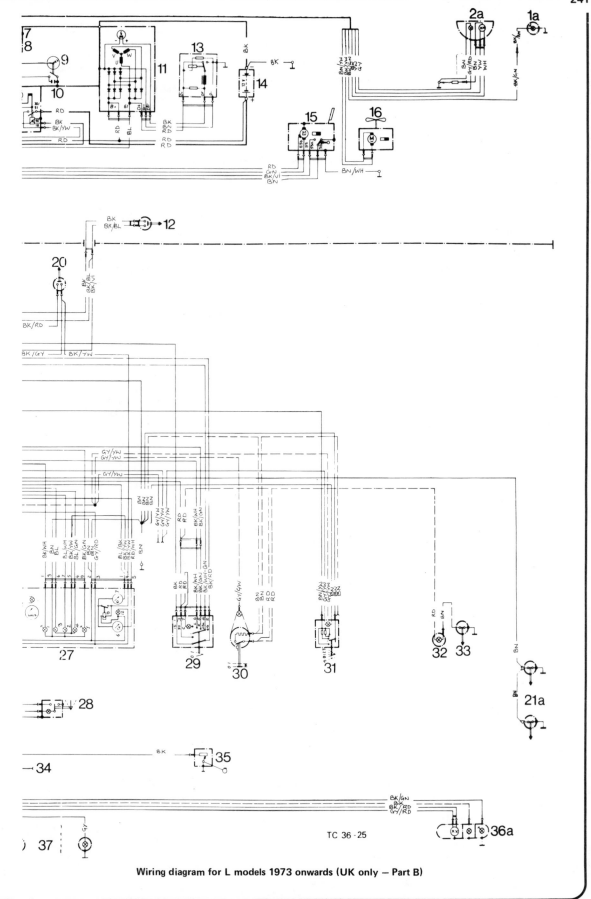

TC 36 - 25

Wiring diagram for L models 1973 onwards (UK only – Part B)

Key to wiring diagram for L models 1973 onwards (UK only)

1	Direction indicator, LH front	23	Light switch
1a	Direction indicator, RH front	24	Switch, windscreen wiper motor
2	Headlamp, LH	25	Variable control (instrument illumination)
2a	Headlamp, RH	26	Steering/ignition/starter lock
3	Horn	27	Instrument cluster
4	Dipping relay		1 Flasher pilot lamp (green)
5	Ignition coil		2 Main beam warning light (blue)
6	Ballast resistance lead—ignition coil		3 Ignition warning light (red)
7	Temperature gauge sender		4 Oil pressure warning light (orange)
8	Oil pressure switch		6 Water temperature gauge
9	Distributor		7 Fuel gauge
10	Starter motor		9 Voltage stabiliser
11	Alternator		12 Instrument lighting
12	Switch — reversing light	28	Interior light
13	Regulator	29	Headlamp flasher switch
14	Battery	30	Cigar lighter
15	Motor—windscreen wiper	31	Switch—heater blower
16	Motor—heater blower	32	Glove compartment lamp
17	Fuse box	33	Switch—glove compartment lamp
18	Flasher unit	34	Connection, heated rear window
19	Connection—heated rear window	35	Transmitter, fuel gauge
20	Stop light switch	36	Tail lamp cluster, LH
21	Door switch, LH	36a	Tail lamp cluster, RH
21a	Door switch, RH	37	Number plate lamp
22	Direction indicator switch		

Fuses (fuse box)

1	Interior lights, emergency flasher, cigar lighter, clock, glove compartment lamp	6	Windscreen wiper motor, reversing lamps, instrument cluster
2	Instrument lighting, number plate lamp	7	Direction indicator light, stop light
3	Side light RH, tail light RH	8)	
4	Side light LH, tail light LH	9)	Dipped beam (RH/LH)
5	Motor — heater blower, horn, heated rear window	10)	
		11)	Main beam (RH/LH)

All unmarked fuses are 8 amps

Colour codes

BK	=	Black	PK	=	Pink	YW	=	Yellow	GY = Grey
WH	=	White	GN	=	Green	BL	=	Blue	BN = Brown
RD	=	Red							VI = Violet

——————————— Standard wire
– – – – – – – – – – L variants

Key to wiring diagram for XL, GXL and 2000E models 1973 onwards (UK only)

1	Direction indicator, LH front
1a	Direction indicator, RH front
2	Headlamp LH
2a	Headlamp RH
3	Horn
4	Dipping relay
5	Two-tone horn relay
6	Ignition coil
7	Ballast resistance lead—ignition coil
8	Transmitter, water temperature gauge
9	Oil pressure switch
10	Distributor
11	Starter motor
12	Engine compartment lamp
13	Switch—reversing lamp
14	Alternator
15	Regulator
16	Battery
17	Wiper motor
18	Motor—heater blower
19	Stop light switch
20	Fuse box
21	Flasher unit
22	Relay, heated rear window
23	Door switch, LH
23a	Door switch, RH
24	Flasher switch

25	Light switch
26	Switch — wiper motor
27	Variable control (instrument illumination)
28	Steering/ignition/starter lock
29	Instrument cluster
	1 Flasher pilot light (green)
	2 Main beam warning lamp (blue)
	3 Ignition warning light (red)
	4 Oil pressure warning light (orange)
	6 Water temperature gauge
	7 Fuel gauge
	9 Voltage stabiliser
	11 Tachometer
	12 Lighting, instruments
30	Interior lamp
31	Clock
32	Emergency flasher switch
33	Cigar lighter
34	Switch—heated rear window
35	Switch—heater blower
36	Glove compartment lamp
37	Switch—glove compartment
38	Transmitter, fuel gauge
39	Heated rear window
40	Tail lamp cluster, LH
40a	Tail lamp cluster, RH
41	Number plate lamp

Fuses (fuse box)

1 Interior lamp, emergency flasher, cigar lighter, clock, glove compartment lamp
2 Instrument lighting, number plate lamps
3 Side light RH, tail light RH
4 Side light LH, tail light LH
5 Motor-heater blower, horn, heated rear window
6 Wiper motor, reversing lamps, instrument cluster

7 Flasher light, stop light
Fuses (dipping relay)
8) 9) Dipped beam (LH/RH)
10) 11) Main beam (LH/RH)
12 Heated window (live)

All unmarked fuses are 8 amps

Colour codes

BK	=	Black	PK	=	Pink	YW	=	Yellow	GY = Grey
WH	=	White	GN	=	Green	BL	=	Blue	BN = Brown
RD	=	Red							VI = Violet

————————— XL
– – – – – – – – – – GXL/2000E

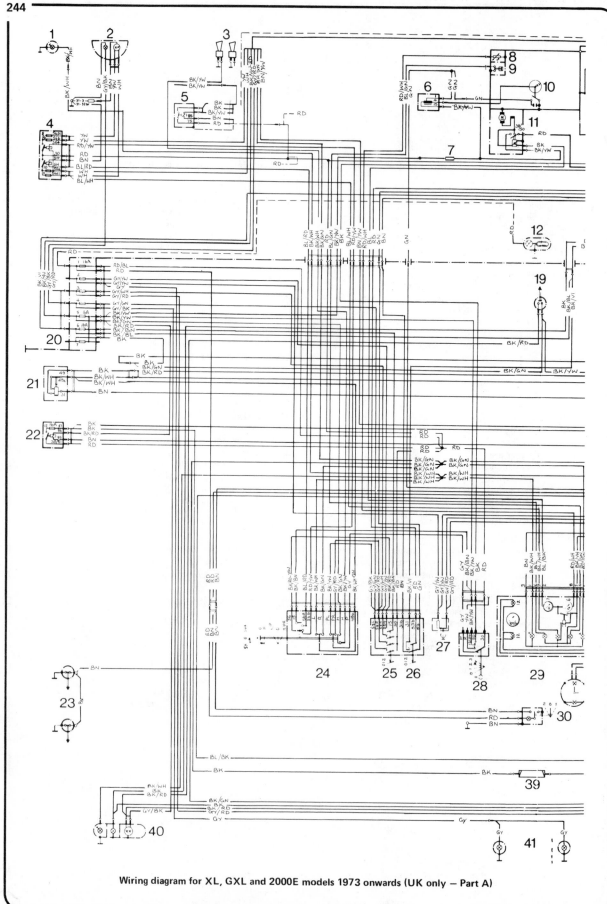

Wiring diagram for XL, GXL and 2000E models 1973 onwards (UK only – Part A)

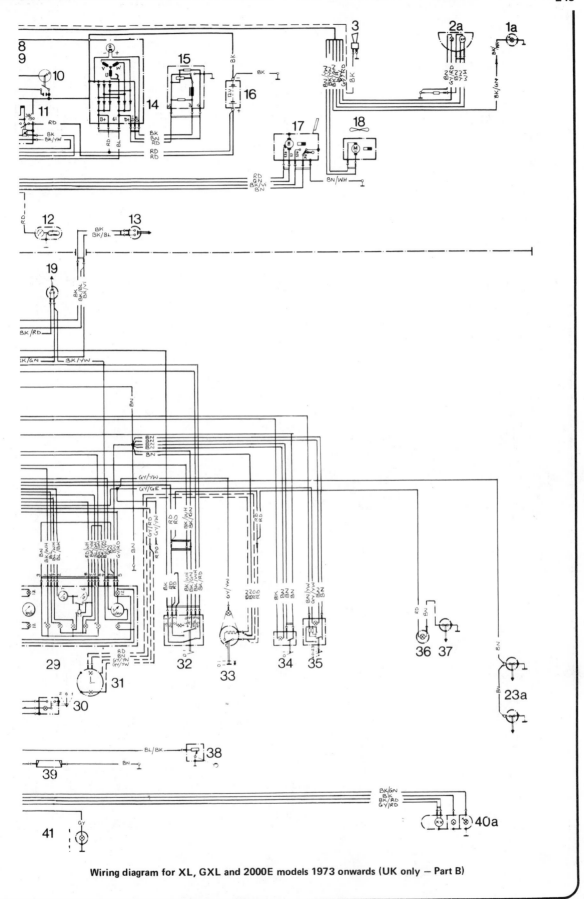

Wiring diagram for XL, GXL and 2000E models 1973 onwards (UK only — Part B)

Wiring diagram for XL and GXL models 1973 onwards (Export only — Part A)

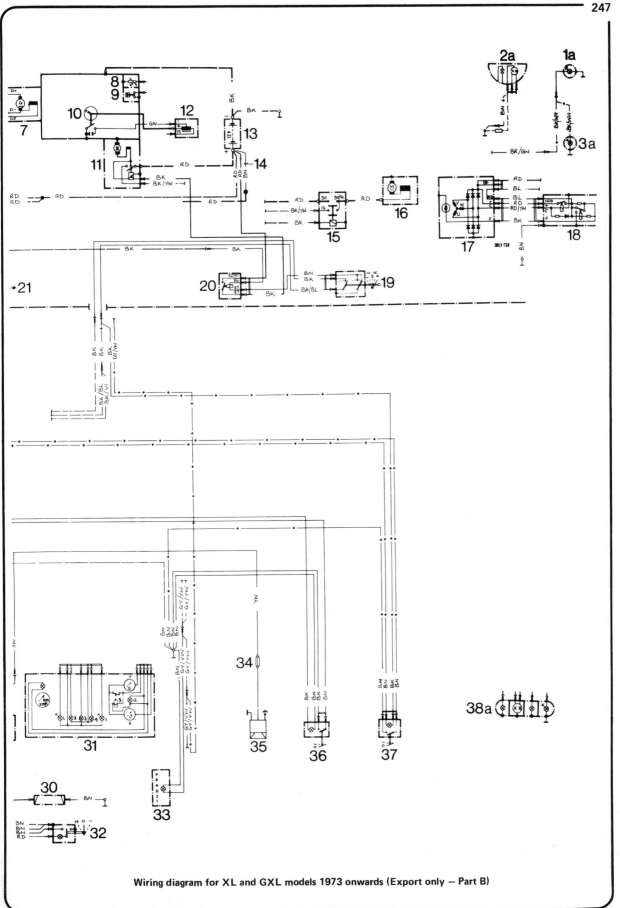

Wiring diagram for XL and GXL models 1973 onwards (Export only — Part B)

Key to wiring diagram for XL and GXL models 1973 onwards (Export only)

1	Direction indicator, LH front	19	Inhibitor switch, automatic transmission
1a	Direction indicator, RH front	20	Relay—automatic transmission
2	Headlamp, LH	21	Test switch, dual-circuit brake warning system
2a	Headlamp, RH	22	Dipping relay
3	Direction indicator, LH side	23	Fuse box
3a	Direction indicator, RH side	24	Flasher unit
4	Wiper motor, headlights	25	Fuse holder
5	Windscreen and headlights washer pump	26	Relay—heated rear window
6	Regulator	27	Foot switch—headlight washer system
7	Generator	28	Door switch—boot lamp
8	Transmitter—water temperature gauge thermometer	29	Steering/ignition/starter lock
9	Oil pressure switch	30	Heated rear window
10	Distributor	31	Instrument cluster
11	Starter motor	32	Luggage compartment lamp
12	Ignition coil	33	Selector dial
13	Battery	34	Fuse holder
14	Fuse link wire (for alternator only)	35	Radio
15	Starter solenoid	36	Switch—heated rear window
16	Starter motor	37	Switch—dual-circuit brake system
17	Alternator	38	Tail lamp cluster, LH
18	Regulator	38a	Tail lamp cluster, RH

Fuses (fuse box)

1	Luggage compartment lamp (cluster)
2	Reversing lamps
	Selector dial illumination
3	Tail light, RH rear
4	Tail light, LH rear
5	Heated rear window
7	Flasher unit

Fuses (dipping relay)

8)	
9)	Straight beam (LH/RH)
10)	
11)	Dipped beam (LH/RH)
12	Headlight washer system
13	Radio
14	Heated rear window

All unmarked fuses are 8 amps

Colour codes

BK	=	Black	PK	=	Pink	YW	=	Yellow	GY	=	Grey
WH	=	White	GN	=	Green	BL	=	Blue	BN	=	Brown
RD	=	Red							VI	=	Violet

——————————— Option
— — — — — — — — — Standard
— + — + — + — + — + Specified for
particular
countries

Index

Printed by
Haynes Publishing Group
Sparkford Yeovil Somerset
England